a history of contemporary praise & worship

understanding the
ideas that reshaped the
protestant church

**Lester Ruth
and Lim Swee Hong**

Baker Academic
a division of Baker Publishing Group
Grand Rapids, Michigan

© 2021 by Lester Ruth and Lim Swee Hong

Published by Baker Academic
a division of Baker Publishing Group
PO Box 6287, Grand Rapids, MI 49516-6287
www.bakeracademic.com

Paperback edition published 2023
ISBN 978-1-5409-6753-4

Printed in the United States of America

The Library of Congress has cataloged the hardcover edition as follows:
Names: Ruth, Lester, 1959– author. | Lim, Swee Hong, author.
Title: A history of contemporary praise & worship : understanding the ideas that reshaped the protestant church / Lester Ruth and Lim Swee Hong.
Description: Grand Rapids, Michigan : Baker Academic, a division of Baker Publishing Group, 2021. | Includes bibliographical references and indexes.
Identifiers: LCCN 2021009315 | ISBN 9780801098284 (cloth) | ISBN 9781493432547 (ebook)
Subjects: LCSH: Public worship—History—20th century.
Classification: LCC BV8 .R88 2021 | DDC 264.009/045—dc23
LC record available at https://lccn.loc.gov/2021009315

Scripture quotations labeled KJV are from the King James Version of the Bible.

Scripture quotations labeled GNT are from the Good News Translation in Today's English Version-Second Edition. Copyright © 1992 by American Bible Society. Used by permission.

Baker Publishing Group publications use paper produced from sustainable forestry practices and post-consumer waste whenever possible.

In memory of four great pioneers
in Contemporary Praise & Worship
who taught and led countless others:

Chuck Fromm
Dick Iverson
James F. White
Charles Green

But thou art holy, O thou that inhabitest the praises of Israel.

Psalm 22:3 KJV

The voice of joy has returned to the church. The sacrifice of praise is again being offered like the sound of the birds on an early spring day.

Reg Layzell, Pentecostal preacher, Canada, February 28, 1952

So I become all things to all people, that I may save some of them by whatever means are possible.

1 Corinthians 9:22b GNT

The only excuse for using anything is if it's going to be effective.

Ralph Carmichael, composer, United States, December 1967

contents

acknowledgments

It is with fear and trembling that we approach this portion of our book. The trepidation does not come from the thought of having to express gratitude. Indeed, as Christians who are scholars, we are quite happy to have an attitude of thanks and appreciation. Thanksgiving is intrinsic to our faith. The worry arises for different reasons: the dread that a limited amount of space does not allow us to thank adequately the innumerable people who have made this work possible and, even if we had limitless pages upon which to gush in gratitude, the anxiety that we would inevitably leave someone out because there have been so many. When this project was first hatched in a hotel room we were sharing at a conference in Toronto ten years ago, we had no idea of all the wonderful people who would speak to us, assist us, and encourage us along the way. To each and every one, thank you.

Notwithstanding the danger of starting to name specific individuals, given the number who have assisted in this project, we will do so because some were especially instrumental. At the top of this list would be our own wives, Carmen Ruth and Maria Ling, who have been untiring in their support and contributions to this book.

We also thank those who have read and offered feedback on various drafts: Matthew Lilley, Fran Huebert, Judith Heyhoe, Adam Perez, Glenn Stallsmith, Jonathan Ottaway, Drew Eastes, and Debbie Wong. Your feedback challenged us, encouraged us, and made the final version much stronger.

Along the way there have been some conversation partners with whom our ability to talk from time to time has proved invaluable. Many of you lived this history and thus are able to make it come alive and be personal in a way that researching it only through published sources would not have allowed. In this category of assistance, we especially wish to thank Steve Griffing, Barry Griffing, Jon Rising, Fred Heumann, Bob Johnson, Sallie Horner, Jim Hart, Howard Rachinski, Stephen (Steve) Phifer, the Reg Layzell family, and Holly Yaryan Hall (who helped us understand fluvial dynamics).

Many also supplied us with materials to supplement our research. In the midst of a pandemic that limited access to libraries and curtailed travel, your graciousness truly and literally made this book possible. For this type of help, we thank those named immediately above as well as the following: Romina Cain and her extended family for background information on and photographs of her grandfather, Judson Cornwall; Eddie Espinosa for photographs and other materials; Tom Kraeuter for access to a complete collection of *Psalmist* magazine; William (Will) Bishop for sharing materials from his own dissertation research on youth musicals and for helping us to make contacts among evangelical musicians; Tom Bergler for sharing his own research and, especially, the elusive Horner thesis on Youth for Christ music; David S. Luecke and Mike Coppersmith for background materials on Missouri Synod Lutherans; Chuck, Stephanie, and Lexi Fromm for materials on *Worship Leader* magazine and Chuck's earlier work; Andrea Hunter for a copy of the George Warnock book, *The Feast of Tabernacles*; Steve Vredenburgh for providing access to Rick Warren's Doctor of Ministry thesis; and numerous university librarians who did yeoman's work in providing creative solutions to accessing key materials. Several other individuals contributed images that the reader will see in this book. Note the names of these contributors—there is a prayer of thanks behind each photograph's source attribution.

We also thank all those we have interviewed for our research on this liturgical topic over the years. Since we conducted our first interviews in 2013, more than 180 people have sat down with us, sharing their time and recollections. From this large wealth of conversations, we used specific information from ninety-seven interviewees for this book and so those persons are named in the bibliography. But all our interviewees have contributed to this project, even if the contribution was more indirect. Each conversation helped orient us to large developments and trends. If we speak with confidence about specifics, it is because all our interviewees collectively have given us a broad picture of the whole.

We also thank John Witvliet, the director of the Calvin Institute of Christian Worship, whose support and encouragement along the way has proved invaluable in helping us deepen our research.

Finally, we thank our contacts at Baker Academic who have shepherded this project. In this regard we extend our gratitude to Robert Hosack, Sarah Gombis, Brandy Scritchfield, Kara Day, and Melisa Blok.

Lester Ruth, Duke Divinity School

Lim Swee Hong, Emmanuel College of Victoria University
in the University of Toronto

preface

This book is a history of how two liturgical theologies—two ideas—reshaped Protestant worship in the second half of the twentieth century. Specifically, it is the story of how these two theologies motivated and guided people to develop the way of worship we will call Contemporary Praise & Worship. In the telling of this history we will emphasize three foci: the theologies, the people captivated by these theologies, and the worship practices these theologies produced and undergirded.

The critical theological ideas can be summarized by two words: "presence" and "purpose." "Presence" highlights how one theology prioritized praise as fulfilling biblical promises about how God's people could expect to experience God's presence in worship. The people who adhered to this theology of worship saw praise-filled worship as a gift from God. "Purpose" underscores how the other theology prioritized using interesting, relevant, and accessible worship practices to attract people to Christian faith and retain them as worshipers. The people who adhered to this theology saw the need for new ways of worship in order to bridge the gap between worship practices and the rapidly shifting tides of culture and society (and the people swept along by those tides). Our book is an attempt to describe these two theologies and the history of their impact on Protestant worship in the latter part of the twentieth century. A look at the theologies allows us to see not only how Contemporary Praise & Worship came about but also why it did.

Though parts of the history of Contemporary Praise & Worship have been told—and sometimes quite well—we believe the theological and liturgical history has remained in large part a hidden history. It is not as if the two theologies have been totally unrecognized. But until now, no study has explored them either in depth or in conjunction with the liturgical changes of the late twentieth century.

How can the hidden aspects of this history be revealed?[1] We have pursued those aspects through a rich, broad collection of primary materials. We have sought out publications written for popular audiences, teaching resources, recordings, and especially interviews with those who lived through and in many cases shaped the history. For these interviews, we have not limited ourselves to names with obvious recognition. Our research has led to the realization that those who worked behind the scenes or who now have been forgotten were often the most instrumental in past times.

A few additional explanations will help the reader know what to expect—and what *not* to expect—in this book.

First, we hope you find this book to be a *comprehensive* history in several respects. We based this history on an aggressive use of a breadth of primary materials so that it goes beyond any other history available to date. We also intend this book to be comprehensive in terms of describing the breadth of the story. By these means we hope to enable you to comprehend the major developments and key plotlines.

Therefore, what we have written is a *detailed* history. We name ideas, people, events, and congregations that have been critical in this history but have often been overlooked. Do not be surprised if some of this information is entirely new. As we researched, we discovered that importance is not always tied to prominence, either in the past or in the present.

Our book is a *sympathetic* history, not in the sense that we agree with everything found in our historical sources but in the sense that we want them to be able to speak for themselves. We have sought to tell the story fairly without predetermining the rightness or wrongness of new liturgical developments and their underlying theologies.

Similarly, this book is a *descriptive* history, leaving to another time the task of assessing how the rise of Contemporary Praise & Worship has been a good thing (or not) for the church.

This book will be a *scriptural* history. By this assertion, we mean that the two theologies that reshaped the face of Protestant worship were biblical theologies. Their adherents relied on the Bible, especially a few key verses, to provide the launching point and the guide for what they were trying to do in bringing about liturgical change. It is not surprising at all that these

---

1. For a discussion of the methodological shifts needed to write better histories of this liturgical phenomenon, see Lester Ruth, "Methodological Insights for the Historiography of Contemporary Praise & Worship," in *Essays on the History of Contemporary Praise & Worship*, ed. Lester Ruth (Eugene, OR: Pickwick, 2020), 176–92.

historical figures would do so, since almost all of them belonged to a liturgical approach called "Free Church" in which the desire to make worship scriptural is a fundamental goal.[2] Consequently, we draw frequent attention to how the various figures used the Scriptures for that end.

Note, finally, that the story we tell in this book is a *different* history than has sometimes been portrayed. Many of the current attempts to tell the story emphasize one possible source or another (Jesus People, baby boomers, certain megachurches, the Charismatic Renewal movement, and youth ministries have been some of the more common options), usually from the 1960s or thereabouts. True, these all played roles, but no single one of these was the sole source for this way of worship. In addition, the story needs to start several decades earlier: not in the late 1960s but in the 1940s.

If these commitments give you as a reader a sense of what to expect, let us also state what we will *not* do in telling this story. For example, our goal is not to provide a *theological* history, although this book is a history of theologies and what these theologies brought about in worship. In other words, we do not tell this story in a way that overtly says "look at what God was doing"—or, as has sometimes been done by opponents of Contemporary Praise & Worship, "look at this unfortunate thing (that thwarted the will of God)."[3]

This book is not a *global* history. The limitation comes not from lack of interest (indeed, one author, Lim Swee Hong, is originally from Singapore) but from the fact that telling the history for North America has proved to be a complicated enough task on its own. We hope that other scholars will not only build on the work we have begun here but tell the other histories of Contemporary Praise & Worship from around the world in their own discrete narratives. Thus, although we focus on North America, by no means do we want to suggest that there were no developments elsewhere or that these developments were unimportant.

2. For a broader historical discussion of Free Church worship, see James F. White, *Protestant Worship: Traditions in Transition* (Louisville: Westminster John Knox, 1989), 80–81, 117–20; and Christopher J. Ellis, *Gathering: A Theology and Spirituality of Worship in Free Church Tradition* (London: SCM, 2004), 27–30, 75–81. Cf. Graydon F. Snyder and Doreen M. McFarlane, *The People Are Holy: The History and Theology of Free Church Worship* (Macon, GA: Mercer University Press, 2005), 20–21.

3. For a fuller description of these sorts of histories, see Lester Ruth, "Divine, Human, or Devilish? The State of the Question on the Writing of the History of Contemporary Worship," *Worship* 88, no. 4 (July 2014): 290–310. For an example of a positive theological history, see Les Moir, *Missing Jewel: The Worship Movement That Impacted the Nations* (Colorado Springs: David C. Cook, 2017). In contrast, see Gordon W. Lathrop, "New Pentecost or Joseph's Britches? Reflections on the History and Meaning of the Worship Order in the Megachurches," *Worship* 72, no. 6 (November 1998): 521–38.

This book is not a history of *music*, in terms of musicians, songs, albums, or the music industry.[4] Indeed, that part of the history is the most thoroughly documented, and so we feel little urgency to rehash it in detail. But neither do we completely ignore it. We do consider music history throughout this story, especially when important persons and pieces—and their theological motivations—have been overlooked. We also look at music history as it reflects the theological commitments of the music makers.

Finally, our history is not an *exhaustive, encyclopedic* history. Everything that could be documented about Contemporary Praise & Worship will not be included in this book. Nonetheless, we hope our efforts here will be an important contribution to what is already a growing topic of scholarly investigation into Contemporary Praise & Worship. In addition, this book is not an all-inclusive account of every major movement that changed Protestant worship at the end of the twentieth century. Therefore, we pay little attention to how the Liturgical movement, gaining strength in Roman Catholicism's Second Vatican Council, spilled over into new Protestant interests in sacraments, lectionaries, enriched yearly calendars, a Word- and Table-centered order of worship, and a renewed connection between worship and social justice.

Two last preparatory comments are needed before you begin reading. First, note that we have coined a neologism to describe the phenomenon about which we write—that is, Contemporary Praise & Worship. We see a new term as necessary since the adherents of the two theologies tended to use their own distinct terms for ways of worship that often looked quite similar. The term of choice for those emphasizing praise as the pathway to God's presence was "Praise & Worship." In contrast, the label most often used by those pursuing a strategic approach was "Contemporary Worship." In the chapters that follow, we will use the term employed by whichever historical figures we are covering at that point of this book. In addition, however, we will use the more comprehensive neologism to describe the whole phenomenon, especially as the dawn of the new century saw the two lines of development flowing together into a kind of confluence. Notice, too, the ampersand (&) whenever this book uses either of the two terms or our new term. The ampersand allows us to put the two respective terms together without an overabundance of the word "and." In other words, the ampersand allows us to write Praise & Worship and Contemporary Worship, not Praise and Worship and Contemporary Worship.

4. To see how the history of this phenomenon can be told using a variety of topics other than music, see our earlier work: Lim Swee Hong and Lester Ruth, *Lovin' on Jesus: A Concise History of Contemporary Worship* (Nashville: Abingdon, 2017).

Second, notice when we refer to the racial or ethnic identity of historical figures. We do so only when we think noting this identity is critical to the liturgical story itself (and it sometimes is). We are trying to undercut the presumption that race or ethnicity should be named only when referring to a person of color and in every such instance, which encourages a subtle assumption that the "normal" historical figures are White since their race is not named. *Simply put, if we do not name a person's race or ethnicity, do not presume that this person is White.*

With these concluding notes, let us begin to tell a story about how two theologies changed Protestant worship.

introduction: a historical overview

As a teacher of Christian worship history, I (Lester Ruth) find that the best serendipitous moments of discovery often come in informal conversations with students after class. And so it was one day about fifteen years ago when a student, a young man in his twenties, approached me after a session of a worship history class and told me the course content had finally made sense to him. He noted the breakthrough awareness that had allowed past forms of Christian worship to be understandable to him now, remarking, "Professor, I finally see what you're trying to say: the pastor is a kind of worship leader, too."

His comment was a eureka moment for me also. I then became aware of how the world of Contemporary Praise & Worship—a liturgical sphere featuring bands, technology, accessibility, worship leaders who were musicians, and all the other normal accoutrements of this way of worship—had flipped several classic liturgical presumptions on their head for a generation of young Christians. What are the normal means by which God's presence is experienced in worship? What are the roles of music and musicians in a service? How dependent is worship on good technology? What is the liturgical leadership a pastor or preacher provides? To these questions and more, Contemporary Praise & Worship of the early twenty-first century gave answers different from those normally given in the past. It had therefore shaped a generation of Christians to have different assumptions than those of the long historical trajectory of Christian worship. What was newfangled had become standard operating practice and what was classic seemed like a novelty to this student and his peers. Thus, he struggled to understand the liturgical world and practices of previous Christians. I had known of this chasm, but I had not really known its breadth. When this student made his comment about pastors and their liturgical role, I became deeply aware of how much something truly new had happened in Protestant worship with the advent of Contemporary Praise & Worship. My eyes were opened to how those nurtured in this world of Contemporary Praise & Worship as the only way of worship they had known were unaware of its relative novelty.

Since that serendipitous moment fifteen years ago, we (Lim Swee Hong and Lester Ruth) have realized, too, how persons such as this student are unaware that Contemporary Praise & Worship has its own history and that its twenty-first-century form is actually a product of a half century of evolution. It did not spring up *ex nihilo* in the late 1990s.

And, indeed, this new approach to worship has an interesting history. What that student knew as normal was in fact a late 1990s merging of two lines of development that had run parallel to each other since the mid-1940s, only occasionally connecting. Each line of development, driven by its own theological vision, had brought about its own new liturgical approach. At times, those involved in one of these lines of development were completely unaware of what was transpiring in the parallel liturgical world. The two theologies provided the motivation to pursue each respective liturgical vision.

Bit by bit, however, the lines of development grew closer until the late 1990s when they came together in an overarching liturgical reality. This approach to worship is easily found in a wide range of congregations, whether mainline, evangelical, or Pentecostal. Some have called this approach "Praise & Worship" and others "Contemporary Worship," but we will use the broader term "Contemporary Praise & Worship" to describe this all-encompassing liturgical phenomenon.[1]

Theology drove the creation of this approach to worship. Thus, this liturgical story is of two ideas that have changed the face of Protestant worship.

Consequently, to be true to this complexity, a single narrative is inadequate.[2] The histories of the two ideas—and their liturgical impact—are like two parallel rivers. Let us associate each "river" with the key notion found in

---

1. "Praise & Worship" tends to be the more global term, the more Pentecostal term, and the term used by non-Whites in North America. "Contemporary Worship" tends to be the term used by Whites in American mainline denominations. For more discussion, see Lim Swee Hong and Lester Ruth, *Lovin' on Jesus: A Concise History of Contemporary Worship* (Nashville: Abingdon, 2017), 1–16; and Lester Ruth, "Introduction: The Importance and History of Contemporary Praise & Worship," in *Essays on the History of Contemporary Praise & Worship*, ed. Lester Ruth (Eugene, OR: Pickwick, 2020), 2.

2. Some prior historiographies have tried to force the narrative into one explanation or the other. One of the broader, more balanced presentations is David Ralph Bains, "Contemporary Worship: Trends and Patterns in Christian America," in *Faith in America: Changes, Challenges, New Directions*, ed. Charles H. Lippy (Westport, CT: Praeger, 2006), 3:1–22, esp. 9–14.

the rivers' respective theological headwaters: gift and gap. The "Gift River" emerged from a particular biblical theology that saw God revitalizing the church by restoring praise as the way worshipers experience God's presence. A foundational biblical vision of worship thus provided the gravitational pull for the waters in this river. This river corresponds with those who normally used the term "Praise & Worship."

The waters in the "Gap River," on the other hand, arose and moved along under the influence of a different force: a theology eager to overcome any gap that had arisen between the church's worship and people living in a changing culture. The pull in this river came from Christians creatively seeking to overcome that gap. This river's proponents typically used the label "Contemporary Worship" for what they were doing.

Because new theological and practical tributaries fed these rivers from time to time, each one became a multifaceted reality. Different "currents" pulled in different directions within each flow. Their banks were sometimes low, allowing a floodplain to form in which the two rivers occasionally met. These floods anticipated the eventual situation: by the end of the twentieth century the two rivers melded into one.

In the appendix to this book the reader will find summaries of each of the histories, aligned in two columns so events occurring at roughly the same time are juxtaposed. With this tool we seek to frame the entire project while allowing the reader to track simultaneous historical happenings otherwise separated by many pages in the book. If you are someone who likes to get an overall picture first, we encourage you to read the appendix at this point. However, to allow each of these histories to have its own integrity, we will unfold each story independently in the first two parts of this book's main text. The concluding chapter of the book will describe the confluence that occurred in the late 1990s.

part 1

the history of praise & worship

one

—

the headwater of praise & worship, 1946–65

A new experience in God was introduced by the Spirit as He restored that wholesale, whole-hearted worship to the Lord. This wholesale praise brought a new experience in God. The sacrifice of praise lifted the church to new heights in faith.

— *Reg Layzell, pastor of Glad Tidings Temple, Vancouver*[1]

Imagine Sunday morning, the day of worship, in countless churches across North America. Now visualize the following modern scene or some variation of it: a band on a platform; music derived from some style of popular music; vocalists and instrumentalists front and center; informality; hands raised in the air; an extended time of congregational singing; reliance upon electronic technology featuring screens, projectors, and large soundboards; updated English and other nods toward establishing accessibility and relevance for worshipers; and the pastor nowhere to be seen until the time for the sermon.

Finding a church whose worship fits this generic pattern was an easy task by the beginning of the twenty-first century. That situation has not changed today. One does not have to look hard to see how widespread some variation of this kind of worship has become. All these elements, in whole or in part,

1. Reg Layzell, *The Pastor's Pen: Early Revival Writings of Pastor Reg. Layzell*, comp. B. Maureen Gaglardi (Vancouver: Glad Tidings Temple, 1965), 206–7.

have combined into a new way of worship that had become ubiquitous in North America and, in fact, around the world by 2000 and has remained so in the time since.

However, if you were to go back to the 1970s, you would discover that this sort of service was not nearly as easy to find. If you did stumble across one, it would have had a different look and feel if for no other reasons than that the technology and the song repertoire were different. But this way of worship was present in the 1970s. Indeed, if you were to visit the late 1940s, you could still come across Christians here and there worshiping in the earliest versions of this way of worship. It might take a few moments of patient discernment, but you would be able to see many later elements in a nascent form. If you were to listen closely, you would hear the various adherents articulate their theological rationales for why it is important to worship in this way.

As a matter of fact, these theologies have been the most stable aspects of the liturgical phenomenon we have been tracing, even as the outward details of worship services have evolved. (Note to reader: whenever we use the term "liturgical" in this book, we simply mean something worship-related.[2]) These theologies have provided the most continuity for more than seventy years, even if their importance has been sometimes overlooked in prior accounts of this phenomenon's history.

Of course, we are talking about the way of worship that many (especially if they are not White or are not part of a mainline denomination) have called "Praise & Worship" and others (especially White members of mainline congregations) have called "Contemporary Worship." The two different names—and the different spheres in which they are used—tell us something about the complexity of the history of this way of worship. This is not a story of a single line of development or even a single point of origin. Neither is it a story of a single strand of theology that led to the creation of this way of worship and gave it the momentum for ever-increasing adoption, even though theological commitments have been a driving force for all its various proponents. Our desire is to tell the complex history of where this way of worship originated and how two different theological visions have propelled it into widespread acceptance. We begin with Praise & Worship.

2. As noted and demonstrated by Daniel Albrecht, although the terms "liturgy" and "liturgical" are seldom used by Pentecostals, nonetheless they are still useful and appropriate terms for this type of Christianity. See Daniel E. Albrecht, "Worshiping and the Spirit: Transmuting Liturgy Pentecostally," in *The Spirit in Worship—Worship in the Spirit*, ed. Teresa Berger and Bryan D. Spinks (Collegeville, MN: Liturgical Press, 2009), 224. We would extend Albrecht's assertion to include evangelicals too.

Headwater: Where Desperation and Bible Met

Notwithstanding the overall complexity of the history, for one line of development—the "river" of Praise & Worship—there was a clear theological headwater: a rainy Wednesday in early January 1946. The place was Abbotsford, British Columbia, Canada, a small town about forty miles east of Vancouver and four miles north of the United States/Canada border. It was a time and place of spiritual desperation for Reg Layzell, a guest speaker in a Pentecostal church in that town. It would become the time and place for the revealing of a Scripture verse that has proved to be the major source for Praise & Worship.

Layzell (b. 1904), who was from the province of Ontario, had recently retired as general manager of the Canadian division of a company that sold machines to print names and addresses on mailing labels, envelopes, and form labels.[3] Toward the end of 1945 he received a letter from the British Columbia superintendent of the Pentecostal Assemblies of Canada, who had heard of Layzell's ministry as a Christian businessman in Ontario. The letter invited Layzell to come to British Columbia and hold meetings in several churches. Layzell decided to do so for three months. The first stop was Abbotsford.

By Layzell's own account, his ministry began dreadfully. Since the host pastor was critically ill, Layzell had responsibility for the entire service, both singing and preaching. Neither went well. Sunday was a flat disaster, as was Tuesday night, the second night of his worship leadership. By Wednesday[4]

3. The details of Layzell's story in Abbotsford have been printed in multiple sources. The most detailed was written by Layzell's son and daughter-in-law: Hugh Layzell and Audrey Layzell, *Sons of His Purpose: The Interweaving of the Ministry of Reg Layzell, and His Son, Hugh, during a Season of Revival* (San Bernardino, CA: privately published, 2012), esp. 30–52. The one published closest to 1946 was written by Layzell's associate pastor, B. Maureen Gaglardi, in collaboration with Reg Layzell and published as *The Key of David* (Vancouver: Glad Tidings Temple, 1966), 9–13. Layzell himself published an account in 1979 in the book *Unto Perfection: The Truth about the Present Restoration Revival* (Mountlake Terrace, WA: King's Temple, 1979), 3, 11–13, 121. The basic details in these accounts are similar and are confirmed by our interviews with Layzell's son and daughter-in-law, daughter (Marion Peterson), and grandson (James Layzell). The story was a foundational one for Layzell's ministry and was a narrative he told many times, as the family affirms (Layzell and Layzell, *Sons of His Purpose*, 36). Unfortunately, the earliest collection of Layzell's writings, compiled by B. Maureen Gaglardi (and printed in 1965 as *The Pastor's Pen*) from his church newsletter articles and sermons from the early 1950s, does not recount the 1946 story. As evidenced by this book, however, praise in general and Ps. 22:3 in particular do play a critical role in Layzell's preaching and teaching from early in his ministry. *The Pastor's Pen*, combined with Layzell's later book, *Unto Perfection*, were edited and re-released in 2019 by Marion Peterson. This combined volume has a different format and pagination than the original publications. This new printing of *The Pastor's Pen* does include an account of 1946.

4. Layzell's 1979 account of the story (*Unto Perfection*, 121) says that the day was January 3, 1946. His dating must be off, since January 3, 1946, was a Thursday.

morning Layzell was desperate. Fasting, he arrived at the church early that morning and began to pray. Feeling sorry for himself, he begged God for some kind of blessing since he was obligated to continue the meetings for the whole week. Around noon a Scripture verse came to mind as he was praying: "But thou art holy, O thou that inhabitest the praises of Israel" (KJV). He did not remember the exact verse reference (Ps. 22:3) at first, but accepted the verse as a gift from God nonetheless.

That Layzell was drawn to this verse is not entirely surprising, given that he was Pentecostal. By the 1940s Pentecostalism was a half-century-old liturgical tradition in which praising had long had an important role. Emerging in the early twentieth century, Pentecostalism had stressed a dramatic infilling of the Holy Spirit that was evidenced outwardly, especially by speaking in tongues (glossolalia or languages supernaturally bestowed). The Pentecostal movement gained its name from the story of the first Pentecost in Acts 2, during which Christian disciples spoke in tongues. Whether in tongues or not, praising God seems to have been a recurring feature of Pentecostal worship. Thus, not surprisingly, there are historical hints that Psalm 22:3 had previously circulated among some Pentecostals. For example, Aimee Semple McPherson, a famous Los Angeles–based preacher at the beginning of the twentieth century, once referenced it when describing the pleasure of being in a service with extensive praising and thus experiencing the presence of God.[5] Moreover, Jack Hayford (b. 1934), a Pentecostal preacher in the second half of the century, noted how when he was growing up he heard leaders exhort people to praise by saying "the Lord inhabits the praises of His people."[6] (Hayford grew up in the denomination that McPherson had started: the International Church of the Foursquare Gospel, often simply known as the Foursquare Church.) It was not until much later that Hayford realized it was actually a Bible verse. Layzell, however, apparently would be the first to make the verse into a cornerstone for a liturgical theology, as we shall see.

On that January day in 1946, Layzell initially focused on the first part of the verse and began to ransack his heart, repenting of every sin that he could remember committing, but "still the heavens were brass."[7] Layzell felt his attention drawn to the second half of the verse: "O thou that inhabitest the

5. Aimee Semple McPherson, *This Is That: Personal Experiences, Sermons and Writings of Aimee Semple McPherson, Evangelist* (Los Angeles: Bridal Call, 1919), 621.

6. Jack W. Hayford, *The Church on the Way: Learning to Live in the Promise of Biblical Congregational Life* (Old Tappan, NJ: Chosen Books, 1983), 81. Despite extensive searching, including the use of the Google Ngram viewer, we cannot find any systematic or widespread use of this verse to create a liturgical theology before Layzell.

7. Layzell, *Unto Perfection*, 12.

praises of Israel." If God does indeed inhabit the praises of his people, Layzell realized, then he ought to fill the church building with the praises of God. He began in the small study room where he had been praying, lifting his hands and praising God aloud. He then ventured into the rest of the church, realizing that he had never quite done anything like this before. He was used to praising God in a prayer room but never in the "open church."[8] He spent the remainder of the day saturating the space with praise, from pulpit to piano ("The pianist is rather dead," Layzell thought), up and down each aisle and pew, and into each room in the whole facility, including washrooms.[9]

Layzell had received the statement of Psalm 22:3 (God inhabits the praises of Israel) as a divine promise ("As you praise me, I will be present with you"), and he was determined to rely on this promise.[10] He continued praising God through the afternoon and through the dinner hour. As people began to gather for that evening's service, he dropped to his knees on the platform and continued praising and worshiping God. He did not stop until it was time for the service to begin.

What happened as the service began at 7:30 confirmed in Layzell's mind that he had understood this scriptural promise correctly. The congregation had barely gotten into the first song, "There's Power in the Blood," before one woman threw up her hands in praise, experienced what Pentecostals call being "baptized in the Holy Spirit," and began to speak in tongues. The first woman was soon joined by another and another. Shortly the entire room was engaged in worship at a higher level. Layzell was delighted since it was the first time he could remember ever seeing someone baptized in the Holy Spirit during this initial part of the service, the "song service."[11]

It was a revolutionary moment for Layzell. He believed God had given him the key to maintaining revival in the church through the continuous presence of God. This realization focused the remainder of his trip to British Columbia and, ultimately, moved Layzell to enter full-time pastoral ministry. Offering praise, irrespective of one's feelings, to experience the presence of God would become the centerpiece of Reg Layzell's ministry, to the point that eventually he became known in his circles as the "apostle of praise."[12] It began with a

8. Layzell, *Unto Perfection*, 13; Layzell and Layzell, *Sons of His Purpose*, 36.
9. Gaglardi, *Key of David*, 12.
10. Gaglardi, *Key of David*, 13.
11. Layzell, *Unto Perfection*, 13.
12. Layzell and Layzell, *Sons of His Purpose*, 134–35; Bill Hamon, *The Eternal Church: A Prophetic Look at the Church—Her History, Restoration, and Destiny*, rev. ed. (Shippensburg, PA: Destiny Image, 2003), 233; Howard Rachinski, "From Praise to Worship," in *An Anthology of Articles on Restoring Praise & Worship to the Church*, ed. David K. Blomgren, Dean Smith, and Douglas Christoffel (Shippensburg, PA: Revival, 1989), 136. Note that Rachinski, the

single verse, Psalm 22:3, about which Layzell testified that "God burned that verse into me, and I preached nothing else but praise, praise, praise."[13]

That journey began with the remainder of the week in Abbotsford. Daily Layzell searched his biblical concordance for other Scriptures that mentioned praise; daily Layzell expounded on these Scriptures to the Abbotsford church. It was during one of these study sessions that Layzell received the second verse that would be critical to the message that he preached for almost forty years. This second verse was Hebrews 13:15 ("By him [Christ] therefore let us offer the sacrifice of praise to God continually, that is, the fruit of our lips giving thanks to his name," KJV), by which Layzell understood that God has commanded us to offer praise regardless of human feelings or emotions. Offering praise, he concluded, was sacrificial because worshipers should offer it as an act of obedience to a divine command regardless of feelings.[14] But, because the command to praise is tied to the promise that God will indeed inhabit praise, this command itself becomes a gift from God to the church. Layzell's own experience on that initial Wednesday in January confirmed the veracity of this theology in his mind. Even though he had not felt like praising God, he chose to do so, trusting in what he saw as a divine promise attached to his act of praising. His—and the church's—experience on that Wednesday authenticated the theology and validated his faith. Layzell now had a fundamental message, one he continued to proclaim for the remainder of this trip to British Columbia. At the end, he returned to his home in Wiarton, a small town north of Toronto.

Shortly thereafter Layzell received a letter from the same Pentecostal superintendent who had first invited him to British Columbia, now asking him to take the pastorate of a small church in the town of Mission, directly across the Fraser River from Abbotsford. Layzell accepted and moved his family west in the summer of 1946. Layzell began his ministry focusing on bringing reconciliation to an internal divide among his church's members. After that breach was healed, the new pastor plunged into sharing what he had learned in Abbotsford: "the truth God had revealed to him of the 'sacrifice of praise'" and "how the Lord had revealed to him the secret of his presence."[15] As Layzell taught his congregation about the connection between praise and God's presence, the church in Mission began to grow. Its renewal confirmed again for Layzell several things: his linkage of Psalm 22:3 and Hebrews 13:15,

---

founder of Christian Copyright Licensing International, grew up in Layzell's longtime pastorate in Vancouver. His father, Ernie Rachinski, was Layzell's choir director from 1953 to 1963.

13. Layzell, *Unto Perfection*, 121.

14. Layzell, *Unto Perfection*, 10.

15. Layzell and Layzell, *Sons of His Purpose*, 46.

the centrality of these verses as a hermeneutic for interpreting Scripture with respect to worship, these verses as the linchpin in perpetuating revival, and the gift of all this insight as a revelation from God. Layzell's first pastorate began to flourish and he made multiple contacts in his time there that would have historical significance in the future, because these contacts would provide the platform for wider dissemination of Layzell's theology.

Latter Rain Produces a River

One of these contacts was George Hawtin, a Pentecostal educator in North Battleford, Saskatchewan, a province in the center of Canada. The men had been introduced during a series of meetings in Terrace, British Columbia,[16] and they renewed their acquaintance in Vancouver at a four-day, city-wide campaign of healing meetings led by itinerant Pentecostal evangelist William Branham in November 1947.[17] Hawtin had come to Vancouver with a group from his institution, the Sharon Orphanage and School. Branham's meetings increased Layzell's and Hawtin's appetites for a greater move of God in each of their locations. The two men shared their common desire and entered into a covenant to seek this move. They also agreed to contact each other when something happened.[18]

That call soon came. In the spring of 1948, George Hawtin called Reg Layzell to describe the revival that had broken out in North Battleford, Saskatchewan, at the Sharon institution. The revival, which would be labeled as the Latter Rain movement or the "New Order of the Latter Rain," had begun.[19]

16. According to Layzell and Layzell, *Sons of His Purpose*, 47, the two first met at a camp meeting while Layzell was touring churches in his early 1946 trip. Reg Layzell's own book, *Unto Perfection* (p. 3), states that this first meeting occurred while he was pastor in Mission—i.e., in mid-1946 or later.

17. Branham is considered the initiator of the post–World War II healing revival. The trip to Vancouver was one of the first after he began emphasizing healing and deliverance as a central part of his ministry. See D. J. Wilson, "William Marrion Branham," in *The New International Dictionary of Pentecostal and Charismatic Movements*, rev. ed., ed. Stanley M. Burgess (Grand Rapids: Zondervan, 2002), 440–41.

18. Layzell and Layzell, *Sons of His Purpose*, 52; Layzell, *Unto Perfection*, 4.

19. The phrase "latter rain" is a biblical term from Joel 2:23 and had been occasionally used previously in the Holiness movement as well as in early Pentecostalism. For background on the Latter Rain movement of the 1940s, the most prolific author has been Richard Riss, who has written multiple books and articles on the movement. See Richard M. Riss, *Latter Rain: The Latter Rain Movement of 1948 and the Mid-Twentieth Century Evangelical Awakening* (Mississauga, ON: Honeycomb Visual Productions, 1987); Richard M. Riss, *A Survey of 20th-Century Revival Movements in North America* (Peabody, MA: Hendrickson, 1988); Richard M. Riss and Kathryn Riss, *Images of Revival: Another Wave Rolls In* (Shippensburg, PA: Revival, 1997); Richard M. Riss, "Latter Rain Movement," in *The New International Dictionary of Pentecostal*

This movement would eventually become the platform by which Layzell's message of praise would be disseminated widely, leading to the development of Praise & Worship as a distinct way of worship.

Having earlier broken with his denomination, the Pentecostal Assemblies of Canada, Hawtin, who had experience as a Bible school administrator, had opened Sharon in October 1947 with the help of several family members and close associates, calling the student body to fasting and prayer.[20] Hawtin's visit the next month to Vancouver to attend the Branham healing meetings only intensified his desire for revival back at the school. That hunger was satisfied on February 12, 1948, as "all Heaven broke loose upon our souls, and Heaven came down to greet us," as Hawtin himself put it.[21] Attending to this move of God soon focused life at Sharon, and an initial camp meeting was held at the end of March. News of the revival had spread and so people from across Canada and the United States flocked to this small town on the Canadian prairie.

At about this time Hawtin fulfilled his earlier promise to Layzell, calling him and telling him about the revival. Hawtin also informed Layzell that a second camp meeting had been scheduled for the upcoming July. Layzell decided to attend.

That same spring, Layzell received a call from a different source, one that would prove instrumental in spreading the Latter Rain revival and placing Layzell at the center of its liturgical impact. This call came from Glad Tidings Temple in Vancouver, a seventeen-year-old Pentecostal church that had recently dedicated a new building in that city's downtown. Glad Tidings was searching for a new pastor. It invited Layzell to come preach a trial sermon. After hearing him speak, the congregation unanimously voted to call him to be its pastor. Layzell and his family moved at the end of June 1948 in anticipation of an official start date in September.[22] The confluence of the North Battleford revival and Layzell's assumption of the Glad Tidings pastorate would make the summer of 1948 an eventful one in the historical development of Praise & Worship.

---

and Charismatic Movements, rev. ed., ed. Stanley M. Burgess (Grand Rapids: Zondervan, 2002), 830–33; and Richard M. Riss, "The New Order of the Latter Rain: A Look at the Revival Movement on Its 40th Anniversary," Assemblies of God Heritage 7, no. 3 (1987): 15–19. For a more recent scholarly summary and appraisal, see D. William Faupel, "The New Order of the Latter Rain: Restoration or Renewal?," in Winds from the North: Canadian Contributions to the Pentecostal Movement, ed. Michael Wilkinson and Peter Althouse (Leiden: Brill, 2010), 239–63. A website organized by Jon Rising also provides a helpful collection of Latter Rain–related articles, pictures, and recordings: The Latter Rain Movement of '48, https://lrm1948.blogspot.com.

20. Faupel, "New Order of the Latter Rain," 240.
21. Quoted in Faupel, "New Order of the Latter Rain," 241.
22. Layzell and Layzell, Sons of His Purpose, 64–65.

In July, Reg Layzell arrived at the North Battleford campground with his two young daughters in tow. Layzell's impressions were favorable as he saw things that fit with his deepest theological commitments. Reflecting on the meeting later, Layzell recalled that a sense of God's presence everywhere was his first strong conviction. Similarly, Layzell appreciated the extensiveness of the prayer and praise, including times of individual prayer giving God thanks and praise before each of the three daily services (morning, afternoon, and evening). Thus, at the North Battleford camp meeting, Layzell saw again a strong connection between praise, prayer, and the experience of divine presence.[23] The strong sense of God's presence in these services reconfirmed for him the veracity of the revelation he had received around praise and Psalm 22:3 two and a half years earlier. Even the acts of spontaneous speech and songs immediately received by revelation from God had a strong praise orientation.

Not surprisingly, a strong affinity developed between Layzell and the emerging revival, including the leaders of the Sharon institution. Indeed, the chorus that usually began the services at North Battleford, "Wonderful, Wonderful Jesus," would become a personal favorite for Layzell; it would soon be sung nearly every Sunday at his church in Vancouver.[24] The leadership in the camp meeting gave Layzell a chance to preach at one afternoon service. He did so but spoke on holiness—not praise!—because he was concerned about the flippant behavior he noticed at the refreshment canteen.[25] Beyond this one sermon, Layzell's connection to the revival would become deep and strong. Within a few months, the *Sharon Star*, which was the newsletter of the North Battleford institution, included Layzell on a short list of ministers who were trusted to be able to bring the revival to new churches as well as to provide "proper instruction from the Word of God as to the new revival."[26]

The affinity between Layzell and the revival went beyond a general sense of experiencing God's presence even as several distinctive emphases began to arise within the revival's message. Layzell shared both the central emphasis of the revival (restoration) and also its main focus of doctrinal application (the church). This doctrinal focus itself had four aspects: the church's nature, mission, authority, and worship. Layzell's writings from the early 1950s express his wholehearted support for Latter Rain theology and practices.[27]

23. Layzell, *Pastor's Pen*, 12, 18–19.
24. Hugh Layzell, Audrey Layzell, and James Layzell, interview by Lester Ruth, January 8, 2018.
25. Layzell, *Pastor's Pen*, 14.
26. The issue of the *Sharon Star* was the May 1, 1949, issue. See Riss, *Latter Rain*, 109.
27. See Layzell, *Pastor's Pen*, for Layzell's writings from this period. By the time he was writing these recollections in the 1950s, Layzell had broken ties with George Hawtin and the

Even before the revival began in February 1948, the North Battleford Sharon leadership already had a view of church history as a series of sequential restorations of truths formerly lost. Returning from the November 1947 Branham campaign in Vancouver, George Hawtin described in the January 1, 1948, edition of the *Sharon Star* the restorations that God was bringing about: Martin Luther had restored the truth of justification by faith alone in the sixteenth century, John Wesley had restored the truth of sanctification, Baptists had restored the truth of the premillennial coming of Christ, the Missionary Alliance had restored the truth of divine healing, and the first Pentecostals at the beginning of the twentieth century had restored the truth of the baptism of the Holy Spirit. Hawtin expected that the next restoration of truth by God would reinforce all of these prior truths as well as bring about a demonstration of all nine gifts of the Holy Spirit as listed in the New Testament.[28]

The outbreak of the revival in February 1948, including the particular demonstrations of the Spirit seen in it, served to confirm in participants' minds the accuracy of this theological idea of restoration. The leaders of the movement would repeat it as the way to place their revival within a larger historical-theological framework.[29] Specifically, what the movement would see as being restored in 1948 were not only the gifts of the Spirit by the laying on of hands but multiple aspects of church life seen in the New Testament: prophecy over individuals by a presbytery, recognition of a full range of offices (including current-day prophets and apostles), and autonomous local church government with elders.[30] The central idea was restoration of and in the church according to Scripture. From the time of the 1948 revival forward, the Latter Rain movement held this concept of progressive restoration of scriptural truth as an underlying hermeneutic shaping its reading of the Bible and approach to ecclesiastical life and practices, including worship.[31]

For long-established Pentecostal denominations like the Pentecostal Assemblies of Canada and the US-based Assemblies of God, among others, this Latter Rain framing of history was infuriating. While it affirmed the vibrancy of the original Pentecostal outpouring at the beginning of the century, it also was an indictment of the general state of Pentecostalism mid-century. In addition, the view that God was granting a new restoration of

---

other leadership in North Battleford. In his eyes, those leaders had fallen into error and left the original emphases of the revival.

28. Riss, *Latter Rain*, 57.

29. Layzell and Layzell, *Sons of His Purpose*, C-1. See also Layzell, *Unto Perfection*, 46–48.

30. An excellent summary of early Latter Rain theology centered on restoration in and of the church is found in Faupel, "New Order of the Latter Rain," 246–59.

31. Riss, *Latter Rain*, 70.

things previously unknown among Pentecostals was itself a not-so-subtle critique of the limitations of the events at the beginning of the century that had launched Pentecostalism. Not surprisingly, in the late 1940s and early 1950s a series of denominational and individual statements denouncing the Latter Rain movement emerged.[32]

This Latter Rain hermeneutic of restoration provided a conceptual home for Reg Layzell and the theology he had developed concerning praise as the means to experience God's presence. As Layzell visited the camp meeting in summer 1948 and continued his association with the North Battleford–based revival, several shared aspects made a syncing between Layzell and the emerging revival possible. One was that Layzell had a prior relationship with George Hawtin. The two had shared aspirations for Pentecostal church renewal. And so, when Layzell saw the new restorations that were manifested in North Battleford, he accepted them (and thereafter decided to chart a course independent of the Pentecostal Assemblies of Canada).

A second shared aspect was that Layzell was already on board with the root notion of restoration of scriptural truth. It was how he framed the revelation of praise given to him in Abbotsford in January 1946. Layzell believed that God had given him a Scripture verse, Psalm 22:3, involving a promise: God will inhabit the praises of his people. His experience in 1946 as well as his broader searching of Scripture made Layzell think that the connection between praise and God's presence was not something totally new but something that had been lost and was now being restored by God's gracious gift. The centrality of praise in North Battleford's worship, along with the pervasive sense of God's presence there, reconfirmed for Layzell that God was indeed restoring the biblical truth of divine inhabitation of praise.

Layzell would also have seen an affinity between his active approach to scriptural promises and the approach seen in North Battleford. Both rejected a former kind of Pentecostal spirituality that relied on tarrying, passively waiting for the Lord to act or waiting for a certain feeling or sense of being led. Instead, both Layzell and the revivalists in North Battleford emphasized an active approach to experiencing the things of God: one should act in faith based on a divine promise or command.[33] For Layzell in 1946, this meant offer-

32. See, for example, the series of scathing denunciations from R. E. (Robert Edward) McAlister, a patriarch in the Pentecostal Assemblies of Canada, printed as *Truth Advocate* newsletters beginning in June 1949. For the Assemblies of God, see the 23rd General Council of the Assemblies of God, *Minutes and Constitution with Bylaws Revised* (Seattle: September 9–14, 1949), 26. Cf. Faupel, "New Order of the Latter Rain," 259.

33. For an example of the conflict between Latter Rain piety and other Pentecostal piety on the necessity of tarrying, see Kevin J. Conner, *This Is My Story* (Vermont, VIC: Conner Ministries, 2007), 220.

ing the "sacrifice of praise" in order to experience God's inhabitation during worship; in North Battleford, this meant active laying on of hands so that people could be baptized in the Holy Spirit and manifest the gifts of the Spirit.

In addition, there was affinity in the strong communal aspects of Layzell's teaching and the North Battleford revival. The belief in the restoration of the true people of God was pervasive in the teaching and practices of the Latter Rain revival. Similarly, what Layzell had perceived in Psalm 22:3 had clear corporate, ecclesiastical underpinnings. What he saw God restoring through the key of Psalm 22:3 was a people of praise, since it was a praising by *Israel* that God inhabited. As praise became foundational to Layzell's liturgical understanding, he understood praise as the true work of all God's people. Thus, North Battleford and Layzell shared the same corporate sensibility in worship, whether in the common act of praising or in the manifestation of the Spirit's gifts.

As Reg Layzell had accepted the restoration of praise given to him in 1946, so he accepted the restorations he saw in the 1948 Latter Rain revival in North Battleford. Harmonizing the two times of restoration, Layzell soon saw the sacrifice of obedient praise as the key to maintaining the revival. As he explained in 1954, although "God always starts a (divine) visitation in His sovereignty," God expects faithful people to continue it according to the pattern given in Scripture.[34] Therefore, for Layzell, not only did his message about praise find a home within the Latter Rain revival; it was the key to perpetuating it.

The alliance that had been formed between Layzell and the leaders of the Latter Rain revival would be reinforced by a visit that took place a few months after Layzell's trip to the summer camp meeting.[35] A team of nine from the Sharon institution came at Layzell's invitation to Glad Tidings Temple, his new pastorate in Vancouver. The team arrived in mid-November 1948, after Layzell had been in this pastorate for less than three months.[36] Members of the team included George Hawtin and his brother, Ern; Violet Kiteley, whose own pastoral ministry would have a tremendous impact on Praise & Worship; and Phyllis and James Spiers, who in the early years seem to have been the

34. Layzell, *Pastor's Pen*, 6. Not surprisingly, Layzell likewise rooted this theology of divine sovereignty and human continuance in its own biblical pattern by citing Exod. 25:40, in which God is addressing Moses: "And look that thou make them after their pattern, which was shewed thee in the mount" (KJV).

35. Riss, *Latter Rain*, 87; Layzell and Layzell, *Sons of His Purpose*, 76.

36. He had accepted the call to the church in the spring, moving his family there in June, but had delayed the start of his work in this congregation until September. He notified the congregation when he began that the "Hawtin party" would be coming in November.

musical face of the Latter Rain revival and its praise and worship. This team ministered for three weeks in Vancouver.

The three weeks of twice-a-day services led by the North Battleford team in November manifested the happy union between Reg Layzell's emphasis on praise and the approach to worship that had been restored in the Latter Rain revival. Reg Layzell's adult son, Hugh, described the harmony, literal and figurative, between the two as he arrived in Vancouver and encountered the team preparing for that evening's meeting:

> Before we reached the second floor [of Glad Tidings], we were riveted by a sound that is hard to describe, of voices blending together in harmonious praise. It is called the Heavenly Choir! There was no instrument, and it wasn't a known song, but the group was singing in beautiful harmony—a spiritual song that literally sent "chills" up and down our spines. It was indeed heavenly and very moving! We were somewhat transfixed, as we stood outside the room, while the team inside blended their voices in this Spirit-inspired song of praise.[37]

All the liturgical aspects of the revival were on display in the Vancouver meeting, in addition to the "heavenly choir," a musical practice first attested at another meeting involving the Hawtins elsewhere in Canada during the previous month (October).[38] This practice, which could continue for long, indefinite periods of time, involved unscripted, ecstatic congregational singing either in one's known language or in tongues.[39] As the voices spontaneously harmonized, the result seemed otherworldly for its participants. As experienced, the essence of such singing was the praise of God, a feature that further solidified the centrality of praise in the worship of the Latter Rain revival.

In addition, George Hawtin's teaching on spiritual gifts within the Body of Christ was accompanied by a display of the same gifts across the congregation. Prophecy and the laying on of hands by the presbytery had imparted the gifts. Prophetic words were spoken over many individuals, including a pastor from Detroit named Myrtle Beall, who herself would soon become a prominent leader in this movement. Through the entire service there was,

37. Layzell and Layzell, *Sons of His Purpose*, 76.
38. Specifically, the meeting was the annual Canadian National Convention of the Independent Assemblies of God, held in Edmonton, Alberta in late October 1948. Richard Riss says that it was the public reading of accounts written by Marie B. Woodworth-Etter of such heavenly singing among earlier Pentecostals that triggered the practice in Edmonton (Riss, *Latter Rain*, 83). After the Edmonton meeting, the "heavenly choir" became a regular and important feature of early Latter Rain Praise & Worship.
39. For a musical analysis of such singing in tongues, see Joel Hinck, "Heavenly Harmony: An Audio Analysis of Corporate Singing in Tongues," *Pneuma* 40, nos. 1–2 (2018): 167–91.

as Hugh Layzell described it, a "high level of corporate praise and worship, including singing in the Spirit."[40] For Hugh Layzell there was a stark contrast between this Latter Rain Praise & Worship and the worship he had seen in other Pentecostal churches. Writing to a friend soon after the end of the meetings, the younger Layzell bemoaned how Pentecostalism had drifted from its original power, substituting program, organization, and choirs for the "liberty and power of the Spirit."[41]

The visits of the Hawtin-led, North Battleford–based team to Vancouver and elsewhere in 1948 and 1949[42] were only the beginning of a quickly growing geographic expansion of the Latter Rain revival and, with it, Layzell's teachings about the sacrifice of praise and God's inhabitation of praise. Some of the new locations for revivals, in return, became regional centers for the distribution of the Latter Rain movement across Canada and the United States in an ever-fuller, intertwined network. Consequently, even as the influence of the North Battleford group waned in the early 1950s,[43] the churches and ministers in this broader network were able to maintain the momentum of the revival and continue to spread the message about praise. It did not take long for these churches to settle into a distinctive way of worship demonstrating Latter Rain emphases, including the centrality of praise.

And, as the years after 1948 would show, not only did Layzell recognize some of his essential commitments in North Battleford—the emerging Latter Rain movement also recognized itself in Reg Layzell and his emphasis on praise. Indeed, as the authority of the original leadership in North Battleford waned after 1950, Layzell remained one of the more active and prominent leaders in the broader movement. His place within the movement would become critical as the restoration of praise was folded into the movement's broader notion of church-centered restoration. The Latter Rain movement's

40. Layzell and Layzell, *Sons of His Purpose*, 111.

41. Quoted in Layzell and Layzell, *Sons of His Purpose*, 104–14. The letter is dated January 6, 1949.

42. Other important visits of the Hawtin-related team were to Hibbing, Minnesota (at the church pastored by E. H. Blomberg), and Portland, Oregon (at Wings of Healing Church, pastored by Thomas Wyatt). At the latter meeting in February 1949, George Hawtin found ninety ministers waiting for him from Montana, Iowa, Kansas, Texas, California, Utah, Idaho, Colorado, Washington, and Canada. The meeting lasted three weeks. In addition, a second summer camp meeting in 1949 in North Battleford again flooded that town with visitors from across Canada and the United States. The local newspaper estimated there were three thousand in attendance. See Faupel, "New Order of the Latter Rain," 243.

43. It appears that George and Ern Hawtin increasingly saw themselves as *the* apostles of the Latter Rain revival and took exception when others took steps without first gaining the approval of the Hawtin brothers, as in the formation of a presbytery for the ministry of prophesying. In addition, the Hawtins began teaching ideas that other Latter Rain participants found troubling.

network of churches, teachers, and pastors would become the network for the propagation of praise-based theology and practices of worship. In a movement that recognized modern-day apostles, Layzell would become recognized as its "apostle of praise."[44]

The Developed Theology of Reg Layzell

Layzell's theologizing on Praise & Worship did not end in the late 1940s. He continued to expound a biblical theology for this approach to worship in his own church, in the yearly camp meeting that it sponsored, and in a variety of speaking engagements elsewhere. Layzell's theological teaching after the 1940s continued to emphasize his cornerstone verses, Psalm 22:3 and Hebrews 13:15, as he introduced them to a widening circle of congregations and instilled a sense that offering praise should be an act of the worshiper's will, not something left to an impulse of feeling. But Layzell did not limit his teaching to these verses. As he taught through the 1950s, these verses were only the core of an integrated biblical liturgical theology that portrayed God's restoration of Praise & Worship as a gracious, powerful gift to the church.

As one would expect, the emphasis on praise was the dominant feature of Layzell's theologizing. His zealous use of a Bible concordance to find all references to praise—a practice he seemingly continued to pursue after that first week in Abbotsford, British Columbia—bore much fruit. If his preserved writings are any indication, several distinct themes can be discerned within his emphasis on praise.[45]

The first theme was the foundational one: the linking of praising God with the coming of divine presence and the worshiping assembly's experience of the same. Indeed, Layzell had such a strong conviction—and experience—of this link that he could portray corporate praise as having a causal instrumentality with respect to God's presence. Because God has promised to be present in the praising of the people (Layzell's interpretation of Ps. 22:3) and because God is faithful to divine promises, God will be present when the people praise in

---

44. For an example, see Hamon, *Eternal Church*, 233.

45. A series of Layzell's teachings through the 1950s can be found in Layzell, *Pastor's Pen*, the anthology compiled by Layzell's associate pastor, Maureen Gaglardi. That book, along with interviews with the Layzell family and Fran and Dave Huebert (January 7, 2018), are the basis for this discussion of Layzell's teaching. Our interviews with the family led us to think that the materials of *Pastor's Pen* generally reflect Layzell's emphases throughout the period, regardless of the setting in which they were taught. According to the foreword of *Pastor's Pen*, the sources for its content were Layzell's early writings plus taped and typed sermons. According to the Layzell family, the book was a collection of his Sunday morning bulletin entries.

Figure 1.1. Reg Layzell preaching in Uganda. His son, Hugh, sits on the platform behind him.

corporate liturgy. Layzell was so sure of the causal connection between praise and presence that he proclaimed that a praising people could bring about the divine presence. Commenting on Psalm 149:6, he stressed the causative link: "High praises in our mouths. Yes!—but not just for a noise or for a good feeling, but because He (Jesus) inhabits the praise of Israel. We produce or release the presence of the captain of the Lord's army."[46] Layzell interpreted the story of Jonah with a similar motif, seeing the prophet's sacrifice of thanksgiving (Jon. 2:9) as an "act of faith producing the special presence of the delivering Lord."[47] Layzell also similarly construed the Acts 2 story of the original outpouring of the Holy Spirit, the foundational narrative of Pentecostal identity. Stating that Psalm 22:3 had come to the disciples "in revelation" after Christ's ascension, Layzell portrayed them spending the intervening ten days praising God, trusting in the promise of that verse: "They knew He [God] had to appear so they did that which produced His appearing."[48] Praising brought about the outpouring of the Holy Spirit. As it was then, Layzell taught, so it is now.

46. Layzell, *Pastor's Pen*, 95.

47. Layzell, *Unto Perfection*, 14. Note that this book was published in the 1970s. The use of Jonah in this way appears to be a continuation of Layzell's early thought, not a development. His daughter, Marion Peterson, affirmed in her interview that the Jonah story was a favorite of her father's.

48. Layzell, *Pastor's Pen*, 150. See also pp. 143–47, 151–52, and 156–59.

Layzell's interpretation of Acts 2 shows how central this causative link between praise and God's presence was for him. For Layzell, what the first Pentecost was about—and thus what the church filled by the Holy Spirit is about—was no other than a confirmation of the promise that God will come and inhabit the praises of his people. In a series of messages from April 1953, Layzell laid out his fusion of Psalm 22:3 and the Pentecost narrative.[49] Noting that before Jesus's ascension he had told the disciples to wait in Jerusalem until the promised Spirit should come and that according to Psalm 65:1 waiting involves praising ("Praise waiteth for thee, O God, in Sion," KJV), Layzell interpreted the pouring out of the Holy Spirit on the day of Pentecost in light of the first disciples' reliance on Psalm 22:3. He framed his interpretation as an exhortation to the church today:

> In Acts 2 we have a great secret yet to be learned by the present day church. It is not more doctrine, or more apostles or prophets that we need, but more of Jesus' manifest presence. Psalm 22:3—He inhabits the praises of Israel. They [i.e., the disciples at Pentecost] so believed it that they did not cease until it became a truth experimentally. Theologically we believe it—mentally we assent to it—experimentally more Christians are strangers to its truth. As the unsaved churchgoer is to salvation—so most Christians are to this great secret of His presence.[50]

Thus when Layzell connected Psalm 22:3 to the Pentecost narrative of Acts 1–2, he connected his theology of God-inhabited-praise with the most essential biblical text in Pentecostalism.

The causal connection behind praise and presence, supported by a sense that this link is what God has scripturally promised, was behind Layzell's insistence that praising God must come before feelings. This thought was the second theme in his teaching on praise and was likewise foundational for his theology. God's people have been commanded to offer a sacrifice of praise. Thus, praise is a volitional act of faith in God's promise on the part of the worshiper. Praise is to be offered as an act of obedience, regardless of feelings or of whether it brings criticism to the worshiper. In this way, Layzell made Hebrews 13:15 the interpretive key to understanding many references to sacrifice in the Bible. Because God is worthy of praise, Layzell taught, worshipers should praise him "feelings or no feelings." Indeed, praising God when there are no feelings is a "bigger crucifixion" and is thus useful as a "great weapon in slaying that carnal mind."[51]

49. Layzell, *Pastor's Pen*, 159–63.
50. Layzell, *Pastor's Pen*, 163. Note, too, how Luke 24:53 describes the disciples' waiting as involving continuing praising and blessing of God in the temple.
51. Layzell, *Pastor's Pen*, 162.

This weaponizing of praise was the third theme found in Layzell's emphasis on praise. Because God will not be passive or impotent when present, praise that brings about God's presence can be used as a spiritual weapon, including the bringing of deliverance. Some of Layzell's favorite Scriptures about praise were linked to praise being the instrument that caused deliverance and aided spiritual warfare. Just as Jonah was delivered through praising God, for example, so were Paul and Silas when they were imprisoned (Acts 16:25–26).[52] Because God promised to inhabit his people's praise, in Layzell's view, praise in the mouth of the worshiping church was an effective weapon against spiritual forces.

In contrast to this militaristic image of praise stood a fourth, gentler theme in Layzell's emphasis on praise—namely, praise as love for God and delight in God. While there could be a hard edge in Layzell's insistence that God be praised regardless of feelings, occasionally he went beyond the issue of volition to suggest that praise results from a transformed desire for God. "Is He precious enough to you to praise Him?" Layzell once asked his congregation.[53] This tenderness is reflected in another of Layzell's favorite praise texts, Jeremiah 33:11, which speaks of voices of joy, gladness, a bridegroom, and the bride who praises the Lord.[54] Indeed, the goal of God's presence and visitation was "a church so in love with God that it is a joy to sit in His presence. . . . A church so in love with God that with joy they serve one another."[55] This church, Layzell explained, was to be so enamored of the goodness and mercy of God that it would become "like David," full of people "after God's own heart."[56]

This church of active praising would be God's gift through the sacrifice of praise. Layzell's emphasis on praise being restored by God was the fifth of his key themes. Layzell was crystal clear that God was the active agent in restoration: "In January 1946, the Lord restored the 'Sacrifice of Praise.'"[57] Commenting on the whole Latter Rain revival, he writes, "A new experience in God was introduced by the Spirit as He restored that wholesale, wholehearted worship to the Lord."[58]

More specifically, Layzell taught that Praise & Worship was the pattern that God gave to continue the revival. Because it was a pattern he found in the Scriptures, Layzell thus rooted the restoration of Praise & Worship in the Bible

52. Layzell, *Unto Perfection*, 14.
53. Layzell, *Pastor's Pen*, 157.
54. Layzell, *Pastor's Pen*, 95, 147; Layzell, *Unto Perfection*, 13.
55. Layzell, *Pastor's Pen*, 182.
56. Layzell, *Pastor's Pen*, 207.
57. Layzell, *Unto Perfection*, 3.
58. Layzell, *Pastor's Pen*, 207.

and not just in his or others' dramatic experiences of God in the revival's Praise & Worship. God may start a major move in sovereignty, but God also "expects us to keep it going as He gave it to us" by the pattern given in the Scriptures.[59] The pattern was not a difficult one; it only required "simple obedience of God's divine recipes: praise and blessing God—with one mind—in one place."[60]

Early Practices of Praise & Worship

In actual liturgical practice, what was the scriptural pattern for Praise & Worship under Layzell's influence? What did his theology on Praise & Worship mean in terms of congregational practices after some time had passed from the original Latter Rain revival of the late 1940s? To answer those questions, we will look at the practices of one of the early church plants spawned by Layzell, a fledging congregation in Chilliwack, British Columbia, sixty miles east of Vancouver and twenty miles east of Abbotsford, to see what Layzell's theology and leadership produced.[61]

Glad Tidings Fellowship Church in Chilliwack, British Columbia, began as a small group of women who met to support each other in a deepened spiritual desire.[62] As the small group began to take root, its members invited Reg Layzell to come and preach. In 1958 the fledgling group began to meet in a storefront. After the newborn congregation had had a series of short-term pastorates, Layzell set Fran and Dave Huebert as elders and pastors of the church in 1961. They would serve in that capacity until 1997, with Fran having main responsibility for the music and Dave preaching and exercising a prophetic gift. By 1964 the congregation had grown to forty members; the church then purchased its first building. The congregation continued to grow and finally gained acceptance within the Christian community of the city—a larger facility was completed in 1975.

Liturgical activities in this congregation in its early years began at 9 a.m., an hour ahead of the scheduled start of the main service. Meeting in a separate

59. Layzell, *Pastor's Pen*, 6.
60. Layzell, *Pastor's Pen*, 153. Notice the allusion to the Pentecost narrative from Acts 2:1.
61. Brief descriptions of other early Praise & Worship services in the Latter Rain movement are available in the following published sources: Hamon, *Eternal Church*, 230–32; and Ernest B. Gentile, *Your Sons & Daughters Shall Prophesy: Prophetic Gifts in Ministry Today* (Grand Rapids: Chosen Books, 1999), 294–95.
62. The history of Glad Tidings Fellowship Church (now called City Life Church) comes from an interview of its longest-serving pastors, Fran and Dave Huebert, by Lester Ruth (January 7, 2018). See also Layzell and Layzell, *Sons of His Purpose*, 99, 221–24; and "(1961–2011)," at the City Life Church website, accessed May 10, 2019, https://www.citylifechurch.ca/what-we-are-all-about/our-story-so-far.

prayer room, members would pray out loud for the hour. Individual expressions of praise dominated the prayer, although members could share prayer requests and pray for each other. This practice of an extended time of pre-service praising was a practice inherited from Reg Layzell's congregation in Vancouver; it was also common in churches impacted by the 1948 Latter Rain revival.[63]

At 10 a.m., those who had gathered for the pre-service praise and prayer would move to the main auditorium to begin the scheduled service. The congregation began by singing, with a strong focus on short choruses and testimonial songs. There were no songbooks in the hands of worshipers and lyrics were not otherwise presented to the congregation.[64] Praise was a dominant motif. There was much repetition of songs. The songs were not preselected and, in the earliest years, neither was the song leader. The Hueberts initially followed Layzell's practice of picking a song leader immediately before the start of the main service.[65] (Over time that changed, as the pastors began to see who was especially gifted for this responsibility. By the late 1960s and early 1970s, these designated song leaders had begun to prepare a bit.) There was no choir, except for the more elaborate, planned Christmas program. Everything was geared toward simplicity and full, active congregational participation; there was nothing that was elaborate or complicated.

The time for congregational singing lasted about an hour, with the first part of the time dedicated to joyful praise. The worshipers' desire was that God would "come and consume the sacrifice of praise" so that the congregation could discern the manifest presence of God. At that time the congregation would move into "high praise" or "high worship" as it exulted in the divine presence. There was a general sense of regular movement from praise to worship in this time of congregational singing, but the order was not tightly scripted or planned. Indeed, in some services there was nothing but joyful praise as the leaders actively discerned the Holy Spirit's leading. When there was movement from praise to worship, the congregation spent the second part of the hour worshiping in the divine presence and exhibiting the Spirit's gifts and movement.

A contemporaneous songbook compiled and used by a musician in Layzell's own church in Vancouver gives a sense of the music and song repertoire of this

63. Marion Peterson, interview by Lester Ruth, February 20, 2018; H. Layzell, A. Layzell, and J. Layzell, interview; Layzell and Layzell, *Sons of His Purpose*, 167. Cf. B. Maureen Gaglardi, *After This Manner* (Vancouver: Glad Tidings Temple, 1963), 95.

64. Most Latter Rain–related congregations eschewed hymnals in their pews. Sabine Tabernacle in Beaumont, Texas, appears to have been an exception. See Jeannie Hilton McWilliams, *From the Past, to the Present, for Our Future* (Beaumont, TX: Sabine Tabernacle, 2005), 114. Cf. Hamon, *Eternal Church*, 231.

65. Ensembles of vocalists were not used until the early 1980s.

daughter congregation. The songbook itself contains pieces from the earliest days of the Latter Rain movement as well as songs from across the 1950s and the early 1960s.[66] The result was an eclectic mix of songs that could have been found in many other Pentecostal or evangelical[67] congregations and of songs circulating in the Latter Rain movement. (Phyllis Spiers was represented, as well as songs rejoicing in the falling of a latter rain.) For many of the songs in the collection, the songbook provided only the lyrics, thus placing a strong demand on the skills of the keyboardist as well as allowing for versatility in terms of which musical key was used for the song. These songs without musical notation were often brief, with only four lines of lyrics. Some consisted of a verse and refrain.

Actively discerning how the Spirit was moving, guiding, and gifting was a common responsibility of the entire congregation, not only the leaders. The specific mix that might be seen on any given Sunday would vary, although certain activities were common. Any of the worshipers could be led by the Spirit to exhort the entire congregation. After the singing, there were often prophetic words (almost every Sunday) or "songs of the Lord" spontaneously given by the Spirit in that moment. Sometimes these Spirit-given songs would become more prolonged, with two or three people contributing to the song. Throughout the service, the foundational praise of God could be musical or spoken. And throughout the first hour of the service, the music served as a backdrop for all the Praise & Worship activity, as songs were strung together and as spoken acts melted back into congregational song. Congregational song provided the sinews connecting the whole service.

This role for music meant instrumentalists needed a critical skill: the ability to provide ongoing flow under the whole service by eliminating gaps between songs or acts of worship. (Initially the church worshiped with a piano and a guitar. After the purchase of its first building in 1964, it added a drum kit.) The task of providing flow meant that the song leaders and Fran Huebert, the main musician, increasingly paid attention to the musical key of the songs, trying to get as many songs as possible in the same key. This desire was especially poignant as the congregation moved into a sense of being in God's presence in worship. When Fran did not know what key was coming next, she improvised musically in order to provide some sort of continuity.

66. Gladys Stone songbook, ms., privately owned. Internal clues indicate a compilation date after 1963. The collection was put together by Gladys Stone, who was involved in Glad Tidings Vancouver and later moved to Chilliwack, British Columbia. H. Layzell, A. Layzell, and J. Layzell, interview.

67. Note that here and elsewhere in the book we use the term "evangelical" without any sort of political connotations. By using "evangelical," we only wish to highlight the spiritual, doctrinal, and ecclesiastical dimensions of a certain kind of Christianity.

Throughout the service, worshipers' physical expression was free and unscripted. They could raise hands, stand, kneel, sit, or even dance as they wished and felt led.[68]

After the hour of Praise & Worship, Dave Huebert would preach and give an altar call. Although the sermon followed the time of Praise & Worship, it would be a grave mistake to see Praise & Worship as merely a preliminary to the sermon, a way of getting people ready to hear some preaching. The time of music-driven Praise & Worship had its own integrity and was an important aspect of the entire liturgy.

For the other Christians in Chilliwack, even (and especially) the other Pentecostals, the worship at Glad Tidings Fellowship Church was strange. No other church in town had the same liturgical practices. No other congregation had teaching for or practice of including a period of unscripted, corporately expressed praise. Such praise was just too loud and indecorous. Consequently, as the fledgling congregation lifted its voices in praise, cars would pass by the building honking, their inhabitants yelling insults. The most deeply insulted threw stones and fruit through the church's open windows.[69] And yet the praise continued unabated, since the congregation was confident that God would come and inhabit its sacrifice of praise. Dodging the rocks and the fruit, little did this flock realize at the time that it was a pioneer in liturgical theology and practices that would sweep across the landscape of continental and global Christianity in the remainder of the century.[70]

The Expanding Embrace of Praise & Worship

To think that the early Latter Rain movement and its practice of Praise & Worship was limited to a few cities and people in Canada would be a false

68. According to Hamon (*Eternal Church*, 232), the Holy Spirit had restored dancing in praise at the Layzell-related Crescent Beach camp meeting in 1954, an event Hamon personally witnessed.

69. According to the Hueberts, the abuse lasted until 1973, when a 1959 prophecy from David Schoch that one day the "wagging tongues" would cease was fulfilled. Huebert and Huebert, interview.

70. Our assertion here stands in contrast to the conclusions of some scholars, who have suggested that the Latter Rain movement's impact was minimal and that it can mainly be seen through the Charismatic Renewal movement (see Faupel, "New Order of the Latter Rain," 259; Riss, *Latter Rain*, 144; and L. Thomas Holdcroft, "The New Order of the Latter Rain," *Pneuma* 2, no. 2 [Fall 1980]: 56–57). It is easy to underestimate the movement's impact if one looks for structural or institutional developments, not liturgical ones. If one looks at the impact on congregational worship, however, the impact has been overwhelming; this is the case we hope to make in the remainder of this book. The problem, perhaps, is a basic methodological one endemic in church historiography: the downplaying of the significance of worship as an organizing and investigating category.

impression indeed. One of the elements that marked this new move of God as a genuine revival for its first participants was the geographic breadth of the people who participated in it, starting with those who traveled from across North America to attend the meetings in North Battleford, Saskatchewan. Those who came to the Sharon institution in 1948 were from the breadth and height of Canada as well as from twenty states in the US.[71]

The cavalcade of license plates from various provinces and states anticipated the further spread of the Latter Rain movement and its approach to Praise & Worship. Pastors, musicians, and other worshipers picked up Praise & Worship in one location, then went home and implemented it in another. In addition, Latter Rain leaders were soon traveling and sending out missionaries across the world to disseminate the theology and practices of Praise & Worship. In other words, as important as Reg Layzell and his church were in its early development, Praise & Worship was not limited to him and his Vancouver congregation. To get a sense of this expansion, it is useful to look at some of the instances in which Praise & Worship migrated from one congregation to another, especially highlighting some figures who would be key players in subsequent waves of this way of worship.[72]

One of the most influential would prove to be Myrtle Beall, a Pentecostal pastor from Detroit. Even before the outbreak of the Latter Rain revival in 1948, she had been leading a growing congregation in that city.[73] Originally named Bethesda Tabernacle, the congregation began in 1934 under Beall's leadership as an Assemblies of God congregation. Through the 1930s and 1940s the congregation grew and prospered so that by 1948 Beall was constructing an eighteen-hundred-seat worship space for the renamed Bethesda

71. Faupel, "New Order of the Latter Rain," 241. The potential for a geographically global expansion of the Latter Rain movement was also present from its beginnings. According to Violet Kiteley, an original participant and subsequently an influential Latter Rain pastor, people came to North Battleford from as far away as New Zealand, Australia, Scandinavia, Britain, and India. See Violet Kiteley, "Remembering the Latter Rain," originally published in 2000 in *Charisma* magazine, accessed February 13, 2019, https://www.charismamag.com/site-archives/24 -uncategorised/9494-remembering-the-latter-rain?fbclid=IwAR0dy_ujPVfxZDTuoSrWVdykyp XKSpje3AKTbf-4tuDS1BnCf9MmZYzQW2k.

72. Lists of early important churches can be found in Faupel, "New Order of the Latter Rain," 243; Riss, *Survey of 20th-Century Revival Movements*, 122; and Hamon, *Eternal Church*, 251–52.

73. The fullest account of Beall's story can be found in Myrtle Dorthea Monville Beall, *A Hand on My Shoulder: God's Miraculous Touch on My Life*, ed. K. Joy Hughes Gruits (n.p.: Embrace His Call, 2014), 114–31. See also James L. Beall, *The Ministry of Worship and Praise* (Detroit: Bethesda Missionary Temple, n.d.); and Layzell and Layzell, *Sons of His Purpose*, 93–95. Beall's inclusion in the Latter Rain movement was significant to Reg Layzell, who called attention to it in his early messages about the significance of the revival. See Layzell, *Pastor's Pen*, 53–54.

Missionary Temple.[74] Beall said that she was working on a God-given imperative to build an "armory" in Detroit.

While the building was being constructed, Beall received a phone call from
a friend, Pentecostal evangelist Vera Ludlum (later Vera Bachle), who told her
about a "move of God" in Canada and invited Beall to travel by car to see what
new thing God was doing. Specifically, Ludlum invited Beall to travel with
her to Reg Layzell's church in Vancouver. This trip would end up impacting
Beall and her congregation dramatically with respect to worship and, through
them, many others. Or as Beall herself put it, "The results of the Revival in
Vancouver brought to the lives of many a complete change in their beliefs
and their mode of worship."[75] Beall and Ludlum arrived in Vancouver in time
to experience the November 1948 meetings being held in Layzell's church by
George Hawtin and the team from North Battleford.

Echoing Layzell's own experience when he first got to the North Battleford
campground, Beall was struck by an overwhelming sense of God's presence in
the Vancouver church, especially in its worship, which she called "heavenly."[76]
She imbibed deeply, and her own church would soon reflect the Praise &
Worship she had seen in Layzell's church. Other Latter Rain distinctives, including the ministry of the laying on of hands by a presbytery accompanied
by prophecy, impressed Beall greatly while she was in Vancouver. A group
of ministers laid hands on Beall and spoke of her being associated with an
armory for God, even though they knew nothing of her almost-completed
building project. Beall was convinced; she returned to Detroit fully within
the sphere of Latter Rain thinking, committed to the liturgical theology and
practices she had seen in Vancouver.

By early December 1948, Beall was back in Detroit. Her congregation
gathered on the first Sunday of the month, December 5, in great expectation
to hear about what was happening in Vancouver. Even before the people heard
Beall's report, however, the congregation would get to see Vancouver's way
of worship in their own midst. James Beall, the pastor's son, reported what
spontaneously happened:

> It was my place to open the service with prayer and to lead the congregation in
> song. I stepped to the pulpit and asked the people to stand for prayer. Instead

74. Beall's church would soon leave the Assemblies of God denomination. The church is
now called Bethesda Christian Church and is located in a suburb of Detroit called Sterling
Heights. Perfecting Church, a congregation pastored by gospel musician Marvin Winans, in
1996 purchased the building that Bethesda had vacated. We extend our appreciation to Jon
Rising for informing us of that fact.

75. M. Beall, *Hand on My Shoulder*, 119.

76. M. Beall, *Hand on My Shoulder*, 120.

Figure 1.2. Worshipers singing at Bethesda Missionary Temple in 1958

of quietly awaiting for someone to lead us to the throne of grace, the congregation spontaneously, under the sovereign leading of the Holy Spirit, raised their hands and began to "sing praises to God," together and in harmony. It was the sound of a heavenly choir as wave after wave of praise swept over the congregation. Since that time we have nurtured and endeavored to develop the ministry of praise and worship in this local church. We have learned the praises of his people provide a habitation for God.[77]

For the people involved, longtime Pentecostals, it was a new experience. As Myrtle Beall's daughter put it, "This spiritual worship and praise [which on this occasion lasted for about an hour] was unheard of at the time."[78] In addition to the congregational singing in the Spirit and immersion in praise, this service also included what would become commonplace in the movement's first decades: spontaneously inspired song.

When Bethesda Missionary Temple's new building opened in mid-February 1949, it became a new center for Latter Rain revival and worship.[79] The

77. J. Beall, *Ministry of Worship*, 17–18. Notice Beall referencing the same extended, ecstatic singing in the Spirit that had marked the Canadian revival. One wonders about the reports that the Detroit congregation had been receiving while Myrtle Beall was gone.

78. M. Beall, *Hand on My Shoulder*, 122.

79. Bethesda Missionary Temple would disassociate from the Assemblies of God by 1950.

congregation reportedly held near-daily services for the next three and a half years, including a stint in the Coliseum at the Michigan State Fairgrounds because the crowds were so large. But the congregation often worshiped without Myrtle Beall in attendance since she traveled extensively after becoming affiliated with the Latter Rain movement. For example, in 1950 alone, Beall traveled to Beaumont, Texas, to speak at Sabine Tabernacle; to St. Louis, Missouri, to speak at the national Latter Rain conference; and to Elim Bible Institute in New York State to give its commencement speech.[80]

Beall's trip to Elim in 1950 was not her first contact with this school, which will be our second example of the spread of Latter Rain Praise & Worship. Elim Bible Institute had been created by Ivan Spencer in 1924.[81] By the late 1940s it was a thriving, yet small, Pentecostal school in New York State. It was also the center for a Pentecostal network, the Pentecostal Prayer Fellowship, which connected ministers across several other smaller networks. In December 1948 in Providence, Rhode Island, this fellowship had gathered to pray and hope for revival when its members heard of what was happening at Myrtle Beall's church in Detroit. After the meeting concluded, Ivan Spencer returned home for his wife and informed their adult son, Carlton, that they were heading to Detroit to see for themselves. Leaving Carlton in charge of the school, the elder Spencers visited Bethesda Missionary Temple. What they saw fulfilled their hopes. Returning to Elim, Ivan told Carlton to go see for himself, and so the son made his own pilgrimage to Detroit with a team from Elim. Between the two visits, the Spencers would become fully immersed in the Latter Rain movement, and Elim would become its own center for the spread of praise-based worship along with the other distinctives of the early Latter Rain movement.[82] Elim multiplied Latter Rain Praise & Worship through its students, the network already associated with the school, special meetings, foreign missionaries associated with the school, and its faculty. Some of the faculty members would play significant historical roles in future decades.[83] Ivan Spencer and his wife, Minnie, spent a good part of early 1949 on a road trip through the United

80. Charles Green, interview by Lim Swee Hong and Lester Ruth, October 13, 2017; Riss, *Survey of 20th-Century Revival Movements*, 189n68; Marion Meloon, *Ivan Spencer: Willow in the Wind* (Lima, NY: Elim Bible Institute, 1997), 162.

81. The best source of information on Elim Bible Institute and the Spencers is Meloon, *Ivan Spencer*, 142–71. The account here is dependent on this source.

82. Many of those ministering at Bethesda would become associates or even faculty at Elim. The Spencers would become friends with the Layzell family and would be instrumental in Hugh and Audrey Layzell's long-term missionary work in Africa. See Layzell and Layzell, *Sons of His Purpose*, 161, 259.

83. Two key examples are Bob Mumford, who would be an influential figure in the Charismatic Renewal movement as well as in the rise of Integrity's Hosanna! Music, and Bob Sorge, who would be a major early teacher and writer on Praise & Worship in the 1980s.

States to see and speak in other regional centers of the expanding Liturgical movement. Their trip took them to South Carolina, Florida, Alabama, Texas (to Beaumont's Sabine Tabernacle), Missouri, Indiana, and Ohio.

Sabine Tabernacle in Beaumont, Texas, had a role in the stories of both Myrtle Beall and Ivan Spencer, as we have seen. It would also play a significant part in Charles Green's history as a conveyor of Praise & Worship.

At the beginning of 1950, Charles Green was a recent college graduate and associate pastor in a United Pentecostal congregation in Baton Rouge, Louisiana.[84] Green's senior pastor, Bill Marshall, had visited Sabine Tabernacle and seen there the Latter Rain approach to Praise & Worship and church life. Marshall instructed Green to go observe on his own. Marshall intentionally did not tell Green anything about what to expect, to avoid prejudicing Green in one way or the other. His intent was to be able to enter into mutual discernment with Green about whether what was happening in the Latter Rain movement was of God and, if so, whether to steer their Baton Rouge church in that direction.

Green was soon convinced that Latter Rain Praise & Worship was indeed of God. He arrived at Sabine Tabernacle on a Wednesday in late February 1950, just before the start of the mid-afternoon service. That service began dramatically with a congregation of hundreds singing simple choruses. After an initial piano arpeggio,[85] the congregation started with the chorus "God Is Moving by His Spirit."[86] By the third time through the chorus, Green was weeping, hands held high. The next chorus was even simpler, organized around only two phrases: "He's all I need" and "all that I need." Singing such short choruses was new to Green, but it had a deep impact on him. Describing the experience later, he confessed these Texas Christians "were freely worshipping and praising God" while previously his own church's efforts at praising God were "very, very small indeed."[87]

This way of worship was not the only thing Green took in from the Latter Rain movement. Green accepted the Latter Rain teaching about the laying on of hands, the gifts of the Spirit, and the fivefold ministry gifts of apostles, prophets, evangelists, pastors, and teachers, learning these things from some of the national leaders in the movement.[88] While Green did come away

---

84. Green, interview. A published account of Green's story can be found at E. S. Caldwell, "Charles Green: Called to Win a Sinful City," *Charisma* 10 (February 1985): 54–57, 58, 60, 62–63.

85. An arpeggio is a chord broken into a sequence of notes.

86. © 1946 Mrs. L. C. Hall. Assigned 1966 to Gospel Publishing House (admin. by Music Services Inc.).

87. Caldwell, "Charles Green," 58.

88. The main speakers at the February 1950 meeting were Raymond Hoekstra and Thomas Wyatt. In April 1950 Green heard Myrtle Beall at this same church. Green, interview; and Charles Green, interview by Lester Ruth, May 3, 2019.

thinking that what he had seen was of God, he had little chance to influence the church in Baton Rouge because he was soon charged with taking a pastorate in Port Arthur, Texas, a town twenty miles southeast of Beaumont.[89] There his ministry flourished. Eventually (in 1953) he would move to New Orleans and in that city lead a Pentecostal congregation that would eventually become a megachurch, Word of Faith Temple.[90]

Beyond the impact of the two churches he would pastor, Green also represents the sort of complex network of guest preaching, personal relationships, and writing that helped to disseminate the Latter Rain revival's praise-based approach to worship. Within a few years of his first exposure in 1950, for example, Green went on a trip across Europe spreading the message and means of Praise & Worship.[91] He also preached extensively across the United States, including more than one hundred times (over the course of five decades) at Bethesda Missionary Temple in Detroit after he became close friends with James, the son of Myrtle Beall.[92] Indeed, Green's friendship network would become widespread, including recognized leaders within and outside the Latter Rain movement. The latter category included David Yonggi Cho (Korean megachurch pastor), Oral Roberts (founder of a university where Green would serve as a regent), Demos Shakarian (founder of the Full Gospel Business Men's Fellowship International), and Jack Hayford (pastor of Church on the Way in Van Nuys, California, and fourth president of the International Church of the Foursquare Gospel).[93]

As these examples show, the Latter Rain movement's lack of organizational unity did not hamper its rapid expansion. It and its liturgical approach, Praise & Worship, spread among those whom one scholar has called the "denominationally dispossessed and the ever-growing crowd of mobile

89. The United Pentecostal denomination dismissed Bill Marshall and Charles Green from its fellowship in the summer of 1950.

90. Green would eventually change the name of the church to Faith Church.

91. The trip included time in Hamburg, Germany, where Green had to overcome the Germans' reluctance to raise their hands in praise because of hand raising's association with the Nazi era under Hitler. Green, interview (October 13, 2017).

92. Jon Rising, "Charles Green's Tribute to James Beall," *The Latter Rain Movement of '48*, October 4, 2013, https://lrm1948.blogspot.com/2013/10/charles-greens-tribute-to-james-beall.html.

93. Hayford opened for Green the sort of writing opportunity that has often exemplified the spreading and mainstreaming of the Latter Rain movement's praised-based approach to worship. Hayford commissioned Green to write a teaching section for the study Bible that Hayford was editing, giving Green the specific assignment to write on praise. Published in the widely sold *Spirit Filled Life Bible* (originally released in 1991), Green's piece was titled "The Pathway of Praise" and used twenty Scriptures, including Ps. 22:3 and Heb. 13:15, to lay out the centrality of praise. See Charles Green, "The Pathway of Praise," in *Spirit Filled Life Bible*, ed. Jack W. Hayford (Nashville: Nelson, 1991), xxix–xxx.

convention-goers."[94] Consequently, even when the older, established Pentecostal denominations such as the Pentecostal Assemblies of Canada or the Assemblies of God rejected the early Latter Rain movement and everything associated with it, there was still a way for Praise & Worship to increase. When these denominations issued formal, harsh repudiations of the Latter Rain revival,[95] those who were reveling in Praise & Worship and absorbing its theology were either independents, who shrugged off such denominational statements as inferior to their newfound experience of God's presence through praise, or those like Myrtle Beall or Charles Green, who left these denominations to become independent. The joy of knowing God's presence in Praise & Worship seemed a much greater gift than an institutional affiliation.

Free of formal denominational support, the Latter Rain movement and its form of Praise & Worship spread by a variety of means. As we have seen, many of the movement's leaders engaged in speaking tours across North America and the world. Reg Layzell himself took European trips in the 1950s to Sweden (traveling with other Latter Rain ministers from St. Louis, Chicago, and Portland), Denmark, Germany, Switzerland, and Italy. His journeys would eventually take him across the globe: he visited India, Uganda, Australia, Taiwan, China, Mexico, Singapore, Japan, Korea, Norway, and South America.[96] Other early Latter Rain leaders reached Fiji, Indonesia, New Zealand, Australia, Liberia, Egypt, India, Russia, Japan, England, and Sweden.[97]

Much of this international focus derived from a missionary impulse seen at the first summer camp meeting in North Battleford as well as at the first National Latter Rain Convention, held in St. Louis, Missouri, in November 1950. Indeed, the missionary impulse within the Latter Rain movement—surely God's gift of restoration for the church was a gift for the worldwide church—was so important that Latter Rain congregations set up their own international missionary efforts, including one in Layzell's own church in the early 1950s, the Glad Tidings Missionary Society.[98] That agency sent long-

94. Mark Hutchinson, "The Latter Rain Movement and the Phenomenon of Global Return," in *Winds from the North: Canadian Contributions to the Pentecostal Movement*, ed. Michael Wilkinson and Peter Althouse (Leiden: Brill, 2010), 268. Hutchinson (p. 267) also notes how the movement fused to some degree with the North American Healing Revival and its global extensions, including figures like William Branham, Oral Roberts, and T. L. Osborn.

95. For an example, see 23rd General Council of the Assemblies of God, *Minutes and Constitution*, 26.

96. Layzell and Layzell, *Sons of His Purpose*, 173, 175; Peterson, interview.

97. Faupel, "New Order of the Latter Rain," 244–45; Riss, *Latter Rain*, 132–35.

98. Layzell and Layzell, *Sons of His Purpose*, 206.

term missionaries promoting Praise & Worship to Asia (especially Taiwan), Africa (where missionaries included Layzell's own son and daughter-in-law, Hugh and Audrey), and, in 1956, to the Inuit in the Canadian Artic when a young woman, Kayy Gordon, felt called to this ministry.[99] Eventually the Glad Tidings–based society would send missionaries to Central America too.[100]

For Reg Layzell himself, perhaps no outlet for him to teach on Praise & Worship was as important as the annual summer camp meeting sponsored by his church. This took place at Crescent Beach, a spot south of Vancouver just above the border with the United States. There Layzell's congregation displayed Praise & Worship in full course and Layzell had an opportunity to instruct pastors and worshipers who came from across Canada, the United States, and even overseas.[101] Although camp meetings generally were a regular feature of Pentecostalism, many other Latter Rain congregations used them similarly to Layzell's to enjoy what they perceived as God's gift of Praise & Worship and to invite others to participate in it.

Regardless of the particular liturgical setting, early Latter Rain Praise & Worship had started to generate new songs too. Collected and published, these new songs were another way by which Praise & Worship was spread. The first such collection was by Phyllis Spiers, titled *Spiritual Songs by the Spiers: Many New Latter Rain Choruses and Hymns*.[102] Spiers, along with her husband, James, had been present at the summer 1948 camp meeting in North Battleford and had been involved in many of the early trips by its leadership to provide musical leadership as they spread the Latter Rain revival. Thus, the couple was present at Glad Tidings Temple in Vancouver as part of the North Battleford group's visit in November 1948. The title of Phyllis Spiers's songbook used a biblical phrase ("spiritual songs") that in Latter Rain thinking emphasized the direct, God-given quality of the new music. Indeed, there is some hint that the emergence of the heavenly choir helped birth the writing of new Praise & Worship songs, including simple ones based on Scripture,

99. Layzell and Layzell, *Sons of His Purpose*, 263; Kayy Gordon and Lois Neely, *God's Fire on Ice* (Plainfield, NJ: Logos International, 1977), 20. Kayy Gordon, interview by Lester Ruth and Lim Swee Hong, May 17, 2019.

100. See William H. Brown, *Bin Der Dun Dat* (Fort Collins, CO: Book's Mind, 2013), loc. 131, Kindle. Note that according to this book (loc. 121) Layzell himself spent a season in Uganda when William and Gerda Brown were back in Canada on missionary furlough.

101. For a description, see Gentile, *Your Sons & Daughters*, 294–95. See also Hamon, *Eternal Church*, 233. Information for this discussion of Crescent Beach has also been drawn from interviews with the Layzell family: one on January 8, 2018, with Hugh, Audrey, and James Layzell and one on February 20, 2018, with Marion Peterson.

102. Phyllis C. Spiers, *Spiritual Songs by the Spiers: Many New Latter Rain Choruses and Hymns* (Chicago: Philadelphia Book Concern, 1949).

in the beginning of the movement.[103] Spiers's collection overall was a mix of popular evangelical hymnody from the previous century (e.g., "Bringing in the Sheaves") and of pieces circulating elsewhere in Pentecostalism, as well as of numbers from the Latter Rain revival itself. Generally, the songs used a four-part harmony hymn form.

Very soon another published collection of songs, Reta Kelligan's *Scripture Set to Music*, advanced the singing of Scripture-derived songs in the Latter Rain movement.[104] Kelligan, a member of the staff at Elim Bible Institute, was the main composer of these Scripture texts set to music. Her compositions arose from a flourishing of Praise & Worship at the school in both its ongoing chapel life and in special meetings from 1949 onward that attracted worshipers from across the nation to New York State.[105] In January 1950, the scheduled week of prayer, for example, lengthened to three weeks as Ivan Spencer taught on revival using the typology[106] of the tabernacle of the Old Testament, and Phyllis and James Spiers contributed with a "richly anointed ministry in song and the Word." Likewise, the January 1951 convention was marked by new dimensions of psalm singing and "praising-through for victories"[107] (i.e., engaging in praise long enough until some sort of spiritual "victory" was experienced). Elim's principal, Carlton Spencer, noted how the Holy Spirit had been inspiring new songs and choruses in service after service and how Kelligan's compositions under this inspiration were being sung across the country.[108] In her published collection of thirteen songs, eight were musical settings for psalms, including six that emphasized the praise of God, based on Psalms 19, 34, 47, 48, 103, and 150. Her musical settings were more diverse and imaginative, too, making use of solos, duets, and quartets as well as metrical changes within songs. Indeed, some of her psalm settings were anthem-like.

103. Riss and Riss, *Images of Revival*, 94. Riss and Riss cite personal correspondence in 1976 from George Warnock, an early Latter Rain participant and teacher, to this effect. In many respects, the Spiers songbook showed overlap with similar works. The fifty-three songs were mainly in a 4/4 or 6/8 meter and emphasized four-part harmony. Some themes were typically Pentecostal: e.g., an eschatologically forward-looking anticipation and an emphasis on the outpouring of the Spirit. Many represented standard evangelical Victorian hymnody: e.g., "Standing on the Promises" and "Sweet By and By." Some, however, declared boldly a new work of Latter Rain: "This Is the Promise" (a hymn by Phyllis Spiers) and two different choruses titled "Rain, Rain, Rain" (one by Spiers and the other by Omar S. Johnson).

104. Reta Kelligan, *Scripture Set to Music* (Lima, NY: Elim Bible Institute, 1952).

105. Meloon, *Ivan Spencer*, 160.

106. Typology is a form of scriptural interpretation that works by analogy: one thing or person in one context (i.e., the type) gives meaning to an analogous thing or person in another context.

107. Meloon, *Ivan Spencer*, 160–61, 171.

108. Kelligan, *Scripture Set to Music*, 3. Spencer's comments are in the foreword to Kelligan's collection.

Recurring Elements in Early Praise & Worship Theology

As we have seen, the Latter Rain movement enjoyed a rapid expansion by a variety of means and persons. Just as Reg Layzell's Vancouver church was not the only center for the early practice of Praise & Worship, so Layzell was not the only theologian within the Latter Rain revival thinking about this movement's emerging way of worship. As foundational as Layzell's advocacy of the sacrifice of praise as the pathway to praise would become, there were others helping to launch trajectories of thought that would become fixtures in Latter Rain liturgical theologizing, especially in subsequent years.

Historian William Faupel provides a useful summary of this early Latter Rain theology on the restoration of true biblical worship, using a twofold concept: worship as sacred space and worship as praise.[109] Worship as sacred space was an important category from the very onset of the revival, because a day before its outbreak a young woman had prophesied that all the Sharon community had to do to enter into a great revival was "open the door." The community grew desirous of finding the key that would open this door. Thus, the community's desire was to find the solution to a spatial problem: to discover the way to move from the place of anticipating revival to the place of experiencing it. As the revival erupted, as discussed above, the people in North Battleford would discover that the key was praise. The result has been long-standing theological tendencies in Latter Rain–related materials to prioritize praise as foundational to Christian worship services and to use notions of space, especially reference to Old Testament tabernacles or temples, to express liturgical theology.

Those tendencies were found in one of the first books produced by the Latter Rain movement, George Warnock's 1951 book titled *The Feast of Tabernacles*.[110] Warnock's inspiration was a message at the July 1948 camp meeting in North Battleford that noted how the Feast of the Passover had been fulfilled in the cross and the Feast of Pentecost had been fulfilled in the original outpouring of the Holy Spirit fifty days after the resurrection of Christ, but the Feast of Tabernacles had not yet been fulfilled. Warnock was

---

109. Faupel, "New Order of the Latter Rain," 255.
110. George H. Warnock, *The Feast of Tabernacles* (Springfield, MO: Bill Britton, 1951). The book seems to have had wide dissemination inside and outside the Latter Rain movement. I (Lester Ruth) received a copy of the book in 2018 from Andrea Hunter, who herself had received it from roving ministers when she was part of the Jesus People movement in Southern California in the late 1970s. Faupel ("New Order of the Latter Rain," 256) gives the background for Warnock's book. Warnock's autobiographical statement can be found at "A Brief Outline of My Life," personal website, accessed February 11, 2019, http://georgewarnock.com/bio.html. See also Riss, *Latter Rain*, 73–74.

in attendance at the camp meeting and was intrigued by the idea. Becoming a staff person in the Sharon institution, Warnock did his own biblical study and eventually published the book to argue that the Latter Rain revival was the fulfillment of that third feast.

In a relatively short passage within his book, Warnock demonstrates both the tendency to prioritize praise and the tendency to use spatial notions. In so doing, he touches on four elements that would be seen repeatedly in later Latter Rain theology, the first being a typological interpretation of the Old Testament to build a theology of Praise & Worship. Warnock focuses on Ezra 3, which deals with the keeping of the Feast of Tabernacles by the exiles who had returned to Jerusalem. In the passage, the people in Jerusalem are on the verge of laying the foundation for a rebuilt temple. Fusing Ezra 3:11 with a passage about musicians in the tabernacle of David (1 Chron. 25:1), Warnock uses a typological interpretation—the restored worship of Jerusalem was equivalent to the restored Praise & Worship of the Latter Rain—to describe the what and how of God's current activity in the church. As Warnock expressed it, "The present work of the Holy Spirit in re-establishing the Temple of God and its spiritual order of worship has really just started."[111] This typological use of the tabernacles and temples of the Old Testament was one of the four elements that became a mainstay in Latter Rain liturgical theology.

Another was the fusion of music and Spirit-inspired prophecy (see 1 Chron. 25:1). By highlighting David's musicians as prophets with instruments, Warnock emphasizes the Holy Spirit's role in the making of music, which would become another commonplace Latter Rain emphasis much developed in following years. Not surprisingly, Warnock also notes that the main activity of Spirit-inspired worship was praise, whether in the Old Testament or in the current revival.[112] This emphasis on praise was the third common element of the movement's liturgical theology, as we have previously seen.

The fourth commonplace element Warnock highlights was to see Praise & Worship as a restoration by God. As Faupel has noted, this concept, restoration, was the centerpiece that brought internal coherence to the entire revival.[113] With respect to the movement's liturgical aspect, the phrase "restoration of

---

111. Warnock, *Feast of Tabernacles*, 91.

112. Warnock reinforces the typology by noting the names, with meanings, of each of the three musicians in 1 Chron. 25:1: Asaph means "Gathered," Heman means "Faithful," and Juduthun means "Choir of Praise." In these meanings, Warnock sees a type for the current restoration of corporate praise, especially in the ecstatic singing of the "heavenly choir": "What a wonderful description of what is generally called the Heavenly Choir. 'The Choir of Praise!' sung by those who are 'Faithful' in their ministry; and to 'Gather' the saints together in the unity of the Spirit." Warnock, *Feast of Tabernacles*, 91.

113. Faupel, "New Order of the Latter Rain," 246.

praise and worship" became a shorthand way to refer to its distinctive way of worship as a gift from God to the church.

The same four elements—typological use of the Old Testament, the connection of music to God-given prophecy, an emphasis on praise, and an assertion of God's restoring of true worship[114]—were present in an early theological reflection by James Beall, the son of Myrtle Beall, at Bethesda Missionary Temple in Detroit. In a small, undated booklet, Beall affirms all four but with different arrangement, emphases, and Scriptures than Warnock used.[115]

Whereas Warnock's theology began with a typological association to the Old Testament, Beall's treatment starts with ecclesiology. Beall asserts that the church, rather than being a human-made organization, is a "spiritual organism" inhabited by God through the Holy Spirit or, more specifically, inhabited by Jesus Christ. Combining Hebrews 2:12[116] with the promise of Christ to be with two or three gathered in his name (Matt. 18:20), Beall lays out his fundamental premise: "Christ declares Himself in the midst of His people by prompting or 'anointing' them in spiritual praise and worship!"[117] Using again Hebrews 2:12 ("In the midst of the church will I [Jesus Christ] sing praise unto thee," KJV), Beall places his emphasis on the prophetic nature of music—specifically on Christ-given songs to the believer (or even Christ-sung songs in the believer)—and on the centrality of praise in Christ's inspiring movement within a worshiping congregation. Not surprisingly, Beall references the key Scriptures learned from Reg Layzell (Ps. 22:3 and Heb. 13:15), presenting them as fundamental givens upon which the particulars

114. Of the four elements seen in Warnock and Beall (and soon to be seen in others)—typological use of the Old Testament, the connection of music to prophecy, an emphasis on praise, and an assertion of God's restoration of true worship—Layzell's emphasis was on the first element and the latter two elements. Of the four elements, Layzell least emphasized the immediate Spirit inspiration of music's prophetic quality, although he could affirm the same. See Layzell, *Pastor's Pen*, 47. Layzell also had a critical difference from Warnock and Beall: although he used types from the Old Testament, he did not emphasize any architectural type from an Old Testament tabernacle or a temple.

115. J. Beall, *Ministry of Worship and Praise*, 9–30. While no publication date is given for this booklet, subtle clues within the booklet place it sometime after the 1940s. See especially pp. 16–17 where Beall comments on his own experience of hearing spontaneously given, prophetic spiritual songs: "It has been my good fortune to be in services in various parts of the country when this same sovereign inspiration took place. As I look back over a number of years, I well remember the first time I ever saw and heard it take place." He then repeats the story of Bethesda Missionary Temple in 1948 and 1949. The book's formatting would seem to place it sometime in the 1950s or 1960s.

116. In the KJV: "I will declare thy name unto my brethren, in the midst of the church will I sing praise unto thee." The author of Hebrews has quoted Ps. 22:22 to call attention to the close affinity between Christ and the church.

117. J. Beall, *Ministry of Worship and Praise*, 11.

of his theology can be laid.[118] Note that Beall carries the prophetic nature of music a step beyond the affirming of the ecstatic singing of the "heavenly choir" to a detailed affirming of the Spirit-given nature of particular worship songs. His specific biblical examples are intelligible, well-constructed songs: the Song of Moses and Miriam (Exod. 15), the Magnificat of Mary (Luke 1), the Benedictus of Zachariah (Luke 1), and the Nunc Dimittis of Simeon (Luke 2). By these examples he lays out a theology for song composition by connecting prophetic impulse and song creation.

Beall also exhibits the two other theological elements seen in Warnock: typological interpretation of the Bible and an affirmation of God's restoration of Praise & Worship to the church. In a discussion of the divine pattern of worship, Beall combines these two elements by referring to multiple patterns for worship given by God in the Scriptures, specifically the patterns given to Moses, David, and Solomon, and in the book of Revelation. By arguing that these patterns should guide the liturgical practices of the church today, he turns them into types of Praise & Worship that have ongoing normative value. And he does so with an edge, using the sense of God's restoration of Praise & Worship as a rebuke to those who will not accept it:

> This [the worship in the book of Revelation] is a far cry from what nominal Christianity calls praise! The majority of Sunday morning worship services has degenerated to the singing of two traditional hymns (and that by only a portion of the congregation), a prayer or two, a sermon and the benediction. . . . I want to openly declare, I DO NOT accept the apostate order of Protestantism [sic] worship as divine order. In fact, it is my firm contention that the church general has drifted so far from the Bible pattern that she wouldn't know divine order if she saw it and heard it. . . . God is pouring out of His Spirit and restoring divine order to those who have an ear to hear "what the Spirit is saying to the church."[119]

Part of Beall's presentation of this restored divine order was a use of proof texts from Psalms to justify specific practices: Psalm 150 to ground the use of a variety of musical instruments, Psalm 134 for the lifting of hands, and Psalm 47 for clapping hands.[120] In the surge of teaching materials in the next historical periods such use of proof texts—especially from Psalms—would become a standard teaching device.[121]

118. J. Beall, *Ministry of Worship and Praise*, 23.
119. J. Beall, *Ministry of Worship and Praise*, 26.
120. J. Beall, *Ministry of Worship and Praise*, 29–30.
121. The appeal to biblical patterns and specific proof texts is an example of a long-standing practice among Free Church liturgical traditions that historian James F. White calls "liturgical biblicism." See his *Protestant Worship: Traditions in Transition* (Louisville: Westminster John

Thus, whether through Layzell, Warnock, or Beall, the early Latter Rain movement was developing a rich, energetic tradition of biblical theologizing about Praise & Worship. Not only did this tradition justify the liturgical practices that had emerged in the Latter Rain—those practices having been given by God, in Latter Rain estimation—but the theology also provided the impulse to revel in them. As Layzell pointedly argued, Praise & Worship was God's gift to the church. The theology also provided the momentum to pass it on to others. In short, early Latter Rain theologizing about Praise & Worship was providing the impetus for its expansion.

This Latter Rain theologizing might have, too, provided a point of attraction to Praise & Worship for other Pentecostals, given how few overarching liturgical theologies there were in Pentecostalism.[122] The early Latter Rain theologians were doing something potentially attractive for Pentecostals looking for an overarching biblical framework to understand praise, if the theology could be disassociated from the Latter Rain movement itself.

Knox, 1989), 81. As here, it involves finding an explicit biblical command, mandate, or example to justify particular liturgical practices.

122. Cf. the opening observations in Marius Nel, "Attempting to Develop a Pentecostal Theology of Worship," *Verbum et Ecclesia* 37, no. 1 (2016): 1–8.

two

—

deepening the channel for praise & worship, 1965–85

The important distinction between praise and worship is not the particular expression which is manifested in a service, but the fact that while praise is often operated as *an act of faith* creating the atmosphere for the presence of God, worship is *the expression of our response* to his presence.

—*Charlotte Baker, pastor of King's Temple, Seattle, Washington*[1]

With his prior earth-shattering experience of a revelation of Psalm 22:3 burned into his memory, Reg Layzell could well understand the frustration and hunger of a younger pastor, Dick Iverson, who asked Layzell to visit his church. Iverson, who was the shepherd of Bible Temple in Portland, Oregon, was desperate to see Praise & Worship in his congregation. This pastor had already experienced the new form of praise-oriented worship in his visits to Latter Rain churches, especially Layzell's congregation in Vancouver and Bethany Chapel, the congregation led by Layzell's close friend David Schoch, in Long Beach, California. After these visits, Iverson hungered for a release of this way of worship in his own church. Determined to reach this goal, Iverson in 1965 invited Layzell and Schoch to come preach in his church. On the last night, Layzell preached on Hebrews 13:15, emphasizing the sacrifice of praise

1. E. Charlotte Baker, *On Eagle's Wings: A Book on Praise and Worship* (Shippensburg, PA: Destiny Image, 1990), 48. Baker's book was originally published in 1979.

as something offered apart from feelings. Iverson was about to have his own memory-burning experience. He describes what happened next:

> For over an hour he [Layzell] quoted scripture after scripture on how we were to offer up our praise to the Lord,—how we were to sing a new song, lifting our hands and worshiping as praises unto God, and how we needed to do so by faith based on God's Word. . . . After the message, I remember him doing something I thought very strange. He brought everybody forward to the front of the church. Then he stood at the altar and said, "Now we know it's God's Word to offer the sacrifice of praise so we're going to do it, as a sacrifice, by faith." He took his watch off his wrist and said, "For ten minutes we're going to offer the sacrifice of praise. I'll keep track of the time and you'll lift your hands, whether you feel like it or not, and for ten minutes sing praises to the Lord."[2]

Iverson reports that the response began awkwardly. Layzell dove right in but the people, himself included, waded hesitantly into these waters. However, within a few minutes the congregation was fully engaged. The experience was everything Iverson had hoped for his congregation: "For a moment I felt like we had gone to heaven. This was what I had wanted more than breath itself. I had wanted the presence of God manifested in the midst of our church, and now we were experiencing it. You could almost physically feel the holy presence of the Lord covering the people as He had truly come into our midst."[3]

Iverson was sorely disappointed when at the end of ten minutes Layzell took the microphone and said, "All right, time's up. Stop now." Layzell had abruptly stopped the praise and the growing sense of being in God's presence in order to teach that praise was to be offered by faith in God's promise and by obedience to scriptural command, not by feelings, and that God indeed would honor the scriptural promise.[4]

Notwithstanding their initial disappointment, Iverson and his congregation received Layzell's lesson, one that transformed the liturgical life at Bible Temple in the years after 1965. (Note to reader: whenever we use the term "liturgical" in this book, we simply mean something worship-related.) Although certainly not the only center for Praise & Worship after the mid-1960s, this Portland congregation would become an important hub for the

2. Dick Iverson, *The Journey: A Lifetime of Prophetic Moments* (Portland, OR: City Bible, 1995), 117–18; Dick Iverson, interview by Lester Ruth, April 19, 2017.

3. Iverson, *The Journey*, 119.

4. Hugh Layzell and Audrey Layzell, *Sons of His Purpose: The Interweaving of the Ministry of Reg Layzell, and His Son, Hugh, during a Season of Revival* (San Bernardino, CA: privately published, 2012), 168. According to Marion Peterson, Layzell's daughter, Layzell used this approach repeatedly, not only in Iverson's church. Marion Peterson, interview by Lester Ruth, February 20, 2018.

further development and spread of the theology and practices of Praise & Worship. While the creation of Christian Copyright Licensing International (CCLI) is perhaps the best known of the developments that originated within Iverson's church, it was not the only important one. Through ministerial associations, a publishing house, a tape ministry, early teaching conferences, and a school (Portland Bible College), Bible Temple played an important role in the continued teaching and transmission of Praise & Worship from the late 1960s onward.

These two terms, "teaching" and "transmission," generally characterize the history of Praise & Worship from the mid-1960s to the mid-1980s. The developments of this twenty-year period would provide foundational elements that have characterized Contemporary Praise & Worship ever since. Foremost among these is the increased musicalization of praise, in the sense that the praise connected to the presence of God became praise offered up musically. A closely related development was a new priestly identity for musicians, especially with a connotation that the role of church musicians was to usher or lead people into God's presence. New theological articulations would lie behind both of these musical changes.

Not surprisingly, this twenty-year period also saw the first uses of the term "worship leader," as the prior role and title of "song leader" morphed into that of "worship leader." Worship leaders shepherded and guided long times of congregational singing as embryonic notions of worship "sets" began to emerge. Popular styles of music also began to increasingly shape music making, especially beyond Latter Rain churches (although some Latter Rain churches had their own resurgence of Praise & Worship with fuller orchestration). Finally, the period also saw an explosion of creativity, both with respect to songwriting and in terms of the resources used to teach others how to lead Praise & Worship. The significance of these developments from the mid-1960s to the mid-1980s should not be underestimated. At the beginning of the period, Praise & Worship existed. By 1985, it was a *thing*—something that was regularly taught and transmitted to others.[5]

Moreover, the teaching and transmission was not limited to Latter Rain congregations. An increasingly intricate web of relationships reflected the spread of Praise & Worship sensibilities and practices. The surge encompassed the nascent Charismatic Renewal movements of mainline denominations as well as other Pentecostal churches, especially those not within long-established

5. Within Pentecostal literature of the period, it is possible to discern the morphing of "praise and worship" (or sometimes "worship and praise") from a general term indicating a worship service to a technical term specifying a distinct liturgical approach.

Pentecostal denominations. But even in long-established denominations, the adoption of Praise & Worship by a gifted Assemblies of God teacher, Judson Cornwall, brought about a theological articulation of Praise & Worship that gained widespread favor. Moreover, the arrival of new channels such as the Jesus People movement (see chap. 3) increased the overall breadth of the phenomenon.

Behind all of these developments and expansion was a continual theologizing from the Bible about Praise & Worship. As it was in its first twenty years, so it would be in the next twenty: a biblical theology associating God's presence with praise would be the impulse by which this "river" flowed. If anything, the power of that momentum increased through new teachings connecting the core praise-to-presence dynamic with two tabernacles of the Old Testament: Moses's and David's.

The Restoration of the Tabernacle of David

The linchpin of theological development within the Latter Rain movement of this period was a liturgical theology based on a typology[6] that focused on a prophetic promise of the restoration of the tabernacle of David. Unlike either the antecedent tabernacle of Moses or the subsequent temple of Solomon in the Old Testament, both of which had separate areas demarcated for different liturgical functions, King David's tabernacle was simply a tent to house the ark of the covenant. The details of this tabernacle's worship practices and its arrangement of personnel for liturgical ministry—the so-called "Davidic order of worship"—became the key materials by which this era of Latter Rain leaders reinforced the movement's approach to Praise & Worship, continued its creative development, and offered it to others for adoption.

Because the theology behind Praise & Worship was a typologically based theology, the identification of the key Scriptures and their interpretation as types were critical. (Typology is a form of scriptural interpretation that works by analogy: one thing or person in one context—that is, the type—gives meaning to an analogous thing or person in another context.) Two

6. Despite its importance in the history of Praise & Worship, few scholars have studied the restoration of the tabernacle of David in Latter Rain theologizing. For the best exception, see chap. 5 in Garry Dale Nation, "The Hermeneutics of Pentecostal-Charismatic Restoration Theology: A Critical Analysis" (PhD diss., Southwestern Baptist Theological Seminary, 1990), 166–95. Tom Craig Darrand and Anson Shupe also discuss Latter Rain typologically based theologizing in this period but do so only in the form of offering a scathing critique. (Darrand had had a negative experience in a Latter Rain church.) Tom Craig Darrand and Anson Shupe, *Metaphors of Social Control in a Pentecostal Sect* (New York: Edwin Mellen, 1983).

biblical passages spoke of the restoration of David's tabernacle: the original prophecy found in Amos 9:11–12 and its quotation by James in the famous Jerusalem Council considering gentile inclusion in the church, recorded in Acts 15:16–17. These passages, with their key notion of the *restoration* of David's tabernacle, spurred Latter Rain teachers to take a close look at the passages describing the original tabernacle of David (1 Chron. 13; 15; 16; 25; 2 Sam. 6) to understand what was to be restored. Also, the tent was the tabernacle of *David*, so Latter Rain teachers used David's status as an exemplary, prototypical worshiper and songwriter to provide the link by which many of the psalms—which could have been authored by David—offer details about proper outward liturgical behavior and inward liturgical disposition. Within these main Scriptures, overlapping and intertwining figurative interpretations provided a wealth of materials with which Latter Rain exegetes worked. For example, the ark of the covenant and King David could both be figurative types for Jesus Christ, disclosing God's presence on the one hand and the fusion of royal and priestly roles on the other.

The result was a more highly developed theology featuring praise as the key to God's presence in the church. For example, an instructor at Bible Temple's Portland Bible College, Kevin Conner, wrote an influential textbook, *The Tabernacle of David*, that provided the most detailed hermeneutic to this theology.[7] The core tabernacle of David passages mentioned above—both Old Testament and New Testament—along with a handful of other passages led to an emphasis on divine presence at the place of worship. The identification of this place as Zion reinforced the connection to praise and liturgical activity through a range of scriptural associations. The centerpiece of the original tabernacle, the ark of the covenant, was likewise central in the interpretation by being a type of Jesus Christ himself, who is present among his people, especially in their praise. The lack of reference to bloody animal sacrifices in the liturgical activity of the tabernacle of David, apart from the initial arrival of the ark, highlighted the centrality of perpetual praise as sacrifice, especially by an arrangement of priests whose work was now musical. The connection of the tabernacle and its way of worship to David reinforced the propriety of fully engaged, physically expressive, and musically offered Praise & Worship.

7. Kevin J. Conner, *The Tabernacle of David: The Presence of God as Experienced in the Tabernacle*, vol. 2 of *Divine Habitation Trilogy* (Portland, OR: City Bible, 1976). For background on the Latter Rain influence on New Zealand and Australia at this time, see Mark Hutchinson, "The Latter Rain Movement and the Phenomenon of Global Return," in *Winds from the North: Canadian Contributions to the Pentecostal Movement*, ed. Michael Wilkinson and Peter Althouse (Leiden: Brill, 2010), 269–79. See also Brett Knowles, *The History of a New Zealand Pentecostal Movement* (Lewiston, NY: Edwin Mellen, 2000).

In other words, a theology based on the restoration of the tabernacle of David took the earlier emphasis on the sacrifice of praise as the key to experiencing God's presence and raised it to the level of a highly developed liturgical ecclesiology in which the church is a corporate priesthood that is praise-oriented and fulfills its priestly ministry in a musical manner.

The precise origins of this theology within Latter Rain circles are ambiguous. Before the Latter Rain revival, evangelical and Pentecostal authors had a long-standing fascination with reading the Old Testament typologically, including doing so to find the language to describe worship.[8] Indeed, some of these earlier authors' typological writings focused on Old Testament tabernacles.[9] Moreover, even the earliest of Latter Rain books, George Warnock's *The Feast of Tabernacles* (1951), mentioned the musicians in David's tabernacle from 1 Chronicles 25. However, instead of developing the idea of the restoration of this tabernacle, Warnock fused the prophetic role of David's musicians with the account of the postexilic rebuilding of the temple in Ezra 3 to affirm in Latter Rain Praise & Worship "the present work of the Holy Spirit in re-establishing the Temple of God and its spiritual order of worship."[10]

Warnock was very close to what the next era of Latter Rain theologians would develop. These theologians, maintaining Warnock's root notion that God was indeed reestablishing or restoring—a foundational Latter Rain notion—right worship in their movement, shifted the emphasis to the tabernacle of David. It is not clear who first made this shift. There is some indication that Violet Kiteley, a preacher who had been at the original North Battleford revival and had been in the group that visited Layzell's Vancouver church later in 1948, had been teaching on the tabernacle of David since the late 1940s or early 1950s.[11] (Kiteley, who had a close relationship with Reg Layzell, would move to Oakland, California, in the 1960s to pastor Shiloh Temple.) On the other hand, Kevin Conner attributed the origins of the teaching to

8. See, for example, Lester Ruth, *A Little Heaven Below: Worship at Early Methodist Quarterly Meetings* (Nashville: Kingswood Books, 2000), 75–76.

9. Consider Ann Taves, *Fits, Trances and Visions: Experiencing Religion and Explaining Experience from Wesley to James* (Princeton: Princeton University Press, 1999), 235–38. Conner drew influence from two earlier books: Philip Mauro, *The Hope of Israel* (Boston: Hamilton Brothers, 1929); and George Smith, *The Harmony of the Divine Dispensations* (New York: Carlton and Porter, 1856). "Tabernacle" was a way of referring to the church assembly in revivalistic traditions from the 1870s onward. Thus, the term was used to refer to Christians worshiping, a use found also in the Latter Rain movement. See Jonathan Ottaway, "Raising Up David's Tabernacle: Theological Hermeneutics as Authority for Theologies of Praise," in *Worship and Power: Liturgical Authority in Free Church Traditions*, ed. Sarah Johnson and Andrew Wymer (Eugene, OR: Cascade Books, forthcoming).

10. George H. Warnock, *The Feast of Tabernacles* (Springfield, MO: Bill Britton, 1951), 91.

11. Mark Chironna, interview by Lester Ruth and Adam Perez, September 30, 2019.

a passing reference by Californian David Schoch in a 1965 speech in New Zealand. What Schoch mentioned briefly was picked up with zeal by several other people, including Conner himself, who began to teach on this tabernacle's restoration.[12]

Graham Truscott, a New Zealander who wrote a classic, widely read treatment on the topic in 1969 (even earlier than Conner's textbook),[13] provided another origin story. According to Truscott, who had moved to India in 1960 for missionary work, it was while he was on a

Figure 2.1. Violet Kiteley, pastor of Shiloh Temple in Oakland, California

Used by permission of David R. Kiteley

speaking trip to Melbourne, Australia, that God opened up the significance of 1 Chronicles 13 to Truscott after he had petitioned God for fresh teaching material. This disclosure seems to have taken place in 1968 since Truscott tied the story to an account of his preaching on David's tabernacle, to the surprise of his Melbourne friends that year. But Truscott did not insist on claiming to have originated the teaching exclusively, noting in 1977 that he had been happy to learn that several others had also been teaching on the restoration of David's tabernacle.[14] Indeed, by 1969 and 1970 the constant

12. Kevin J. Conner, *This Is My Story* (Vermont, VIC: Conner Ministries, 2007), 199–200; Conner, *Tabernacle of David*, iii. See also Vivien Hibbert, *David's Tabernacle: God's Plan for Glory* (Texarkana, AR: Judah Books, 2015), 3.

13. Graham Truscott, *The Power of His Presence: The Restoration of the Tabernacle of David* (San Diego: Restoration Temple, 1982). Truscott originally published this work in 1969 while in India.

14. See the author's preface to the fourth printing in Truscott, *Power of His Presence*. There is some question about whether Graham Truscott ought to be considered part of the Latter Rain movement. He certainly was not part of the original North America–based first or second generation of leaders and their networks. Truscott, too, is cautious about an identification, noting that when he uses the term "latter rain" he does not mean any group or organization by that name (see Truscott, *Power of His Presence*, 350n5; and Graham Truscott, *You Shall Receive Power: A Fresh Study of the Holy Spirit in Light of the New Awakening in the Historic Churches* [Poona, India: New Life Centre, 1967], 16n16). After Truscott moved to San Diego in 1977, however, he was absorbed into the West Coast Latter Rain network and became a regular speaker in Latter Rain churches and conferences. Truscott relates how he was already involved in ministry when he rejected Praise & Worship on his first exposure to it, thinking it would be off-putting to people. He changed his mind as others reported having experienced

theme in most of the California Latter Rain churches was the tabernacle of David, according to Kevin Conner.[15] Not surprisingly, when Conner moved in 1972 from New Zealand to the United States to take a teaching position at Portland Bible College, he spent his first weekend in North America with Violet Kiteley and David Kiteley (Violet's son) speaking on the truths of the tabernacle of David.[16] (That same year, in Violet Kiteley's church in Oakland, Graham Truscott had preached a sermon on the restoration of the tabernacle of David, associating this restoration with the Latter Rain movement.)[17]

By the late 1970s, this teaching of a "Davidic order of worship" was part and parcel of the Latter Rain approach to Praise & Worship. Both Truscott's and Conner's books on the subject were especially widely known and influential. Truscott's book, *The Power of His Presence*, had seen five printings by 1982; it would be translated into at least three languages: Japanese, Chinese, and Amharic (spoken in Ethiopia).[18] Conner's treatment, *The Tabernacle of David*, would become a standard textbook at Portland Bible College, Bible Temple's school, at which Conner would teach from 1972 to 1976 and again from 1977 to 1981. The book was available for wider purchase through order forms found at the rear of the numerous Bible Temple publications. Conner's book circulated widely, influencing later significant leaders in Praise & Worship (like John Wimber of the Anaheim Vineyard and Bill Johnson of Bethel Church in Redding, California).[19]

Notwithstanding their prominence, Truscott's and Conner's books and teaching were not the only outlets for teaching about the restoration of David's tabernacle. Other Bible Temple–affiliated persons, including Pastor Dick

---

the presence of God in praise: "According to His promise God had indeed dwelt in the praises of His people" (see Graham Truscott, *Every Christian's Ministry* [Calgary: Gordon Donaldson Missionary Foundation, 1977], 69). For more information on Truscott, see Graham and Pamela Truscott, *Kiwis Can Fly! Celebrating over 50 Years of Marriage, Ministry and Miracles* (privately published, 2013).

15. Conner, *This Is My Story*, 199.

16. Conner, *This Is My Story*, 202.

17. Darrand and Shupe, *Metaphors of Social Control*, 135.

18. Truscott's other widely known book, *Every Christian's Ministry* from 1977, eliminated the focus on the tabernacle of David while still highlighting every Christian's involvement in Praise & Worship.

19. Howard Rachinski, interview by Lester Ruth and Lim Swee Hong, April 17, 2017. Conner wrote several other books, especially in his role as a Bible-college instructor. His book on the tabernacle of David was part of a three-volume series (the *Divine Habitation Trilogy*) that looked also at the tabernacle of Moses and the temple of Solomon. In his look at the two tabernacles and the one temple in the series, Conner believed it was the tabernacle of David that established a divine order of worship. Cf. Kevin J. Conner, *The Temple of Solomon: The Glory of God as Displayed through the Temple*, vol. 3 of *Divine Habitation Trilogy* (Portland, OR: City Bible, 1988), 20.

Iverson and David Blomgren, one of the original teachers at Portland Bible College, released books featuring the theology.[20] Similarly, LaMar Boschman highlighted King David's organization of priestly musicians in his 1980 guide on the role of music in Praise & Worship.[21] Beyond publications, the restoration of David's tabernacle became a central motif in the teaching in workshops, conferences, and consultations that began in the late 1970s and early 1980s. The emphasis, however, was not universal among Latter Rain writers at the time.[22]

Several points of affinity with previous Latter Rain emphases help explain the rapid rise and spread of the liturgical theology based on the restoration of the tabernacle of David within the Latter Rain movement. At the most essential level, the theology tapped into the fundamental notion driving Latter Rain piety: restoration. Since the earliest days of the revival, the view that God was returning the church to critical aspects of proper ecclesiastical life and organization through this revival was an organizing principle.[23] Indeed, both the original Amos passage and its quotation in Acts 15 in some Bible translations included the word "restore," providing an easy connection between these passages and the category of "restoration" so critical in Latter Rain thinking. At a more specific level, emphasizing the tabernacle of David reaffirmed the earlier connection that Latter Rain teachers, starting with Reg Layzell, had made between God's presence and praise. Indeed, the tabernacle of David—a single space with a single object (the ark of the covenant) that served as the symbol for God's presence among the people—was an exceptionally fine way to reinforce the critical Latter Rain connection between presence and praise. David's tabernacle was unencumbered with the division of spaces and multitude of liturgical accoutrements found in Moses's tabernacle or in the temple built by Solomon.

20. Dick Iverson and Bill Scheidler, *Present Day Truths* (Portland, OR: City Christian, 1976); David K. Blomgren, *Restoring God's Glory: The Present Day Rise of David's Tabernacle* (Regina, SK: Maranatha Christian Centre, 1985). Iverson's book was available in Spanish by 1978, according to the order form found at the back of contemporaneous Bible Temple publications.

21. LaMar Boschman, *The Rebirth of Music: A Unique View of the Real Meaning and Purpose of Music* (Little Rock: Manasseh Books, 1980), 26. In contrast, Charlotte Baker did not emphasize David's tabernacle in her book.

22. For example, see Baker, *On Eagle's Wings*. Reg Layzell also did not see the restoration of the tabernacle of David as being associated with Praise & Worship. See the appendix in Layzell and Layzell, *Sons of His Purpose*, C-8.

23. See D. William Faupel, "The New Order of the Latter Rain: Restoration or Renewal?," in *Winds from the North: Canadian Contributions to the Pentecostal Movement*, ed. Michael Wilkinson and Peter Althouse (Leiden: Brill, 2010), 246–59. Key to this concept was the notion that this restoration occurred as part of a special eschatological time in human history. We thank Jonathan Ottaway for pointing this out. See Ottaway, "Raising Up David's Tabernacle."

The nature of proper praise was the third point of affinity. David's organization of priests into musical groups to offer praise without ceasing, all day every day, linked nicely to the second of Reg Layzell's favorite verses: the exhortation in Hebrews 13:15 to offer a sacrifice of praise *continually*.[24] Even Layzell's emphasis from Hebrews 13:15 on praise as a volitional act, an act carried out by choice and an act of the will apart from feeling or some sense of inward leading, easily matched what one could imagine as the motivation for David's cohorts of music-making priests. They offered praise musically to fulfill their vocation.

Such human obedience was matched with divine blessing, a fourth point of affinity between the teaching on David's tabernacle and earlier Latter Rain liturgical thought. Layzell's 1954 instruction that faithful following of scriptural patterns was the way to maintain a revival of the divine visitation[25] found its counterpart in later uses of the teaching about the tabernacle of David. That teaching about the tabernacle was supplemented by passages from other Old Testament books that spoke about the specific practices of worship, for example, raising hands. The result was a system of Praise & Worship called the "Davidic order of worship."[26] As Layzell had connected the command of offering a sacrifice of praise from Hebrews 13:15 to the promise of God's inhabitation of praise in Psalm 22:3, so later the teachers of the Davidic order of worship were effusive in their sense of its promise as the sure way to experience God's presence. Take the 1966 pronouncement of Maureen Gaglardi, Layzell's associate pastor: "To venerate His name in singing, joy and victory is to be able to put a law of God into operation which immediately produces His Divine unction. . . . One may practice the presence of God by the recognition that He inhabits the praises of His people." This is matched by Kevin Conner's optimism ten years later that "God's will done in God's way will never lack God's blessing."[27]

24. Neither Reg Layzell nor Latter Rain theologians of the 1970s seems to have taken this continual aspect literally and advocated perpetual 24-7 worship. It would take a subsequent generation of worshipers interested in the tabernacle of David to implement this vision literally.

25. Reg Layzell, *The Pastor's Pen: Early Revival Writings of Pastor Reg. Layzell*, comp. B. Maureen Gaglardi (Vancouver: Glad Tidings Temple, 1965), 6.

26. For example, see Conner, *Tabernacle of David*, 19. By "order," neither Conner nor other Latter Rain teachers meant an order of worship in the sense of a sequential list of acts of worship within a liturgy. The Davidic order of worship refers rather to a system or model of worship.

27. B. Maureen Gaglardi, *The Key of David* (Vancouver: Glad Tidings Temple, 1966), 115; Conner, *Tabernacle of David*, 104. For a more nuanced approach to the automatic, causative efficacy of human liturgical activity, see Baker, *On Eagle's Wings*, 32: "It must be noted that mere mortal man can never 'create the presence of God.' Praise is only the means by which we create the *atmosphere* in which God loves to dwell."

The development of the teaching of the restoration of David's tabernacle and its accompanying Davidic order of worship was critically significant in the history of Praise & Worship in two ways, both of which are derived from the status and activity of the ministers within this tabernacle. The first was a musicalizing of praise. While there had been a prior assumption and practice in the Latter Rain movement that the praise associated with God's presence could be musical, the increased focus on the tabernacle of David—and its musical priesthood—made the connection between praise and music essential. The second way was closely related. It was the presumption that church musicians held a priestly function of mediating God's presence to the people, an idea that was sometimes expressed spatially as leading people into God's presence. If David's priests were musicians, then our musicians today can be priests. Even those who have never adopted the Davidic tabernacle teaching wholesale are likely to have imbibed the connections between praise and music, on the one hand, and, on the other, musicianship and priestly ministry. Because these developments arising from the teaching about David's tabernacle have been important, let us consider each in more depth.

Praise as Music and Musicians as Priests

As just mentioned, the teaching on David's tabernacle reinforced the perspective that praise is essentially musical. While musical expression of either praise or worship was never discounted in earlier Latter Rain teaching, prior teaching was mainly concerned with a basic vocalization of praise that was both loud and free. As Gaglardi argued in 1966, reverence in the Bible is not portrayed by silence but by praise that was both vocal and loud, not "confined only to some place deep in our heart or deep in the basement of the church."[28] Her concern was the same as Layzell's: that praise should be out loud and exuberant, whether spoken or sung.

In the tabernacle of David, however, the priests who offered praise continually were also musicians. Therefore, according to this biblical type, offering praise (and its intimate counterpart, worship) is essentially a musical act. Thus, the widespread notion that corporate liturgy means doing something musical—what some scholars have called the "sonicization of worship"[29]— emerged not only from the widespread prominence of music-making in

28. Gaglardi, *Key of David*, 84–91, esp. 86–87.
29. Cf. Joshua Kalin Busman, "(Re)Sounding Passion: Listening to American Evangelical Worship Music, 1997–2015" (PhD diss., University of North Carolina, 2015), 45–46; and Monique M. Ingalls, *Singing the Congregation: How Contemporary Worship Music Forms Evangelical Community* (Oxford: Oxford University Press, 2018), 18.

Pentecostal settings for Praise & Worship but also from a specific theological vision. One can sense the essential role of music in Graham Truscott's effusive descriptions of what God was restoring in Praise & Worship: "By the Power of the Spirit, Who is given to glorify Christ, the Presence of Christ is being restored today to His people. The Ark of the Covenant and its contents are being restored today in spiritual application. As a direct result of this Restoration, there is praise, worship, song and rejoicing in the Church as never before."[30]

This musicalization of praise was in harmony theologically with a long-standing distrust of liturgical ceremony among some Protestants in Free Church liturgical traditions. For Latter Rain theologians the tabernacle of David, being free of ongoing bloody animal sacrifices (except at its beginning), had a purer simplicity.[31] Its priests had a straightforward task not wrapped up in the ceremonies of the "formal way of worship" found in the tabernacle of Moses. David's priests were musicians: they handled musical instruments, not animals and knives. Making music was how they offered the sacrifices acceptable to God. Indeed, for Graham Truscott, the tabernacle of Moses with its ceremonies and nonmusical sacrifices was a type for Christians still committed to their former, formal way of worship even though God had "moved on" to the restoration of musical Praise & Worship.[32] Truscott saw the Mosaic tabernacle as a type for Christian liturgical history before God's restoration of Praise & Worship: this prior worship was essentially silent and formal, with a distinct order of service to which people rigidly adhered.[33] But the ark of God's presence was no longer there in the tabernacle of Moses; it was in the tabernacle of David.

Kevin Conner agreed that God was restoring something in Praise & Worship and that that something was essentially musical. In his 270-page book about the tabernacle of David, he dedicated more than one-quarter of the contents to a close consideration of music. Describing the twenty to thirty years before the publication of his book in 1976, Conner emphasized the musical developments that had taken place in what God was doing around the world in restoring praise by the people of God: spiritual songs, sung congregational praises, and instrumental music. Conner gloried in the result, noting, "God's people are seeing that there is a new level of worship in music and song that the Lord is wanting to bring His people into."[34] In other words,

---

30. Truscott, *Power of His Presence*, 221–22.

31. This dimension of the tabernacle of David would also play into a deeply valued Protestant emphasis about the completed atoning sacrifice of Christ—that is, there is no need for ongoing bloody sacrifices to appease God.

32. Truscott, *Power of His Presence*, 218–19.

33. Truscott, *Power of His Presence*, 74.

34. Conner, *Tabernacle of David*, 179.

the gift of God was Praise & Worship restored according to the model of the tabernacle of David; that model was essentially musical.

The second impact the teaching on the restoration of the tabernacle of David had was to strengthen the priestly identification for church musicians who help mediate the access of God's people to God's presence. Kevin Conner demonstrated one way of conceiving how this association could be done. First, he described the organization of the priests into twenty-four courses in 1 Chronicles 15 and 16 so that "there was a continual service of praise ascending to the Lord as the Levites waited in their particular course. What a glorious atmosphere to live in. God inhabits the praises of His people (Ps. 22:3)." Conner's next step was to identify this continual service of praise in David's tabernacle as a "service of song (or song service)" since it was musical and involved singing.[35] The slight adjustment of label so that Conner could see the ancient priests as conducting a "song service," which was a well-known term in Pentecostal and evangelical churches in the 1970s, provided the link by which the priestly association could pass to musicians today. Thus, there was an ambiguity of time as Conner noted that "there are those whom the Lord gives a distinct ministry for leading the song service in His house" since this ministry vocation applied in his mind equally to either the ancient priesthood or modern church musicians. Modern musicians not only lead the songs but also lead people in a priestly way: in the "service of song" musicians "lead God's people into the realms of worship which God desires" and, we might add, in which God dwells.[36]

Also writing in 1976, Dick Iverson (Conner's supervising pastor at Bible Temple) and Bill Scheidler (Conner's faculty colleague at Portland Bible College) agreed and stated straightforwardly the case for a priestly musical class in the church: "There are those in the House of God today whose ministry it is to lead into spiritual song and worship. Their ministry is to lead the congregation into the Presence of the Lord. These singers lead the way into the gates of praise."[37] This priestly function of church musicians could be used for desirable liturgical ends, according to the two men. They describe the importance and role of music at Bible Temple: "We have found that Churches that have a strong emphasis in the area of music have no trouble maintaining a heavy anointing and a constant flow of Body ministry. Music does create an atmosphere. The world knows it and misuses it, but we want to use music to draw people into the presence of God."[38]

35. Conner, *Tabernacle of David*, 184.
36. Conner, *Tabernacle of David*, 184.
37. Iverson and Scheidler, *Present Day Truths*, 204. For the identification of Scheidler, see Conner, *This Is My Story*, 203.
38. Iverson and Scheidler, *Present Day Truths*, 208.

Beyond the theologizing on the restoration of the tabernacle of David, Latter Rain teachers in this period also began to express other theological developments that both reflect what was happening in the liturgy of Latter Rain churches and also helped shape the ongoing spread of Praise & Worship. One such development was the making of a technical distinction between "praise" and "worship" as forms of liturgical interaction with God. Iverson and Scheidler, for example, were already making this distinction in their 1976 instructional guide for other churches. Basing the distinction on word studies of the various Hebrew and Greek words in the Bible, they offered up a technical distinction: "Praise is specifically that act of worship or service unto God in which we audibly render thanks to God with the lifting up of our hands. Worship in the specific sense involves a humble adoration, a bowing of the spirit before the Almighty God."[39] Charlotte Baker, pastor of King's Temple in Seattle, likewise noted a distinction between the two activities, lodging the distinction not in biblical word studies but in "further outpourings of the Holy Spirit" since the first days of the Latter Rain revival.[40]

Charlotte Baker's 1979 discussion of the difference is particularly interesting in that it shows the distinction's connection with the prior history of Praise & Worship, the then-current state of its practice, and its future development. With respect to the past, Baker draws on her understanding of praise's efficacy learned from Reg Layzell and his teaching on Psalm 22:3 and Hebrews 13:15: "Praise, an operation of faith, is an instrument which will create the atmosphere for the presence of God, where He is pleased to dwell. . . . In contrast, worship is the expression of our response to His presence. Worship involves . . . expressing love for Him (i.e., Jesus)."[41] Baker's discussion of the difference between praise and worship also was a window into the current status of Praise & Worship as done in 1979 as well as its future adoption in many contexts. Simply put, Baker was disgruntled with the formulaic and "natural" (i.e., not of the Holy Spirit) way some churches at that time implemented Praise & Worship: "One distinction which is often made when the natural mind tries to analyze the moving of the Spirit of God is that of labeling part of a worship service *praise* and another part *worship*. We often call slow songs worship and fast songs praise."[42] Notwithstanding Baker's complaint, this slow-versus-fast distinction would be one many churches would adopt.

39. Iverson and Scheidler, *Present Day Truths*, 218.
40. Baker, introduction to *On Eagle's Wings* (introduction unpaginated).
41. Baker, *On Eagle's Wings*, 46–47.
42. Baker, *On Eagle's Wings*, 48. Perhaps part of this formulaic approach about the tempo of songs was due to another secondary theological emphasis among Latter Rain thinkers: an occasional use of the notion of intimacy to describe the nature of the liturgical interaction

The Davidic Order of Worship

This simplistic (Baker would say overly simplistic) distinction between praise and worship based on the tempo of songs, sung together in sequence, hints at what had indeed happened by the late 1970s: Praise & Worship according to a "Davidic order of worship" had become a liturgical approach that could be taught, appropriated, and implemented. From this time forward, more and more Latter Rain efforts in a variety of outlets would be made toward this end; from this time forward, more and more churches would adopt Praise & Worship as their liturgical life on Sundays.

A critical dimension of this pedagogical surge was in the systematization of the Davidic order of worship. The fact that it was the tabernacle of *David* that was being restored opened up a rich vein of Scriptures, especially the psalms, that Latter Rain proponents of Praise & Worship used in teaching a Davidic liturgical order. It helped greatly that many of the psalms were ascribed directly to David's authorship, while others were to the musical priests serving in his tabernacle. The psalms were combined with the various biblical passages, noted above, in which David had organized the liturgical life in his tabernacle. The scriptural pinnacle was how the Bible portrayed David himself as a consummate worshiper.

The result was an all-encompassing, scripturally derived vision for Praise & Worship within a congregation. For instance, Kevin Conner, writing on a "divine order of worship" based on the tabernacle of David, highlighted the different dimensions in this vision. His full list that named and described the possible liturgical dimensions filled four pages.[43] Conner listed sixteen elements found within Praise & Worship, noting that not all would occur in every service but that they should occur as the Spirit leads on a particular occasion:

- ministry of the singers and singing
- ministry of the musicians with instruments
- continual ministry before the ark (i.e., continual, praise- and music-driven access to the divine presence)

---

between Christ and the church as the church was responding to a sense of Christ's liturgical presence achieved through praise. Surely, in a North American cultural perspective, slower songs were more fitting for intimate banter. Both Iverson and Baker utilize this notion of intimacy. See Iverson and Scheidler, *Present Day Truths*, 196; and Baker, *On Eagle's Wings*, 88. Remember that the notion of intimacy had not been absent in earlier teaching: it can be found in Layzell's use of Jeremiah 33:11 to speak about the reciprocating voices of the bridegroom (Christ) and bride (the church) in Praise & Worship.

43. Conner, *Tabernacle of David*, 151–55. Cf. Iverson and Scheidler, *Present Day Truths*, 192.

- ministry of recording (i.e., the recording of new songs of Praise & Worship, especially those given spontaneously in prophetic moments)
- thanksgiving
- praise
- psalms
- rejoicing
- clapping of hands
- shouting
- dancing
- lifting up of hands
- worship (i.e., "a bowing before the Lord, a prostration of themselves in deep adoration and devotion")[44]
- seeking God's face
- spiritual sacrifices
- the ministry of saying "amen"

Conner's list gives us a sense of the practices that characterized Latter Rain Praise & Worship at the time. In this way of worship, worshipers experienced God's presence continually and perpetually by means that were communal, music-driven, vocal, and noisy. Worshipers also participated in a variety of liturgical postures of the soul (thanks, praise, and worship) that were expressed through the body.

Other leaders offered even greater summarization and systematization to describe a Davidic order of worship. For example, Dick Iverson in Portland and Ernest Gentile, a Latter Rain pastor at Christian Community Church in San Jose, California, each organized the long list of scriptural practices of Praise & Worship into a ninefold expression categorized into three groups (the mouth, the hand, and the body).[45] Worshipers used their mouths to sing, shout, and express audible praise. As for the hands, a Davidic worshiper lifted them, clapped, or played musical instruments. And the body of a worshiper could stand, bow or be prostrate, and dance.

44. Conner, *Tabernacle of David*, 154.
45. Iverson and Scheidler, *Present Day Truths*, 200; Ernest B. Gentile, *Charismatic Catechism* (Harrison, AR: New Leaf, 1977), 148. Gentile was inspired to write a catechism by looking at Martin Luther's catechism and a Roman Catholic catechism. He also drew guidance from educational material of other Latter Rain teachers: Patricia Beall Gruits, daughter of Myrtle Beall, who had written a catechism from her teaching at Bethesda Missionary Temple in Detroit titled *Understanding God* (Springdale, PA: Whitaker House, 1962); and Maureen Gaglardi's "Church School Bible Course," used at Reg Layzell's Glad Tidings Temple in Vancouver. Ernest B. Gentile, email message to Lester Ruth, September 16, 2019.

Such systematic summaries were not purely theoretical. They described the activities commonly found within Latter Rain congregations at the time. What such lists do not portray is the intense inward dynamic of worshipers and their leaders as they sought the Holy Spirit's movement and responded to what they sensed to be the Spirit's direction. Charlotte Baker described such a scene in 1979, focusing on the Spirit's "anointing" of musicians and emphasizing the Latter Rain distinction of immediate, "prophetic" inspiration of even instrumental music making. For her such moments were wondrous: "It is a wonderful blessing to find a pianist or organist who will abandon his or her talent unto God, and play anthems of praise under the anointing, while the congregation listens in quiet worship. There have been occasions when a pianist or organist has led an anthem of worship; as the playing progressed every instrument began to play under the same anointing, not following a musical score but playing spontaneously and forming an anthem of orchestral praise unto the Lord."[46] Within Baker's account, notice the presumed orchestral instrumentation and the priority of keyboard instruments like the piano and organ.[47] The predominance of pop- and rock-band instrumentation often associated with the rise of Praise & Worship should be associated with other practitioners of Praise & Worship, as will be seen shortly.

In addition, the sort of ninefold summary put forward by Iverson and Gentile was not limited to Charlotte Baker's church but described the worship at leading Latter Rain churches by the late 1970s and early 1980s. A 1983 account of the worship based on participant observation at many of these churches highlighted how standard these practices were.[48] According to this

46. Baker, *On Eagle's Wings*, 93. Latter Rain authors liked to recount stories of musicians playing under the spontaneous inspiration and enabling of the Spirit. One of the more dramatic is Bill Brown's account of two untrained trumpet players playing a forty-five-minute duet in Mexico. See William H. Brown, *Bin Der Dun Dat* (Fort Collins, CO: Book's Mind, 2013), under "Mexico," Kindle. Other art forms someone might not normally consider "prophetic," such as dance and mime, could be included under this label. For an example of the latter, see Todd Farley, *The Silent Prophet: The Prophetic Ministry of the Human Body* (Shippensburg, PA: Destiny Image, 1989).

47. For a reappraisal of the role of keyboard instruments within the historiography of Praise & Worship, see Adam Perez, "Beyond the Guitar: The Keyboard as Lens into the History of Contemporary Praise and Worship," *Hymn* 70, no. 2 (Spring 2019): 18–26.

48. Darrand and Shupe, *Metaphors of Social Control*. Darrand, the book's primary author, visited Reg Layzell's Glad Tidings Temple in Vancouver; Charlotte Baker's King's Temple in Seattle; Ernest Gentile's Christian Community Church in San Jose, California; Bible Missionary Temple in San Diego; Myrtle Beall and James Beall's Bethesda Missionary Temple in Detroit; Olen Griffing's Shady Grove Church in Grand Prairie, Texas; Bible Fellowship in Surrey, British Columbia; and, especially, Violet Kiteley's Shiloh Temple in Oakland. See Darrand and Shupe, *Metaphors of Social Control*, 7. Kiteley's church had been Darrand's home church from 1969 through 1976. Note that Darrand had rejected Latter Rain teachings as "social control." Thus,

account, in Latter Rain worship "the first thing one notices is the atmosphere of spontaneity and the intensity of the meetings. The whole congregation seems to be alive and participating in the group's ritual activities—singing, clapping, lifting their hands, sometimes marching or 'dancing' (often more like jumping), and above all chanting glossolalic 'praises' to God." The first part of the service, which could last from fifteen to forty-five minutes or longer as the leaders discerned appropriate, was driven by music as the atmosphere built "through the enthusiastic repetition of choruses sung by the congregation while a small orchestra" continued to play. At occasional breaks in the singing, prophecy or "a song of the Lord" (i.e., a sung version of a prophetic word from God) could occur.[49]

Praise was the most crucial and unifying aspect of the services in Latter Rain churches, including the times of unscripted, ecstatic congregational singing either in the congregation's known language or in tongues—that is, what early Latter Rain worshipers had called the "heavenly choir." To arrive at this point was desirable for the congregation, as worshipers harmonized together "usually in a major key with spontaneous crescendos and decrescendos."[50]

According to this 1983 account, those leading congregational singing used subtle vocal cues to lead the congregation in Praise & Worship (from praising to worshiping). Such cues amounted to a word or phrase (such as "We praise you, O Lord" or "Hallelujah") sung by the leader with a gradually rising intonation. The leader usually drew out the last syllable to bridge the transition to spontaneous congregational praising and worshiping expressed using a variety of vocal means.[51]

Such a description hints at the existence of Latter Rain Praise & Worship patterns and practices—as well as perspectives—that could be taught. Even if the Holy Spirit was actively directing and shaping such a corporate liturgy and the responsibility of these early musicians was to discern and respond to this leading, Latter Rain musicians began to articulate these patterns and practices as a technique to be taught and shared with others.

Perhaps the first to do so in published form was David Blomgren in his 1978 book, *The Song of the Lord*.[52] This book reflects a significant step in Praise & Worship publications (which had previously been dominated by

some sense of a personal feud with this movement colors the book. His description of worship practices and their supporting theology, however, is still helpful.

49. Darrand and Shupe, *Metaphors of Social Control*, 61–62.

50. Darrand and Shupe, *Metaphors of Social Control*, 89. For a fuller musical analysis of such times in other settings, see Joel Hinck, "Heavenly Harmony: An Audio Analysis of Corporate Singing in Tongues," *Pneuma* 40, nos. 1–2 (2018): 167–91.

51. Darrand and Shupe, *Metaphors of Social Control*, 140.

52. David K. Blomgren, *The Song of the Lord* (Portland, OR: Bible Temple, 1978).

pastors who dealt with theological topics) by being an accomplished musi-cian's attempt to articulate and teach others the musical techniques needed to lead Praise & Worship. Blomgren himself had been grafted into the Latter Rain movement. Blomgren's roots had been thoroughly Baptist: first growing up in the home of a Baptist pastor and then attending a Baptist seminary in Portland. While studying at the seminary, however, he was exposed to the Charismatic Renewal movement. As soon as he graduated from this seminary in 1967, he became one of the two original faculty members of Portland Bible College, the school affiliated with Dick Iverson's church, Bible Temple. There he became one of the school's main administrators, teachers, and textbook writers.[53]

The first half of *The Song of the Lord* is a scriptural and theological overview of "the significance of singing as a ministry in the Spirit" (as the title of his first chapter declares). In this overview, Blomgren teaches about the role of music in Praise & Worship within a theology of the tabernacle of David, while also theologizing beyond it.[54] The book's last three chapters contain Blomgren's detailed description of the musical techniques involved in handling each of the three kinds of songs Latter Rain churches saw as ap-propriate for use in Praise & Worship: psalms, hymns, and spiritual songs.[55] For each category, Blomgren provided a technical definition explaining the distinctions between the types of songs, illuminating their role within the long times of music-driven Praise & Worship. Blomgren defined "psalms" as not only the Psalms per se, but "all songs from Scripture." That seem-ingly included not only songs found as songs in the Bible, but all "scriptural

---

53. Biographical information on Blomgren was ascertained from Conner, *This Is My Story*, 204; the back cover of Blomgren's book *Prophetic Gatherings in the Church: The Laying on of Hands and Prophecy* (Portland, OR: Bible Temple, 1979); and an interview of Mike Herron on September 24, 2019, by Lester Ruth.

54. For example, Blomgren argued for the unique qualification of singing as a channel of the Holy Spirit's ministry on the basis of the movement of music toward resolution and rest, concepts that Blomgren interpreted musically and as scriptural motifs. Blomgren eventually would publish his own study on the restoration of the tabernacle of David: *Restoring God's Glory*. The title page of *The Song of the Lord* shows an image of David playing a harp.

55. This threefold distinction in types of songs was widespread among Latter Rain people (and not only them). It is based on two passages in the New Testament: Eph. 5:19 and Col. 3:16. It is interesting to compare Blomgren's book to a songbook published by Blomgren's church in 1980 titled *Psalms, Hymns, and Spiritual Songs*. Much of this collection is doxological (praise) or devotional (worship). Most songs are a single stanza, though a few have multiple stanzas. There are occasional songs in verse-chorus form. Several songs that would later be well-known songs (e.g., Laurie Klein's "I Love You, Lord") were included but without composer attribution, a fact attesting to the informal networks of circulation and distribution of Praise & Worship songs in the period. Wenceslaus Farlow, Rich Fleming, and Mike Herron, eds., *Psalms, Hymns, and Spiritual Songs* (Portland, OR: Bible Temple, 1980).

choruses" consisting of lyrical material drawn from the Bible.[56] Hymns might contain praise (a strong emphasis presumed in scriptural choruses) along with a variety of other themes. In contrast to "psalms" (i.e., choruses), there was often a strong horizontal, person-to-person dimension in hymns. Blomgren's examples pulled from standard strophic songs typically found in a hymnal (i.e., hymns and "gospel songs").[57] Finally, Blomgren defined spiritual songs as "songs of praise of a spontaneous or unpremeditated nature, sung under the impetus of the Holy Spirit" or, using a romantic motif also used by other Latter Rain authors, as the adoring "love songs of the Bride, the church, to the Bridegroom, the Lord Jesus Christ."[58] A specialized kind of spontaneous, Spirit-inspired song reflected the deeply rooted Latter Rain emphasis on prophetic expression. This was the "song of the Lord," meaning "a spiritual song directed primarily to God's people as the singer becomes a channel for the Lord to convey a message in song."[59]

Songs of the Lord were not incidental or peripheral to Blomgren's discussion of musical technique. Indeed, they were highly valued. Consequently, much of Blomgren's musical technique aimed to lead the congregation to a point at which such musical prophetic expressions would take place. The preponderance of the discussion of musical technique came in his discussion of psalms, which, as you remember, included all scriptural choruses. This weight is not surprising, since the offering of the sacrifice of praise (musically in scriptural choruses) was how God's presence was presumed to be manifested to and experienced by the worshiping congregation. Once in God's presence, the congregation desired to be blessed by the movement and work of the Holy Spirit, especially in prophetic utterances including spiritual songs and the song of the Lord.

Within Blomgren's discussion of musical techniques with psalms, hymns, and spiritual songs, three emphases can be seen. The first dealt with the basic methods to achieve protracted periods of congregational singing with good, uninterrupted flow.[60] Some of the methods Blomgren described would become standard in this type of literature to the present day. The key element in leading a flow of successive choruses (Blomgren presumed choruses, not hymns, were the main type of song for the first part of a service) was to keep a list of choruses organized by Scripture reference, theme, and key signature. Kept in

56. Blomgren, *Song of the Lord*, 25–26. For a summary definition of all three types, see also p. 5 in *Song of the Lord*.

57. Blomgren, *Song of the Lord*, 33–34.

58. Blomgren, *Song of the Lord*, 37.

59. Blomgren, *Song of the Lord*, 37, 43.

60. Blomgren, *Song of the Lord*, 29–30.

the leader's Bible or taped to the pulpit for quick access, this list allowed the leader to respond to the Spirit's leading in the moment, based on what was happening in the congregation. Blomgren advocated linking songs to each other by key signature in order to avoid interruptions between songs. Tempo was a final musical consideration, which Blomgren said the leader of worship must be careful to use well to make the environment fitting for the Spirit's moving. He advocated that leaders not indiscriminately switch back and forth between fast and slow tempos but instead group choruses together by tempo to match the emotional tone of what God is trying to say in the moment.

The second emphasis involved the nature of the lengthy period of congregational singing. Blomgren utilized a series of related semitechnical terms to assert what direction—assessed inwardly by affections—needed to be achieved in the congregational singing. Such terms included "flow," "atmosphere of worship," "spirit of worship," "intensity and momentum," "high flow of worship," "high peak of worship," "level of worship," and "direction of the service." It seems unlikely that Blomgren originated either the terms or the concepts; it is more likely that a level of technical language and perspectives already existed in his own and other Latter Rain congregations.

Guiding and facilitating the singing to achieve a certain end was critical in Blomgren's approach: "The flow of worship should be paced so that a high peak of worship may be realized. A high flow of worship is not automatic in any service but must be raised in the singing of choruses and spontaneous praise. It is usually better to begin with faster choruses and then change to a series of slower choruses."[61] Knowing when to stop was just as critical: "The worship leader should be careful to not continue the singing so long that there is an overpeaking of the flow of worship. The leader in worship should purpose to give the service back to the leadership for the ministry of the Word at a high peak of the spiritual tide. A sensitivity to know when a peak of worship occurs comes with increased experience and greater spiritual understanding."[62] Simply stated, the worship leader's responsibility was to match the flow of Praise & Worship with the flow of the Spirit.[63]

This mention of the Spirit of God highlights the third emphasis in Blomgren's approach: ideally the flow and direction of the service should lead to a congregational environment ("atmosphere" is the term that several Latter Rain authors use) in which there is an awareness of God's direct movement, especially in spontaneous or prophetic expression. In other words, the

61. Blomgren, *Song of the Lord*, 30.
62. Blomgren, *Song of the Lord*, 30–31.
63. Blomgren, *Song of the Lord*, 31.

musician's priestly stewardship was to lead the congregation to a heightened
state for the sake of prophetic expression, not a heightened state for its own
sake. Although Blomgren did not describe specific musical techniques for
playing music during spiritual songs and the song of the Lord, other Latter
Rain musicians would soon be teaching the elements of how to use instrumental music during the times of spontaneous or prophetic singing, whether
by individuals or by the congregation.

It would be wrong to say either that Blomgren's book was *the* book that
launched the discussion of how to do periods of congregational singing or
that it was *the* book that all future worship leaders referenced for proper
technique. However, it is a good window into Praise & Worship musical
technique at one of the leading Latter Rain churches in the late 1970s. In addition, it described musical techniques that would become standard across
Praise & Worship since that time, especially for the purpose of achieving good
flow. Blomgren wanted his readers to take ownership of their music making,
moving from merely replicating what was already extant to creating musical
self-expressions of adoration in new "spiritual songs." The exceptional aspect
of the book was perhaps Blomgren's emphasis on the prophetic, including
the singing of the song of the Lord. As Latter Rain musicians increasingly
began to teach their approach, it would be the distinctiveness of the Latter
Rain emphasis on the prophetic in and through music that would gain less
acceptance among other churches at the end of the century.

There was one other item in Blomgren's book that would be increasingly
evident from the late 1970s onward: the use of the term "worship leader" for
the main musician responsible for the long periods of congregational singing.
Blomgren's discussion is useful for seeing one of the origins of this term and a
reason why it arose. In *The Song of the Lord*, Blomgren used three terms for
the chief vocalist in a service: "song leader" (the older, more widespread term),
"leader in worship," and "worship leader." In his use of the terms there is an
evolution from the older term (song leader) to the new term (worship leader).
Blomgren rejected the former in favor of the latter. The reason had to do with
the responsibility of the main vocalist: this person's task was not simply to
lead the singing of songs but to be truly and personally engaged in worship
(to "enter into a true spirit of worship and exalt the Lord with your whole
heart").[64] Therefore, what a worship leader did was not just lead songs but
lead the congregation into true Praise & Worship. Behind this definition lay
a Pentecostal assumption that the actual inward engagement of the musician

---

64. Blomgren, *Song of the Lord*, 30. Compare, favorably, Nelson Cowan, "Lay-Prophet-
Priest: The Not-So-Fledgling 'Office' of the Worship Leader," *Liturgy* 32, no. 1 (2017): 24–25.

constitutes the key difference between being merely a song leader and being a true worship leader. What Blomgren wrote in 1978 has become a standard emphasis in worship leader training materials since then.

Judson Cornwall and the Tabernacle of Moses

Notwithstanding how this period's Latter Rain theologizing on and advocacy of Praise & Worship was increasing the number of congregations practicing it, there remained a potential drag on its momentum. Specifically, long-standing and vehement repudiation of the Latter Rain movement by established Pentecostal denominations like the Pentecostal Assemblies of Canada or the (US-based) Assemblies of God could cause any Latter Rain development like Praise & Worship to be suspect. For many Pentecostals, knowing that Praise & Worship derived from the Latter Rain movement caused them to consider it contaminated. However, as proponents of Praise & Worship separated it from obvious Latter Rain association, it could become more palatable to mainstream Pentecostals. The period from 1965 to 1985 saw both teaching venues and teachers who did exactly that. Foremost among the teachers who helped popularize Praise & Worship for a broad audience was Judson Cornwall. By the early 1980s he was perhaps the most popularly disseminated Pentecostal author on Praise & Worship.

Originally an Assemblies of God minister serving churches in Washington and Oregon, Judson Cornwall had become by the 1970s an independent Pentecostal author and speaker who traveled the world. By 1984, he had written seventeen books, including his two seminal liturgical books, *Let Us Praise* (1973) and *Let Us Worship* (1983). Moreover, his books were also appearing in four languages besides English by 1984: French, German, Spanish, and Dutch. (The following year would see his work published in Chinese too.) Indeed, such was his prominence that the Pentecostal magazine *Charisma* tapped Cornwall to write a historical retrospective about the rise of Praise & Worship for a 1985 issue.[65] Simply put, Cornwall was one of the main voices of Praise & Worship by the mid-1980s. Not as apparent—but just as important—was how Cornwall was an example of the spread of Latter Rain ideas about Praise & Worship beyond the Latter Rain movement. Not only did Cornwall receive insights on Praise & Worship from the Latter Rain movement; he also mediated them. Thus, he became a key conduit of Praise & Worship across Pentecostalism, disseminating both Latter Rain emphases

---

65. Judson Cornwall, "Trend toward Praise & Worship," *Charisma* 11, no. 1 (August 1985): 22–26.

Used by permission of Justine Sentfleben

Figure 2.2. Judson Cornwall

and his own theological interpretation featuring a typology built on the tabernacle of Moses (not David).[66]

Cornwall was born in San Jose, California, in 1924 into a Pentecostal family; his father was an Assemblies of God minister. The oldest of five children, he began preaching in his early childhood. He was married in 1943 and ordained by the Assemblies of God in the same year. He spent his early ministry in the Pacific Northwest, with pastorates in Kennewick, Washington; Yakima, Washington; and at the Santa Clara Assemblies of God church in Eugene, Oregon.[67] It was in this last church, probably in the early to mid-1960s, that Cornwall had an encounter with a guest speaker that revolutionized his approach to praise. In his first book, *Let Us Praise*, Cornwall relates the story.

66. Some prior histories of Praise & Worship have noticed Judson Cornwall but have not treated him or his work in any substantial detail. See, for example, Birgitta Joelisa Johnson, "'Oh, for a Thousand Tongues to Sing': Music and Worship in African American Megachurches of Los Angeles, California" (PhD diss., University of California Los Angeles, 2008), 507; Wen Reagan, "A Beautiful Noise: A History of Contemporary Worship Music in Modern America" (PhD diss., Duke University, 2015), 248–50; and Monique Ingalls, "Awesome in This Place: Sound, Space, and Identity in Contemporary North American Evangelical Worship" (PhD diss., University of Pennsylvania, 2008), 90, 93.

67. Cornwall dedicated his 1982 book to these three churches, listing them by name. Judson Cornwall, *Let God Arise* (Old Tappan, NJ: Revell, 1982).

He had reluctantly assumed the pastorate of the Oregon congregation only after he perceived God telling him that there would be a divine revelation of a "safe way" into God's realm and presence. Sometime after that, during a midweek service, Cornwall noticed a visitor—someone he had known in Bible college, a friend who had been in ministry in South America. Cornwall invited this acquaintance to give his testimony, which he did that night. Cornwall then invited him to give a series of meetings. The friend agreed to stay for a week.

It was to be a transformative week for Cornwall and his congregation, although initially it was distressing to Cornwall and his Assemblies of God congregation. What the speaker taught on this occasion (and two months later on a second visit) had all the fingerprints of standard practices and perceptions of the Latter Rain movement: lengthy periods of praising in the Spirit, protracted periods of singing Scripture choruses (not hymns) until there was deep inward resonance with the songs, an assembling of the people at the front of the church for times of raising hands and offering up individual expressions of praise and adoration, and congregational marching and dancing.[68] The speaker also played a tape for Cornwall so he could hear another church engaged in this type of praise.[69]

Cornwall does not identify this guest speaker in his book, but the introducer of praise was likely R. Edward Miller, an American missionary to Argentina.[70] Both Miller and Cornwall attended Southern California Bible School, an Assemblies of God school in Pasadena, in the early 1940s.[71] In the mid-1960s (likely 1964–65) Miller was on furlough in the United States, traveling east to west across the country. A few years later (in 1968), Miller and Cornwall would reconnect when the latter ministered in Argentina.[72]

Miller had clear connections to the Latter Rain movement, especially through Elim Bible Institute in New York State and through World MAP (Missionary Assistance Plan), an independent Pentecostal support organization for missionaries.[73] In fact, Miller had been cut off by his original sponsoring

68. Judson Cornwall, *Let Us Praise* (Plainfield, NJ: Logos International, 1973), 15–21.

69. Cornwall, *Let Us Praise*, 17.

70. Robert Miller, son of Edward Miller, has identified his father as the man portrayed in Cornwall's account. Robert Miller, interview by Lester Ruth, November 21, 2019. Similarly, Cornwall's descendants have confirmed that the guest speaker was Edward Miller. Jon Cain, email message to Lester Ruth, November 25, 2019.

71. Since then the school has moved to Costa Mesa, California, and been renamed Vanguard University.

72. This information is from an email message from Cornwall's descendants. Faith Cain, email message to Lester Ruth, September 10, 2019.

73. See Marion Meloon, *Ivan Spencer: Willow in the Wind* (Lima, NY: Elim Bible Institute, 1997), 196; and Richard Riss, "The New Order of the Latter Rain: A Look at the Revival Movement on Its 40th Anniversary," *Assemblies of God Heritage* 7, no. 2 (Fall 1987): 18.

denomination, the Assemblies of God, when he adopted Latter Rain practices and perspectives out of sync with that denomination. Moreover, it is highly probable that the tape Miller played for Cornwall was from Myrtle Beall and James Beall's Bethesda Missionary Temple in Detroit. In the mid-1970s and a couple of years after writing *Let Us Praise*, Cornwall once spoke at this church: at that time, he noted that the first time he had ever heard the kind of Praise & Worship about which he taught was when he had heard a tape recording of Bethesda.[74] Cornwall noted that it was a missionary who had played the tape for him.[75]

After Miller left Cornwall's Eugene church, Cornwall, although he felt like a novice himself, began to teach his congregation on praise. What he reported as his emphasis shows both the influence of prior Latter Rain teaching and his own distinctive take, which itself would become highly influential across Pentecostalism. Cornwall made sure his congregation understood that the place of God's habitation was in the "courtyard of praise," since according to Psalm 22:3 God inhabits the praises of his people. Thus Cornwall instructed his fledgling praise givers that if they wanted to approach God, the approach had to be through praise.[76]

The distinctive element in Cornwall's teaching was how he connected strong notions of spatial movement by the people—and not God—to this root notion of encountering God's presence through praise. Specifically, Cornwall taught his congregation to combine an understanding of the tabernacle of Moses, including its distinct areas and entrances, with Psalm 100:4, which spoke of entering God's gates with thanksgiving and his courts with praise. Thus, unlike Latter Rain theologians in the 1970s who were increasingly emphasizing the restoration of the tabernacle of David, Cornwall emphasized the Mosaic tabernacle instead. He would continue to do so as a linchpin of his theological discussion of Praise & Worship, starting with his first book, *Let Us Praise*, in 1973.

In his books in the 1970s and 1980s, Cornwall continued to show a relative disinterest in the tabernacle of David even when he was considering David

---

74. Jon Rising, "Bethesda Celebrates Its 75th Anniversary," *The Latter Rain Movement of '48* (blog), September 26, 2009, https://lrm1948.blogspot.com/2009/09/bethesda-celebrates-its-75th-anniversary.html.

75. Jon Rising, email message to Lester Ruth, November 21, 2019. Note that Cornwall continued to have several points of close interaction with Latter Rain people in this period, most notably serving on the staff with Fuschia Pickett at the Plano, Texas, Fountain Gate church in the early 1980s. Cornwall's sister, Iverna Tompkins, likewise had a ministry often associated with the Latter Rain.

76. Cornwall, *Let Us Praise*, 24–25. Note the emphasis on the tabernacle of Moses in this, his first book.

as a worshiper. In contrast, the tabernacle of Moses held an important place within his whole theological world, whether he was discussing worship-related matters or not. Indeed, one of his early books, *Let Us Draw Near*, was a detailed commentary (in story form, sometimes from the mouth of Moses!) on the significance of this first tabernacle as a type for understanding the dynamics of salvation mediated by Christ. While there is nothing particularly exceptional in this typological use of the Mosaic tabernacle—even Latter Rain authors had done the same[77]—Cornwall used the notion of the mediation of Christ as the linchpin for making the tabernacle of Moses the critical type for considering Praise & Worship. As people are dependent on Christ to mediate a saving relationship with God, Cornwall argued, so too people are dependent on Christ to mediate acceptable praise that connects them to the presence of God. Commenting on Hebrews 13:15 ("By him therefore let us offer the sacrifice of praise to God continually, that is, the fruit of our lips giving thanks to his name," KJV) and combining it with Hebrews 2:12 ("In the midst of the church will I [Jesus Christ] sing praise unto thee," KJV),[78] Cornwall argued in *Let Us Draw Near* for the utter necessity of Christ's mediation in any relationship with God: "We need the mediation of Christ as much for getting our praises into the presence of God as we do to get our prayers before Him. He praises for, with, and in the midst of the believer-priest, but His praises are always assured of getting through to the Father. By Christ Jesus the church is enabled to worship, not merely work, for He makes our worship available and acceptable unto God."[79]

Since the areas and furnishings of the tabernacle of Moses spoke to Cornwall of what God had provided in Christ to restore humanity's relationship with God and since *restored relationship* was at the center of Cornwall's theologies both of Praise & Worship and of salvation, this tabernacle played a central role in Cornwall's continuing exposition on either praise or worship. As he expressed it in his seminal book on worship, *Let Us Worship*, the dynamics of salvation and Praise & Worship are inextricably linked on the basis of the atonement:

> True worship is possible only on the basis of the divine atonement that was provided by God at Calvary. Through the self-offering of God in the Son, the

77. See, for example, B. Maureen Gaglardi, *The Path of the Just: The Tabernacle of Moses* (Vancouver: New West, 1963); or Kevin J. Conner, *The Tabernacle of Moses: The Riches of Redemption's Story as Revealed in the Tabernacle*, vol. 1 of *Divine Habitation Trilogy* (Portland, OR: City Bible, 1975).

78. As we saw in chap. 1, James Beall had made this same combination but did so without emphasizing the essential mediation of Christ.

79. Judson Cornwall, *Let Us Draw Near* (Plainfield, NJ: Logos International, 1977), 129–30.

believer now stands in a personal relation of sonship to God on the basis of a new birth. Prayer, then, ceases being merely a pleading for mercy and becomes the praising of our merciful God. Through His High Priestly office, Christ enables men to offer acceptable worship unto God. Our restoration becomes the basis of our rejoicing, and Christ's finished work becomes the foundation of our worship.[80]

Simply put, Cornwall seems attracted to the Mosaic tabernacle in discussing Praise & Worship because it provides an easier connection between his liturgical theology and his theology of salvation.

Cornwall used the tabernacle of Moses to describe a good shape for the times of congregational singing that characterized Praise & Worship. Whether Cornwall originated this teaching cannot be determined, but he certainly helped popularize it, given the extent of his speaking engagements and the proliferation of his books.[81] Not within Latter Rain circles at the time but elsewhere in Pentecostalism, it became commonplace to organize congregational singing by a sense of moving from thanksgiving to praise to worship, visualized by a sense of moving through the different areas of Moses's tabernacle. For Cornwall—and many other Pentecostals—the key biblical passage was Psalm 100, especially verse 4: "Enter into his gates with thanksgiving, and into his courts with praise: be thankful unto him, and bless his name" (KJV). While Cornwall's earlier books did not articulate whose responsibility it was to lead a congregation through this musical architectural journey, his 1983 book, *Let Us Worship*, made it quite clear: the one leading the singing had this liturgical responsibility.[82] Cornwall dedicated a whole chapter (chap. 17, "Leading Others into Worship") to describing the musical process, noting, "Almost anyone can lead songs, but it take someone special to be able to lead *people* as they sing. This person must be a worshipper himself if he is to lead others into worship, and he must know where he is, where he is going, and when he arrives."[83]

To make his architectural model work for shaping times of congregational singing, Cornwall had begun to make a clear distinction between the terms "praise" and "worship" by the early 1980s. He was explicit about the shift in

80. Judson Cornwall, *Let Us Worship: The Believer's Response to God* (South Plainfield, NJ: Bridge, 1983), 17.

81. For a similar treatment, see British author Graham Kendrick, *Learning to Worship as a Way of Life* (Minneapolis: Bethany House, 1984), 141–51.

82. Cornwall did not use the term "worship leader" in 1983; he still used the older term "song leader." By 1985, however, he was acknowledging that many were "upgrading" the older term to "worship leader." See Judson Cornwall, *Elements of Worship* (South Plainfield, NJ: Bridge, 1985), 131.

83. Cornwall, *Let Us Worship*, 154.

his thinking and when it had occurred. When he had published *Let Us Praise* in 1973 he had used the terms synonymously, but by 1983 he was convinced that the Scriptures did not use the two terms to mean the same thing. In the Bible, Cornwall wrote, "praise prepares us for worship" or "praise is a prelude for worship."[84] Cornwall could maintain the distinction even if he wanted to connect it to the root notion of Psalm 22:3: "Praise is the vehicle of expression that brings us into God's presence, but worship is what we do once we gain an entrance to that presence."[85] Similarly, the distinction easily fit into the architectural model of the Mosaic tabernacle: "We traverse God's courts with praise, but when we are drawn into the holy place with God, worship is the prescribed response."[86]

Cornwall's distinction between "praise" and "worship" helped reinforce "Praise & Worship" as a technical term describing a particular approach to a congregational liturgy.[87] His teaching became an important part of the demise of the term's use as a generic way of describing a congregational service, a use that had been common in previous decades. As an increasing number of Pentecostal congregations sought someone to lead them musically from thanksgiving to praising to worshiping, consciousness continued to grow that "Praise & Worship" was a thing to seek.

And seek it congregations did. We should not underestimate Judson Cornwall's role in popularizing Praise & Worship across Pentecostalism. In many ways, he absorbed the core notions and practices of Latter Rain–shaped Praise & Worship and reshaped them in a way that a wide swath of other Christians found accessible and compelling.

Cornwall had some sense of this vocation and, indeed, had been commissioned to do it, starting with his first book, *Let Us Praise*. He explained the story on the back cover of the book's original 1973 printing as well as in a 1985 retrospective article, "Trend toward Praise & Worship."[88] The book's publisher, Logos International, wanted to build on the success of two earlier books it had printed on the power of praise for individual discipleship.[89]

---

84. Cornwall, *Let Us Worship*, 143.

85. Cornwall, *Let Us Worship*, 149.

86. Cornwall, *Let Us Worship*, 61.

87. Cornwall was not the only one at the time making a distinction between "praise" and "worship." See Iverson and Scheidler, *Present Day Truths*, 216–18.

88. Published in the August 1985 issue of *Charisma* magazine. See p. 23 in this article. Prior to publication of *Let Us Praise* in 1973, Cornwall had already begun to speak and write on the subject of praise. See, for example, a series of four addresses given at a 1971 charismatic conference and published in vol. 4, nos. 4–7 (April–July 1972) of *New Wine* magazine.

89. The books were two best sellers by an Army chaplain, Merlin R. Carothers. The books were *Prison to Praise* (Plainfield, NJ: Logos International, 1970), his autobiography; and *Power*

Sensing that an eager readership awaited more works on praise, the publisher asked Cornwall to write a book helping congregations and worshipers know how to praise. Cornwall accepted the assignment; the result was *Let Us Praise*. Throughout the book, Cornwall showed his pastoral sensitivity in addressing the various obstacles—both individual and corporate; both his own and others'—he had seen that made accepting a Latter Rain–inspired approach to Praise & Worship difficult.

Steady dedication to that sense of purpose continued to drive his writing. For example, noting that *Let Us Praise* had opened many doors for him to teach on praise, he wrote *Let Us Arise* to address a spiritual problem he had noted in his congregational speaking trips. Although he had taught churches new corporate expressions of praise, he discovered on second visits that many had not maintained the praise. He decided the problem was a lack of the deep relationship with God needed to "maintain a life of praise."[90] Meanwhile, Cornwall's own sense of vocation was being sharpened. Through the latter half of the 1970s, he shifted his concern increasingly to worship rather than praise.[91] Although Logos International encouraged him to write a book on worship, it was seven years before he felt the liberty from the Holy Spirit to do so. *Let Us Worship* was the result, published in 1983. By then Cornwall was a fixture in the growing world of Praise & Worship.

Cornwall himself was aware of the broadening parameters of this world. While he acknowledged the role of the Latter Rain and maintained close professional and personal relationships with the people in that movement—for example, he once described Charlotte Baker as "a long-time personal friend"[92]—Cornwall did not think the restoration of Praise & Worship culminated in or was limited to the Latter Rain movement. This breadth of thinking was reflected in his 1985 published retrospective on the rise of Praise & Worship. Cornwall's portrayal was one crowded with an array of Pentecostals and even Charismatics (mainline or evangelical Christians who had had Pentecostal experiences).[93] Where are the people, Cornwall

in Praise (Plainfield, NJ: Logos International, 1972). Carothers was a Methodist who had become part of the Charismatic Renewal movement. Carothers's basic theological emphases were those of Reg Layzell. How Carothers became aware of this teaching is unclear. *Prison to Praise* was made into a movie.

90. Judson Cornwall, *Let Us Abide* (Old Tappan, NJ: Revell, 1977), 11.

91. Cornwall, *Let Us Worship*, ix.

92. Cornwall, *Let Us Worship*, v. Surely it was in the camp meeting sponsored by Baker's church in Seattle that the "forceful prophetic word" spoken over Cornwall that God had called him to be a worshiper occurred. The event occurred in the early 1970s. See p. ix in *Let Us Worship*.

93. Highlighting the cross-denominational Charismatic Renewal movement was a recurring feature of Cornwall's work during the period. See Cornwall, *Let Us Draw Near*, 166–67; and

asked, who have learned that praise brings worshipers into God's presence? His answer was expansive: everywhere.[94] In other words, Praise & Worship was surging.

Increasing Venues for Disseminating Praise & Worship

As critical as theological authors like Cornwall, Truscott, Conner, Baker, and Blomgren were in teaching others about Praise & Worship, several other outlets for instructing others about this liturgical approach contributed to this surge.[95] By the late 1970s, musicians and pastors had something to teach and disseminate—namely, an approach to Praise & Worship that fused a robust biblical theology of worship with specific techniques they found useful in leading this kind of liturgy. And teach it they did. Starting in the 1970s, they used more and more outlets to reach ever increasing numbers of people and to encourage them to adopt Praise & Worship. The theology and practices of Praise & Worship became less associated with the Latter Rain movement over time and, as they lost this association, they began to sweep up even more congregations within Pentecostalism. The surge began to include more Pentecostal churches within old-time Pentecostal denominations and even some congregations in broader evangelicalism.

Let Us Worship, 167–77. He had been a speaker at some of this movement's largest meetings. For example, see his presentation to the 1973 Greater Pittsburgh Charismatic Conference: Judson Cornwall, "Into the Holy of Holies," in *The Spirit Is a-Movin': 16 Charismatic Descriptions of How, Where, and Why*, ed. R. Russell Bixler (Carol Stream, IL: Creation House, 1974), 170–75. Not surprisingly, Cornwall consistently used the tabernacle of Moses and its furnishings to frame his understanding of how the Charismatic Renewal movement fit into larger church history.

94. Cornwall, "Trend toward Praise & Worship," 24–25.

95. During this period, Glad Tidings Temple and its pastoral staff increasingly slid toward the margins of developments within Latter Rain Praise & Worship. Reg Layzell left Glad Tidings in 1970, and by the late 1970s he was pastoring in Yuba City, California. At the age of eighty he died on November 2, 1984, while visiting a pastoral friend, Mike Servello, in upstate New York. When Layzell left Vancouver, he was replaced by his associate, Maureen Gaglardi, who had been influenced by Layzell's ministry since the original revelation of Ps. 22:3 in 1946. See Gaglardi, *Key of David*, 5–6. Layzell never accepted the growing theological emphasis of the period: the restoration of the tabernacle of David as referring to the emergence of Praise & Worship. He remained adamant that biblical references to this restoration applied to the reestablishment of the nation of Israel in the late 1940s. In addition, disagreements over several other theological and administrative points isolated Layzell, Gaglardi, and Glad Tidings to a degree, especially from Portland's Bible Temple, which continued to grow in influence. See Layzell and Layzell, *Sons of His Purpose*, 250–53. Gaglardi herself eventually developed difficulties in the pastorate of Glad Tidings and was removed from her position in 1987, a process supervised by Charles Green of New Orleans.

Increased publication of books and magazines was one outlet. For example, Dick Iverson's Portland church, Bible Temple, released a steady stream of Praise & Worship materials under its own publishing imprint. These tapes, books, and other teaching materials were obviously intended for the students at the church's Bible college, but by the early 1980s a mail-in order form standardly included in the materials made acquiring these materials easy. Bible Temple's national and international prominence opened up a wide market for this imprint's releases.

Authors gained another publishing outlet in the eastern United States in the early 1980s with the start of Destiny Image Publishers in Shippensburg, Pennsylvania. Don Nori Sr. founded the company in 1983. At the time, Nori was a co-pastor of a Latter Rain–type church in Shippensburg named Deliverance Temple.[96] Nori went on to publish materials on Praise & Worship under the Destiny Image imprint and, eventually, under the Revival Press imprint too. (By 1989 Revival Press was the "worship and praise division" of Destiny Image.)[97]

Latter Rain dissemination of Praise & Worship also spawned early attempts at periodicals. The first issue of the quarterly *Praise Magazine* came out in late 1981, for example. It included an interview by Reg Layzell, labeled "the apostle of praise."[98] Another early magazine was David Blomgren's *Restoration Magazine*, which he started in 1982 after he had left Bible Temple in Portland and had begun to pastor in Regina, Saskatchewan, Canada. Both magazines seem to have had limited print runs and circulation.[99]

A third periodical seems to have had a little more success, probably because it was linked to a subscription tape service for Latter Rain–derived music. This newsletter, *Music Notes*, was compiled and edited by Barry Griffing, the music pastor at Violet Kiteley's Shiloh Temple in Oakland. First printed in December 1979, *Music Notes* accompanied the ZionSong cassette tapes featuring songs contributed by musicians from across the Latter Rain network. By coupling the tapes and the newsletters, Griffing sought to provide an early

---

96. Deliverance Temple (renamed as Oasis of Love Church) had been founded by Latter Rain church planters Harrison and Elvira Miller in 1953. For information on the start of Destiny Image, see Destiny Image, "Destiny Image Founder Promoted to Glory: The Story of Don Nori Sr. and Destiny Image Publishing," April 18, 2018, https://www.destinyimage.com/2018/04/18/destiny -image-founder-promoted-to-glory-the-story-of-don-nori-sr-and-destiny-image-publishing/.

97. This latter publisher had been started by another Latter Rain figure, Don Lewis, who had been mentored by Violet Kiteley, a prominent Latter Rain pastor in Oakland, California. Chironna, interview.

98. [Barry Griffing], "New Products Review," *Music Notes* 4, no. 1 (Winter 1982): 3.

99. Blomgren was ministering at Maranatha Christian Centre in Regina. *Restoration Magazine* had a print run from 1982 to 1988.

outlet for the dissemination of new
music by Latter Rain–related composers as well as for information on events
and resources related to Praise & Worship, on the theological underpinnings
of Praise & Worship, and on practical
tips for doing Praise & Worship. In
its typical four-page layout, this periodical included the latest news about
conferences and happenings, a list of
resources, a review of the history and
theology of Praise & Worship, and
discussions of the best musical technique to facilitate a flowing service to
get to the song of the Lord. In other
words, *Music Notes* was an articulation of Reg Layzell's root teaching
on praise, fused with the typological
expositions of later teachers, centered
on the narrative of the tabernacle of
David, and tempered by the actual
experience of musical leadership, all

Figure 2.3. An example of a book from Destiny Image Publishers written by a popular
Praise & Worship teacher, Myles Munroe

to articulate a method for entering into heightened spiritual and prophetic
awareness of God's presence through music.

The newsletter's initial growth was promising. It began with twenty-four
subscribers in 1979, and a year later there were two hundred representing one
hundred churches across the continent. *Music Notes* reported that forty-eight
new choruses had gone out to these subscribers, along with twenty-five choir
specials and twelve instrumental pieces.[100] By 1983 there were four hundred
subscribers in two hundred churches.[101] Much of the expansion came through
promotion at the growing number of worship conferences associated with
Griffing and others.

In the 1970s and early 1980s other means beyond publications reinforced
Praise & Worship among its own adherents as well as extending it to others
more broadly within Pentecostalism and, eventually, evangelicalism. A key
part of this web of dissemination was the network of Latter Rain ministers

100. [Barry Griffing], "ZionSong's First Year: Praise Him for His Mighty Acts," *Music
Notes* 2, no. 6 (December 1980): 1.
    101. [Barry Griffing], "ZionSong Has Moved!," *Music Notes* 5, no. 2 (1983): 1.

and their annual conferences. These conferences not only allowed ministers to maintain close relationships with each other but also provided ongoing opportunities for classes and shared evening worship services. The conferences were a critical link that allowed the circulation of new songs across churches.[102] One key network with a conference was the one centered in the Los Angeles area and known as the Revival Fellowship. Another important network and conference arose from the Revival Fellowship when Dick Iverson started the Northwest Ministers Fellowship, initially for those ministers in the Pacific Northwest of the United States who had been traveling the thousand miles to Southern California to attend the Revival Fellowship conference. Eventually, the Northwest Ministers Fellowship would attract between eight hundred and nine hundred ministers from across the United States, both from independent Pentecostal churches like Latter Rain congregations and from long-established Pentecostal denominations.[103]

Not every ministers' network instrumental in spreading Praise & Worship was congregation-centered. An important example is World MAP (Missionary Assistance Plan), an organization started by Ralph Mahoney, who had been pastor of a church in Louisiana. This organization gained prominence during the 1970s, especially through its summer camp ministry in the United States. The organization's forte was providing financial and prayer assistance to missionaries who had had charismatic experiences that made them distasteful to their non-charismatic sending denominations.[104] Attendance at World MAP's meetings could range in the thousands, purportedly, and the camps' worship services exposed participants to Praise & Worship. Speakers included known names within the Latter Rain movement (e.g., Charlotte Baker) but also Pentecostal teachers increasingly prominent in the broader Pentecostal world of Praise & Worship, such as Judson Cornwall, Iverna Tompkins (Cornwall's sister), Bob Mumford, and Ern Baxter.[105]

Within the growing world of Latter Rain promulgation of Praise & Worship, Iverson's Portland church, Bible Temple, would play an increasingly important role. We have already mentioned the Northwest Ministers Fellowship and the publishing house connected with Bible Temple. Another component of the church's impact was its cassette tape ministry. Unlike many other churches that only recorded the sermon on the tapes that they distributed, Bible Temple recorded the entire service. Distributed without cost, the tapes

102. Rachinski, interview.
103. Iverson, interview.
104. Kenneth Cain, interview by Lester Ruth, November 9, 2019.
105. Conner, *This Is My Story*, 220.

were sent around the world and introduced many to this congregation's approach to Praise & Worship.[106]

If cassette tapes disseminated Bible Temple's liturgy by being sent out, their counterpart was the congregation's school founded in 1967, Portland Bible College. Students came from across the continent and overseas to attend the college. While there, they were exposed to Bible Temple's Praise & Worship in services while their teachers and textbooks provided the theological and technical exposition of the same.

While Portland Bible College was a particularly important piece in the larger Latter Rain matrix that was standardizing and disseminating Praise & Worship, it was not the only school teaching Praise & Worship. Indeed, since formal accreditation seems not to have been a concern for the organizers of such colleges, they were easily started and became widespread among congregations wanting to provide a venue for a more thorough grounding in their own approach to Scripture. Reg Layzell's congregation in Vancouver, for example, ran such a Bible college for years. Its students included Howard Rachinski, the eventual founder and first chief executive of Christian Copyright Licensing International, who attended from 1973 to 1976, and LaMar Boschman, who also attended in the 1970s. Both men would play prominent roles in the spread and establishment of Praise & Worship from the 1980s onward.[107]

However, not all the educational institutions instilling Praise & Worship were congregation-based. In western New York State, Elim Bible Institute, a school affiliated with the Latter Rain movement since the earliest days of the revival (as seen in chap. 1), would emerge again as another center for the dissemination of Praise & Worship through one of its faculty members, Bob Sorge. Neither were all the colleges found within the United States. La Nueva Esperanza, a Bible college near Allende, Mexico (not far from the border with Texas), became a center where Spanish-speaking students from across a range of denominations experienced Latter Rain–style Praise & Worship in their chapels, learned it in their classes, and encountered it at special conferences beginning in 1973.[108]

Even as Bible colleges taught their residential students in this period, pastors and musicians teaching Praise & Worship traveled to a variety of settings:

106. Iverson, interview.

107. Rachinski, interview; LaMar Boschman, interview by Lim Swee Hong and Lester Ruth, August 3, 2017. Note that Rachinski had attended Layzell's church since his birth in 1951. Boschman had begun attending this same church in the mid-1970s after Layzell had turned pastoral authority over to Maureen Gaglardi.

108. William H. "Bill" Brown, interview by Lim Swee Hong and Lester Ruth, August 20, 2019. Brown, *Bin Der Dun Dat*, under "Mexico." For a list of other Mexican Bible colleges with which Brown worked, see *Bin Der Dun Dat*, under "Mexico."

local church consultations, local church demonstrations, small regional conferences, and, increasingly, large-scale national conferences. From the late 1970s onward, there was an ever-growing surge in such educational activity. LaMar Boschman, for example, was perhaps one of the first Praise & Worship musicians to have an itinerant worship ministry. Traveling church to church with Kayy Gordon, the missionary to the Arctic from Layzell's Glad Tidings Temple, Boschman would play worship music and teach on a theology of worship.[109] Participating in the first Praise & Worship conferences also enriched Boschman's ministry. Attending one of the first of such conferences and hearing Dick Iverson preach on music sparked Boschman to do his own biblical study that resulted in a 1980 book, *The Rebirth of Music*. This book anticipated the direction of some Latter Rain Praise & Worship material. While the Latter Rain roots and articulation of key concerns are evident in Boschman's book, in comparison to Blomgren's book from two years earlier, Boschman rounded off the sharp edges of Latter Rain distinctives, thus making the material potentially more accessible for a broader Pentecostal audience.

By no means was Boschman the only traveling Latter Rain musician and teacher of Praise & Worship.[110] In Central America, for example, Bill Brown and the other faculty from La Nueva Esperanza would spend six months in residence and then six months ministering across the region, including holding worship seminars in countries like Guatemala, Costa Rica, and Cuba. On occasion, preachers from Canada and the United States would assist. Brown liked to work with Dave Huebert, the pastor from Chilliwack, British Columbia, discussed in chapter 1.[111]

An increasingly important teaching outlet for such speakers and musicians was a growing number of Praise & Worship–focused conferences. The first was one at Portland's Bible Temple, organized by that church's musician, Mike Herron, in August 1977. Though he was aiming primarily for Latter Rain musicians in the Pacific Northwest, Herron also invited a number of musicians from California.[112] The impulse was to more directly cater to musicians' concerns in a way not done in the various fellowships for ministers.

109. Boschman, interview.

110. Many of the speakers traveling and teaching during this period were associated with some of the most significant Latter Rain churches. These included Barry and Steve Griffing, musical brothers associated with Shiloh Temple in Oakland, California; Mike Herron from Bible Temple in Portland, Oregon; Hazel and Sam Sasser from the Rock Church in Virginia Beach, Virginia; Dean Demos from Hope Temple in Findlay, Ohio; and David Fischer at Living Waters Tabernacle in Pasadena, California.

111. Brown, *Bin Der Dun Dat*, under "Mexico."

112. [Barry Griffing], "Seeing Regional Worship Conferences as Part of Your Music Ministry," *Music Notes* 3, no. 2 (April 1981): 1; Herron, interview.

The number of conferences quickly grew from there. By the mid-1980s there were numerous Praise & Worship conferences across the United States and Canada. Some were one-time events while others, like the Northwest Music Ministers Conference at Bible Temple, became part of a regular annual cycle. Some were in large churches while others were held in smaller venues.[113] Despite the variety, what became clear was that these conferences were critical outlets for sharing theology, musical technique, and new songs, not only within the Latter Rain movement but increasingly across a range of denominations. For example, the first conference held at Elim Bible Institute in 1983 featured Barry Griffing speaking to more than three hundred delegates from East Coast states. These delegates represented "Pentecostals, charismatic Catholics, Mennonites, Baptists, and Messianic Jews."[114] Similarly, the Conference on Charismatic Worship in Santa Ana, California, in 1981 attracted two hundred participants, an estimated eighty percent of whom were "charismatics or classical Pentecostals who had no previous exposure to the Song of the Lord and Davidic worship."[115]

The most significant of the Praise & Worship conferences was held annually, changing its location each year, and was eventually known as the International Worship Symposium.[116] Its origin was a resolve birthed out of the 1977 conference at Bible Temple to hold an annual, national worship conference every August.[117] Soon a four-man team organized and led these meetings: Barry and Steve Griffing, Larry Dempsey, and David Fischer.

The 1978 meeting at Shiloh Temple in Oakland attracted 120 participants. The 1979 meeting was in Findley, Ohio, at Hope Temple; it attracted fewer than one hundred participants. After the 1979 meeting, the annual meeting began to be known as a "symposium," picking up on a term that the Findley church's pastor had applied to a separate conference at his church in 1978.[118]

---

113. An example of a smaller venue would have been Deliverance Temple in Shippensburg, Pennsylvania, the church of Destiny Image Publishers' founder, Don Nori Sr. See the notice under "Upcoming Events" in *Music Notes* 5, no. 1 (Spring 1983): 2.

114. See the notices of recent conferences in *Music Notes* 5, no. 3 (1983): 2.

115. [Griffing], "Seeing Regional Worship Conferences," 1.

116. See Adam Perez, "'All Hail King Jesus': The *International Worship Symposium* and the Making of Praise and Worship History, 1977–1989" (ThD diss., Duke Divinity School, 2021), 148. We are indebted, too, to Steve Griffing, who agreed to multiple interviews on October 13, 2017, and February 13–15, 2018, to supply the data for this history. An interview of Barry Griffing and David Fischer on May 25, 2017, has also been very helpful, as has been the periodical *Music Notes*.

117. The name morphed from "National Music Leadership Conference" to "National Music Symposium" to "International Worship Symposium."

118. Our account is based on the history provided in *Music Notes*, since it was written close to the events in question. For a different spin on this history, see Moses Vegh, *The Chronicles of Moses: The Acts of an Apostolic Journey* (Fort Wayne: Weaver, 2013), 116.

Used by permission of Barry Griffing and Steve Griffing

Figure 2.4. The organizers of the International Worship Symposium (left to right: Larry Dempsey, Barry Griffing, Steve Griffing, David Fischer)

The 1980 symposium was at Larry Dempsey's church in Santa Ana, California, with just under two hundred in attendance.

Attendance began to climb steadily after 1980. The 1981 meeting at Shady Grove Church in Grand Prairie, Texas (a suburb of Dallas), had about four hundred in attendance. The 1982 symposium in Clawson, Michigan, had about eight hundred in daily attendance and twice that number in the evening services. Similarly, the 1983 meeting in Pasadena, California, grew in both the daytime attendance for the workshops (about nine hundred people) and the evening services (around sixteen hundred in the Pasadena City Auditorium). Having Jack Hayford as the keynote speaker in the evening along with the choir from his church (Church on the Way in nearby Van Nuys) singing Hayford's recently written song "Majesty" spurred the large evening attendance and would have made the meeting feel more pan-denominational to a breadth of Pentecostals.[119]

The 1983 symposium was the last one hosted at a church for several years, as the number of participants continued to swell and the conference's reach spread ever more broadly across Pentecostalism. The 1984 symposium was held at Oral Roberts University with more than one thousand delegates

119. Griffing and Fischer, interview; Barry Griffing, "Symposium '83: Excitement Mounts in Pasadena," *Music Notes* 5, no. 1 (Spring 1983): 1.

©1988 ZionSong Music

Figure 2.5. Music during an extemporaneous "song of the Lord" during an International Worship Symposium (left to right: Steve Griffing, Barry Griffing, JoAnne Griffing, Vikki Marchi)

attending the daytime teaching portion and more than two thousand in attendance for the evening services. The 1985 conference was held at Duquesne University in Pittsburgh, Pennsylvania, and the 1986 symposium, the largest in terms of attendance, was held at the Sheraton Hotel in Washington, DC. This 1986 meeting had about 2,200 participants for the daytime sessions and more than 3,800 at the evening services.

The significance of the International Worship Symposium resides not only in the number and range of registrants it attracted but also in the number and range of teachers it utilized. Over the years, several hundred different faculty members taught in at least one of the conference's meetings.[120] The effect in the 1980s was a small whirlpool where Latter Rain teachers mixed with the ever-growing number of proponents of Praise & Worship from across Pentecostalism. This eddy effect within the annual symposia allowed circulation of Latter Rain emphases more broadly with the teaching of other Pentecostals beyond the Latter Rain movement, the exchange rounding off the edges of the teaching from all directions. With the rounding off came ever wider adoption.

This broadening was not without controversy. The use of speakers beyond Latter Rain networks caused some consternation among members of the

120. Chironna, interview.

established Latter Rain pastoral leadership, such as Dick Iverson, especially after the 1983 meeting that had featured Jack Hayford (a Foursquare pastor). Despite pressure from Iverson and others to bring the meetings and speakers back solely within the Latter Rain umbrella, the four organizers (the Griffing brothers, Dempsey, and Fischer) kept on the broad track they had chosen. The result was a break in fellowship between those involved in the International Worship Symposium and Iverson's network organized around his Portland church, Bible Temple. Serendipitously, even as the disgruntled Latter Rain pastors widely circulated a letter instructing others to disassociate from the symposium, an invitation came from the head of the music department at Oral Roberts University in Tulsa, Oklahoma, and several Pentecostal megachurches in that area, offering to host the 1984 International Worship Symposium.[121] The organizers accepted the invitation and booked Judson Cornwall to be one of the featured speakers.[122]

And thus, while from 1965 to 1985 the energy applied to theologizing about praise and God's presence had deepened the channel in which the river of Praise & Worship ran, an increasing breadth of congregations and denominations worshiping in this way was at the same time widening the stream of Praise & Worship. Like the old children's chorus, this liturgical river was running deep and wide by the mid-1980s. Let us now review the variety of Christians adopting Praise & Worship in the period.

---

121. Steve Griffing, interview by Lester Ruth and Lim Swee Hong, October 13, 2017; Steve Griffing, interview by Glenn Stallsmith and Jonathan Ottaway, February 15, 2018.
    122. See the notices regarding meetings in *Music Notes* 5, no. 3 (1983): 1.

three

—

increasing currents in praise & worship, 1965–85

By all means, sing! God inhabits (is at home in) the sung praises (*tehillahs*) of his people.

—*Jack R. Taylor, Spirit-filled pastor of Southcliff Baptist Church, Fort Worth, Texas*[1]

As noted previously, perhaps the strongest contemporaneous witness that there had been a broadening of Praise & Worship was Judson Cornwall's 1985 retrospective article in *Charisma*, the popular, trans-Pentecostal magazine.[2] The article's title highlighted the broadening by suggesting that there was a *trend* toward Praise & Worship. The article's introduction summarized what had taken place: "The past decade has witnessed the discovery of new dimensions of worship. Congregations have risen beyond praise into a higher worship." The entire framing of this ten-year period (1975–85) underscored that this spread of Praise & Worship was a significant, new, and ever-widening development. According to Cornwall, before churches had discovered the

1. Jack R. Taylor, *The Hallelujah Factor* (Nashville: Broadman, 1983), 146. Note that *tehillah* is the Hebrew word found in Ps. 22:3. Interpreted as sung praise, this word in this verse was another way teachers were reinforcing a sense that the praise that God inhabits is essentially musical.

2. Judson Cornwall, "Trend toward Praise & Worship," *Charisma* 11, no. 1 (August 1985): 22–26.

renewal of worship, they had discovered praise, its "forerunner." (One can sense the technical distinction Cornwall made between "praise" and "worship"; see chap. 2.) He described the musical changes brought about by this first discovery: hymnbooks had been replaced by overhead projectors "beaming newly written Scripture choruses"; laggardly singing had been replaced with fervent congregational singing; and spontaneous singing in English and in glossolalia, by individuals and by congregations, had sprung up from time to time. Cornwall compressed this first discovery into a pithy summary: "Praise became popular." Stating it in terms of experienced theology, he stressed the now-expected sequence from praise to an experience of God in which the people worshiped: "We have learned that praise brings us into God's presence, and when we are standing before Him, we worship!"[3]

Who was this "we" who had learned how to praise and how to worship? Cornwall was exuberant about how ubiquitous those who practiced Praise & Worship had become: such worshipers were now found "in churches large and small, denominational and independent."[4] Indeed, Cornwall could have increased the scope of his description and it still would have been accurate. By the early 1980s, the theology and practices of Praise & Worship were not only in a wide range of churches, but also in renewal movements, schools, colleges, youth and campus ministries, home meetings and Bible studies, missionary organizations, parachurch organizations, meetings led by itinerant evangelists and musical groups, and an emerging worship music industry.

Cornwall was not only the one who noticed and exulted in this widening of the "river" of Praise & Worship; voices from within the Latter Rain movement were likewise rejoicing. For example, in 1982 Barry Griffing, one of the organizers of the International Worship Symposium and the editor of *Music Notes*, exulted in the surge of praise he had seen arising in the previous twenty years. Ecstatic about what he called the "Praise Movement," Griffing noted how, despite a diversity of Pentecostal and Charismatic viewpoints on a myriad of issues, there was yet one common denominator that had expanded since the 1960s: "the primacy of dynamic and demonstrative praise and worship in their church life."[5] He saw evidence for this surging "Praise

3. Cornwall, "Trend toward Praise & Worship," 23–24.
4. Cornwall, "Trend toward Praise & Worship," 25.
5. [Barry Griffing], "The Praise Movement of the '80s: Past Roots, Present Problems, Future Promise," *Music Notes* 4, no. 1 (Winter 1982): 1. Compare the assessment of well-respected evangelical author Paul E. Billheimer in *Destined for the Throne: A New Look at the Bride of Christ* (Fort Washington, PA: Christian Literature Crusade, 1975), 128n2. Billheimer noted the expansive pervasiveness of praise across Pentecostalism and attributed this tradition's growth to the praise. Pentecostal scholar Vinson Synan endorsed Billheimer's judgment in a 1986 article: "Pentecostalism: Varieties and Contributions," *Pneuma* 9, no. 1 (Fall 1986): 37. More scholarly

Movement" in many places, especially in Charismatic Protestants and the Jesus People movement. In Griffing's view, the leadership in Praise & Worship by early Latter Rain pioneers like Reg Layzell, Violet Kiteley, Charlotte Baker, and Myrtle Beall had rebounded in abundance among Charismatic Protestants and the Jesus People.[6] These newcomers in Praise & Worship were already making their contributions to the "Praise Movement," Griffing said, including the pace-setting praise albums of Maranatha! Music. In contrast, Griffing felt as if Praise & Worship had made little headway in the long-standing Pentecostal denominations. His pessimism was premature. As we shall see, even in these denominations Praise & Worship was advancing, as Praise & Worship became a distinct "thing" in its own right and its connections to the Latter Rain movement grew more obscure. As more and more congregations began to hold to the theology and practices of Praise & Worship—and a wider range of teachers advocated it—those roots would evaporate from view.

Clearly by the early 1980s Praise & Worship had spilled beyond its Latter Rain origins and was influencing a range of early adopters from across Pentecostalism and the emerging Charismatic Renewal movement of mainstream denominations. To get a sense of the broadening reach of Praise & Worship, this chapter will look at examples in this period of how the theology tying praise to God's presence captivated a range of Pentecostals and those with Pentecostal-type experiences. Such case studies are useful for gaining a sense of the variety of people and movements caught up in Praise & Worship and motivated by its theology. Therefore, this chapter will not be an exhaustive review of everyone caught up in this surge, but it does give a sense of Praise & Worship's multiple "currents" by the 1980s.[7] These examples will also not be given in strict chronological order. Moreover, we will intentionally delay consideration of the Jesus People movement until the end of the chapter, lest we reinforce the misconception that the rise of Praise & Worship was mainly

work needs to be done on praise itself as a defining propensity in the history of Pentecostal worship.

6. Griffing, "Praise Movement," 2. Griffing also mentioned Milford Kirkpatrick as one of these pioneers. Kirkpatrick had been on the staff at the Sharon institutions in North Battleford, had participated in the original revival in 1948, and had been part of the traveling team that helped spread the revival in its earliest years.

7. Two outlets in particular cry out for further scholarly work, both related to institutions geared for young adults: Youth With A Mission, a global missions organization, and Christ for the Nations Institute, a school in Dallas. Several important songwriters (e.g., Twila Paris and Karen Lafferty) have been involved with Youth With A Mission. Not only has Christ for the Nations Institute trained a series of important songwriters and worship leaders, but the recordings produced by this school, including of its chapel services, have been influential to many.

or exclusively tied to this movement. Important as it was, it was but a tributary feeding into a much larger, already-existing system.

In addition to demonstrating the pervasiveness of the theology connecting praise to God's presence, these early adopters picked up and reinforced some of the developments of the period that had been taking place in the practices of Praise & Worship. These other currents contributed other elements that eventually would sweep across the entirety of this liturgical phenomenon: the use of popular styles of music making, widespread songwriting out of these popular styles, an emphasis on "intimacy" as a critical aspect of the dynamics of being in God's presence, a highlighting of how praise can enthrone God, and an emphasis on the seven Hebrew words for praise.

By the mid-1980s the various currents of Praise & Worship had their own temperature and pace of flow. Yet they were all moving in the same direction and were propelled by the momentum of the same core theological commitment. It is impossible, however, to always decipher clear lines of influence, given how these currents swirled in and around each other. Let us examine some examples from across the growing breadth of Praise & Worship, beginning with how the theology was capturing the imagination of songwriters.

Singing the Tie between Praise and Presence

Perhaps nothing shows as much what worshipers love about God than what they sing about in a song. If that is the case, an increasing number of songs in the late 1970s and early 1980s revealed that worshipers from a range of backgrounds were enamored with the link between praising God and experiencing God's presence. While the songs obviously never referenced Psalm 22:3 directly—lyrics do not lend themselves to chapter and verse citation—they nonetheless show how the root notion of God inhabiting the praises of his people had swept up an increasing number of songwriters and worshiping congregations.

The writing of songs with this idea apparently began in the mid-1970s and has continued to the present day.[8] From the mid-1970s to 1985 at least fourteen songs were written by North American composers that explicitly mention God inhabiting praise. This proliferation of worship songs perhaps indicates better than anything else the wide circulation of this core theology of Praise & Worship. In addition, given how worship songs are fluid across lines that often separate one group from another, the flow of songs across a variety of

8. An example is "There Is a Name" by Benjamin Hastings, Pat Barrett, and Sean Feucht (2017).

congregations would have helped spread this theology broadly, thus further loosening the theology's bonds to the Latter Rain movement.

The first two of these songs, both dating from 1977, left no doubt about the underlying theology. These songs shared the same title, which was not at all subtle: "The Lord Inhabits the Praises of His People." The two composers, Thurlow Spurr and Jeannie Clattenburg, could not have been more different in background. Spurr was an older, experienced evangelical composer whose work with a touring singing group for youth, the Spurrlows, had been a fixture in evangelicalism since 1959 (see chap. 5). Clattenburg, on the other hand, was a thirty-two-year-old church musician at an Assemblies of God congregation (Calvary Assembly) outside Orlando, Florida.[9] Spurr's song was part of a larger composition for yet another touring event, the *Festival of Praise*.[10] Clattenburg's offering was a single composition—although she, too, recorded it on a solo album.[11]

These two 1977 songs seemingly opened the floodgates: they were followed by many songs incorporating the same idea, although the titles were usually less direct.[12] Some of these songs came from well-established composers and recording artists like Brown Bannister and Michael Hudson's song "Praise the Lord," which was made well known on the 1979 album *Heed the Call* by the Imperials. Similarly, in 1985 Dove Award–winning composers Lanny Wolfe and husband-wife duo Dick and Melodie Tunney all wrote songs based on the tie between praise and God's presence. Wolfe composed "I'm Gonna Praise the Lord" and the Tunneys composed "Let There Be Praise." This latter song was recorded by Sandi Patty on the 1986 album by the same name.

Some songs came from the circles associated with the Jesus People movement, as when Maranatha! Music composers Judi and Bruce Borneman contributed "Don't You Know It's Time to Praise the Lord" in 1981. The song exulted

9. Also in 1977, Brent Chambers, a New Zealander, wrote "The Celebration Song," also known as "In the Presence of Your People," based on Ps. 22:3. Chambers's song was published in David Garratt and Dale Garratt, eds., *Scripture in Song*, vol. 2, *Songs of the Kingdom* (Auckland, New Zealand: Scripture in Song, 1981), 156. See "Brent Chambers," Hymnary.org, accessed February 4, 2021, https://hymnary.org/person/Chambers_B.

10. Thurlow Spurr, *Festival of Praise* (Waco: Lexicon Music, 1977). In addition to being released in this songbook, the musical was released as an album, an eight-track tape, and a cassette tape. There were also an accompaniment tape, a fully orchestrated score, and a choral songbook.

11. Jeannie Clattenburg, *Chosen Generation*, Mission, KS: Tempo Records, 1977, 33⅓ rpm.

12. Other songs based on this theology were "We Worship You O God" (1979, Larry Dempsey; note that Dempsey was one of the organizers of the International Worship Symposiums); "Lord Jesus We Enthrone You" (1980, Paul Kyle); "Praise You Lord" (1981, Lynn DeShazo); "Lord God You're Holy" (1983, Dick Grout); "I Will Sing I Will Dance" (1984, Coleen Sacy and Warren Hastings); "Communion Prayer" (1985, Gary L. Bruce); "Yahweh Is Holy" (1985, Lynn DeShazo); and "Give Him Praise" (1985, Myrna and Delton Alford).

in how God lives in the praises of worshipers. That same year, Carl Tuttle, the worship leader in John Wimber's congregation, Calvary Chapel in Yorba Linda, California, recorded this song on the training tapes for the worship leaders in that congregation's small groups. He used it, too, in the congregation's Sunday services.[13] The song was the first track on the *Praise 5* album released by the Maranatha! Music company, increasing its circulation even more.

Whether by recordings, traveling musicals, or informal sharing of songs, the theology of God inhabiting the praises of worshipers was celebrated in song. This theology was captivating the hearts of a growing number of song-writers, both well-known composers and those with more limited exposure.

The Charismatic Renewal Movement

Cornwall's 1985 retrospective in *Charisma* magazine, mentioned at the beginning of this chapter, was not the first time that this glossy, pan-Pentecostal periodical had looked at the spread of Praise & Worship. In 1977 this fledgling magazine dedicated a theme issue to "praise power." Thurlow Spurr contributed one of the feature articles.[14] In it he described his Festival of Praise musical as well as his belief in the theology that coupled praise to God's presence. Spurr also mentioned where he had first been introduced to this idea: Merlin Carothers's best-selling book from 1972, *Power in Praise*.[15] (This book was one of the books by Carothers whose sales had led the publisher to ask Judson Cornwall to write something similar for congregational worship. See chap. 2 for that story.) According to Spurr, reading Carothers had led him to understand the "fundamental truth" that God "inhabits the praises of His people."[16] Carothers's significance was not only in how widely his books disseminated this theology, but that he shows how widely this idea had already spread outside Pentecostal congregations. Carothers was not a Pentecostal per se but a Methodist Army chaplain who had had an experience of baptism in the Holy Spirit through the Charismatic Renewal movement that swept through the mainline denominations in the 1950s and after.[17] (Carothers's

13. Wimber's congregation would shift affiliations in 1982 and become the Anaheim Vineyard. The information on the congregation's song usage is based on the unpublished training tapes and recordings of congregational services.

14. Thurlow Spurr, "Praise: More Than 'Festival.' It's a Way of Life," *Charisma* 2, no. 6 (July/August 1977): 12–14, 26.

15. Merlin R. Carothers, *Power in Praise* (Plainfield, NJ: Logos International, 1972).

16. Spurr, "Praise: More Than 'Festival,'" 13.

17. For a general history of the Charismatic Renewal movement, see Stephen Hunt, *A History of the Charismatic Movement in Britain and the United States of America* (Lewiston, NY: Edwin Mellen, 2009).

experience occurred around 1965.) He serves as an important witness to how the theology based on Psalm 22:3 had seeped into mainline and evangelical circles through the Charismatic Renewal movement.[18]

It is not surprising that this praise-to-presence theology can be found in authors who were part of the Charismatic Renewal movement or similar movements in the mid-twentieth century that emphasized the Holy Spirit. For one thing, those seeking charismatic experiences sometimes noted their own inadequacy in praising well.[19] Robust praising, too, characterized charismatic worship.[20] Dennis Bennet, the Episcopal priest who in the early 1960s became a public face of the Charismatic Renewal movement (even though it preceded him in several places by several years), described the pervasive quality of praise among his charismatic parishioners at their home meetings:

> The singing might continue for a half-hour or even an hour. . . . Chorus would follow chorus, and it was a rare evening in which a new song or two was not learned. After the singing came another completely new thing, praise. Not thanksgiving, but just plain praise, which not only permeated the meetings but our personal everyday affairs also. . . . This new activity of praising God was seen to be the source of power and freedom in our meetings. "Father, I love you!" "Jesus, you're wonderful!" "Blessed be God!" "Glory be to God!" "Thank you, Jesus!" "Hallelujah!" Perhaps twenty or thirty persons at a time could be heard spontaneously uttering words of praise. Most eyes would be closed, some faces lifted to heaven, a number of hands raised in this ancient gesture of prayer. The voices blended in a murmur. . . . Such praise might continue for five minutes, or ten, and be repeated several times during the evening.[21]

Such persons were ripe for introduction to a theology that would place praise within a larger biblical framework.

Multiple continuing points of interaction provided opportunities for that introduction. Prominent Latter Rain pastors as well as early non–Latter Rain adopters of Praise & Worship were frequent speakers at charismatic organizations and events.[22] The connections began early in the Charismatic Re-

18. Starting in 1970, Carothers published four books that applied the theology to individual life and discipleship: *Prison to Praise* (1970); *Power in Praise* (1972); *Answers to Praise* (1972); and *Praise Works!* (1973). Logos International was the publisher of all four. He did not address corporate liturgy in these books, although some of his readers applied his insights in that way.

19. For example, see John L. Sherrill, *They Speak with Other Tongues* (Grand Rapids: Chosen Books, 1985), 87–88 and 133–44.

20. Sherrill, *They Speak with Other Tongues*, 134, 161.

21. Dennis J. Bennett, *Nine O'Clock in the Morning* (Plainfield, NJ: Logos International, 1970), 37–38.

22. The most complete list can be found in Richard M. Riss, "The Latter Rain Movement of 1948," *Pneuma* 4, no. 1 (1982): 42–45; and Richard M. Riss, *Latter Rain: The Latter Rain*

newal movement. For example, Carlton Spencer from Elim Bible Institute (see chap. 1) was a speaker at a 1953 meeting of the Full Gospel Business Men's Fellowship International. The use of speakers who held a praise-to-presence theology continued in charismatic meetings from those early years through the 1980s. Thus, the large 1973 Greater Pittsburgh Charismatic Conference featured plenary talks by James Beall from Bethesda Missionary Temple in Detroit, and Judson Cornwall. Cornwall spoke on one of his trademark topics, the tabernacle of Moses.[23] Joseph Garlington, a musical Pittsburgh-area pastor who would become a fixture in the broad world of Praise & Worship, led worship in this 1973 meeting.[24] Because the Charismatic Renewal movement crossed denominations, such speaking and leading of worship had the potential to widely disseminate the theology and practices of Praise & Worship.

As Spirit-filled non-Pentecostals began to publish their theologies of Praise & Worship, these books expressed well-established features of the praise-to-presence theology circulating in Praise & Worship. Perhaps the first to publish such a book was Jack R. Taylor, a Southern Baptist. His 1983 book, *The Hallelujah Factor*, was published by his denominational imprint, Broadman Press. Taylor was well known in the Southern Baptist Convention, having led large churches and been elected as the first vice president of the convention in 1980.[25]

Taylor's book derived from a series of sermons he had preached on praise while serving as an interim pastor in a Fort Worth, Texas, Baptist congregation in the early 1980s. Taylor's book and sermons used Psalm 22:3 repeatedly as a key verse. For example, while explaining why God seemed so active during

---

Movement of 1948 and the Mid-Twentieth Century Evangelical Awakening (Mississauga, ON: Honeycomb Visual Productions, 1987), 140–41. It would be false to say that the Latter Rain movement and those closely associated with its way of Praise & Worship were the sole theological influences on the liturgical theology and practices of the Charismatic Renewal movement. However, the level of influence seems strong nonetheless. Compare the assessment of Bill Hamon, a Latter Rain–related author, in *The Eternal Church: A Prophetic Look at the Church—Her History, Restoration, and Destiny*, rev. ed. (Shippensburg, PA: Destiny Image, 2003), esp. pp. 231 (Charismatics "came into the Latter Rain type of worship more than the Pentecostal ways of worship") and 239 ("The Charismatic Movement was an extension and an expansion of the Latter Rain Movement").

23. R. Russell Bixler, ed., *The Spirit Is a-Movin': 16 Charismatic Descriptions of How, Where, and Why* (Carol Stream, IL: Creation House, 1974), 170–75. Beall's address is on pages 10–17.

24. Joseph L. Garlington, interview by Lester Ruth, February 13, 2020.

25. C. Douglas Weaver, *Baptists and the Holy Spirit: The Contested History with Holiness-Pentecostal-Charismatic Movements* (Waco: Baylor University Press, 2019), 271. Note that Weaver (pp. 268–72) does not identify Taylor as a Charismatic per se because he did not speak in tongues, did not affirm tongues as a necessary sign of having received the Holy Spirit, and did not identify a secondary experience of the fullness of the Spirit as "the baptism of the Holy Spirit." Nonetheless, under influence of the related Holiness movement, Taylor promoted and testified to a dramatic infilling of the Spirit after 1964.

times of congregational praising, Taylor gave an answer in which God both inhabits praise and is enthroned on praise: "While God is everywhere, he is not everywhere manifested. He is at home in praise, and, being at home, he manifests himself best as God! . . . He is enthroned and liberated to act mightily in praise."[26] This latter emphasis linking praise to God's enthronement was a growing one during the early 1980s, when it was being promoted by other Praise & Worship teachers as well as found within some new translations of the Bible.[27]

The remainder of Taylor's book reflected the method and theologizing commonplace in Praise & Worship. His method rested on using a concordance to find biblical passages about praise and then organizing and synthesizing these into a schema.[28] The Scriptures with the most prominence in his method were the Psalms (which provided many of the root ideas), 1 and 2 Chronicles (which furnished the types to make concrete the conceptual schema pieced together in the Psalms), and Revelation (which gave a cosmic and heavenly significance to congregational praising). Of special note in Taylor's theology was his discussion of the seven different Hebrew words for praise. Although Taylor did not originate this teaching, his use of it reflected a new development in Praise & Worship theologizing.[29]

Prosperity Gospel Pentecostals

A better candidate for the source of the seven Hebrew words teaching would be Charles Trombley, a Pentecostal minister who had started as an Assemblies of God pastor in the early 1960s and then migrated through a variety of ministries. Along the way he had absorbed the teaching of the line of Pentecostal thinking that has become known as the prosperity gospel.[30] In 1976 Trombley published a book, *How to Praise the Lord*,[31] that showed how thoroughly—

26. Taylor, *Hallelujah Factor*, 29.

27. For example, the New American Standard Bible.

28. See, especially, Taylor, *Hallelujah Factor*, 26–32.

29. We are indebted to conversations with Jonathan Ottaway on these insights about scriptural method and the seven Hebrew words for praise. This teaching notes the different Hebrew words translated as "praise" and their nuances of meaning. See Jonathan Ottaway, "The Seven Hebrew Words for Praise: Pentecostal Interpretations of Scripture in Liturgical Theology," *Worship* (forthcoming).

30. Note that adherents in this movement often prefer the term "Word of Faith" rather than "prosperity" to identify their approach. However, because the term is so widespread in scholarly literature, we use the latter term rather than the former.

31. Charles Trombley, *How to Praise the Lord* (Harrison, AR: Fountain, 1976). Its foreword is by Kenneth E. Hagin, one of the key figures in the rise of the prosperity movement in the mid-twentieth century.

and easily—prosperity preachers had picked up the standard aspects of Praise & Worship thinking and fused them with their prosperity emphases.[32] (The book, too, appears to be the first published version of the teaching about the seven Hebrew words for praise.) *Charisma* magazine published an excerpt from this book in its 1977 theme issue on praise, eliminating the strongest statements of the book's prosperity teaching. What it did provide was a piece that allowed the reader to experience the novelty of praise, to have a growing desire for it, and to develop a commitment to engage in it.

Trombley began his book's exposition of praise by describing his own first encounter with Praise & Worship. This exposure occurred at a conference in Atlanta, Georgia, in the latter half of the 1950s. Driving from Vermont (probably Bellows Falls, Vermont, where Trombley pastored his first church, an Assemblies of God congregation) to Georgia, Trombley was shocked by what he saw in the worship. Although he did not identify the conference, the worship he saw had the earmarks of Latter Rain Praise & Worship: the "heavenly choir" singing in the Spirit, the lifting up of hands (in which Trombley only hesitantly participated), and a quick sense of being in God's presence. According to Trombley, what used to take hours of "waiting on God" and "praying through" happened in less than three minutes of this Praise & Worship.[33] He was amazed and hooked. Trombley wrote his book to lay out the biblical basis for prioritizing praise and to help his readers overcome any reluctance in adopting it.

In multiple respects Trombley's theological discussion of praise was unexceptional. There was the quotation of Psalm 22:3 as the cornerstone of the theology[34] as well as a discussion of the necessity of the sacrifice of praise from Hebrews 13:15.[35] Trombley even worked in a discussion of the restoration of David's tabernacle.[36]

What was exceptional was Trombley's reframing of these standard Praise & Worship elements into a larger prosperity gospel system. Trombley's theology

32. Kate Bowler, *Blessed: A History of the American Prosperity Gospel* (Oxford: Oxford University Press, 2013), 45. Bowler's book is the best treatment of the prosperity movement.

33. Trombley, *How to Praise the Lord*, 7–12. Trombley would also serve ministries in Sarasota, Florida; Ottumwa, Iowa; and Tulsa, Oklahoma. Another description of this meeting started his 1978 book, *Praise: Faith in Action* (Indianola, IA: Fountain, 1978), 7–8. Unfortunately, neither these books nor Trombley's autobiography (*Kicked Out of the Kingdom* [Springdale, PA: Whitaker House, 1974]) help clarify the matter about what conference he had attended. There are two likely possibilities: (1) a Full Gospel Business Men's Fellowship meeting or (2) a conference held July 15–22, 1956, at Christian Fellowship Evangelistic Center in Atlanta, Georgia. We are grateful to Jon Rising for helping us identify the possibilities. Jon Rising, email message to Lester Ruth, December 6, 2019.

34. Trombley, *How to Praise the Lord*, 48. For Hagin's citation of the verse, see p. 5.

35. Trombley, *How to Praise the Lord*, 79.

36. Trombley, *How to Praise the Lord*, 53.

picked up on a latent aspect of a Latter Rain theology of praise: specifically, Reg Layzell's emphasis on the causal instrumentality of praise bringing God's presence. Trombley used this latent aspect to recast praise as a "release for true faith," such faith being the key in a prosperity approach to unlocking the already-given blessings of God. Trombley brimmed with confidence in the system: "Ending prayer with praise is sealing what you've asked in faith with a period while you wait expectantly for delivery."[37] Trombley could state the matter even more forcefully, quoting E. W. Kenyon, the "theological architect" of the prosperity gospel movement: "Prayer asks but praise takes. Prayer talks about the problem but praise takes the answer from God."[38]

Another prosperity gospel preacher, Terry Law, would have an even wider influence on the entirety of the Praise & Worship movement than did Trombley.[39] In the 1970s Law was an evangelist who traveled with a music group called Living Sound. The sudden death of Law's wife in a car accident in September 1982 precipitated his investigation of Praise & Worship as a source of healing for his grief. Part of Law's encouragement at the time was a direct exhortation by Oral Roberts to begin to praise God.[40]

The morning after Roberts's exhortation, Law began to praise God. Initially he found it an excruciating, hollow experience. Eventually, however, Law experienced what he described as an inner healing. His commitment to Praise & Worship was born out of his own experience: "It was through the power of praise and worship that I found healing and deliverance in all areas of my life—emotional, spiritual, physical, psychological."[41] Law decided to use Praise & Worship in his own speaking events. He instructed Don Moen, who had become Living Sound's primary worship leader in January 1983, to switch all the music from a focus on evangelism to a focus on Praise & Worship. To give Moen a chance to learn more fully what this switch meant, Law sent him to attend the 1983 International Worship Symposium in Pasadena, California.[42] As

37. Trombley, *How to Praise the Lord*, 71, 79.

38. Trombley, *How to Praise the Lord*, 77. See Bowler, *Blessed*, esp. 250, for the identification of Kenyon in this way.

39. For this account, we are dependent on the research of Adam Perez. See Adam Perez, "Sounding God's Enthronement in Worship: The Early History and Theology of Integrity's Hosanna! Music," in *Essays on the History of Contemporary Praise & Worship*, ed. Lester Ruth (Eugene, OR: Pickwick, 2020), 84–89.

40. Terry Law, *The Power of Praise and Worship* (Tulsa: Victory House, 1985), 16–17. Law also tells the story in Terry Law and Shirley Law, *Yet Will I Praise Him* (Old Tappan, NJ: Chosen Books, 1987), 252–57. According to *Yet Will I Praise Him* (p. 257), Law's first "Praise and Healing" crusade with Don Moen was in February 1983.

41. Law, *Power of Praise and Worship*, 19.

42. Terry Law and Jim Gilbert, *The Power of Praise and Worship*, exp. and rev. ed. (Shippensburg, PA: Destiny Image, 2008), 46. To hear Law interviewed about his journey from grief

we will see in chapter 4, Moen's trip would have a huge impact on the history of Praise & Worship through the rise of Integrity's Hosanna! Music.

As in Trombley's earlier work, the theology in Terry Law's 1985 book showed the clear influence of earlier teachers of Praise & Worship now fused with distinctive prosperity gospel emphases. The basic theological premise is the association of praise with an experience of God's presence. Law cited Psalm 22:3 on multiple occasions, even offering alternative translations: God inhabits praise or is enthroned on praise.[43] Law also discussed the need to go beyond feelings or desires in offering the "sacrifice of praise" (Heb. 13:15) and used the architectural layout of the tabernacle of Moses to discuss the proper sequencing of thanksgiving, praise, and worship, whether in individual or corporate practice.[44] Law even included the increasingly common discussion of the seven Hebrew words for praise.[45]

But Law gave these commonplace Praise & Worship themes a distinct prosperity gospel framing, as did Trombley in his earlier book. For Law, providing a throne for God through praise was not simply a way to experience the divine presence; it was a necessity to experience the *power* of God's presence. Consequently, Law felt he could rely absolutely on the causal instrumentality of praise: "As I hear the sacrifice of praise from the people, I know beyond all shadow of a doubt that I'm going to see miracles. Never, in any miracle service that I have held, where people entered into a sincere sacrifice of praise, has there not been healing or manifestation of God's power."[46] Law realized the tension in his approach but was unwilling to back away from the causal optimism, noting that "we must be very careful at this point. We cannot make praise a source for the manipulation of God. It is not a coin in a cosmic vending machine. But according to Scripture, it is absolutely correct to praise God for expected results and promises on the basis of the law of faith."[47] Indeed, praise was the most effective of weapons in spiritual warfare because it was

---

to Praise & Worship, see Terry Law, "Getting through Life's Tragedies," interview by Moira Brown, three YouTube videos, posted by "100 Huntley Street," May 26, 2009: 9:02, https://www.youtube.com/watch?v=pDLIAXjcgRs#action=share; 8:39, https://www.youtube.com/watch?v=d7UdXtaoh98; and 9:45, https://www.youtube.com/watch?v=_yNdsDmArZU. At the 1983 International Worship Symposium in Pasadena, Moen joined others from the prosperity gospel sphere of Tulsa, Oklahoma, including Macon Delavan (the head of the music department at Oral Roberts University) and Billy Joe Daugherty (pastor of Victory Christian Center). Also in attendance, as one of nearly one thousand participants at the 1983 symposium, was Steve Young, the music director at John Osteen's Lakewood Church in Houston.

43. Law, *Power of Praise and Worship*, 117, 156.
44. Law, *Power of Praise and Worship*, 166, 243–54.
45. Law, *Power of Praise and Worship*, 130–35.
46. Law, *Power of Praise and Worship*, 170.
47. Law, *Power of Praise and Worship*, 230.

"the taking of God's thoughts and superimposing them over the thoughts from the enemy"—that is, the devil.[48]

In these ways, Law and Trombley voiced a clear prosperity gospel accent within the theologizing of Praise & Worship. The increasing breadth of Praise & Worship had added another current that would have continuing impact.[49]

Pentecostals in Established Denominations

Although we often have highlighted in this book persons who were historically significant in the past but might not be well known now, we draw attention now to Jack Hayford, a leader who has stayed well known for decades. He is also an important example of someone from a long-established Pentecostal denomination who entered into Praise & Worship and yet remained within his denomination.[50] Hayford, who had a long pedigree in the International Church of the Foursquare Gospel, represents an increasing number of classic Pentecostal denominations that moved from earlier ways of worship to the Praise & Worship of the 1970s and 1980s. In addition, Hayford himself would become a major influencer within Praise & Worship as a well-known composer of Praise & Worship songs (including "Majesty," his best-known song), a prolific speaker and author on Praise & Worship, and the president of his denomination. His influence came, too, through his congregation, the First Foursquare Church of Van Nuys, California, an assembly more widely known as Church on the Way. He came to this pastorate in March 1969 when it was a small, struggling congregation and when he was at the beginning of his entrance into Praise & Worship.

Hayford's first step was his own study of Psalm 22:3. In his 1983 book describing the dynamics of congregational life in his church, Hayford noted how in his upbringing he had often heard leaders exhort the congregation to

48. Law, *Power of Praise and Worship*, 50.

49. For an assessment of the impact of prosperity gospel churches on the recent history of Praise & Worship, see Kate Bowler and Wen Reagan, "Bigger, Better, Louder: The Prosperity Gospel's Impact on Contemporary Christian Worship," *Religion and American Culture: A Journal of Interpretation* 24, no. 2 (Summer 2014): 186–230. Bowler and Reagan focus on the period since the 1990s.

50. As discussed previously, both Judson Cornwall and Charles Trombley began as Assemblies of God pastors but eventually launched into independent ministries. Our interviews have shown us more broadly how exposure to Praise & Worship in this period sometimes led people out of the established Pentecostal denominations to independent ministries (Kenneth Cain, interview by Lester Ruth, November 9, 2019), sometimes into Latter Rain–related congregations (Bob Johnson, interview by Lester Ruth, April 8, 2017), and sometimes to renewed ministries within the original congregation (Stephen R. Phifer, interview by Lester Ruth and Lim Swee Hong, December 12, 2017).

praise the Lord by saying "the Lord inhabits the praises of His people" but without citing the specific verse.[51] Sometime early in his ministry, Hayford returned to this notion and, after expending some effort to find where it was in the Bible, did his own exegetical study of the verse. Hayford decided the Hebrew verb translated "inhabitest" in the King James Version of the Bible was actually a more fluid action depending on who the subject was, and he began to think of God being enthroned on praises, emphasizing the royal majesty of God as heavenly king.[52] This enthronement theme would stay as an important feature of Hayford's theology of Praise & Worship.

The second step was Hayford's recently acquired commitment to emphasize worship, not evangelism, as the goal of Sunday morning. Hayford later said that up to 1968, he was a "typical evangelical" in his "approach to worship," meaning he focused on evangelism and thought actual worship was an "auxiliary activity" of the church.[53] After hearing the president of an Assemblies of God Bible college, G. Raymond Carlson, speak at a convention on the priority of worship, Hayford changed his mind and his approach: "When God calls us to worship, His goals are encounter and action. He wants to meet with us and move among us, interacting with and transforming His people."[54] Thus, Hayford arrived in his small California congregation already convinced that praise and God's presence were connected and that, when present, God intended to interact with and transform the congregation.

Hayford began his ministry at Church on the Way with a commitment to reinvigorate the praise offered by this congregation. For Hayford, it was not a matter of teaching the people something entirely new. Instead, he recognized that the members had a tradition of "worshiping God openly and expressively" but believed that this tradition had become stale and undynamic. Their

---

51. Jack W. Hayford, *The Church on the Way: Learning to Live in the Promise of Biblical Congregational Life* (Old Tappan, NJ: Chosen Books, 1983), 81. Hayford, who was born in 1934, grew up in Southern California and in the Oakland area. His book is scanty on details but raises the possibility that other mid-century Pentecostals utilized Ps. 22:3 as a liturgical promise. Hayford belonged to the denomination that Aimee Semple McPherson began. In her 1923 book, McPherson quotes Ps. 22:3 (without citation) as a description of services in which she had seen God's presence experienced in a robustly praising congregation. Aimee Semple McPherson, *This Is That: Personal Experiences, Sermons and Writings of Aimee Semple McPherson, Evangelist* (Los Angeles: Bridal Call, 1919), 621.

52. Hayford, *Church on the Way*, 81.

53. Quoted in "What Others Say about Praise and Worship," *Charisma* 11, no. 1 (August 1985): 25.

54. Quoted in "What Others Say about Praise and Worship," 25. See also S. David Moore, *Pastor Jack: The Authorized Biography of Jack Hayford* (Colorado Springs: David C. Cook, 2020), 127–28.

praise over time had become "perfunctory and programmed."[55] Therefore, Hayford worked toward instilling Praise & Worship in this congregation not as a completely new discovery, but as a recovery of practices latent in the people's spiritual heritage as Pentecostals.

Through Hayford's leadership—including his commitment to liturgical principles he found in 1 Corinthians 14[56]—the congregation developed patterns for its three weekly services with strong Praise & Worship.[57] Hayford strove to maintain a sense of order throughout while allowing for response to the Holy Spirit's leading. The main service on Sunday morning began with a robust time of congregational singing, commonly lasting for twenty to twenty-five minutes; Hayford himself sometimes led the singing. Because Hayford had perfect pitch, he sometimes signaled to the organist to change keys to a key he felt would be more fitting to accomplish one of his main goals, the full participation of the entire congregation. Spoken praise could sprinkle the singing. In the first years, until the congregation grew larger, there was no choir. Throughout the sung Praise & Worship, Hayford had a concern for the content of the songs. To care for that concern, Hayford always included one hymn to anchor the congregation in historic truth.[58] In addition, he aimed to thematically connect the more contemporary songs to the day's message. Hayford sought coherence throughout the whole service.

Next came a time of sharing, personal interaction, and praying in spontaneously created small groups. Hayford usually provided instruction, drawing on some truth from the Bible, to guide the groups. Hayford saw engagement in these groups as another way to have full participation of the entire assembly: as worshipers had ministered to God in Praise & Worship, so then they ministered to each other in prayer. The service concluded with the pastor's scriptural teaching, a sermon.

In the congregation's liturgical life and in his writing and speaking, Hayford forged his own approach to Praise & Worship. What he offered was an accessible, yet still biblically rooted, theology of Praise & Worship. Hayford's

55. Hayford, *Church on the Way*, 81–82.

56. On the basis of this passage, Hayford aimed for "orderly services which release worship, release the flow of gifts, and develop the ministry-mindedness of the individuals present." See Hayford, *Church on the Way*, 102. See also Moore, *Pastor Jack*, 145–52.

57. Hayford, *Church on the Way*, 102–6. Notice how, in terms of sequencing the songs, Hayford did not make an absolute distinction between "praise" and "worship." Other details about worship in this congregation come from an interview of Jimmy Owens, Carol Owens, Jamie Collins, and Dan Collins by Lim Swee Hong and Lester Ruth, September 21, 2017.

58. "All Hail the Power of Jesus' Name" was a very common hymn, again reinforcing the theme of majestic royalty for the divine. See Jack W. Hayford, *Manifest Presence: Expecting a Visitation of God's Grace through Music* (Grand Rapids: Chosen Books, 2005), 87.

personal disposition facilitated the communication of his approach too. He thus joined Judson Cornwall as one of the main popularizers of Praise & Worship in the period, further loosening any exclusive connection Praise & Worship might have had to the Latter Rain movement. Hayford would become a prolific author of Praise & Worship materials, offering numerous songs, teaching media, and books, including the widely sold *Spirit Filled Life Bible* (originally released in 1991). This study Bible included Charles Green's Latter Rain–inspired teaching titled "The Pathway of Praise"[59] (see chap. 1, note 93). Church on the Way also held pastor conferences with church musicians in attendance in which a key point was the dissemination of new music. Workshops at these conferences reinforced the dissemination of Praise & Worship to attendees.[60] Less obvious—but as important—was the impact this congregation's worship would have on West Angeles Church of God in Christ, which in the late 1980s would model Praise & Worship for African American congregations across the United States (see chap. 4).

The Jesus People

Of the various currents that had emerged within Praise & Worship in this period, the one identified as the Jesus People movement—that dynamic adoption of Christianity among the hippie subculture and other disenfranchised young adults—has been the one previous scholars have documented best. The development of a new way of worship and a new genre of songs among the Jesus People is well known and often told. Indeed, the commonplace approach has been to portray this movement of the late 1960s and early 1970s as *the* source for the development of Praise & Worship, especially its music. However, while the Jesus People movement was important, it was only one current among many. In addition, rather than being the originating headwater, it was more of a tributary flowing into an existing river whose multiple currents were already providing strong momentum forward.

We have held off describing the Jesus People until this point of the book in order to portray the complexity of Praise & Worship's history and to describe a different origin for it. We have even suspended a strict chronological approach in this chapter to avoid letting the typical story—what Adam Perez calls the "music-industrial" discourse[61]—overwhelm a more accurate

59. Charles Green, "The Pathway of Praise," in *Spirit Filled Life Bible*, ed. Jack W. Hayford (Nashville: Nelson, 1991), xxix–xxx.
60. Denise Hammack and Doug Hammack, interview by Lester Ruth, December 5, 2018.
61. See Adam Perez, "'All Hail King Jesus': The *International Worship Symposium* and the Making of Praise and Worship History, 1977–1989" (ThD diss., Duke Divinity School, 2021), 6.

narrative. But, having now brought Jesus People into the story, we will slow down and provide a drawn-out examination so that this movement's important contributions of practice to Praise & Worship can be put into a larger historical context, noting easily overlooked details of how those practices arose. The slower pace will also allow us to show how the liturgical theology that arose in the Jesus People current connected it to the broader liturgical phenomenon and its already widely circulating biblical theology.

In the standard portrayal of the Jesus People movement's liturgical impact, two networks of congregations, Calvary Chapels and Vineyard Fellowships, have played the central role. And, within these two networks, two Southern California congregations have occupied the spotlight of scholarly consideration: Calvary Chapel of Costa Mesa, pastored by Chuck Smith Sr. and the "mother church" of Calvary Chapels, and the Anaheim Vineyard (originally known as the Calvary Chapel of Yorba Linda), pastored by John Wimber.[62] (Wimber's congregation shifted its affiliation to the Vineyard Fellowships in 1982, and it also moved to a neighboring city around the same time. Thus, it

62. To list every scholarly and popular treatment that follows this standard narrative would take too much space. However, several significant works in particular seem to have made it commonplace and should be mentioned. An in-depth sociological study of the mid-1990s by Donald E. Miller (*Reinventing American Protestantism: Christianity in the New Millennium* [Los Angeles: University of California Press, 1997]) lauded these congregations as "new paradigm" churches unveiling landmark changes, including worship-related ones. After Miller's study, three later authors are often cited. The first two were former executives with Maranatha! Music (a company started by Calvary Chapel of Costa Mesa), who naturally place Calvary Chapel and Maranatha! Music at the center of their narratives. See Robb Redman, *The Great Worship Awakening: Singing a New Song in the Postmodern Church* (San Francisco: Jossey-Bass, 2002); and Charles E. "Chuck" Fromm, "Textual Communities and New Song in the Multimedia Age: The Routinization of Charisma in the Jesus Movement" (PhD diss., Fuller Theological Seminary, 2006). Fromm, too, is the nephew of Chuck Smith of Calvary Chapel. Also frequently cited is the work of social historian Michael S. Hamilton in "The Triumph of the Praise Songs: How Guitars Beat Out the Organ in the Worship Wars," *Christianity Today* 43, no. 8 (July 12, 1999): 29–35; and in "A Generation Changes North American Hymnody," *Hymn* 52, no. 3 (July 2001): 11–21. Recent dissertations, especially from musicologists, have picked up on the Calvary Chapel / Vineyard narrative and reinforced it. See, for example, Monique Marie Ingalls, "Awesome in This Place: Sound, Space, and Identity in Contemporary North American Evangelical Worship" (PhD diss., University of Pennsylvania, 2008). A useful body of secondary literature on Jesus People generally facilitates the work of any scholar who wishes to focus on them. The standard works are Larry Eskridge, *God's Forever Family: The Jesus People Movement in America* (Oxford: Oxford University Press, 2013); and David Di Sabatino, *The Jesus People Movement: An Annotated Bibliography and General Resource* (Westport, CT: Greenwood, 1999). Thus, the amount of supporting secondary literature on the Jesus People is much more than is available on any of the other currents of Praise & Worship. The most detailed study on worship in Wimber's congregation is Andy Park, Lester Ruth, and Cindy Rethmeier, *Worshiping with the Anaheim Vineyard: The Emergence of Contemporary Worship* (Grand Rapids: Eerdmans, 2017). No comparable study of Chuck Smith's Calvary Chapel exists.

is more commonly remembered as the Anaheim Vineyard.) These networks, congregations, and pastors indeed had a significant impact on the development of Praise & Worship in this current. Consequently, in continuity with this chapter's focus on case studies, we will likewise emphasize these two networks, including these two congregations. Note, however, that although we focus on Calvary Chapels and Vineyard Fellowships, we do not intend to imply (as some scholarly works have) that Praise & Worship music was either solely or mainly the creation of those in the Jesus People movement or of these two congregations. Nor do we accept the insinuation of some scholarly literature that the rise of Praise & Worship was mainly about a repertoire of songs, the instruments that accompanied them, and the industry that promoted them.

As we slow down and provide an examination of early Calvary Chapels and Vineyard congregations, we will discuss how their liturgical theology meshed with that of Praise & Worship elsewhere. We will also consider easily overlooked details of their liturgical history, including, among other topics, Chuck Smith's conservative approach to Sunday morning worship at Calvary Chapel of Costa Mesa; the importance of Calvary Chapel Bible studies in generating a new way to worship; and the nature of Praise & Worship in Vineyard congregations before John Wimber, including how the important category of liturgical intimacy comes from the Vineyard's very origins. With the help of these hidden details, we can understand more fully the context for the contributions that the Jesus People did indeed bring to Praise & Worship: informality, intimacy as a technical category to describe being in God's presence, the rise of popular forms of music making involving bands, and the first steps toward a music industry connected to Praise & Worship.

Before we look at these specific contributions, we should recognize the theological continuity this current had with broader Praise & Worship, to see how Calvary Chapels and Vineyard congregations fit into this larger history. We have already mentioned briefly some tangential aspects of this connection—for example, the impact Kevin Conner's book on the tabernacle of David had on John Wimber.[63] A look at the first theological expositions arising from within the Calvary Chapel / Vineyard matrix elevates this discussion by revealing their clear resemblance to the theology of the larger phenomenon of Praise & Worship. (From the 1970s until the very early 1980s, Calvary Chapels and Vineyard churches have a somewhat shared history, as the pastors from each denomination fellowshiped together.)

The first written theological exposition from this shared matrix seems to have been teaching materials from the late 1970s that were originally used in

63. Howard Rachinski, interview by Lester Ruth and Lim Swee Hong, April 17, 2017.

the Calvary Chapel Bible School in Twin Peaks, California, and were quickly shared with John Wimber's congregation sixty miles to the southwest. What was being taught was a biblical theology in which certain verses were critical. One instructor, Ralph Kucera, has noted, "There were certain Scriptures that the Holy Spirit really highlighted and . . . generally shined the light on." Among these highlighted verses was Psalm 22:3, understood to promise that God inhabits or is enthroned on the praises of his people.[64] Consequently, early Calvary Chapel / Vineyard theologizing rested on many of the same Scripture verses that had mesmerized others within Praise & Worship.

Systematic teaching on a theology of worship began in the linked worlds of Calvary Chapels and Vineyard congregations in the 1978–79 school year, when Ralph Kucera offered a seminar on a biblical theology of worship to students at the Calvary Chapel Bible School. Some of the students, who were from Calvary Chapel of Yorba Linda, told their instructor about the similarity between his emphases and those of their pastor, John Wimber.[65] Kucera's connection to Wimber's congregation increased around 1980 when Kucera became affiliated with Wimber's church and joined Carl Tuttle, Yorba Linda's worship leader, to begin teaching an expanded seminar on worship. Kucera and Tuttle took the former's outline of materials and combined it with insights from Tuttle, who had previously done his own examination of biblical texts on Praise & Worship to create a booklet titled *Worship Seminar*.[66] The booklet consisted mainly of a lengthy outline organizing key Scripture verses around theological insights on praise, worship, and rejoicing. Kucera and Tuttle, singly and jointly, used the resource to teach in-house, in other Calvary Chapels, and, beginning in the early 1980s, in seminars offered on the congregation's overseas mission trips.[67]

64. Ralph Kucera, interview by Lester Ruth, January 22, 2020. This interview is the source for the description of this early theologizing in Calvary Chapels and Vineyards.

65. Ralph Kucera, email message to Lester Ruth, January 13, 2020.

66. Kucera has graciously provided us a copy of this *Worship Seminar* booklet. Produced in-house, the document carried no publication information. Parts of the booklet can be found in Park, Ruth, and Rethmeier, *Worshiping with the Anaheim Vineyard*, 110–12; and in Carl Tuttle, "Introduction to Worship," in *Worship Leaders Training Manual* (Anaheim: Worship Resource Center/Vineyard Ministries International, 1987), 5–26. Some of the outline's contents also form the basis for a later essay by Carl Tuttle, titled "Foundations of Praise and Worship," in *In Spirit and in Truth: Exploring Directions for Music in Worship Today*, ed. Robin Sheldon (London: Hodder & Stoughton, 1989), 133–50.

67. See, for example, Tuttle's teaching schedule in the 1981 South Africa trip in Park, Ruth, and Rethmeier, *Worshiping with the Anaheim Vineyard*, 55. Note that Wimber's role in teaching on worship was fulfilled mainly through sermons in these early years; later he would expand to other modes of instruction on this subject. With respect to Chuck Smith, early Calvary Chapel worship leader Holland Davis noted how he never taught systematically on worship, although

Kucera's and Tuttle's theology lay within the pale of the sort of liturgical theologies expressed more broadly within the Praise & Worship of the late 1970s. There was much overlap in theological method and conclusions, especially with praise and worship identified as the key corporate activities. Like other Praise & Worship theologians, Kucera and Tuttle used detailed biblical word studies, guided by concordances that allowed them to review every instance of a word (e.g., "praise") in its English, Greek, or Hebrew forms, across the entirety of the Bible. These theologians used these biblical word studies to identify shades of meaning for critical terms as well as to synthesize these shades of meaning into overarching definitions. This method of scriptural study also highlighted key typological examples like David, who provided an image for biblical Praise & Worship. The biblical word studies also led the two men to emphasize outward bodily expressions of worship, organized into broader categories: for instance, clapping was part of rejoicing while lifting hands was part of praise. And, like theologians in other currents of Praise & Worship, Kucera and Tuttle saw this biblically derived liturgical theology as providing a biblical pattern from God that faithful Christians should obey.

There was overlap with other Praise & Worship theologians, too, in how Kucera and Tuttle understood the goal of Praise & Worship done in a biblical manner: it was to experience God's presence. As the introduction of the *Worship Seminar* booklet stated, "We are coming together with the expectation of His manifest presence to give expression to this reality."[68] This root sentiment would have gained an amen of assent from across the entirety of Praise & Worship, especially as the experience of encounter occurred primarily through a protracted, flowing time of singing to God. The key was a desire to "stand in His presence." Without it, Kucera and Tuttle only saw a "fruitless style of worship—worship without expectation, worship without the manifest presence of God."[69] But Kucera and Tuttle shared a hopefulness that characterized all the currents in Praise & Worship—namely, since God indeed was renewing the church "by restoring a Biblical form of worship to His church," a fruitless style of worship was not the only or inevitable option.[70] Praise & Worship in which worshipers experienced the presence of God was the two theologians' hope and expectation.

This commonality Kucera and Tuttle shared with the broader phenomenon of Praise & Worship did not mean there were no differences. The most striking

---

it would come up in his teaching occasionally and naturally. Holland Davis, interview by Lester Ruth, March 6, 2015.

68. Kucera and Tuttle, *Worship Seminar*, 4.
69. Kucera and Tuttle, *Worship Seminar*, 3.
70. Kucera and Tuttle, *Worship Seminar*, 4.

difference was the lack of interest Kucera and Tuttle showed for either David's or Moses's tabernacle as providing the key analogy to press a biblical theology of Praise & Worship into actual liturgical practices.[71] Instead, they used terms of personal relationship with God, including "intimacy," in a general way as the principle to guide and assess a liturgy. They did not press those terms of an organized order through which a worship service progressed (as we will see in chap. 4). Notwithstanding these differences from the other currents of Praise & Worship, a shared theological vision drawn from the Bible provided the underlying background to the way of worship being developed among Calvary Chapel and Vineyard Fellowship thinkers.

This basic commonality was not surprising, given the Pentecostal or Charismatic background of the Jesus People generally and of those involved in Chuck Smith's and John Wimber's congregations specifically.[72] Their descriptions of the experiential encounter with God through praise paralleled those of other Pentecostals and Charismatics. For example, Calvary Chapel worship leader Holland Davis, a young teenager in the mid-1970s, experientially learned this theology while playing choruses on his guitar in the privacy of his bedroom. Davis would play the songs, allowing them to flow from one to the other, until he felt the presence of God. When he was asked to lead worship in a Calvary Chapel just a few years later, he transplanted this approach to the congregational setting.[73]

71. Yet awareness and use of these architectural types was not totally foreign to Calvary Chapel–Vineyard theologizing. For an example, see how in a later essay Tuttle connects the holy of holies of Moses's tabernacle to intimacy in "Foundations of Praise and Worship," 146. Similarly, Chuck Smith Sr., when appointing Holland Davis as worship leader in 2001, used the Mosaic tabernacle categories as expressed in Ps. 100 to give direction to Davis about how to lead worship. Davis described the episode in his 2015 interview and has shown us the notes he took on that occasion. See also Holland Davis, *Let It Rise: A Manual for Worship* (Alachua, FL: Bridge-Logos, 2006), 69.

72. Richard Bustraan makes a convincing case that Jesus People were overwhelmingly—although not entirely—Pentecostal in their piety. See *The Jesus People Movement: A Story of Spiritual Revolution among the Hippies* (Eugene, OR: Pickwick, 2014), 36, 57–107; and "The Jesus People Movement and the Charismatic Movement: A Case for Inclusion," *PentecoStudies* 10, no. 1 (2011): 29–49. Chuck Smith's background was in the International Church of the Foursquare Gospel. For a description of the journey of John Wimber and his wife, Carol, from their evangelical Quaker roots to Pentecostal piety, see Carol Wimber, "How the Vineyard Began," Vineyard USA, accessed February 4, 2021, https://vineyardusa.org/library/how-the-vineyard-began/. See also Connie Dawson, *John Wimber: His Life and Ministry* (privately published, 2020), 31–51. For an account of how Carl Tuttle began to speak in tongues around 1977, see Carl Tuttle, *Reckless Mercy: A Trophy of God's Grace* (N.p.: Coaching Saints, 2017), 44. Similarly, the original Vineyard church planter, Kenn Gulliksen, had been filled with the Spirit in the early 1960s as part of a charismatic Lutheran youth group, as he described in Kenn Gulliksen, interview by Lester Ruth and Lim Swee Hong, January 7, 2017; and Kenn Gulliksen and Joanie Gulliksen, interview by Lester Ruth, May 27, 2017.

73. Davis, interview.

Members of the home group that provided the eventual nucleus for John Wimber's congregation, Calvary Chapel of Yorba Linda, reported having a similar experience as they began to meet in late 1976.[74] The group's routine was simple: sing and then pray for each other. One night, praising God in song led to a dramatic sense of God's presence. While Carl Tuttle led on guitar the singing of the chorus "Praise You, Father," the worshipers were overwhelmed by a sense of God's presence filling the room.[75] This was a turning point for the worship of the group, as its members discovered the standard theology of Praise & Worship: praising God led to a sense of experiencing God's presence. The group began to associate deeper experiences with God to songs that praised and adored God or Jesus in direct address; they learned to differentiate between songs *about* God and songs *to* God. The participants used terms like "personal" and "intimate" to describe these sorts of songs to God. As Bob Fulton, one of the original participants, put it, singing songs directly to God "caused a face to face encounter with God."[76]

While many elements of the theology experienced in these early Calvary Chapel and Vineyard settings were common to Praise & Worship, as seen in these two stories, there was one striking difference between them and other currents in Praise & Worship: a guitar led the praise through which the people experienced God's presence. The guitars in both the Davis story and the Tuttle story hint at a distinct contribution of the Jesus People to the Praise & Worship of the 1970s—namely, the use of popular forms of music making, particularly bands based on pop or rock models. In contrast, the other currents of Praise & Worship at the time tended to reflect other forms of music making, so they usually featured a keyboard instrument like piano or organ as the main instrument.[77] Indeed, many of the people who most ardently promoted the theology of the restoration of the tabernacle of David were using full orchestras. Congregations filled with folks from the Jesus People

74. For descriptions of these early meetings, see Tuttle, *Reckless Mercy*, 34–37; and Park, Ruth, and Rethmeier, *Worshiping with the Anaheim Vineyard*, 62–67.

75. The song "Praise You, Father" was written by Jim Stipech and recorded on *Praise 2*, the second of the praise chorus albums released by Maranatha! Music, the company created by Calvary Chapel of Costa Mesa. Notice that the lyrics themselves mention both praising God and petitioning for the Spirit's presence.

76. Bob Fulton, "The Genesis of Vineyard Kinships," *First Fruits*, February 1985, 6–7. Quoted in Park, Ruth, and Rethmeier, *Worshiping with the Anaheim Vineyard*, 66.

77. See Adam Perez, "Beyond the Guitar: The Keyboard as a Lens into the History of Contemporary Praise and Worship," *Hymn* 70, no. 2 (Spring 2019): 18–26. For a visual representation, see the cover of the first edition of Bob Sorge, *Exploring Worship: A Practical Guide to Praise and Worship* (Canandaigua, NY: Bob Sorge, 1987). The cover is reprinted in the photographs included in Lim Swee Hong and Lester Ruth, *Lovin' on Jesus: A Concise History of Contemporary Worship* (Nashville: Abingdon, 2017).

movement, however, tended to draw on their own pop culture and talents in how they made music. (Some Charismatics adopted this approach too.) At the same time some of the strongest Praise & Worship voices beyond the Jesus People were expressly rejecting music making that reflected pop culture.[78]

Popular music making was not the only contribution the Jesus People made to the larger breadth of Praise & Worship. The emphasis on intimacy, noted above, as a technical term to describe the experience of participating in true worship was another. While the notion could be found among previous Praise & Worship practitioners,[79] it never received the level of stress as it did among Jesus People, especially those in Vineyard Fellowships.

The worshipers in Calvary Chapels and Vineyard congregations also brought to Praise & Worship a higher comfort level with informality in dress and behavior. Congregants with hippie backgrounds, who often had no real prior church experience, simply brought over the ethos from their pre-Christian days. But acceptance of informality reached even to those who had not been hippies: the broader culture was trending toward more informality. Calvary Chapels and Vineyard congregations absorbed this general trend, an attitude that distinguished them from many others in Praise & Worship who maintained an older Pentecostal ethos about liturgical dress and behavior. But the tension between formality and informality could be seen in Calvary Chapel of Costa Mesa, where it played out in differences between the church's morning and evening services.

The Jesus People in Praise & Worship also made a fourth contribution, the contribution that had the most immediate effect on the other currents of Praise & Worship. Spurred by an explosion of songwriting and new music groups in their midst, the leaders among the Jesus People very quickly took the first steps, beginning with Maranatha! Music, toward a music industry to record, publish, and distribute the songs that in many minds have characterized the whole of Praise & Worship. The impact was so large, then and now, that this

78. For example, see Kevin Conner's (from Bible Temple in Portland, Oregon) diatribe against the use of rock, "Satan's counterfeit music," in *The Tabernacle of David: The Presence of God as Experienced in the Tabernacle*, vol. 2 of *Divine Habitation Trilogy* (Portland, OR: City Bible, 1976), 213–19. For a broader context for this sort of criticism, see Anna E. Nekola, "Between This World and the Next: The Musical 'Worship Wars' and Evangelical Ideology in the United States, 1960–2005" (PhD diss., University of Wisconsin–Madison, 2009).

79. See E. Charlotte Baker, *On Eagle's Wings: A Book on Praise and Worship* (Seattle: King's Temple, 1979), 88; and, especially, Dick Iverson and Bill Scheidler, *Present Day Truths* (Portland, OR: City Christian, 1976), 196. Reg Layzell, too, had drawn from Jeremiah 33:11 to speak about the reciprocating voices of the bridegroom (Christ) and bride (the church) in Praise & Worship. During his speaking engagements, Judson Cornwall would use the related notion of human lovemaking as a metaphor for the progression from praise to worship. Steve Griffing, interview by Lester Ruth and Lim Swee Hong, October 13, 2017.

contribution was one of the reasons why some have inaccurately reduced the history of Praise & Worship to the history of the Jesus People. Notwithstanding this misconception born from incomplete information, Maranatha! songs did begin to circulate throughout the entirety of Praise & Worship very quickly.

Having recognized four distinct contributions of the Jesus People to the breadth of Praise & Worship in this period, let us backtrack and look at how these contributions came about. They arose naturally and organically within the Calvary Chapels of Costa Mesa and of Yorba Linda, emerging from the people's culture, spirituality, dispositions, and talents. Let us begin with Calvary Chapel of Costa Mesa before it had connected with any hippies and before it became the first in a growing network of Calvary Chapels.

This Costa Mesa, California, congregation began in 1961 as a small Pentecostal church meeting in a mobile home park in order to accommodate some older women who had trouble traveling to other congregations.[80] Chuck Smith, a minister with prior experience in several Foursquare churches, arrived in December 1965 to be the congregation's second pastor. Smith's prior pastoral experience had made him wary of anything he viewed as a human-created gimmick or program to bring church growth or congregational renewal. Thus, even before arriving in Costa Mesa, he had dedicated himself to verse-by-verse expository preaching and teaching of the Bible as the centerpiece of pastoral ministry and congregational liturgy. In addition, despite practicing classical Pentecostal practices like glossolalia in private, in family devotions, and in corporate "afterglow" meetings, Smith was guarded about Pentecostal behavior he considered excessively demonstrative in congregational worship. On occasion, he asked those exercising charismatic gifts on Sunday morning to quit and sit down.[81] Under his leadership, the fledgling congregation had quadrupled in size even before the arrival of any hippies in spring 1968.[82] The ongoing growth necessitated a succession of moves and building projects that continued through the mid-1970s. The arrival of the hippies accelerated the pace of these moves and projects.[83]

Smith first connected with the hippies when he met Lonnie Frisbee, who would become a dynamic evangelist to this subculture, in March 1968.

---

80. A useful source for background details of the early history of Calvary Chapel is Sharon Gardner Fischer, *I Remember . . . : The Birth of Calvary Chapel* (privately published, 2014). Fischer was one of the original participants. She and her husband remained strongly involved through the early years, including participating in the lay governance of the church.

81. Sharon Gardner Fischer, interview by Lester Ruth, March 7, 2015.

82. Fischer, *I Remember*, 69.

83. Fromm, "Textual Communities and New Song," 173. Fromm's dissertation, based on his insider knowledge (he was the nephew of Chuck Smith Sr. and was head of Maranatha! Music), is an excellent source of historical information on the development of music in this congregation.

Frisbee and his wife moved into the Smith home at that time. Through Frisbee, more and more hippies came into contact with Smith and Calvary Chapel, leading to Smith's decision to rent a house and start a Christian commune in May 1968, the first in a series of over two hundred Christian halfway houses the congregation would sponsor.[84] It was in communal living and in the multiple weeknight Bible studies at Calvary Chapel of Costa Mesa where the music of the hippie subculture would have its strongest impact. Beginning in 1971, regular outreach concerts, especially on Saturday nights, highlighted the new music even more.[85] The houses, the concerts, and the weeknight Bible studies were the first outlets for new songs to be sung, new instruments to be played, new soloists to express their art, and new bands to perform. Little, if any, of it directly impacted Calvary Chapel of Costa Mesa's Sunday morning worship. Nonetheless, the Jesus People still came on Sunday mornings, attracted by what had drawn them in the first place: the loving welcome of the congregation (the hippies were allowed to remain informal in dress and behavior), the authenticity of Chuck Smith in his ministry, and the simplicity of the way he opened the Bible to address their spiritual questions.

These other settings beyond Sunday mornings were the main outlets for the hippies' contributions because Smith's liturgical sensibilities for Sunday mornings remained conservative and traditional even after the hippies' arrival. Sunday morning featured Smith wearing a suit and expositing the Scriptures in a simple, straightforward way while the congregation sang three hymns with piano and organ accompaniment.[86] Even Sunday evening was not radically different. The hallmark of the Sunday evening service was still expository teaching, but Smith allowed himself to dress down somewhat, to the level of business casual, which often meant his trademark turtleneck sweater. On Sunday nights the music did change, however. Instead of hymns there were choruses, especially choruses based directly on Scripture so as to reinforce Smith's and the congregation's knowledge of the Bible. Often the choruses were those written by the Jesus People. Smith himself led the singing with a rich baritone voice; the congregation followed him a capella. He chose and improvised the sequence of songs into a flowing, seamless stream. The entire

84. Fromm, "Textual Communities and New Song," 174.
85. Fromm, "Textual Communities and New Song," 219. Compare the contemporary description of Sunday worship services at Calvary Chapel of Costa Mesa to the account of concerts and Bible studies in Brian Vachon, *A Time to Be Born* (Englewood Cliffs, NJ: Prentice-Hall, 1972), 84–119. For examples of variety of worship among different Jesus People congregations, even within close proximity to each other, see also Vachon, *Time to Be Born*, 36–45, 66.
86. Fischer, interview; Cheryl Brodersen (Smith's daughter), Kathy Gilbert, and Kim Linn, interview by Lester Ruth, March 10, 2015.

congregation would be caught up in a robust sound of praise without musical instruments.[87]

Thus, the arrival of the Jesus People and their bands at Calvary Chapel of Costa Mesa had the greatest impact on liturgical life, especially in the manner of making music, on days other than Sundays. This music most shaped a new form of congregational liturgy during the Bible studies held several nights every week on the church's main campus.[88]

This impact was also felt in the growing number of new congregations being planted out of the mother church in Costa Mesa. John Wimber once noted in a sermon that there had been sixty new worshiping groups in the last eight months of 1978 alone.[89] Wimber, showing his typical tongue-in-cheek humor, described how easy it was to start one of these new churches: to have an "insta-church," all that was needed was a Bible, a teacher, and a rock band. Notwithstanding Wimber's overstatement, his comment highlighted the connection of these new congregations to the Bible studies at Costa Mesa.

Despite Wimber's "insta-church" comment, not all the church plants arising out of Calvary Chapel of Costa Mesa had rock bands to lead worship.[90] Closer geographical proximity to this original Calvary Chapel increased the likelihood that a church would have such a band, but it was no guarantee. Indeed, these church plants—and this includes the first Vineyard Fellowships, since the Vineyard also was derived from Calvary Chapel—used the musicians who were attracted to the recently started congregations or the musical skills of whoever planted the new church. Thus, there was variety in the music of these new congregations. Sometimes the planters themselves were the original musicians, usually leading with a single acoustic guitar. Sometimes the singing would be a capella. In other cases, it might be to recordings. The music arose organically from within the congregations as it had in Costa Mesa's communal houses and Bible studies, although it is fair to grant that much of the music had pop, folk, or rock connections since the musicians did too. In addition, many of the new pastors wanted popular forms of music since

87. Fromm, "Textual Communities and New Song," 186.

88. The failure to differentiate clearly between the musical worlds of Sunday mornings and other settings at Calvary Chapel is a common one in the secondary literature.

89. See Park, Ruth, and Rethmeier, *Worshiping with the Anaheim Vineyard*, 105. For a directory of early Calvary Chapel church plants, see *Last Times Magazine* 3, no. 1 (1980): 19–23. The magazine was the bimonthly magazine from Calvary Chapel of Costa Mesa. The directory lists eighty-four churches and fellowships in California and fifty-nine outside California, almost all Calvary Chapels but also including five Vineyards in California: Big Bear Lake, Desert (Lancaster), West LA, San Fernando Valley, and San Luis Obispo.

90. This fact, along with much of the description of early Calvary Chapel church plants, comes from Holland Davis, interview by Lester Ruth and Lim Swee Hong, August 24, 2018.

many of them came out of the evening Bible studies at Calvary Chapel of Costa Mesa. What they all shared, however, was an emphasis on an expository approach to the Bible, whether in studies or in preaching. Simply put, what happened in the new Calvary Chapels was a move of the liturgical activities of Costa Mesa's midweek Bible studies to Sunday morning, using the best musical resources available.

Some of the earliest church plants to come out of Calvary Chapel of Costa Mesa were those led by Kenn Gulliksen, one of the original congregation's Bible teachers.[91] The impact of Gulliksen's experiences in the nighttime Bible studies at Calvary Chapel shaped the worship in his new congregations. In 1974 he sensed a desire to begin a new ministry on the opposite side of Los Angeles from Costa Mesa. (Calvary Chapel of Costa Mesa is in Orange County, which is south of Los Angeles.) Sent with Chuck Smith's blessing, Gulliksen began with a Bible study in the home of Chuck Girard, a member of Love Song, one of the most influential bands at Calvary Chapel of Costa Mesa. Gulliksen was a longtime friend of Girard, having gone to college with Girard's wife. The Bible study began in the summer of 1974. Drawing on Girard's acquaintances and network of musicians, the original participants had begun to invite others by the third meeting.

As this first study grew, one of the participants, Pam Norman (the wife of Larry Norman, a musician in the Jesus People movement), invited Gulliksen to start a second study at the Norman home. This process kept repeating as the studies grew. By 1975, Gulliksen had decided to bring the studies together and an assembly met at the Beverly Hills Women's Club.[92] From these first Bible studies and this first assembly would come the first Vineyard congregation. Gulliksen's fledgling flock was incorporated as the Vineyard Christian Fellowship of Beverly Hills in March 1975.[93] Continuing to grow, the congregation moved several times in its first few years. It eventually began sharing

91. The details for this early Gulliksen-Vineyard history are drawn from the two interviews with Kenn Gulliksen (January 7, 2017, and May 27, 2017), unless otherwise attributed. The best published source for understanding Kenn Gulliksen and his ministry in the earliest Vineyard Fellowships is Thomas W. Higgins, "Kenn Gulliksen, John Wimber, and the Founding of the Vineyard Movement," *Pneuma* 34, no. 2 (2012): 208–28. This article is a distillation of Higgins's much fuller paper, titled "Kenn Gulliksen and the Beginning of the Vineyard Christian Fellowship" (master's thesis, Gordon-Conwell Theological Seminary, 2005). An interview with Bill Dwyer (September 21, 2017) by Lim Swee Hong and Lester Ruth enriches the details of this description.

92. Higgins, "Kenn Gulliksen, John Wimber," 212.

93. Higgins, "Kenn Gulliksen, John Wimber," 212. Gulliksen's first plant was in El Paso, Texas, in 1972, when Calvary Chapel of Costa Mesa sent him to respond to an invitation from a burgeoning, interdenominational youth meeting under the sway of the Charismatic Renewal movement.

a building with a Methodist church in Tarzana, California, renting the space for two afternoon services.

Notwithstanding the location or the occasion—whether home Bible study, home group, or larger worship assembly—Gulliksen began a meeting the same way: with a lengthy time of congregational singing, usually including choruses and an occasional hymn and sometimes a special number by a soloist. This was followed by exposition of the Bible. The church's congregational worship felt much like a weeknight at Calvary Chapel moved to a congregation's main service. Gulliksen himself served as the worship leader in many instances. Given the wealth of musical resources in the congregation, others served in this same role, including some of the most well-known names in contemporary Christian or secular music at the time.[94] The leadership of the music evolved through the second half of the 1970s, moving from constantly rotating leaders to more stable leadership and from a single musician to a band. This same approach to congregational worship could be found in new Vineyard congregations being planted from Gulliksen's original group in the late 1970s.[95]

A comparable evolution from worshiping as a home group to worshiping as a congregation was taking place contemporaneously in Yorba Linda, a town northeast of Costa Mesa and southeast of Los Angeles. Something was different about this group, however. Its first participants, by and large, were not drawn from Calvary Chapel of Costa Mesa but from the Yorba Linda Friends (Quaker) Church. This was the group that would eventually be led by John Wimber and was mentioned earlier in this chapter.

John Wimber was not involved at the very beginning, and the group first met with no grand plans to plant a church.[96] Indeed, there was not even a systematic study of the Bible—it was just a very small group of family and friends meeting in the evening to discuss their dissatisfaction with their own spiritual state. In fact, Carl Tuttle, who would become the group's worship leader, just happened to stumble on the first meeting because it was at his

94. For example, see the account of Keith Green's relationship with Gulliksen and the early Vineyard in David W. Stowe, *No Sympathy for the Devil: Christian Pop Music and the Transformation of American Evangelicalism* (Chapel Hill: University of North Carolina Press, 2011), 153–55. For a secular example, two members of the rock band Eagles once played in the worship band in Gulliksen's church.

95. For an account of these first Vineyard church plants, see Higgins, "Kenn Gulliksen, John Wimber," 214–18.

96. The most thorough documentation of this home group's worship is in Park, Ruth, and Rethmeier, *Worshiping with the Anaheim Vineyard*, 62–67. Carl Tuttle's autobiography, published since the release of *Worshiping with the Anaheim Vineyard*, also provides helpful insider information. See Tuttle, *Reckless Mercy*, 34–49.

sister's house and he had gone there with a friend to scrounge for food.[97] His coming would be providential for the group, however: someone asked him to bring his guitar to the group's second meeting the following week. Tuttle brought his guitar and began to lead the group, which kept increasing in size, in the choruses he knew, many of which came from songwriters at Calvary Chapel of Costa Mesa about twenty miles away.

The group continued to grow, worshiping under Tuttle's leadership, until it launched as a public congregation on Mother's Day 1977. (John Wimber was one of the newcomers who joined the group after it had been meeting for several weeks.) Even after the launch, these worshipers continued the sensibility developed in their earlier home-based singing—namely, connecting praise with a sense of experiencing the divine presence. As a public congregation, the group also acquired a new affiliation as a Calvary Chapel, because John Wimber, Bob Fulton, and Carl Tuttle had been ordained by a Calvary Chapel pastor, Don McClure, a few weeks previously. It was McClure who had suggested to his friend John Wimber that the new congregation be a Calvary Chapel.[98] Thus, the congregation started with a new name: Calvary Chapel of Yorba Linda.

It also started with a new worship band, using the skills of those who were attending. Wimber, an accomplished pop musician, added a portable piano to the mix and another friend, Dick Heying, was on drums. That first Sunday's worship was the first time the ensemble had played together.[99] There was no rehearsal and there was no prepared song list. Another musical friend, Jerry Davis, walked by the musicians at the end of the service; he was invited to bring his bass and play with them too. Soon Eddie Espinosa would add a lead guitar to the band's sound. When the song called for it, Cindy Rethmeier added the female vocal line. From that first Sunday forward, the congregation never retreated from having band-led worship.

The congregation continued to grow, holding services every Sunday morning and evening, and it moved several times in its first years to accommodate the number of worshipers. The congregation reaffiliated in 1982, ceasing to be a Calvary Chapel and becoming the Anaheim Vineyard (it had moved from Yorba Linda to Anaheim). At that time Gulliksen handed over leadership of the entire emerging Vineyard movement to Wimber.

97. Tuttle, *Reckless Mercy*, 34; Carl Tuttle, interview by Lester Ruth, February 1, 2013.

98. Tuttle, *Reckless Mercy*, 41; Fromm, "Textual Communities and New Song," 263. The Wimbers were friends with McClure for several years, occasionally attending his church, Calvary Chapel of Twin Peaks, which was close to their second home near Lake Arrowhead, California. See Tuttle, *Reckless Mercy*, 33.

99. Tuttle, interview.

Recordings of worship from Wimber's congregation in the early 1980s reflect the worship's setting and nature. Many of the songs were not brisk but had a warm and laid-back feeling that conveyed a sense of intimate worship. Generally, over the extended period of congregational singing the songs moved from brisker tempos to something more calm and reflective. The songs were mainly sung in unison, with strong congregational participation. Occasionally there was singing in parts; the recordings suggest that some of this harmonization was improvised. Some songs used a call-and-response form; some of these call-and-response songs worked by separating male and female voices.

The fact that Gulliksen's nascent Vineyard movement (there were several Vineyard congregations at the time) and Wimber's congregation would find common ground liturgically is not surprising. Both were more open to demonstrations of spiritual gifts in corporate worship than Calvary Chapel of Costa Mesa had been. Both, too, used relational terms, especially the category of intimacy, to define the nature of the encounter with God's presence through Praise & Worship. While worship as intimacy with God was already a theological idea in broader Praise & Worship, it was the Vineyard—first with Gulliksen and then with others in the movement—that placed intimacy at the center of an approach to Praise & Worship, an idea gaining broader traction in the 1980s.

Indeed love, expressed in terms of close relationships with others, was the dominant aspect in Kenn Gulliksen's spirituality.[100] It was what he admired in those who shaped his own Christian experience and it was what he was known for in his pastoral ministry. Not surprisingly, Gulliksen used intimacy with God as a liturgical category from the very beginning of his independent work in the Vineyard. As the essence of worship, intimacy shaped what songs he considered most appropriate for his congregation and helped steer him toward a predilection for slower songs that expressed adoration directly to God or Jesus.

Gulliksen highly valued the Old Testament book Song of Solomon as a key text for describing the relationship between God, the church, and individual worshipers. Its language of intimate communion between the bridegroom and the bride shaped Gulliksen's theological and liturgical worlds in a fundamental way. This shaping was strongly evident in his 1974 album titled *Charity: Songs of Love to Jesus and the Family*.[101] The first song began with him singing "We

---

100. This assessment of the role of intimacy in Gulliksen's approach to worship is drawn from two interviews with him (January 7, 2017, and May 27, 2017) and one with Bill Dwyer (September 21, 2017), a close associate of his from the 1970s.

101. Kenn Gulliksen, *Charity: Songs of Love to Jesus and the Family*, Irvine, CA: Maranatha! Music, 1974, 33⅓ rpm.

have come to worship you, Lord, in the beauty of your holiness, to know your presence, hear your voice, and praise your precious name." Immediately following these lyrics, Gulliksen added a voice-over as the instruments continued: he noted that God wants an "intimate love relationship" with his people and used marriage as the central metaphor. The next song reinforced that notion of marriage to describe the relationship between God and God's people. The concluding song on the album was perhaps Gulliksen's best-known worship chorus, "Charity," based on 1 Corinthians 13 and included in the first songbook printed by Calvary Chapel of Costa Mesa, *Rejoice in Jesus Always! Songs of Worship & Praise*. Wimber, too, used romantic and sensual images in his preaching on worship in the late 1970s.[102]

Note the publisher for the *Rejoice in Jesus Always!* songbook and for Gulliksen's album: Maranatha! Music. This company would become one of the main distributors of Praise & Worship materials across the spectrum of congregations worshiping in this way.[103] It would be joined in the early 1980s by a Vineyard-connected outlet, Mercy Records/Vineyard Publishing.[104] Both companies emerged from congregations related to the Jesus People movement: Maranatha! Music from Calvary Chapel of Costa Mesa and Mercy Records/Vineyard Publishing from the Anaheim Vineyard.

The degree of impact these companies would have was little imagined at their beginnings, especially in the case of Maranatha! Music. The arrival of Jesus People at Calvary Chapel had brought about the emergence of much new music sung by talented artists. Concerned about providing his musicians with adequate financial support given the uncertainties of congregational giving, Smith led the congregation to organize Maranatha! Corporation in December 1970 to facilitate making recordings that the artists could sell as they traveled to perform.[105] The company was soon releasing albums recorded by various musicians in the church, including the widely popular *Everlastin' Living Jesus Music Concert* in 1971.

The company also quickly expanded into releasing materials more directly related to congregational worship. In 1973 it published the *Rejoice in Jesus Always!* songbook, most of whose songs came from writers within Calvary Chapel. An expanded songbook came in 1983 with the release of

102. For multiple examples, see Park, Ruth, and Rethmeier, *Worshiping with the Anaheim Vineyard*.

103. Although this is not directly germane to our study of liturgical developments, the reader should note that Maranatha! Music—among other companies—was also instrumental in the development of the broader genre of Contemporary Christian Music.

104. The precise name the publisher used in the 1980s varied: e.g., Worship Resource Center/Vineyard Ministries International or Mercy Publishing.

105. Fromm, "Textual Communities and New Song," 217–18.

Maranatha! Music Praise Chorus Book. The company also began releasing albums featuring Praise & Worship songs, beginning with the album simply titled *Praise* in April 1974.[106] This album presented some of the strongest congregational choruses that had emerged in the evening studies at Calvary Chapel. This first *Praise* album would be followed by an entire series, which used a straightforward scheme for titles: *Praise II, Praise III*, and so forth. *Praise II* was released in 1976. These albums allowed congregations elsewhere to hear the potential of these new songs for worship. Church musicians, too, could learn the songs by listening to the album. The series so flourished that by 1980 Maranatha! Music had ceased recordings of individual artists singing non-worship-related songs, instead concentrating its efforts on musical resources for congregational worship.[107]

Similarly, John Wimber's congregation quickly launched into the production of materials to train musicians and provide resources for congregational worship. The effort began in 1981 when Carl Tuttle and Cindy Rethmeier recorded (in a bathroom, because of the acoustics) two cassette tapes of the main songs in the congregation's repertoire. The tapes were intended to train the musicians leading worship in the congregation's home groups.[108] Production values increased dramatically in the following year with the release of a studio album, *All the Earth Shall Worship: Worship Songs of the Vineyard*, featuring ten congregational choruses, eight of which were written by Carl Tuttle, John Wimber, or Eddie Espinosa.[109] A songbook, *Songs of the Vineyard*, soon followed. Like Maranatha! Music, Vineyard products to supply resources for worship leaders would increase and diversify in future years.

These companies increased the musical impact of Calvary Chapels and Vineyard Fellowships across the breadth of Praise & Worship. They were also the first steps toward what would become a huge music-related industry by the end of the century.

The Surge at Shady Grove

By the early 1980s the ever-expanding phenomenon of Praise & Worship involved multiple overlapping and intertwining currents. To see how this com-

---

106. Fromm, "Textual Communities and New Song," 230.

107. Charles E. Fromm, "New Song to Contemporary Christian Music Entertainment" (master's thesis, Fuller Theological Seminary, 1996), 74.

108. Park, Ruth, and Rethmeier, *Worshiping with the Anaheim Vineyard*, 71.

109. *All the Earth Shall Worship: Worship Songs of the Vineyard*, Mercy Records, 1982, 33⅓ rpm.

plex flow of currents actually interacted, let us consider a single example, Shady Grove Church in Grand Prairie, Texas. In multiple respects, this congregation encapsulates the complexity of what was happening at the time. At Shady Grove, we can see the influence of key figures within the Latter Rain movement, of the International Worship Symposium, and even of Judson Cornwall. Moreover, Shady Grove shows (1) the dynamics of the appropriation of Praise & Worship, (2) the adaptation of prior teaching, and (3) shifting ecclesiastical relationships brought about by becoming a Praise & Worship church.[110]

Shady Grove's pastor was Olen Griffing, a former Texas state trooper.[111] Griffing had grown up in a Baptist parsonage, but his religious commitments had waned as he became an adult. A spiritual experience in his late twenties, however, changed the direction of his life—and he also received a call to ministry. In 1970 he left his law enforcement position and enrolled at Southwestern Baptist Theological Seminary in Fort Worth. In his last semester there, Griffing came under the sway of the Charismatic Renewal movement among Baptists and received the baptism of the Holy Spirit. Nonetheless, his first two pastorates were in Baptist churches, initially in Johnson City, Texas, and then at Shady Grove in Grand Prairie (a city between Fort Worth and Dallas), beginning in March 1974.

At Shady Grove, Griffing's charismatic spirituality began to shape the direction of his ministry and, through him, the worship of this small church. By the summer of 1975, he felt led to preach on the tabernacle of Moses and teach on it in the congregation's adult Vacation Bible School. Griffing grew mesmerized by the ark of the covenant and its association with the presence of God. On his own, Griffing began to read the Bible and its description of David and his bringing of the ark to Jerusalem. Griffing and the church musician began to explore how contemplating the ark could provide direction to this congregation. Inspiration from Merlin Carothers's 1972 book, *Power in Praise*, led the men to introduce into Shady Grove the singing of joyful praise choruses. Several choruses in a row were sung before the sermon.

Griffing's and the church's growing charismatic proclivities soon gained the attention of the Dallas Baptist Association, but not favorably. In fall 1975 the association cut off fellowship with the congregation, removing Shady Grove from its membership. But a series of events would soon produce another fellowship for Griffing and Shady Grove.

110. In March 2013 Shady Grove merged with Gateway Church, becoming the fourth extension campus for the latter. Gateway Church is one of the largest churches in Texas.
111. Olen Griffing, interview by Lester Ruth and Lim Swee Hong, October 10, 2017.

About the same time as the Baptist disassociation, one of the members of the church asked Olen Griffing if he had heard of Judson Cornwall. This man said he would be willing to pay the expenses for Griffing to go hear Cornwall speak at a camp meeting sponsored by a church called King's Temple in Seattle, Washington. (This was Charlotte Baker's church.) Griffing accepted the offer. He arrived at his hotel in Washington but lacked a ride to the camp meeting. Noticing another man in the hotel's lobby who appeared to also be going to the camp meeting, Griffing asked for a ride. The man, Ernest Gentile, agreed.

Arriving in time for the Monday night worship service, Griffing was not at all pleased with what he experienced. He was interested only in hearing Judson Cornwall speak but was "subjected" to a worship service featuring an orchestra, lots of physical movement and expressiveness (including clapping, marching, and bowing), banners, prophetic words and songs, and a stretched-out time of congregational singing with songs whose lyrics, projected on an overhead, seemed to Griffing to be endlessly repetitive. In other words, he had stepped into a full-blown Latter Rain Praise & Worship service influenced by the artistically minded Charlotte Baker. Griffing at times felt totally disgusted and isolated; he considered returning home. A turning point came on Wednesday morning. Griffing sensed God cleansing him, releasing him to engage in praise exuberantly, hands raised in the air. Griffing felt as if he was truly understanding what he had already been preaching at Shady Grove about the ark, the tabernacle of David, and the presence of God. (And he did get to hear Judson Cornwall speak too.)

Griffing's experience at the camp meeting opened up a new religious fellowship for him. He contacted Charlotte Baker after the camp meeting and she directed him to the Revival Fellowship, the Latter Rain pastors' network in Southern California. Griffing began to attend the meetings in 1976, and there he had the chance to hear Reg Layzell speak, as well as Dick Iverson, Kevin Conner, David Blomgren, and Frank Damazio (Iverson's successor at Bible Temple). Griffing also participated for a season in the Northwest Ministers Fellowship meeting at Bible Temple in Portland.

Increasingly, however, Griffing focused his attention on his own—now independent—congregation, Shady Grove, especially after revival broke out there in 1978. The services at this time could consist of two hours of congregational singing with a sermon at the end. As the congregation grew, so did its musicality as it attracted additional gifted musicians such as Warren Hastings and Kirk Dearman. The church also began to host its own set of conferences around 1980. Eventually it had three annual conferences: a prophetic conference, a missions conference, and a worship conference. The first worship conference was held in late fall 1980 and featured Mike Herron (a musician at Bible Temple) and LaMar Boschman.[112]

The organizers of the International Worship Symposium selected Shady Grove to be the site for the 1981 annual meeting, held the first week of August. Graham Truscott and Charlotte Baker were scheduled as the featured evening speakers. An "all-time high" of twenty daytime workshops were held, including sessions on worship leading, dancing, vocal technique, and songwriting. There was even a session on orchestration by Fletch Wiley, an arranger associated with Andraé Crouch. Also in the lineup of activities were three song-sharing sessions: two for congregational choruses and one for group arrangements. Shady Grove's music department itself debuted a multimedia pageant titled *David's Tabernacle*.[113]

This symposium can be remembered especially for three things. The first was a prophetic parable delivered through Charlotte Baker that was later titled "The Eye of the Needle."[114] Spoken spontaneously by Baker under, as she called it, a "special anointing of the Holy Spirit," the parable exhorted church musicians to make a critical choice. God wanted to know if they were willing to minister only to people or, laying everything aside and passing through the gate of true worship called "the eye of the needle," to minister to God through their music: "Thou canst minister unto men, and I will cause thee to sway the hearts of men with thy talent. Or thou canst humble thyself as one passing through a very low gate and become a worshiper of God. Then thou shalt minister unto the King."[115] Behind the parable one can sense the growing role of musicians—and the tensions they faced—in the development of Praise & Worship at the time.

The second item of significant note was a new song the pianist at Shady Grove, Kirk Dearman, shared at the symposium: "We Bring the Sacrifice of Praise." Immediately the song was in demand, requested by many of the symposium's 350 participants (who represented twenty-three states, Canada, and Mexico and 101 congregations). Because of the "countless" requests, the song was included in the fall 1981 release of ZionSong, the subscription tape service managed by Barry Griffing, one of the organizers of the International

112. [Barry Griffing], "Go Tell It on the Mountain: Music Ministry on the Move," *Music Notes* 2, no. 6 (December 1980): 1.

113. [Barry Griffing], "Symposium '81 in the Big 'D,'" *Music Notes* 3, no. 3 (June 1981): 1.

114. Along with other prophetic parables that Baker gave over the years, this most well-known of her prophetic words can be found in E. Charlotte Baker, *The Eye of the Needle and Other Prophetic Parables* (Hagerstown, MD: Parable, 1997), 125–32. As of this book's publication, a sound recording of Baker delivering the prophecy, along with an instrumental backdrop, can be found at https://godfire.net/Audio/EyeOfTheNeedle.mp3.

115. Baker, *Eye of the Needle*, 131–32.

Worship Symposium.[116] This song would become a favorite across Praise & Worship churches in the 1980s and 1990s.[117]

Finally, the symposium's concluding banquet made a lasting impression on the participants. Feasting on Texas-style barbecue chicken and ribs, several hundred enjoyed the food in the banquet hall at the top of Texas Stadium, the home of the Dallas Cowboys professional football team. While participants ate, the stadium's electronic scoreboard encouraged them with exhortations like "Sing a New Song unto the Lord." On the field beneath, the Cowboys held a scrimmage and the team's cheerleaders practiced.[118]

Access to Texas Stadium was surely due to the fact that the owner of the Dallas Cowboys, Clint Murchison, and his wife, Anne, were members at Shady Grove. Indeed, Anne Murchison said it was at Shady Grove that she learned to enter into Praise & Worship. Struck by the power of this way of worship, she decided to write a book based on her experience in this congregation's worship. In this book, which was titled *Praise and Worship in Earth as It Is in Heaven* and published in the same year that her church hosted the International Worship Symposium (1981), Murchison sought not only to inform her readers but to advocate for Praise & Worship and to encourage its adoption.[119]

If Shady Grove is a window into the complexity of the congregational spread of Praise & Worship at the time, Murchison's book likewise offers a view into the complexity of a single individual's appropriation and adaptation of this way of worship. The complexity is immediately apparent in the wide range of authors whose writings influenced Murchison's thinking, sources she tried to fuse into a single, coherent description of the theology and practices of Praise & Worship. In an appendix to her book, she listed the most influential authors and books.[120] She included on the list such evangelical stalwarts as A. W. Tozer (author of *Worship: The Missing Jewel of the Evangelical Church*) and Andrew Murray (devotional writer of *God's Best Secrets* and *Abide in Christ*, and a nineteenth-century missionary to South Africa) as well as key Latter Rain authors (Kevin Conner and Graham Truscott) and their texts. Murchison also acknowledged Judson Cornwall and his book *Let Us Praise*. Throughout her book, Murchison also referenced other Pentecostal and evangelical authors and their materials that had shaped her thought.

116. [Barry Griffing], "Symposium '81 in Dallas: The Keynote Word Was 'Overflow,'" *Music Notes* 3, no. 4 (Fall 1981): 1.

117. Ethnomusicologist Monique Ingalls includes a musical description of this song as part of her analysis of 1980s-era praise songs. See Ingalls, "Awesome in This Place," 88–89.

118. [Griffing], "Symposium '81 in Dallas," 1.

119. Anne Ferrell Murchison, *Praise and Worship in Earth as It Is in Heaven* (Waco: Word, 1981).

120. Murchison, *Praise and Worship*, 140.

The result in Murchison's book was a fusion emphasizing passionate desire for God expressed in Praise & Worship, understood by both the tabernacle of Moses and the tabernacle of David, and reflecting the liturgy of heaven.

Murchison's book is important in the historical development of Praise & Worship but not because of the theology she reproduced. In most respects her approach was the passionate rearticulation of those who had influenced her. Her book is important because it hints at the continuing surge of Praise & Worship. Specifically, her book is important because it seems to have been one of the first Praise & Worship books based on Pentecostal sensibilities published by a mainstream evangelical publisher. Prior Pentecostal Praise & Worship literature had appeared from Pentecostal publishers, but Murchison released her book through Word Books in Waco, Texas.[121] A release from Word had the chance to reach an audience across the breadth of evangelicalism. Indeed, Praise & Worship would sweep up increasing numbers of evangelicals in the years after Murchison wrote and even while she wrote. The breadth also hints at a future confluence with Protestants beyond Praise & Worship.

To influence her readers, Murchison not only articulated her theology of Praise & Worship but also provided her personal testimony of having first experienced it. Sometime after becoming a Christian in 1976, she had become part of a Bible study that practiced a Davidic way of worship. Uncomfortable at first, she learned to like the songs, the clapping, and the lifting of hands.[122] She wrote in the hope that others would learn to appreciate such a Davidic pattern too. Given the continuing spread of Praise & Worship, her aspiration would be a well-founded hope, as we will see.

---

121. On p. 12 of her book, Murchison mentioned that Word's vice president and editorial director was a good friend.

122. Murchison, *Praise and Worship*, 90.

four

—

a swollen river, surging
and sweeping, 1985–95

God is restoring praise and worship throughout His Church, enlivening
the liturgy of the mainline denominations as well as the praise time of the
independent churches with His Holy Spirit.

—*Jenny Howard, head of music, St. David's Episcopal Church,*
Jacksonville, Florida[1]

"God, come, live in and inhabit the praises that I sing on this drum." Since
1995, this sentiment derived from Psalm 22:3 has been the recurring prayer of
worship leader Jonathan Maracle.[2] Indeed, Maracle has known this verse for
even longer, having first heard it in a Canadian Pentecostal church in 1986. At
that time, he was a new Christian, having just begun to lead worship using
songs in wide circulation. He led in a variety of congregations for several
years. Up to 1995 his path and his prayer mirrored the journey of countless
other worship leaders. Even using Psalm 22:3 to frame heartfelt convictions
about Praise & Worship was commonplace.

It was the final phrase in Maracle's prayer that was exceptional: "on this
drum." The drum Maracle had in mind was not the customary set of drums
found in worship bands. Maracle is a Mohawk, and so the drum through which

---

1. Jenny Howard, "The Sleeping Giants," *Psalmist* 3, no. 6 (December 1988/January 1989): 7.
2. Jonathan Maracle, interview by Lim Swee Hong and Lester Ruth, October 28, 2019.

Figure 4.1. Jonathan Maracle (center) with Bill Pagaran on his right and Jaymi Millard on his left. Robert Soto dances in the rear.

he wanted to pray was a First Nations / Native American instrument. His prayer arose after a spiritual experience in December 1995 launched him on a new trajectory toward more Indigenous ways of music making in Praise & Worship.[3] Since then, Maracle has followed a divinely given sense that the drum will be the restoration of First Nations people across Turtle Island (North America). He has found it a hard journey since First Nations Christians have been told for centuries that they must give up their own culture, including their musical instruments, in order to be true Christians. The fact that most First Nations Christians have accepted this colonizing fallacy has underscored the difficulty of recovering their drums. Only in the last several years has Maracle noticed a growing acceptance of Indigenous music making while leading Praise & Worship.

The novelty in Maracle's worship leadership is the manner of making music, not the existence of Praise & Worship in First Nations congregations

3. The experience came during the Sacred Assembly organized by Elijah Harper on December 6–9, 1995, in Hull, Quebec, Canada. Harper had invited Maracle to attend in order to sing "Amazing Grace" in Mohawk for the assembly. Maracle was prepared to sing this until he heard one of the keynote speakers, John Sandford (who was half Osage), address the assembly. Listening, drum in hand, Maracle sensed the Holy Spirit showing him the importance of being true to being Native and also spontaneously giving him a new song, "Broken Walls." Maracle sang this new song instead of the hymn originally planned.

or the underlying theology of Praise & Worship. Indeed, after the mid-1980s, Praise & Worship overwhelmed Pentecostalism and a good bit of evangelicalism too. To return to the river metaphor, what had been a Mississippian liturgical phenomenon by 1985 went on to become Amazonian in its breadth, depth, and power by the latter half of the 1990s. Pentecostal liturgical fields everywhere have been watered by the swollen river of Praise & Worship, a river that has swept up everything before it.

Accordingly, from across the continent, congregational testimonies about experiencing the presence of God marked Praise & Worship's expanding breadth. The testimonies came from a diverse array of congregations:

- megachurches such as West Angeles Church of God in Christ in Los Angeles, California: "The Lord has been manifesting Himself in a new and powerful way"
- small assemblies such as Indonesian Full Gospel Fellowship in Temple City, California: "When we lift up the name of Jesus, we feel the presence of the Lord"
- independent Pentecostal congregations such as Croydon Center in Croydon, Pennsylvania: God's "Power and Presence are always manifested in a supernatural way during praise and worship"
- congregations within the long-standing Pentecostal denominations such as Victory Chapel El Cajon Foursquare Church in El Cajon, California: "We are increasingly becoming aware of God's total presence being manifested in our midst"
- Black congregations such as Abundant Life Church of Christ in Richmond, Virginia: "A renewed, refreshing sense of God's presence has permeated our services"
- White congregations such as New Life Christian Center in Milwaukie, Oregon: Praise & Worship "establishes the glory and presence of God in the service"
- evangelical congregations of Charismatics such as Immanuel Baptist Church in Baton Rouge, Louisiana: "Worship ushers in the presence of God and you never know what is going to happen"
- congregations of mainline denominations such as Episcopal Church of the Messiah in Chesapeake, Virginia: "The effect of worship in our service is a calling forth of the Holy Spirit and a sense of His manifest presence"
- congregations that had long practiced Praise & Worship such as Bible Temple in Portland, Oregon: "In these times of deep worship unto God, it's as if their praises go up to the throne room [of God]"

- congregations that were new adopters such as Fidelity Church in Diamond, Missouri: "For the past 2 years we've been teaching the people what praise and worship is . . . as we experience the presence of God in our midst"[4]

The river had become a flood.

The Developed Theology

Not only was there a surge of Praise & Worship after the late 1980s, but the main features of the theology underlying this liturgical approach had been settled by this time. The myriad of Praise & Worship proponents shared a set of core theological convictions as well as a theological method. Although, of course, the proponents differed in how they expressed certain particulars, they all held four core theological convictions.

The first was a fundamental expectation in Praise & Worship: through praising God, worshipers can encounter the presence of God.[5] Both the means (praise) and the end (a deep experience of the divine presence) were clear in how Praise & Worship theological voices expressed this expectation. This root notion, which we have traced in Praise & Worship's development back to Reg Layzell in the late 1940s, was ubiquitous by the late 1980s. Indeed, making a connection between praise and God's presence had become so widespread that many of the references to God inhabiting (or being enthroned on) praise did not even bother to cite Psalm 22:3, the main verse that had grounded the theology for Layzell. With or without the biblical citation, seeing praise as the preeminent way to facilitate an experience of God's presence was the air that

4. All of these congregational reports come from a regular feature titled "America Worships: Regional Church Reports on Praise and Worship" in the magazine *Psalmist*. The specific reports come from the following issues: West Angeles Church of God in Christ: vol. 6, no. 3 (June/July 1991): 45; Indonesian Full Gospel Fellowship: vol. 1, no. 6 (April/May 1986): 14; Croydon Center: vol. 5, no. 3 (June/July 1990): 29; Victory Chapel El Cajon Foursquare Church: vol. 5, no. 6 (December 1990/January 1991): 26; Abundant Life Church of Christ: vol. 2, no. 6 (December 1987/January 1988): 25; New Life Christian Center: vol. 5, no. 5 (October/November 1990): 26; Immanuel Baptist Church: vol. 1, no. 4 (December 1985/January 1986): 15; Episcopal Church of the Messiah: vol. 7, no. 1 (February/March 1992): 37; Bible Temple: vol. 1, no. 5 (February/March 1986): 16; Fidelity Church: vol. 4, no. 3 (June/July 1989): 29. By no means were such testimonies exceptional; if fact, they were the standard fare in this magazine. The examples here are a representative, not exhaustive, sample.

5. As for what it means to encounter the presence of God, the emphasis varied among proponents and between settings: some understood this to mean that *God's* presence was experienced in worship, others that the presence of one of the persons of the Trinity (Father, Son, or Holy Spirit) was experienced in worship.

the entire Praise & Worship world breathed at this time. This world relied on a link between praise and God's presence as a divinely given promise. Because it was God-given, the promise was sure and reliable.

One young musician in this world reported reinvesting himself in an unbreakable praise-to-presence association after a direct challenge from the Lord on the matter. According to the musician's testimony, God had asked him, "Do you believe that Psalm 22:3 really happens, that I inhabit the praises of My people?" After the young man asked for a revelation of how praise can lead to experiencing the presence of God, he described the divine explanation that he received.[6] There is nothing in the account's source, *Psalmist* magazine, that undercuts the propriety of either the praise-to-presence link or the idea God would query someone about it. In fact, the magazine in its ten-year print run from 1985 to 1995 often repeated this theology.

The nature of experiencing the divine presence through praising is described not as a mere light brush between parties but as a direct meeting of humanity with God; it is an *encounter* with a living God. To experience God's presence in Praise & Worship was not understood as something that happens merely conceptually or abstractly. This encounter is actual, discernable, and, in the estimation of worshipers, even sensible on occasion. Thus, the report from one Missouri church expressed what many would have affirmed in some way: "There are times during our worship when the presence of God is so strong that there seems to be a sweet aroma in the sanctuary and the people respond in a deeper understanding of what praise and worship is."[7]

To highlight the vivid nature of this encounter with God's presence, Praise & Worship theology often relied on a distinction between affirming divine omnipresence and testifying to God's "manifest presence." For example, Bob Sorge, a teacher of growing importance in this period, succinctly witnessed to the distinction: "The Scriptures reveal that God is everywhere at all times (omnipresent), but yet there are different degrees to which God manifests his presence. He manifests himself on one level 'where two or three are gathered.' But when a group of God's people congregate to sing his glorious praise, he 'inhabits' those praises and reveals his presence in a very particular way among his praising people (see Ps. 22:3)."[8] In distinguishing God's omnipresence and manifest presence, Sorge expressed a widespread theme.

6. Bob Mason, "I Inhabit Your Praises," *Psalmist* 2, no. 3 (April/May 1987): 20.

7. Report from Abiding Branch of Crescent Lake, Excelsior Springs, Missouri, in "America Worships: Regional Church Reports on Praise and Worship," *Psalmist* 5, no. 6 (December 1990/January 1991): 27.

8. Bob Sorge, *Exploring Worship: A Practical Guide to Praise and Worship* (Canandaigua, NY: Bob Sorge, 1987), 110. The term "manifest presence" by itself provided the title for a

To see praise as the unique "pathway"[9] to God's presence led Praise &
Worship teachers to distinguish between "praise" and "worship." It was commonplace to distinguish the two terms, although there was not total agreement about the precise difference between the two. Accordingly, Praise &
Worship advocates often cautioned against making too strident a distinction.
Nonetheless, generally there was a sense that praise is the activity that honors
God for his nature and his acts and that worship is the loving expression of
adoration for God. Because praise as its own activity was understood as the
path to experiencing God's presence, a corporate service began there and,
once God's presence had been manifested, the congregation moved into the
adoring worship of the God who was present. Thus, the mature theology of
the late 1980s generally saw a liturgical sequence from praising to worshiping.
Many supported this sequence by referring to Psalm 100:4 or to the tabernacle
of Moses. (See chap. 2 for the origins of this line of teaching.)

Although praise and worship were understood to be different activities,
Praise & Worship theology saw one essential commonality between the two:
music is the primary mode for expressing each. This musical emphasis was the
second core theological conviction of Praise & Worship proponents. While
Praise & Worship theologians in the era acknowledged that these liturgical
activities could be spoken or even done through other art forms, the pervasive
assumption was that Praise & Worship was a corporate musical enterprise.

Perhaps the most pointed theological expression of this assumption was
the approach some took in explicating the seven Hebrew words for "praise."
While teaching on these seven Hebrew words was widespread, some instructors made the point that the critical word for "praise" (the one found in Psalm
22:3, *tehillah*) meant musical, sung praise. In this respect, Judith McAllister
at West Angeles Church of God in Christ taught in 1994 that *tehillah* was
the "song that lives in your spirit" and was the type of praise in which "God
inhabits, settles, dwells, and fellowships."[10] In this way, this kind of word

book written by Don Nori, himself an important publisher of Praise & Worship literature:
His Manifest Presence: Discovering Life within the Veil (Shippensburg, PA: Destiny Image,
1988).

9. Charles Green, "The Pathway of Praise," in *Spirit Filled Life Bible*, ed. Jack W. Hayford (Nashville: Nelson, 1991), xxx. See also Jack W. Hayford, ed., *Hayford's Bible Handbook*
(Nashville: Nelson, 1995), 722. Decades after penning these pieces, Charles Green could still
recite from memory the Scriptures upon which they were based. Charles Green, interview by
Lim Swee Hong and Lester Ruth, October 13, 2017.

10. Judith McAllister, unpublished teaching outline titled "The Seven Levels of Praise" for
the See His Glory Worship Symposium, West Angeles Church of God in Christ, Los Angeles,
California, October 5–8, 1994. Cf. LaMar Boschman, *The Prophetic Song* (Shippensburg, PA:
Revival, 1986), 64, 66; and Boschman, *A Passion for His Presence: Keys to Living in God's Presence* (Shippensburg, PA: Destiny Image, 1992), 162–63.

study reinforced the notion that had arisen in the teaching of the restoration of David's tabernacle in the 1970s that God-inhabited praise is essentially musical (see chap. 2).

The notion that music is the primary mode of expression, therefore, means that musicians—especially a chief musician, known as a "worship leader"—have a crucial, priestly role in leading the congregation to an encounter with God's presence. One Assemblies of God worship leader, surely speaking for all worship leaders, affirmed this God-given stewardship in a 1986 poem: "I am a worship leader. / Not by my own doing, God has set me apart to lead his people into His presence."[11]

A favorite way of speaking about this liturgical stewardship was with the idiom of ushering. Perhaps the image was drawn from the spatial descriptions of moving from the outer areas of the Mosaic tabernacle into the holy of holies. Musicians, especially worship leaders, were to usher the congregation into the presence of God. Worship leader Mark Conner affirmed this widely used idiom in 1993, saying, "I see my role as a worship leader a bit like an usher at an important event. . . . We are to bring them [i.e., the worshipers] to a place of worship in the presence of God."[12]

In the mature theology of Praise & Worship, this responsibility was weighty since this theology saw being in the presence of God as being in the middle of a dynamic environment. Simply put, where and when God is present, God is active. This affirmation anchored the third core theological conviction. Praise & Worship theologians and congregations regularly testified to what they saw God doing when present (redeeming, healing, and delivering). One Ohio congregation exuded stories of God's action at the beginning of the 1990s: "Praise and worship sets the climate for redemption, healing and deliverance. We have experienced the manifest presence of the Holy Spirit. . . . His glory is filling His Temple! The prophetic anointing has been released."[13]

Even when the divine activity was not as dramatic, the theology of Praise & Worship expected the people to be active before God too. One necessary dimension was the active discerning of the Spirit of God, especially by the worship leader. To adjust, to shift plans, to gauge the Spirit's leading: all were the presumed liturgical responsibilities of the worship leader. Discerning the

11. Stephen R. Phifer, "I Am a Worship Leader," *Psalmist* 1, no. 5 (February/March 1986): 26.

12. Quoted in "Frontline Worship," *Psalmist* 8, no. 4 (July/August 1993): 14. Mark Conner was the son of Kevin Conner. See chap. 2 for the elder Conner's importance in the theological development of Praise & Worship.

13. Report from Christian Assembly Church of Columbus, Ohio, in "America Worships: Regional Church Reports on Praise and Worship," *Psalmist* 5, no. 6 (December 1990/January 1991): 27.

Spirit's guidance was not solely the musician's responsibility, however. That assessment was a joint liturgical responsibility of the entire congregation, especially in prophetic moments and in the times of spontaneous songs of the Lord.

The other necessary dimension of corporate activity before God was active response. To feel affectively and to express physically were expected responses from all worshipers. In fact, the theology had developed a schema from biblical texts, especially passages from the Psalms, for physical expression before God like raising hands, bowing down, dancing, clapping, and shouting.[14]

The use of psalm proof texts to develop a liturgical schema points to the fourth core theological conviction: Praise & Worship was approached as a biblically derived, God-given pattern for worship. Convinced that this was the way of worship God had given in the Bible, its practitioners taught it with the confidence they had in the Scriptures themselves. Their tone was neither experimental nor cautious since Praise & Worship was not human-created, according to this theology. Rather, it was God's gift to renew the church. Consequently, the Bible as God's Word outlined its underlying promise (God desires to dwell with his people and does so through their praise) and its specific methods.

Not surprisingly, this conviction about the biblical basis for Praise & Worship generated a method for theologizing. It had three regular features: The first was a predilection for undertaking studies of biblical words and then using key words to compile a group of passages from which to form a synthesis. For example, what Reg Layzell did in 1946 (see chap. 1), Judith McAllister did forty years later when the criticalness of praise first hooked her: she immersed herself for days in Bible study tools like concordances, skipping nearly a week of college classes.[15] Her goal was to see when and how the Bible used the word "praise." The second regular feature was an attraction to typology drawn from Bible stories, especially from the Old Testament and especially from narratives about David. (The book of Revelation was a favorite of some too.) Praise & Worship teachers used these stories to develop types instructive for how and why Christians should worship. The third regular feature of the theological method was, as mentioned above, a predilection for using the Psalms to provide the details about the specific dimensions of

14. For an example, see Ken Barker, ed., *Songs for Praise & Worship*, Worship Planner Edition (Waco: Word Music, 1992), 472–73. For an earlier example, see Ernest B. Gentile, *Charismatic Catechism* (Harrison, AR: New Leaf, 1977), 148. Gentile is not exceptional. Such a schema goes back at least to Graham Truscott, *The Power of His Presence: The Restoration of the Tabernacle of David* (San Diego: Restoration Temple, 1969).

15. Judith McAllister, interview by Lester Ruth and Lim Swee Hong, June 7, 2018.

Praise & Worship, especially those involving physical expression. Therefore, the biblically derived theology of Praise & Worship was a very embodied theology, because the Psalms drew a picture of worshipers fully engaged with their whole persons.

In summary, by the late 1980s Praise & Worship theologizing had given rise to a set of four core beliefs, widely held and widely shared: (1) God's people can encounter and experience the divine presence through praise; (2) praise and the subsequent liturgical activity, worship, are primarily musical activities; (3) when and where God's presence is manifest, God is active among the people, who should be thoroughly active to God in return; (4) this whole approach to Praise & Worship is God's gift to the church, as can be seen and understood in the Bible. These stable convictions provided the essential momentum for Praise & Worship.[16]

If this theology was stable, however, it was not static. For example, this period saw both a restatement of one critical point and an expansion of another. The restatement emerged in one Vineyard congregation and the expansion in another.

The restatement arose in the Anaheim Vineyard congregation and was applied to the congregation's earlier sense of distinguishing between singing *about* God and singing *to* God. In the early years of the congregation, this distinction was a way to describe a common ordering of songs, a sequence that generally followed a flow from praise to worship. By the mid-1980s, the congregation had a new worship leader, Eddie Espinosa, whose prior church background was in a Spanish-speaking congregation with close ties to the Latter Rain movement and its more developed theology of Praise & Worship.[17] As Espinosa brought the specifics of that theological background into the leadership mix at the Anaheim Vineyard, a new statement about ordering worship emerged that used relationship terms to name the progression in the service.[18] Espinosa included this new Vineyard articulation as one model among multiple options for ordering congregational singing that he summarized in a 1987 educational essay for other worship leaders. In that essay, he first highlighted

16. Cf. Gerrit Gustafson, "A Charismatic Theology of Worship," in *Twenty Centuries of Christian Worship*, vol. 2 of *The Complete Library of Christian Worship*, ed. Robert E. Webber (Nashville: Star Song, 1994), 309–12.

17. Eddie Espinosa, interview by Lim Swee Hong and Lester Ruth, May 2, 2015; Eddie Espinosa and Joey Arreguin, interview by Lim Swee Hong and Lester Ruth, March 12, 2018.

18. Compare the explanation offered by Barry Liesch, who was in close proximity to this development. See Barry Liesch, *People in the Presence of God: Models and Directions for Worship* (Grand Rapids: Zondervan, 1988), 91; and Barry Liesch, "A Structure Runs through It," in *Changing Lives through Preaching and Worship: 30 Strategies for Power Communication*, ed. Marshall Shelley (Nashville: Moorings, 1995), 245.

Figure 4.2. Eddie Espinosa on guitar, Debby Smith (center), and John Wimber leading worship in South Africa, late 1980s

models based on the tabernacle of Moses or on the older Vineyard approach (which called for starting with songs about God, continuing with songs to us, and ending with songs to God).[19] Then he explained the new model, the "relationship approach," which involved an invitation or call to worship (to focus worshipers and remind them why they were together); engagement (to start drawing near to God); exaltation (to magnify and glorify God); adoration (love songs); and, ultimately, intimacy (a "quiet time together" with God).[20] The use of the term "intimacy" tied this model to a foundational Vineyard sensibility, present from Vineyard beginnings, as we saw in chapter 3. Having a relational term like "intimacy" as foundational set this church on a natural course to restate the entire order of Praise & Worship in relationship terms.

John Wimber, Espinosa's pastor and the leader of the Vineyard movement, began to publish his own version of the relationship model in 1987

19. Eddie Espinosa, "Worship Leading," in *Worship Leaders Training Manual* (Anaheim: Worship Resource Center/Vineyard Ministries International, 1987), 81–82. According to Espinosa, the Ps. 100 model started with encampment outside the fence (fun songs), then entered the gates with thanksgiving (gratitude songs), then entered the courts with praise (upbeat praise songs), then went into the holy place (worship songs), then climaxed by entering the holy of holies in which was the ark of God's presence (intimate songs). He also gave a Ps. 95 model that involved moving from rejoicing to thanking to praising to reverencing.

20. Espinosa, "Worship Leading," 81–82.

too. In the same educational manual where Espinosa's version appears, Wimber described a version involving seven stages.[21] Earlier in that same year, in the denominational magazine, Wimber had published another explanation involving five "phases." The five phases were, in order, the call to worship, engagement with God and each other, the expression before God of what's deeply in us, the visitation of God, and a giving of substance (i.e., our giving ourselves as a way of life in response to God).[22] As described by Wimber, these were the phases "through which [worship] leaders attempt to lead the congregation" with a clear goal of "intimacy with God."[23] In subsequent years this fivefold version was included in other teaching materials and republished several times.[24] Consequently, it has been the version most people identify as the Vineyard approach to Praise & Worship.[25]

If this one Vineyard congregation restated commonplace Praise & Worship theological commitments, then another, Metro Vineyard Fellowship in Kansas City, Missouri, expanded them. This expansion is a second example of how Praise & Worship theology was stable but not static.

By the early 1990s in this Missouri congregation, a line of theologizing had arisen that accepted the earlier notion connecting Praise & Worship to God's presence but joined it to an emphasis on intercessory prayer. The point of connection was Revelation 5:8, which envisioned the elders around the throne of God in heaven each holding a harp and a bowl, the harp representing worship and the bowl, as the text says, representing the prayers of God's people. The result of this line of theologizing was a vision for congregational

21. John Wimber, "The Worship Experience," in *Worship Leaders Training Manual* (Anaheim: Worship Resource Center/Vineyard Ministries International, 1987), 171–83. By 1984, at least, Wimber had been using these labels for the phases in an undeveloped manner in his teaching. See his teaching on tape 4 in volume 2 of *Worship Seminar* (Placentia, CA: Vineyard Ministries International, 1984).

22. John Wimber, "Worship: Intimacy with God," *Equipping the Saints* 1, no. 1 (January/February 1987): 4–5, 13.

23. Wimber, "Worship: Intimacy with God," 5.

24. The 1987 article was included in the teaching manual titled *Worship Conference* (Anaheim: Vineyard Ministries International, 1989) as an article titled "Worship: Intimacy with God." It was also republished in a volume edited by John Wimber, *Thoughts on Worship* (Anaheim: Vineyard Music, 1996), 4–7; and in *The Way In Is the Way On: John Wimber's Teachings and Writings on Life in Christ* (Atlanta: Ampelon, 2006), 121–24.

25. Note that Wimber's article doesn't state that the fivefold phase explanation was explicitly taught in the first years of the Vineyard. However, because Wimber introduces it in a discussion of the worship of the original home group, a reader might think that Wimber is implying that the fivefold phase model was explicitly taught during the early years. That does not appear to be the case, on the basis of available contemporaneous primary sources. See Andy Park, Lester Ruth, and Cindy Rethmeier, *Worshiping with the Anaheim Vineyard: The Emergence of Contemporary Worship* (Grand Rapids: Eerdmans, 2017). This relationship model appears to be a secondary theological development within the Vineyard.

worship in which prayer expressions of praise and adoration moved naturally back and forth with intercession. Both praise and intercession were seen as particularly potent instruments of spiritual warfare.

The novelty of this theology lay not in the emphasis on intercession, since a dedication to intercession was a common aspect of Pentecostal spirituality and, indeed, intercession had been an emphasis in the early Latter Rain movement. Nor did it lie in the idea of praise and intercession as instruments of spiritual warfare. Nor did it lie in using the Bible typologically to theologize about Praise & Worship. The novelty—and theological expansion—lay in the fusion, as corporate liturgical activities, of praising and worshiping with active, ongoing intercession. This fusion can be seen in the name by which the approach came to be known: Harp and Bowl, a name obviously taken from the Revelation 5:8 passage.

Once sprung, it took little time for this Harp and Bowl expansion of Praise & Worship theology to be disseminated. Published forms began appearing from one of Metro Vineyard Fellowship's pastors, Greg Mira, at the end of 1991.[26] He had earlier taught on the topic at a national worship conference in July 1991 (the Third Annual Kent Henry/Psalmist Resources Worship Conference in St. Louis, Missouri), a videotape of which was available for purchase by phone or mail order from *Psalmist* magazine.[27]

Eventually the Harp and Bowl theology would be connected with another earlier theological emphasis, the notion of unceasing, around-the-clock worship in the tabernacle of David. This second fusion would later serve as a basis for the 24-7 worship movement that began to emerge by the end of the decade. Perhaps the best-known representative of this movement has been Kansas City's International House of Prayer (commonly known as IHOP), pastored by Mike Bickle, who had been the senior pastor at Metro Vineyard Fellowship.[28]

26. Greg Mira, "Spiritual Warfare through Worship," *Psalmist* 6, no. 6 (December 1991/January 1992): 41–43. A longer explication came the following year in the publication of Mira's book titled *Victor or Victim: A Fresh Look at Spiritual Warfare* (Grandview, MO: Grace!, 1992). In the book's preface (p. iii), Mira mentions that he had begun ruminating on Revelation 5:8 after hearing the verse read at a conference in 1990.

27. Back cover ad for the conference, *Psalmist* 6, no. 5 (October/November 1991).

28. A brief review of Bickle's and his congregation's journey into and out of the larger Vineyard network can be found in Jack W. Hayford, *The Charismatic Century: The Enduring Impact of the Azusa Street Revival* (New York: Warner Faith, 2006), 266–67. A good source for background information on Bickle and his thoughts on Praise & Worship at that time can be found in Mike Bickle, *Growing in the Prophetic* (Lake Mary, FL: Creation House, 1996). Bickle was also one of the original regular columnists for *Psalmist* magazine (he was good friends with the editor, Kent Henry) and so his articles, usually on prayer, can found in that magazine's first year of publication (1985–86). Note that in 1986 Bickle was already affirming

The Settled Practices of Praise & Worship

As the theology of Praise & Worship settled into a fairly established paradigm, so did its form as corporate liturgical activity.[29] Consider Mike Bickle's description of Praise & Worship as he saw it in 1996:

> Most churches I've visited that allow for the expression of prophetic gifts do so by having a programmed pause for the prophetic. The service begins with exuberant praise, slows down to tender worship songs and finally slows down even more to a silent pause in the service waiting for prophetic words to be given. There are two types of pauses in a worship service. One is a programmed silence to make room for a prophetic word. On the other hand, times of silence come because we sense the presence of God.[30]

Of course, given the breadth and variety in Praise & Worship, not all congregations would have had a clear emphasis on or allowance for the prophetic. Other congregations, too, would have responded to a sense of the manifest presence of God not by silence but by exuberant expression. And other congregations would have had a more obvious role for a variety of nonmusical arts. Nonetheless, the general tone, movement, and structure Bickle describes matched what had emerged by the late 1980s as the typical form of Praise & Worship. A stable theology now undergirded a set of specific Praise & Worship practices, especially musical, that were likewise widespread and settled. Note, for example, how Bickle spoke of the pause or silence being "programmed," hinting at a sense that there was an established pattern to which the theological expectations of God's presence were attached. The title of a 1993 book suggests this link between pattern and expectation even more bluntly: *God's Presence through Music*.[31] This title was not considered presumptuous because it so well matched the theology and practices of Praise & Worship, which by this time had diffused throughout

---

Revelation 5 as a "model" for the church's worship without specific reference to Harp and Bowl theology or practice. See Mike Bickle, "The Secret Place: Revelation of the Throne," *Psalmist* 1, no. 7 (June/July 1986): 17.

29. We recognize that those practicing Praise & Worship would not normally have used the terms "liturgy" or "liturgical" to describe what they did. We do so here in the most generic way possible to speak of Praise & Worship as corporate, participatory worship-related activity (i.e., the work of the people of God). We do not intend by the use of these terms to adopt any of their other common connotations or imply that worship is text-based, eucharistically oriented, or tied to levels of formal ceremony.

30. Bickle, *Growing in the Prophetic*, 152.

31. Ruth Ann Ashton, *God's Presence through Music* (South Bend, IN: Lesea, 1993). Ashton built her theology on the Mosaic tabernacle typology.

much of Pentecostalism and, eventually, would spread through even broader evangelicalism.[32]

Five widespread practices characterized the Praise & Worship of the late 1980s and early 1990s. Multiple theological commitments shaped each of the practices.

The first of the commonplace practices involved having a musical worship leader—not a minister of the Word of God or of the sacraments (i.e., a pastor)—perform the central role in directing a congregation's liturgical activity. This musician, *the* worship leader, was normally assisted by a team of vocalists as well as by other instrumentalists. These musicians had the responsibility to guide and direct the congregation's liturgical participation. The historical novelty of this practice has been the displacement of the minister responsible for the Word—whether preacher, pastor, elder, presbyter, or bishop—as the main leader of a congregation's worship. (Younger Christians may not recognize this Praise & Worship practice as a novelty, since it became widespread so quickly that they may never have seen the older practice.)

The elevation of musicians—literally, in terms of the liturgical space, and metaphorically, in terms of their central role as liturgical leaders—was a natural outgrowth of the theologizing taking place in Praise & Worship. As we saw earlier, this elevation of musical leadership naturally grew from associating typologically today's church musicians with the priestly musicians of David's tabernacle. Thus Marcos Witt, the primary face for Praise & Worship in Spanish-speaking Central and South America at the time, could assume both the practice and its biblical theology underpinnings in 1989 when he spoke of musicians as "Levites, on whose shoulders rests the responsibility of carrying the Ark of God's presence."[33]

---

32. There is some indication that by the late 1980s this standard approach to Praise & Worship practices was labeled a "charismatic" approach to worship. See, for example, the essay by the well-embedded Praise & Worship practitioner Gerrit Gustafson: "A Charismatic Theology of Worship," in *Twenty Centuries of Christian Worship*. "Charismatic" in this sense should not be limited to the Charismatic Renewal movement that emerged in mainline and evangelical denominations in the 1960s, although this movement did practice forms of Praise & Worship. Why and how the term "charismatic" became applied to Praise & Worship generally are questions awaiting further research.

33. J. Mark Witt, "Wanted: Christ-Like Musicians," in *An Anthology of Articles on Restoring Praise & Worship to the Church*, ed. David K. Blomgren, Dean Smith, and Douglas Christoffel (Shippensburg, PA: Revival, 1989), 153–54. Despite being the preeminent person in Spanish-speaking Praise & Worship at the end of the twentieth century, Marcos Witt is the child of English-speaking missionaries from the United States to Mexico. Witt most often goes by the name Marcos rather than his birth name. Witt's parents came from a Latter Rain–affiliated church in San Antonio, Texas. Our thanks go to Adam Perez for this background information on Witt.

The theological support for elevating musicians as the primary worship leaders was not confined to the theology of the restoration of the Davidic tabernacle, however. The support came also from more general theological commitments. Key among those other commitments was the sense that, according to the Bible, music is the primary mode of expression for both praise and worship. Since music was considered essential to fulfill the biblical vision for Praise & Worship, it followed that those who lead the music were likewise essential. This rationale was especially critical since, in the theology, praise leads to God's presence, experienced liturgically as the manifest divine presence. Experience thus paralleled the biblical theology in making musicians' leadership central.[34]

The second widespread practice that had come to characterize Praise & Worship in its mature form of the late 1980s was a related musical one: worship leaders primarily fulfilled their liturgical responsibility in a time of congregational singing, which was referred to as "worship" or, eventually, as a "worship set." Praise & Worship regularly involved having a lengthy time, created and managed musically, to fulfill the biblical pattern needed to get to a point of discerning God's manifest presence.

A regular feature of the magazine *Psalmist* gives us a glimpse of how standard the practice was and the range of time taken for congregational singing. From its inception in 1985 through the early 1990s, this magazine, which was the primary journal for worship leaders at the time,[35] included a feature titled "America Worships: Regional Church Responses on Praise and Worship" in which churches from across the United States reported on the state of their Praise & Worship. Two of the standard questions dealt with the overall length of a congregation's service and the length of the time of "worship," meaning the time of congregational singing. While these reports do not

---

34. Of course, the particular musical practices of those using pop- or rock-style bands too would reflect normal cultural practices for these bands with respect to their placement.

35. *Psalmist* was an outgrowth of the ministry of Kent Henry, a worship leader from Missouri who developed it as part of his wider teaching ministry. In addition to the magazine, Henry created media-based teaching resources for worship leaders, traveled extensively to speak and conduct worship seminars, and held an annual Praise & Worship conference. He had close ties with important historical figures like Mike Bickle, on the one hand, and Tom Brooks, who was the producer of the early Integrity's Hosanna! tapes, on the other. *Psalmist* used authors from across the breadth of Praise & Worship and is therefore one of the best windows into the entire phenomenon for that time. The managing editor for most of its print run was Tom Kraeuter, another worship leader from Missouri, who eventually developed his own writing and workshop ministry. By 1992 the magazine had close to eight thousand subscribers and was distributed internationally (Tom Kraeuter, interview by Lester Ruth and Adam Perez, September 30, 2019). The magazine ceased publication in 1995. The particular feature of church reports ended a little bit earlier.

provide a scientific sampling of congregational practices across the nation (since the congregations self-selected in sending in the reports), nonetheless they clearly confirm how pervasive a drawn-out time of singing was. Across the magazine's print run, 309 church reports indicated an average worship time of 38.91 minutes and a median time of 38 minutes.

Of course, in order to handle such long periods of singing, worship leaders had to become stewards of large collections of congregational songs, including a growing repertoire of new songs. *Psalmist* magazine supplies information showing how critical this practice was for worship leaders in a series of surveys that ran from 1990 to 1992.[36] In each year, respondents named seeking out, selecting, and organizing new songs for the church as their second-most-common duty, ranking below only the actual leadership of music for corporate gatherings. In 1990, 75 percent listed this responsibility for songs as one of their main functions; in 1991, 79 percent did so; and, in 1992, the number was 84 percent. In each year this responsibility for handling new songs outweighed the task of overseeing vocalists and instrumentalists. Not surprisingly, the magazine began running advertisements offering aids for song management like computer programs that could assist in the task of managing songs. INFOsearch, for example, could index each song in its database by title, topic, Scripture reference, key, tempo, and the original recording on which the song was first released. The result was greater ease for worship leaders wanting to plan song medleys "centered around Scripture passages, topics, musical keys or meters, specific words and phrases, or titles and names ascribed to our Lord."[37]

Several theological emphases lay behind the practice of a long period of congregational singing: on seeing praise as the preeminent way to facilitate an experience of God's presence, on making a distinction between praise and worship, and on holding music as the primary mode for expressing biblical Praise & Worship. Combined, these theological commitments required time: both time to cultivate an expression of true, heartfelt praise and time to move from praise to worship. This combination explains the attractiveness of architecture-based schemas like the tabernacle of Moses or Psalm 100:4 as biblical expressions of this theology. Imagining moving through an architectural space paralleled worshipers' sense of moving through the liturgical time of Praise & Worship.

36. See these issues of *Psalmist*: vol. 5, no. 1 (February/March 1990): 27; vol. 6, no. 3 (June/July 1991): 35; and vol. 7, no. 4 (August/September 1992): 7.

37. See the inside front cover of *Psalmist* 7, no. 3 (June/July 1992). For a competitor product, see the advertisement for Maestro the Worship Workshop in *Psalmist* 5, no. 1 (February/March 1990): 11.

The third standard practice that characterized Praise & Worship concerns how musicians sequenced and played the songs in the time of singing. The goal in both sequencing and playing was to create a flowing progression in the medley of songs so as to help the congregation discern and experience the presence of God. Good flow was critical since it assisted the corporate discernment of God; a lack of flow disrupted this discernment. As one resource for worship leaders explained, "Creating a musical worship flow is crucial in helping a church sense God's presence throughout a service." It added that congregations should not think of worship as simply a "song service" but "as a progression into the manifest presence of God."[38] Similarly, Tom Brooks, the producer for early Hosanna! tapes, described the sequencing not as a "formula" but as a "loose framework or road map to help lead people into God's presence."[39]

Not surprisingly, Brooks and countless other instructors regularly included in their teaching explanations about how to create and maintain a sense of good musical flow in leading Praise & Worship. The goal was not simply to allow one song to lead into the next but to have the musical skill to change and shift the affective dynamics as the congregation more fully developed a growing sense of entering into God's presence.

Many of the core theological convictions discussed earlier shaped this practice also and made it commonplace. For instance, the distinction between praise and worship was reflected in the sense of a proper sequence of songs. Whether any one song was praise or worship depended not only on its expressed content but also on its general musical feel. However, the strictness with which worship leaders applied a praise and worship sequence and the rules by which a song was sorted into one or the other category could and did vary among worship leaders. Nonetheless, other theological convictions made universal some concern with proper sequencing. The whole theology rested on the trust and experience that worshipers could move from not sensing God's presence to encountering God's manifest presence, and that this move should be done musically in praising and then worshiping.

38. Barker, *Songs for Praise & Worship*, 453, 464. For a historical overview of the emphasis on flow, see Lim Swee Hong and Lester Ruth, *Lovin' on Jesus: A Concise History of Contemporary Worship* (Nashville: Abingdon, 2017), 32–36; and Zachary Barnes, "How Flow Became the Thing," in *Flow: The Ancient Way to Do Contemporary Worship*, ed. Lester Ruth (Nashville: Abingdon, 2020), 13–23.

39. Tom Brooks, "Worship Forum: Spontaneity in Worship," *Worship Times* 1, no. 2 (Summer 1986): 4. Compare Barry Griffing, "Releasing Charismatic Worship," in *An Anthology of Articles on Restoring Praise & Worship to the Church*, ed. David K. Blomgren, Dean Smith, and Douglas Christoffel (Shippensburg, PA: Revival, 1989), 96–97. Griffing utilizes the listing of "psalms, hymns, and spiritual songs" as the framework for sequencing songs in Praise & Worship.

The fourth standard practice also involved a developed sense of musical skill in that, once a sense of God's manifest presence had been discerned, the worship leader and other musicians had a responsibility to foster musically the ongoing engagement and interaction with God. In other words, music was not only to lead a congregation to the threshold of encounter with God, it was to provide the dynamic backdrop while the congregation remained in God's presence. The theological dimensions of this approach to Praise & Worship music, on the one hand, saw God as being active once the divine presence had been felt by the worshiping assembly and, on the other, expected whole-person response by worshipers.

Thus, worship leaders should plan musically but should also be willing to adjust their plans as seems fitting. The repetitive nature of the songs and the use of other forms of musical repetition help worshipers move beyond awareness of only the surface dimension of what is happening to see more fully the spiritual dynamics of the moment. A skillful worship leader is understood to be one who has developed the musical techniques necessary to discern and respond to the ebb and flow in the encounter with God. Thus, this person shapes the song selection and musical performance practice, deciding the following: repetitions, key and tempo changes, and when to "linger" in the presence of God. Of special importance (in this view) are the skills required to handle "open worship" or "free style worship," during which there is an open-endedness to what might take place and how long those liturgical actions might last.[40] These times might include singing in the Spirit, spontaneous sung or spoken expressions of praise or adoration, and prophetic words or songs. Regardless, the responsibility of the worship leader is to assist musically what is happening between God and God's people.

The fifth widespread practice of the developed form of Praise & Worship of the 1985–95 era was enabling worshipers' bodies to be free to be fully engaged in worship. Worshipers' bodies were to be the outlets to express the inward spiritual experience of interaction with God. In practice, this theological vision meant that worshipers' bodies needed to be free from the holding of liturgical books, even hymnals or songbooks. While it might seem a simple thing, the holding of a book was a form of physical restraint inhibiting movement and gesture, and reorienting the worshiper's eyes downward, not upward. Consequently, songs tended to be sung from repertoires already internalized by the congregation or, increasingly during the period from the late

40. Discussing such techniques was a regular consideration in *Psalmist* magazine. See, for example, an article in the first edition of *Psalmist*: Tom Brooks, "Inside Music: Practical Applications of Theory in Worship," *Psalmist* 1, no. 1 (1985): 14–15.

1980s into the 1990s, by using some early form of projection. The projection technology most commonly used in this period was the overhead projector, which had become widespread in military, business, and educational venues in the 1960s. A page-sized sheet of transparent plastic film containing the lyrics of a song was placed on the glass surface of the projector, which had a light source below the glass and a projecting mirror and lens above it. A single person usually operated the overhead projector, ready with the transparencies needed for the service and with a box containing the congregation's whole repertoire in case the worship leader changed plans. Until the advent of computer-based projection later in the 1990s, the other viable alternative for song projection was a slide projector.

The simplicity of Praise & Worship songs in this period also helped enable fuller engagement of worshipers. Shorter songs with a simple structure (verse + chorus or chorus only) were easy to memorize and internalize. Cycles of repetition, too, helped foster deeper participation in singing, as did musical techniques like call-and-response or echoing by parts (e.g., men sing a line first and then the women repeat it). The simplicity of the songs and the musical repetitiveness seemed to facilitate a congregation's sense of the presence of God.

The theological roots for this physical expressiveness involved more than the long-standing Pentecostal tendency toward liturgical exuberance and ecstasy. Rather, the roots were a theological system that fused (1) biblical passages, especially from the Psalms, suggesting certain outward behaviors like the raising of hands or clapping with (2) scriptural exhortations about appropriate inward dispositions before God like purity and singleness of heart. Helping to make this instructive biblical material more compelling to worshipers was its link with key biblical types that allowed worshipers to imagine what appropriate engagement with God should look like. In this regard, the story of David dancing before the ark of God on its arrival to Jerusalem was a particular favorite (2 Sam. 6).

A River of Many Colors

We have described the period from 1985 to 1995 as the era in which the river of Praise & Worship swelled tremendously, increasing from an impressive Mississippian size in the mid-1980s to an overwhelming Amazonian juggernaut ten years later. This expansion came not only in terms of the number of people involved but also in terms of the number of ethnic groups. These ten years were when non-White expressions of Praise & Worship became more public. It was also when non-White leaders with large spheres of influence emerged. Of course, Praise & Worship was not entirely new to non-White congregations,[41] but the time after the mid-1980s was when this way of worship became easy to find in African American, Latino, and Asian contexts in North America. Simply put, Praise & Worship had developed into a river of many colors.

Even as Praise & Worship expanded racially, neither its shared theology nor its shared practices were lost. The common theology and practices provided the link between these new "currents" and the larger phenomenon of Praise & Worship. Indeed, the most prominent leaders in the various ethnic and racial currents of Praise & Worship were clear proponents of the standard elements of its theology and practices.

Consider, for example, Stream of Praise Music Ministries in Southern California, a global leader since 1993 in songwriting for Chinese-speaking Christians.[42] The title song "Let Praise Arise" on the ministry's first album (1995) encapsulated many of the standard sentiments of Praise & Worship's theology.[43] The song's single verse quoted directly from a much-used biblical

41. For an example of earlier Praise & Worship in a Spanish-speaking context, see the discussion in chap. 2 of Bill Brown and his work in Mexico in the 1970s. With respect to a Black context, there was perhaps no greater pioneer than Joseph Garlington, founding pastor of Covenant Church in Pittsburgh, Pennsylvania. Garlington first came into contact with Latter Rain–inspired Praise & Worship after meeting Violet Kiteley in the late 1960s and visiting Bethesda Missionary Temple in Detroit (Myrtle Beall's church) in the early 1970s. Garlington was enthralled and adopted Praise & Worship for his new Pittsburgh congregation. Soon Garlington was involved in a network of teaching and leading Praise & Worship that lasted through the 1970s and 1980s. He was involved in the Charismatic Renewal movement, *New Wine* magazine, the early development of Integrity's Hosanna! Music, and, later in the 1990s, as a worship leader at Promise Keepers rallies (Joseph Garlington, interview by Lester Ruth, February 13, 2020). Garlington in his interview also pointed to the important role Andraé Crouch played in this earlier period by introducing a different sound for Praise & Worship songs to White congregations and familiarizing Black congregations with songs from this type of repertoire. Other early Black pioneers of Praise & Worship include Evangel Temple in Washington, DC (a large congregation); Don Lewis (influenced by Violet Kiteley) of Little Rock, Arkansas, who would begin Revival Press; and Andrew Merritt (influenced by Myrtle Beall), who planted Straight Gate International Church in Detroit.

42. For more information on Stream of Praise, see Lim and Ruth, *Lovin' on Jesus*, 83; Lim Swee Hong, "Nashville and Sydney Are Not the World: The Transnational Migration of Sources for Chinese Contemporary Praise & Worship Songs," in *Essays on the History of Contemporary Praise and Worship*, ed. Lester Ruth (Eugene, OR: Pickwick, 2020), 152; and Connie Oi-Yan Wong, "Singing the Gospel Chinese Style: 'Praise and Worship' Music in the Asian Pacific" (PhD diss., University of California, 2006). An interview with Sandy Yu by Lim Swee Hong (September 16, 2017) provided useful background information on this ministry.

43. Historical documentation of the song can be found at "About," Stream of Praise Music Ministries, accessed February 5, 2021, https://www.sop.org/en/about. The song was written by Sandy Yu (the founder of Stream of Praise), Chuck Hong, and Steven Chen.

Used by permission of Dennis Chou and Stream of Praise Music Ministries

Figure 4.3. Sandy Yu, founder of Stream of Praise Music Ministries

verse, Psalm 100:4, speaking of entering God's gates with thanks and his courts with praise. The song also reveled in an encounter with God through praise and the enjoyment of God's manifest presence. Specifically, the lyrics exulted in a "face to face" meeting in which the worshipers could feel the divine "sweet embrace" as the Holy Spirit filled the worship space. The song expressed, too, the propriety of worshipers' full-bodied engagement with the divine presence through singing, opening of hands, opening of hearts, and dancing. Notwithstanding that the song was in Chinese, its theology was soundly within the bounds of customary Praise & Worship thought.

The same was the case for the theology of Marcos Witt, who emerged as the preeminent public face for Spanish-speaking Praise & Worship in this period.[44] We have already quoted from Witt's 1989 essay in which he described worship leaders as "Levites, on whose shoulders rests the responsibility of carrying the

44. As mentioned in an earlier note, Witt was the son of an Anglo missionary couple from the United States serving in Mexico. He had strong ties to the Latter Rain expression of Praise & Worship, and was included in that stream's 1989 book, edited by David K. Blomgren, Dean Smith, and Douglas Christoffel, titled *An Anthology of Articles on Restoring Praise & Worship to the Church* (Shippensburg, PA: Revival, 1989). He had also attended conferences at Bible Temple, Dick Iverson's church in Portland, Oregon, in the 1980s, according to Howard Rachinski (Howard Rachinski, interview by Lester Ruth and Lim Swee Hong, April 17, 2017). In 1987 Witt founded CanZion Producciones and seven years later the CanZion Institute. He has been one of the most popular Praise & Worship leaders and recording artists since the late 1980s. See Adam Perez, "Beyond the Guitar: The Keyboard as a Lens into the History of Contemporary Praise and Worship," *Hymn* 70, no. 2 (Spring 2019): 25–26. Witt has published an autobiography, titled *Enciende Una Luz* (Lake Mary, FL: Casa Creación, 2000).

Ark of God's presence." Witt's subsequent book-length writings reiterate this core notion and combine it with other commonplace convictions of Praise & Worship theologizing. His seminal book, *Adoremos*, republished in English as *A Worship-Filled Life*, expresses most of the key aspects of a theology of encountering God's presence through musical praise.[45] The book begins with the universal question of Praise & Worship (How do we enter into the presence of God?) and immediately answers by citing Psalm 100:4.[46] Having used Psalm 100:4 to connect thanksgiving and praise with experiencing God's presence, Witt next distinguishes between praise and worship, using studies of biblical words.[47] Moreover, as done widely in other Praise & Worship theologizing, Witt employs two standard biblical types: the tabernacle of Moses to speak about the goal of being in God's presence by entering into the holy of holies, and David as an example for being a true worshiper.[48] Psalm 22:3 is a recurring biblical citation in Witt's discussion. He interprets the verse by saying that praise builds a throne that God then inhabits, a framing of the theology also found in some other authors.[49] Witt's approach thus mediates between the two common translations of this verse (i.e., God inhabits the praises of his people or God is enthroned on the praises of his people). The overall effect of Witt's biblical method is the same as in other Praise & Worship theologizing: he presents Praise & Worship as a biblically derived, God-given approach to corporate liturgy.[50]

A comparable approach to Praise & Worship can be found in the writings of African American theologians. For instance, Judith McAllister, a popular

45. Marcos Witt, *Adoremos* (Miami: Editorial Caribe, 1993), reprinted in English as *A Worship-Filled Life: Making Worship a Way of Life Rather Than Just a Manner of Expression* (Orlando: Creation House, 1998). We will cite from this English reprint.

46. Witt, *Worship-Filled Life*, 1–2.

47. Witt, *Worship-Filled Life*, 19–21.

48. Witt, *Worship-Filled Life*, 77–78, 62.

49. Witt, *Worship-Filled Life*, 75, 199.

50. A hallmark of Witt's theologizing is his highlighting of a needed Christlikeness or holiness in the life of the musician. In this regard Witt emphasizes repeatedly that true Praise & Worship is not just music. Even here, however, this concern serves the underlying theology presuming that music, to use Witt's own terms, is "one of the most effective vehicles" to discern and enjoy the presence of God. Consequently, Witt is capable of speaking of musicians as both priests and prophets. See chap. 7 ("El músico como sacerdote") and chap. 8 ("El músico como profeta") in Marcos Witt, *¿Qué hacemos con estos músicos? Respuestas a los problemas que enfrenta la iglesia en cuanto al ministerio musical* (Nashville: Grupo Nelson, 1995), 117–39. The title of this book in English would be "What do we do with these musicians?" Witt has continued these themes in recent interviews. See Marcos Witt, "Marcos Witt on the Change in Music and Lyrics of Worship among Hispanics," interview by Jaime Lázaro, Calvin Institute of Christian Worship, November 21, 2013, https://worship.calvin.edu/resources/resource-library/marcos-witt-on-the-change-in-music-and-lyrics-of-worship-among-hispanics/.

worship leader and recording artist, was a keynote speaker at the annual "See His Glory" Praise & Worship training event at her church, West Angeles Church of God in Christ.[51] Throughout the 1990s her sessions paralleled standard Praise & Worship teaching with her dual focus on the practical aspects of leading worship (e.g., how to achieve good flow in a service through attentiveness to tempo and keys) and the theological underpinnings for Praise & Worship.[52] With respect to theology, McAllister covered topics that had long been considered important, such as explaining the prophetic nature of the "song of the Lord," the proper ordering of musicians as seen in David's arrangements in the tabernacle he had raised, David's role himself as prototypical worshiper and worship leader, the difference between praise and worship, and the various levels of praise based on the seven Hebrew words for praise. The last discussion climaxed with McAllister's treatment of *tehillah*, the word found in Psalm 22:3 and other verses.[53]

McAllister's story is useful for seeing how Praise & Worship circulated into and through the Black church. McAllister had acquired her Praise & Worship theology as a student at Oral Roberts University in Tulsa, Oklahoma, in the mid-1980s. After an initial exposure to Praise & Worship in that school's chapel services during the fall 1985 semester,[54] McAllister happened to hear Myles Munroe, a preacher from the Bahamas, speaking in a local church about the seven Hebrew words for praise. She hurriedly wrote down everything he said, filling her legal pad with Scripture references. She was hooked.

51. West Angeles was not the only African American congregation to hold such training events. Perfecting Church, a Detroit, congregation pastored by Marvin Winans, held an annual Praise & Worship Weekend each year during the 1990s rooted in the theology of Ps. 22:3 (Beverly Ferguson, email message to Lester Ruth, March 2, 2020; see also Deborah Smith Pollard, *When the Church Becomes Your Party* [Detroit: Wayne State University Press, 2008], 47). Interestingly, Perfecting Church purchased the building originally constructed by Myrtle Beall for Bethesda Missionary Temple.

52. Judith McAllister kindly showed us her teaching outlines for this event from 1991 to 1997. The information in the description above is based on those unpublished outlines.

53. McAllister, "Seven Levels of Praise." Again, as with Marcos Witt, this focus on a single individual is not meant to imply that there were no other significant African American theological voices at the time. Writings of contemporaneous voices would include the following in chronological order of publication: John W. Stevenson, *The 2nd Flood: The Discipline of Worship* (Shippensburg, PA: Destiny Image, 1990); Kenneth C. Ulmer, *A New Thing: A Theological and Personal Look at the Full Gospel Baptist Church Fellowship* (Los Angeles: FaithWay, 1994); Joseph Garlington, *Worship: The Pattern of Things in Heaven* (Shippensburg, PA: Destiny Image, 1997); Rodney A. Teal, *Reflections on Praise & Worship from a Biblical Perspective* (privately published, 1999), reprinted in *Readings in African American Church Music and Worship*, vol. 2, ed. James Abbington (Chicago: GIA, 2014); and Myles Munroe, *The Purpose and Power of Praise & Worship* (Shippensburg, PA: Destiny Image, 2000).

54. The reader should remember that a year earlier, this university had hosted the International Worship Symposium (see chap. 2).

McAllister skipped classes the following week, instead going to the university library and poring over Bible study tools to search out scriptural passages on praise. That week "changed my life," McAllister later said.[55]

In 1988 McAllister graduated from Oral Roberts University, moved to Los Angeles, and eventually joined the music staff at West Angeles Church of God in Christ, a flagship megachurch. When she arrived, she discovered that its pastor, Charles Blake, had already been teaching on the restoration of the tabernacle of David and encouraging the church's music minister, Patrick Henderson, to explore Praise & Worship more fully. This Henderson did by visiting congregations like Jack Hayford's Church on the Way, reading Hayford's books and other descriptions of the reestablishment of praise,[56] and learning new Praise & Worship songs. Henderson even had some exposure to the Latter Rain–rooted International Worship Symposium when the meetings were held in Southern California.[57] To achieve the specific musical technique needed for flowing song medleys, Henderson drew on his past concert tour experience playing with Leon Russell,[58] a rock artist who often wove medleys into his concerts. From that concert experience, Henderson knew how timbre, theme, a combination of new and old songs, and overall musical feel could work in song medleys.

The combination of Blake with Henderson—and, eventually, McAllister—would be a potent one. Through their efforts, their West Angeles congregation had its own worship transformed into a vibrant form of Praise & Worship that impacted area churches, including other prominent Black megachurches.[59]

---

55. McAllister, interview.

56. Specifically, Blake gave Henderson a copy of the following book to read: Paul W. Wohlgemuth, *Rethinking Church Music*, rev. ed. (Carol Stream, IL: Hope, 1981), 61–70. Wohlgemuth was a Mennonite music professor at Oral Roberts University. Patrick Henderson, interview by Lester Ruth and Lim Swee Hong, November 8, 2018. Cf. Paul W. Wohlgemuth, "Praise Singing," *Hymn* 31, no. 1 (January 1987): 18–23.

57. See Adam Perez, "'All Hail King Jesus': The *International Worship Symposium* and the Making of Praise and Worship History, 1977–1989" (ThD diss., Duke Divinity School, 2021), 173n101.

58. Henderson, interview. Henderson was a keyboardist for Russell. On occasion, the two would share twin grand pianos on stage. See Patrick Henderson, "Praising God for What He Has Done, Worshipping Him for Who He Is," in *Messengers: Portraits of African American Ministers, Evangelists, Gospel Singers, and Other Messengers of the Word*, ed. David Ritz (New York: Doubleday, 2005), 199.

59. Birgitta J. Johnson, "'This Is Not the Warm-Up Act!': How Praise and Worship Reflects Expanding Musical Traditions and Theology in a Bapticostal Charismatic African American Megachurch," in *The Spirit of Praise: Music and Worship in Global Pentecostal-Charismatic Christianity*, ed. Monique M. Ingalls and Amos Yong (University Park: Pennsylvania State University Press, 2015), 120. Johnson has also documented this church's transition to Praise & Worship in "Singing Down Walls of Race, Ethnicity, and Tradition in an African American Megachurch," *Liturgy* 33, no. 3 (2018): 37–45; "Back to the Heart of Worship: Praise and

Perhaps an even more widespread impact of this congregation, however, came through release of three recordings featuring Praise & Worship medleys: the *Saints in Praise* CDs, which were released in 1989 (volume 1), 1990 (volume 2), and 1992 (volume 3) and were significant projects spearheaded and produced by Patrick Henderson.[60] Although the congregation's leadership was anxious about the acceptance of the first volume, it exceeded all expectations and won industry honors.[61] More importantly for the history of Praise & Worship, the church's recordings modeled how to achieve good flow in medleys within long periods of congregational singing, doing so with a musical sound that fit the sensibilities of Black churches and their propensity to use choirs and keyboards. Perhaps the testimony of another African American megachurch pastor provides the best witness to the recordings' impact: "'Saints in Praise' launched a revolution within the black church" in teaching it how to do Praise & Worship.[62]

The efforts of Stream of Praise Music Ministries, Marcos Witt, and West Angeles Church of God in Christ (and comparable ministries) brought about another surge of Praise & Worship in the late 1980s and early 1990s. This liturgical phenomenon, which had already acquired great momentum in White congregations, swelled with the inclusion of a wider range of races.

Mainstreaming Praise & Worship

After 1985 the momentum of shared theology and practices across a range of church bodies increased the extent of Praise & Worship. In both White and non-White churches, the increase came from the burgeoning number of people and institutions teaching and promoting this way of worship. In other

---

Worship Music in a Los Angeles African-American Megachurch," *Black Music Research Journal* 31, no. 1 (Spring 2011): 105–29; and "'Oh, for a Thousand Tongues to Sing': Music and Worship in African American Megachurches of Los Angeles, California" (PhD diss., University of California Los Angeles, 2008).

60. The CDs were handled by Sparrow Records. The project began with a dream of Billy Ray Hearn, the CEO of Sparrow Records, who had a desire to do an African American Praise & Worship album. When he contacted Andraé Crouch and Bill Maxwell (a producer and drummer for Crouch), Hearn was told that West Angeles was *the* congregation to do the album. Hearn called Patrick Henderson, who consulted with Blake. This backstory was gained from the interview of Henderson. For a musical analysis of *Saints in Praise*, volume 1, see Lim and Ruth, *Lovin' on Jesus*, 71.

61. Indeed, the album won the 1990 award for traditional gospel album of the year from the Gospel Music Association. See Johnson, "Oh, for a Thousand Tongues," 352.

62. Kenneth C. Ulmer, "Transformational Worship in the Life of a Church," in *Worship That Changes Lives: Multidisciplinary and Congregational Perspectives on Spiritual Transformation*, ed. Alexis D. Abernethy (Grand Rapids: Baker Academic, 2008), 184.

words, there was an increasing mainstreaming of Praise & Worship. However, even as Praise & Worship grew more extensive, there remained a clarity about both why it should be pursued (the theology connecting God's presence to corporate praise) and how it could be done (the musical techniques and skills needed for this liturgical form).

Of course, one would have expected that clarity from the earlier generation of Praise & Worship teachers, figures like Judson Cornwall, LaMar Boschman, Barry and Steve Griffing, and David Fischer, all of whom continued their teaching ministry into the late 1980s. Indeed, some of these teachers launched into new endeavors, as Boschman did with the creation in 1986 of his annual training event, originally known as the National Worship Leaders' Institute and advertised as a "Holy Spirit school for worship leaders."[63]

This first generation of promoters would soon be joined by teachers like Marcos Witt and Judith McAllister, as well as by Kent Henry, John Stevenson, Tom Kraeuter, Vivien Hibbert, and Bob Sorge among many others. Sorge's work exemplifies the range of outlets for promotion these advocates for Praise & Worship were using. One of his outlets for teaching Praise & Worship was his travels as a conference speaker. Another was the publication of short articles in Praise & Worship–based magazines like *Psalmist*, which were emerging in this period. Perhaps his strongest influence came as a result of his 1987 book, *Exploring Worship: A Practical Guide to Praise and Worship*. For many people, the book would be a seminal one, codifying their initial explorations into Praise & Worship.[64]

In both content and structure, *Exploring Worship* was representative of Praise & Worship by the late 1980s. Even though the subtitle labels the book as a practical guide, Sorge actually begins with seven chapters of biblical theology. The first chapter, not surprisingly, answers the question "What is Praise?" The second chapter is called "Entering the Presence of God." Sorge's approach is classic Praise & Worship theologizing:

> It is true that God inhabits our praise, that he dwells and abides in our praise, in the sense that he loves our praises, bathes in our praises, and surrounds himself with our praises. He so delights in and relishes our praises. And note the NASB [i.e., the New American Standard Bible] rendering, which is truer to the original Hebrew: he is "enthroned" on our praises. He is made King when

63. LaMar Boschman, interview by Lim Swee Hong and Lester Ruth, August 3, 2017. See also the advertising insert in *Psalmist* 2, no. 2 (February/March 1987). This annual training event would eventually be renamed the International Worship Institute.

64. Bob Kauflin, interview by Lester Ruth and Lim Swee Hong, October 17, 2019. Sorge's book would be reprinted multiple times and, by the late 1990s, translated into Spanish, Chinese, Russian, Korean, Indonesian, and Bulgarian.

we praise him, for we are declaring his Kingship and Lordship to a world that does not recognize him as Lord.[65]

The second half of Sorge's book provided practical guidelines for implementing Praise & Worship as a worship leader, touching on topics like "The Art of Leading Worship," "The Worship-Leading Team," "Planning the Worship Service," "Sources for New Choruses," "Chord Progressions in Worship," and "Chordal Hand Signs." Sorge concluded the book by providing a list of strong choruses organized by tempo and key as well as a list of sources for new choruses. Taken as a whole, *Exploring Worship* exemplified the mature form of integrated theologizing and cultivation of musical technique that propelled Praise & Worship in this period.

In addition to publishing a book, Sorge exemplified a new outlet for teaching Praise & Worship, an outlet that would be especially useful for teaching technical musical skills—that is, multimedia resources. About the same time as his book's publication in the late 1980s, Sorge released a teaching resource, *Piano Improvisation Techniques for Worship*, as a two-tape set (in VHS videocassette tapes).[66] Recorded in a church sanctuary on a handheld camera, Sorge's videos sought to help pianists learn to make music by "ear" rather than by relying on notated music scores. His teaching encompasses music theory that enables this approach, such as introducing the circle of fifths, as well as keyboard performance practices like the stride piano style from the jazz piano musical tradition.[67] He spent time explaining the role of the pianist and the sonic abilities of the piano (that is, the instrument) to provide melody, rhythm, and harmonic leadership in music making. He emphasized the need to develop critical listening skills, including the ability to discern chord types, harmonic progression, and so forth.

Through this approach, Sorge worked on introducing to the learning keyboardist music-making devices that create sonic texture and ambience to enhance Praise & Worship, especially during times of "free worship" when

---

65. Sorge, *Exploring Worship*, 33.

66. Bob Sorge, *Piano Improvisation Techniques for Worship* (Canandaigua, NY: n.d.), 2 videocassettes (VHS). Sorge's tape set was near the start of a growing stream of media resources intended to teach the musical technique for leading Praise & Worship. For example, Kent Henry soon contributed a series of tapes aiming for piano and guitar players at several levels of playing ability. See the advertisement in *Psalmist* 4, no. 3 (June/July 1989): 32; or on the back cover of *Psalmist* 4, no. 5 (October/November 1989).

67. For an explanation of what these are musically, see "Circle of Fifths Guide: Why and How Is It Used?," *Musicnotes Now* (blog), accessed February 5, 2021, https://www.musicnotes.com /now/tips/circle-of-fifths-guide/; and Noah Kellman, "5 Killer Stride Exercises [Jazz Piano Tutorial]," YouTube video, June 25, 2020, 8:08, https://www.youtube.com/watch?v=6kUq5RqUu _8&feature=youtu.be&ab_channel=NoahKellman.

musicians respond to the movement of God among the congregation. Examples of these techniques included the use of arpeggios, modulations, and chord progressions. Sorge's emphases moved the pianist away from the printed page and to "feeling the music" and producing music fitting for the moment. (Though this use of jazz piano music technique for worship was exceptional for much music making in White worship settings, it had been prevalent in African American churches for some time.)

Sorge's publications, while influential, were not the only resources released in this period. The rising level of Praise & Worship was matched—and surely, in part, caused—by a growing body of published literature advocating and teaching this form of worship in its theological and technical dimensions. Whereas about a dozen books on Praise & Worship were published up to the mid-1970s and about thirty from 1975 to 1984, more than sixty new books were disseminated from 1985 to 1995. While many of these later books were general treatments (like Sorge's volume), others were more specialized in their focus: these included volumes on mime, books on banners and dance, study Bibles emphasizing Praise & Worship, and hymnals organized so as to make song medleys easier to construct.[68]

Magazines dedicated to Praise & Worship also appeared in this period. Chuck Fromm, associated with Maranatha! Music, began two of these magazines: *Worship Times* in 1986 and *Worship Leader* in 1992.[69] Another journal, *Psalmist*, began in 1985 as part of the teaching ministry of Kent Henry. Henry's connections across Praise & Worship allowed this magazine to be a combined clearinghouse and meeting ground for Praise & Worship in its ten-year print run. Its contributors read like a who's who of Praise & Worship of the late 1980s and early 1990s, featuring well-established teachers (e.g., Charlotte Baker, Judson Cornwall, Steve Griffing)[70] and those whose influence was still rising (e.g., John Wimber,[71] Tom Brooks, Mike Bickle, Gerrit Gustafson, Don Moen, and

68. Respectively, Todd Farley, *The Silent Prophet: The Prophetic Ministry of the Human Body* (Shippensburg, PA: Destiny Image, 1989); Lora Allison, *Celebration: Banners, Dance and Holiness in Worship* (New Wilmington, DE: SonRise, 1987); Jack W. Hayford, ed., *Spirit Filled Life Bible* (Nashville: Nelson, 1991); and Barker, *Songs for Praise & Worship*.

69. *Worship Times* was a newsletter published quarterly for subscribers to Maranatha! Music's early copyright clearinghouse, Music Net. *Worship Leader* remains an active periodical.

70. It is interesting and important that the magazine did not indicate Latter Rain connections for any of this older generation of teachers. The omission was likewise reflected in virtually all other sources for the period. That lack of mention indicates that eventually Praise & Worship as a liturgical form had been freed of the possible taint attributed to it because of its association with the Latter Rain movement. Remember that, in its early years, the Latter Rain movement had been rejected by established Pentecostal denominations and its adherents derided for being part of it.

71. Wimber's active role in teaching about worship seems to have increased in the second half of the 1980s as compared to his earlier activity on this topic.

David Ruis). Regardless of the
contributing authors, however,
the magazine routinely had
three recurring features: articles
and testimonies reaffirming the
core tenets of Praise & Worship theology, articles on how
to do Praise & Worship musically, and resources to support
Praise & Worship.

Regarding the last of these
recurring features, *Psalmist*
regularly ran advertisements
for the surging number of
Praise & Worship conferences.
It also carried a list of upcoming conferences compiled by its
managing editor, Tom Kraeuter. The high-water mark for
the conference list probably
came in the magazine's fifth

Figure 4.4. The cover of the second *Psalmist* magazine (vol. 1, no. 2), 1985

anniversary issue for April/May 1990. The magazine's five thousand subscribers received a list of sixteen national and regional conferences to be held
in the near future.[72] The magazine also occasionally ran composite lists of
Praise & Worship resources. The 1988 list included seventeen organizations
providing resources for Praise & Worship. Some were well known (e.g., Maranatha! Music, Vineyard Worship Resource Center, Scripture in Song, Zion-
Song Music, and Revival Press, a part of Destiny Image Publishers), whereas
others reflected the growing edge of Praise & Worship developments like
handling copyright licensing for songs (LicenSing! and StarPraise Ministries).[73]
The growing number of sources for Praise & Worship materials, many of
which also purchased advertisements in the magazine, indicates the surging
level of Praise & Worship by the late 1980s. In fact, for the reader looking
for an easier path to access the increasing number of resources, there was
one mail-order company whose twenty-four-page catalog sought to make
the search simpler. The name of this company should come as no surprise:
it was the Praise Connection.

72. See *Psalmist* 5, no. 2 (April/May 1990): 30.
73. "Praise and Worship Resource Organizations," *Psalmist* 3, no. 4 (August/September
1988): 30–31. Compare the list in Sorge, *Exploring Worship*, 261–66.

Although the number of resources to bolster Praise & Worship was rapidly increasing in this period, two deserve special attention for the important roles they played in the history of this way of worship. Each provided critical infrastructure that rapidly propelled Praise & Worship forward in the latter half of the 1980s and has continued to shape it ever since.

The first of the two resources, Integrity's Hosanna! Music, sprang innocently enough from requests made to a well-established charismatic magazine, *New Wine*, to provide cassette tapes of choruses to its readers.[74] That this "music tape ministry" flowed out of the fundamental

Figure 4.5. Insert from *Psalmist* magazine (vol. 7, no. 2), showing resources for sale in 1992

theological convictions of Praise & Worship was crystal clear from its first promotion in a two-page advertisement in *New Wine*'s June 1985 issue, which went out to the magazine's sixty thousand subscribers. Under a bold heading ("*New Wine* Introduces Hosanna!") came a statement of theological purpose: "A New Praise and Worship Music Tape Program Designed to Bring You Into the Presence of God."[75] In the opening announcement, this purpose was expressed twice more—each time as a theological aspiration. A sidebar describing the historical origins of the new tape ministry expressed its creators' hope: "It's our desire that as you sing along with these tapes, you'll be drawn into the presence of the Lord." Similarly, an endorsement from one of the magazine's main figures, Bob Mumford, relied on a standard theological framing of praise's potential: "Praise and worship are the highest callings of

74. The best historical overview of these origins is Adam Perez, "Sounding God's Enthronement in Worship: The Early History and Theology of Integrity's Hosanna! Music," in *Essays on the History of Contemporary Praise and Worship*, ed. Lester Ruth (Eugene, OR: Pickwick, 2020), 74–94. Our account is very dependent on this groundbreaking essay by Perez.

75. *New Wine* 17, no. 6 (June 1985): 6–7. *New Wine* was a publication of Integrity Communications, a company located in Mobile, Alabama. Thus, the tape series became known as Integrity's Hosanna! Music.

a believer. Music can either help or hinder you from entering God's presence. I believe that the music in this tape ministry will help you fulfill your calling and draw you into His presence."[76]

A connection between this music and God's presence soon became a regular tagline used to promote the tape series in other venues. The advertisement in the February/March 1986 issue of *Psalmist* magazine, for example, used the same affirmation found in the series' opening announcement the previous year: this was a tape ministry designed to bring listeners into the presence of God.[77] Soon, increasing numbers of subscribers were paying $7.95 per tape to receive a cassette tape every other month.

The Hosanna! tape series represented a convergence of several Praise & Worship currents in the mid-1980s.[78] The move toward the tape series began when *New Wine* conducted an interest survey of its readers and learned that there was a desire for more articles on Praise & Worship. Consequently, the magazine ran a three-part series of articles by Terry Law, the prosperity gospel evangelist who had become a vocal advocate for Praise & Worship (see chap. 3). Law's articles led the magazine's leadership to consider providing its readers with recordings of actual worship music—not simply, as historian Adam Perez has put it, "so that they could demonstrate or reference the kind of musical worship that was discussed in Law's articles but rather so that people could, through the music, have an experience of the presence of God."[79]

The search for suitable recordings that could be released was satisfied when the magazine's leadership had Law and Don Moen, who led the musical group associated with Terry Law, connect with Tom Brooks, a music producer at Grace World Outreach Center in St. Louis, Missouri, and a close friend of Kent Henry (who also had been associated with this church at one time). Brooks's congregation had undergone its own revitalization through Praise & Worship in the early 1980s and Brooks had made several recordings of its services. One of these would become the first Hosanna! Music release, *Behold*

76. Quoted in *New Wine* 17, no. 6 (June 1985): 6–7. Bob Mumford was one of five Pentecostal teachers known as the Fort Lauderdale Five. It was this group that launched *New Wine* magazine and would organize as the Christian Growth Ministries. These teachers would be instrumental in the development of the controversy known as the Shepherding Movement. For more information, see S. David Moore, *The Shepherding Movement: Controversy and Charismatic Ecclesiology* (London: T&T Clark, 2003).

77. *Psalmist* 1, no. 5 (February/March 1986): 32.

78. See Perez, "Sounding God's Enthronement," 80–82.

79. Perez, "Sounding God's Enthronement," 81. According to Perez, providing this kind of experience through music was the expressed aim of Mike Coleman, the president and publisher of *New Wine*.

His Majesty. Brooks himself played a key role in subsequent tapes, arranging, producing, recording, and regularly playing keyboard for the entirety of the series, which ran into the mid-1990s.[80] Kent Henry also became involved in Hosanna! tape series, serving as the worship leader for the third release, *All Hail King Jesus.* Don Moen would become the icon for the series.

The Hosanna! tapes were wildly successful. By the third year, using only direct-to-consumer marketing, sales for each tape had reached 150,000 units.[81] By seven years after its launch, the series reportedly had distributed more than fifteen million recordings, which could be heard in sixty-two nations.[82] Even after such success, the original theological motivation remained strong. Explaining his goals when producing the tapes, Brooks in 1993 highlighted not only a desire to supply church musicians with usable songs and introduce them to new sounds in music, but also to promulgate Praise & Worship's underlying theological conviction: "Our ultimate goal is to lead people into the presence of God, for it's in His presence where people can be healed, saved and delivered from sin."[83]

Because of its wide dissemination, Integrity's Hosanna! tape series provided a key infrastructure for Praise & Worship after 1985 by supplying a steady source of singable songs. This role was increased by its other products, including lead sheets, songbooks, and full orchestrations, which were regularly advertised in *Psalmist* magazine and offered to congregations wishing to use the songs they had heard on the tapes.[84] The series also contributed to the development of Praise & Worship by helping congregations hear a certain approach to the underlying theology of praise. Although Integrity's music products would eventually offer a range of musical styles, its early recordings intentionally sought to express sonically a sense of praise as the enthronement of God,[85] which was one of the two readings of Psalm 22:3.

However, by the mid-1980s, Praise & Worship practitioners began to realize they were courting potential legal trouble by using all the choruses circulating among churches. This growing awareness eventually led to the second major infrastructure development. The problem arose from a standard Praise & Worship practice: instead of having worshipers hold a published songbook

80. Perez, "Sounding God's Enthronement," 80.

81. Perez, "Sounding God's Enthronement," 74.

82. Tom Brooks, "An Interview with Tom Brooks," interview by Marcie Gold, *Psalmist* 8, no. 4 (July/August 1993): 18. Note that Brooks was one of the original contributors for *Psalmist* when it started.

83. Brooks, "Interview with Tom Brooks," 20.

84. Eventually, Integrity would provide leadership in Praise & Worship by maintaining a large cadre of songwriters as well as venturing into the education of worship leaders.

85. Perez, "Sounding God's Enthronement," 88–91.

or hymnbook, congregations routinely appropriated choruses from wherever and made their own unauthorized reproduction of each song on a transparency to use with an overhead projector. However, after some well-publicized lawsuits in which publishers sued over the unauthorized use of copyrighted songs, pastors and musicians began to worry about what they were doing. A string of magazine articles warning of the potential legal liability heightened this anxiety. (The first issue of *Psalmist* included one such warning;[86] articles on the same topic followed regularly.) Because of the multiple songs used in a typical period of Praise & Worship, the legal liability that even a single service generated could have been devastating if a church was sued.

A congregation could seek permission from each copyright holder of every song, which some did, paying whatever fee the holder required. At least one congregation (a church outside Pittsburgh, Pennsylvania) hired a full-time staff person to handle the copyright clearances for the songs it was singing.[87] Another, in Missouri, put up a chart with the congregation's favorite songs and asked worshipers to "adopt" a song and donate the money needed to pay its copyright holder.[88] With the typical fee per song ranging from twenty-five to fifty dollars and with a constant rotation of new and old songs, such song-by-song solutions were cumbersome, expensive, and soon outdated. Moreover, congregations had to determine who held the copyright and how to contact this holder—often a difficult process in pre-internet days. Many songs circulated widely and wildly, making a search for their copyright pedigree nearly hopeless. Tom Kraeuter, the worship leader at the Missouri church mentioned earlier, aptly summarized the exasperation this situation caused: "The vast majority of the songs were songs that were learned by somebody who had heard them from somebody else who heard them from somebody else. . . . Trying to find who held the copyright on these songs was crazy."[89]

Of course, the needed infrastructure solution was to try to find a way to pay a single subscription fee to a single source and gain permission to use the songs controlled by that source. Not surprisingly, *Psalmist* magazine began to carry announcements, advertisements, and articles about companies offering

---

86. "Noteworthy News," *Psalmist* 1, no. 1 (1985): 20. This article noted how one church had lost such a suit and been forced to sell its parking lot to pay the fees for its unpermitted song reproduction. More troubling, however, was the 1984 award in a lawsuit against the Roman Catholic Archdiocese of Chicago in which the publisher, F. E. L. Publications, was initially awarded over three million dollars.

87. Kauflin, interview. The congregation was Northway Christian Community in Wexford, Pennsylvania.

88. Kraeuter, interview. The congregation was Christian Outreach Center in Hillsboro, Missouri.

89. Kraeuter, interview.

such a service. Its first issue in 1988, for example, had information on Music Net from Maranatha! Music, on another company named LicenSing!, and on yet a third, StarPraise Ministries, whose prepaid, pullout send-me-more-information postcard touted it as "a legal answer for transparency usage."[90] The difficulty with several of these early companies was that their collections of songs were limited.[91] It was on that point that StarPraise soon gained a competitive advantage.

StarPraise Ministries began in a congregation with one of the strongest heritages in Praise & Worship: Bible Temple in Portland, Oregon, pastored by Dick Iverson (see chap. 2). StarPraise's origins were in the late 1970s as church staff began to document the copyrights for the songs the congregation was using, initially keeping this information on handwritten note cards. Eventually the information was compiled to form StarPraise's original database. Because Bible Temple was the center of a broader network of Praise & Worship, StarPraise was easily promoted in this network at the church's conferences for music ministers and pastors.[92]

StarPraise launched in May 1985.[93] For three years it worked as a prototype, with a fairly low public profile. Nonetheless, the membership grew to almost 1,600 churches. In January 1988, it became an independent organization, changing its name to Christian Copyright Licensing Inc. (hereafter CCLI) in May of that same year. The competitive advantage for StarPraise/CCLI came from its discussions beginning in April 1988 with the Church Music Publishers' Association, an umbrella organization for the industry. By August, that organization had endorsed CCLI's program, giving CCLI a chance to begin full, public operations

90. See *Psalmist* 3, no. 1 (February/March 1988): 15, 17. StarPraise Ministries' postcard was between pp. 18 and 19.

91. Music Net from Maranatha! Music only covered songs from Maranatha! Music, Scripture in Song, Thankyou Music, Celebration, and some "other major companies." LicenSing! only covered songs by Bill and Gloria Gaither, Steve Fry, Jack Hayford, Greg Nelson, Dick and Melodie Tunney, John Michael Talbot, Anne Herring, Lanny Wolfe, Dallas Holm, "and others." LicenSing!'s ad encouraged people to write to get its "complete listing of over 120 songs."

92. We are indebted to Adam Perez for this research. See especially his dissertation "'All Hail King Jesus.'"

93. StarPraise began with twenty-five churches, which signed up at the Northwest Ministers Conference held at Bible Temple. In September 1985 (with fifty-three churches having joined), it sent out its first music book publication (Howard Rachinski, email message to Lester Ruth, October 2, 2020). See also the sidebar article by Howard Rachinski titled "Christian Copyright Licensing, Inc.: One Solution," *Psalmist* 4, no. 1 (February/March 1989): 21. Rachinski's adjoining article ("Relief for Your Copyright Headache," 20–21, 27) laid out the larger legal situation that made Christian Copyright Licensing Inc. a useful salve for the "copyright headache." See also "All about Howard Rachinski," personal website, accessed February 5, 2021, https://howard rachinski.com/about/. At some time the name of the company was changed to Christian Copyright Licensing International.

in October 1988. For an annual fee ranging from seventy-five dollars for churches under one hundred in attendance to three hundred dollars for churches over three thousand, a copyright license from CCLI allowed a congregation a variety of cleared uses for authorized publishers' songs, including the all-important making of "slides, transparencies and any other means of projection." Howard Rachinski, the music minister at Bible Temple and someone with his own deep pedigree in Praise & Worship,[94] was CCLI's first president and CEO.

With the advent of a licensing agency with a large corpus of songs, countless congregations exhaled in relief, the fear of lawsuits gone. In addition, this solution meant screens would continue as a permanent feature of an increasing number of sanctuaries, and CCLI emerged as and remained a dominant feature of Praise & Worship infrastructure.[95]

The company's first list of songs reported as most used by the churches between October 1988 and April 1989 highlighted songs that evidenced a clear praise-to-presence theology. Indeed, the lyrics of the top four songs on this list themselves could have served as a medley based on Psalm 100:4, with emphases on thanksgiving, praise, and adoration. The number one song in reported usage was "I Exalt Thee" (Pete Sanchez Jr.), number two was "We Bring the Sacrifice of Praise" (Kirk Dearman), number three was "All Hail King Jesus" (Dave Moody), and number four was "Give Thanks" (Henry Smith). Thus, Praise & Worship's core theological commitments were embedded even in its growing infrastructure.

A Lurking Danger

Even as Praise & Worship surged in both numbers and developments between 1985 and 1995, a danger began to lurk. The peril arose from within the growth

94. Rachinski grew up with Reg Layzell, the key instigator of the praise-to-presence theology, as his pastor. See Howard Rachinski, "From Praise to Worship," in *An Anthology of Articles on Restoring Praise & Worship to the Church*, ed. David K. Blomgren, Dean Smith, and Douglas Christoffel (Shippensburg, PA: Revival, 1989), 135–36. Rachinski attended the Bible college attached to Layzell's Vancouver church, Glad Tidings, and his parents, Ida and Ernie Rachinski, were some of Layzell's original parishioners in British Columbia and served as pastors of Glad Tidings' church plant in Abbotsford. Ernie Rachinski had also served as Layzell's choir director from 1953 to 1963. Indeed, Rachinski's mother-in-law had been a student at the school in North Battleford (see chap. 1) at which the original 1948 Latter Rain revival broke out. Rachinski, interview; Hugh Layzell and Audrey Layzell, *Sons of His Purpose: The Interweaving of the Ministry of Reg Layzell, and His Son, Hugh, during a Season of Revival* (San Bernardino, CA: privately published, 2012), 221; Fran and Dave Huebert, interview by Lester Ruth, January 7, 2018.

95. For an assessment of CCLI's role and impact, see Wen Reagan, "Christian Copyright Licensing, Inc.," in *The Encyclopedia of Christianity in the United States*, ed. George Thomas Kurian and Mark A. Lamport (Lanham, MD: Rowman & Littlefield, 2016), 530–31.

itself. By the time of its swelling in the late 1980s, the standard form of Praise & Worship had such clear features and practices, bolstered by a growing body of teaching on how to do them, that this form could be followed and adopted without its underlying theology and its expectation for dynamic encounter with God. The danger was that Praise & Worship would be adopted without its grounding in a biblical theology.

The danger did not go unnoticed at the time. A piece in a 1987 issue of *Psalmist* magazine, for example, worried that Praise & Worship had "for all practical purposes become a tradition" or a new "liturgy," terms with negative connotations in most Pentecostal and Charismatic circles.[96] Soon after, longtime worship leader Tom Kraeuter wondered whether the theological concept of Psalm 22:3 (God inhabits the praises of his people) was so "overused" that some were at risk of forgetting its truth and real power. He warned others to not take this oft-quoted sentiment for granted.[97] By the early 1990s, Vineyard worship leader Eddie Espinosa too was worrying that all the developments of the 1980s had not been good ones. Framing the issues in a typical Vineyard way, Espinosa worried that the decade had been a time in which people had learned about "worship itself" rather than about the better thing of "worshipping the Lord Jesus." He continued, "We began to enjoy worship instead of enjoying the presence of God and the intimacy with the Lord Jesus Christ. Many of us fell more in love with the process of worship instead of falling more and more in love with the Lord Jesus."[98] Thus, Espinosa cast the threat in terms of a misdirected love.

Of course, these worship leaders' warnings were nothing new in the long history of worship. Leaders have often challenged worshipers to not lose sight of the real object and subject of worship: God. Nonetheless, the caveats expressed by Kraeuter and Espinosa manifested how by the late 1980s Praise & Worship had entered a developed phase, one in which the novelty could wear off and people could forget the whole point, according to its theology.

Churches practicing Praise & Worship could have easily fallen into this error. Ironically, the growing wealth of teaching resources on *how* to do Praise & Worship, especially in terms of required musical technique, heightened the risk. The jeopardy seemed particularly acute as mainstream evangelical publishers began to distribute materials. Although the *Songs for Praise & Worship* songbook, released by mainstream evangelical publisher Word Music in 1992, included sections on the classic theological moorings for Praise &

96. "Worship Analysis," *Psalmist* 2, no. 5 (Fall 1987): 28.
97. Tom Kraeuter, "Music: Emotionalism or Real Spiritual Power?," *Psalmist* 2, no. 6 (December 1987/January 1988): 7.
98. Eddie Espinosa, "Worship in the 90's," *Psalmist* 6, no. 2 (April/May 1991): 20.

Worship, for example, it also provided 131 pre-chosen song medleys that a church musician could have simply appropriated without the theology.[99] Similarly, Barry Liesch's abbreviated presentation for ordering a service based on the Vineyard model, printed in 1995 in a book sponsored by the evangelical magazines *Leadership* and *Christianity Today*, lacked the rich underpinning of biblical theology found in his earlier treatment of the same.[100]

This divorce between the form of Praise & Worship and its underlying theology would only increase as Praise & Worship swelled in the mid-1990s and began to converge with the other river of Contemporary Worship.

Large Event Propulsion

By the mid-1990s, Praise & Worship—in form, if not in theology—had swept the field, flooding all of Pentecostalism and, increasingly, some of evangelicalism. In the middle of that decade three large Pentecostal and evangelical happenings—the revival known as the "Toronto Blessing," the Brownsville Revival, and the Promise Keepers rallies—show us how widespread Praise & Worship had become. These events helped disseminate Praise & Worship even more, sometimes directly by teachings and recordings and other times indirectly by allowing the uninitiated to experience this way of worship for the first time.

Several commonalities tie these events to each other in the historical development of Praise & Worship. For one thing, each was large in terms of the numbers of people participating: each reportedly attracted at least hundreds of thousands within its first few years. Moreover, two of the three events (the ones overtly Pentecostal in context and public face: the Toronto Blessing and the Brownsville Revival) presumed Praise & Worship from the beginning and the other, Promise Keepers, soon incorporated it as its standard approach. Thus, each of the events provided an opportunity for new worshipers unfamiliar with Praise & Worship to experience and appropriate it. And, in the case of one of the events (Promise Keepers), this indirect form of teaching was supplemented by intentional sessions to hand over Praise & Worship theology and practices.

The Toronto Blessing was a revival that emerged in the Toronto Airport Vineyard, a Canadian Vineyard church, in January 1994. The revival's name

99. See Barker, *Songs for Praise & Worship*, 530–48. Similarly, even *Psalmist* magazine suggested medleys in its presentation of new songs in every issue. The organization of songs into medleys had occurred as early as a 1981 album by Scripture in Song, *Songs of the Kingdom*. Similarly, in the same general time period, The Continentals' album *Come Bless the Lord* and two album/songbook combinations from Portland's Bible Temple, *Worship Alive*, provided medleys.

100. See Liesch, "Structure Runs through It." See also Liesch, *People in the Presence of God*.

was coined by media covering the phenomena that took place there, which had quickly drawn attention for their unusual nature. They included laughter, violent shaking, animal-like sounds, and massive numbers of people falling by the power of the Spirit (being "slain in the Spirit"). Thousands attended the nightly evening meetings for the first several years, and the revival spawned a series of conferences held around the world titled "Catch the Fire."[101] Those who visited the revival experienced not only the ecstatic demonstrations that attracted most of the attention but also a Vineyard style of worship. The musical sets were provided by the Toronto Airport Vineyard's own music team as well as by the music team from the nearby Thornhill Vineyard.[102]

While the public's eye was drawn to the dramatic evening meetings, other outlets were introducing pastors to Praise & Worship and teaching them to desire it for their congregations. In addition to the large-scale, intense evening sessions, the Toronto Airport Vineyard began to hold a smaller, more low-key weekly meeting for pastors from Toronto's greater metropolitan area.[103] The meetings pulled from the same song repertoire as the nighttime assemblies but reduced instrumentation to a keyboard. (A guitar was sometimes added.) The flow followed a standard shape, usually starting with lively praise about God and moving to more intimate statements of love expressed directly to God. The approach was classic Vineyard. Some ministers nourished by this Praise & Worship began to copy it in their congregations.

The year after the start of the revival in Toronto, another erupted in Pensacola, Florida, at the Brownsville Assembly of God. This revival, which began in June 1995, was similar to Toronto in how its nightly evening meetings attracted large crowds. Reportedly two and a half million people had visited the congregation by 1998.[104] After arriving, these liturgical pilgrims

---

101. For more information, see Hayford, *Charismatic Century*, 269–71; David Hilborn, ed., *"Toronto" in Perspective: Papers on the New Charismatic Wave of the Mid 1990s* (Carlisle, UK: Acute, 2001); and Michael McClymond, "After Toronto: Randy Clark's Global Awakening, Heidi and Rolland Baker's Iris Ministries, and the Post-1990s Global Charismatic Networks," *Pneuma* 38, no. 1–2 (2016): 50–76. See also multiple works by Martyn Percy: "Sweet Rapture: Subliminal Eroticism in Contemporary Charismatic Worship," *Theology and Sexuality* 6 (March 1997): 71–106; "The Morphology of Pilgrimage in the 'Toronto Blessing,'" *Religion* 28 (1998): 281–88; and "Adventure and Atrophy in a Charismatic Movement: Returning to the 'Toronto Blessing,'" in *Practicing the Faith: The Ritual Life of Pentecostal-Charismatic Christians*, ed. Martin Lindhardt (New York: Berghahn, 2011), 152–78. The revival was not without controversy. In late 1996 John Wimber, the leader of the larger Vineyard movement, withdrew his earlier endorsement; afterward, the Toronto congregation withdrew from the Vineyard association.

102. Alan Wiseman, interview by Lim Swee Hong and Lester Ruth, December 20, 2019.

103. Wiseman, interview.

104. Steve Rabey, *Revival in Brownsville: Pensacola, Pentecostalism, and the Power of American Revivalism* (Nashville: Nelson, 1998), 5.

experienced a congregational liturgy firmly rooted in Praise & Worship. They also experienced an eclectic convergence of songs and musical styles that reflected the breadth of Praise & Worship by the mid-1990s. Drawing especially on his background in gospel music, worship leader Lindell Cooley drew together songs from one current of Praise & Worship and combined them with the sound of another.[105] A favorite technique was arranging Vineyard songs to sound like gospel. One consequence of Cooley's leadership was the introduction of songs written by Vineyard composers to a wide breadth of Pentecostalism.

Cooley's approach to music was apparent in the Brownsville Assembly of God's live worship CD, recorded and released by Integrity's Hosanna! Music in 1996.[106] The sequencing of the songs reflected common practice: the CD starts with driving praise and slowly melts into adoring appreciation for the presence of God. Indeed, the set's opening affirmation ("We've come to praise him") and closing sentiments ("Right here in your presence is where I belong . . . I just want to thank you, Lord") truly represented the whole phenomenon of Praise & Worship. At the beginning of the CD, Cooley also reinforced classic Praise & Worship theology, using Old Testament typology, by a voice-over during the first song explaining that the congregation had "entered into the Temple to give you glory, Lord." The mixture of songs reflects Cooley's normal breadth of song selection. Pieces by two Black composers (Richard Smallwood's "We've Come to Praise Him" and Andraé Crouch's "Take a Little Time") bracketed songs by White songwriters like Andy Park, Paul Baloche, and Rich Mullins. The sound throughout, however, was thoroughly gospel.[107]

Promise Keepers rallies were the third happening that served to promote and reinforce Praise & Worship in this mature stage of its development. These rallies, which had begun as smaller events during the Promise Keepers

105. Rabey, *Revival in Brownsville*, 109; and Lindell Cooley, interview by Lim Swee Hong and Lester Ruth, July 6, 2015. Cooley, who is White, reports having continuing formative experiences in Black churches as he grew up. In the 1990s he also was influenced by West Angeles Church of God in Christ, according to Judith McAllister in her interview by us. Cooley notes in his interview that he was also influenced as a young adult by Grace World Outreach Center in St. Louis, the congregation that played a significant role in the origins of Integrity's Hosanna! Music.

106. *Revival at Brownsville*, recorded live in Pensacola, Florida (Mobile, AL: Integrity Music, 1996), CD.

107. To see Praise & Worship at this church, go to "Lindell Cooley—Live from Pensacola," YouTube video, posted by "Chaz Smith," September 20, 2017, 1:05:59, https://www.youtube .com/watch?v=22iASTH4p7E&feature=youtu.be&ab_channel=ChazSmith. For comparison, listen to this praise break in the African American gospel tradition: "Hot Praise Break—Tye Tribbett, Beverly Crawford, Ricky Dillard, Kevin Terry," YouTube video, posted by "The House," April 21, 2013, 8:51, https://www.youtube.com/watch?v=6lQex-inTN4&feature=youtu.be &ab_channel=TheHouse.

organization's first two years (1991 and 1992) to promote Christian disciple-ship among men, blossomed in 1993 into a large-scale sports stadium event involving approximately fifty thousand men. It was at this event that a business agreement with Maranatha! Music would launch these rallies as occasions for Praise & Worship teaching and dissemination.[108] The impact was large, given the numbers who attended the organization's gatherings. Through 2000 the organization had sponsored one hundred stadium conferences; by 2004 an estimated five million men had attended a Promise Keepers event.[109]

The juncture with Maranatha! Music came in December 1992 as Promise Keepers sought a company to provide a cassette of worship music to which the Promise Keepers name could be licensed for the upcoming 1993 rally.[110] Maranatha! acquired the order for seventy thousand cassette tapes to be distributed ahead of time so the men would know the songs when they ar-rived. As planning continued, so did Maranatha! Music's liturgical role. Soon Promise Keepers tapped the company to provide the music during the rally's worship and so Buddy Owens, the Maranatha! executive running point for the company, promised to put a band together. Maranatha! Music then arranged for the rally to be broadcast on several hundred radio stations. Eventually, Owens successfully pitched to the Promise Keepers organization the idea of releasing a live recording two months after the event.

This cassette was a compilation of songs and included excerpts of the spoken presentations too.[111] Its editing highlighted classic Praise & Worship sensibilities. The first track, an opening medley of three songs, focused the rally on praise, starting with a hymn ("Crown Him with Many Crowns") before flowing into two praise choruses: "All Hail King Jesus" (originally composed by Dave Moody at Glad Tidings Temple in Vancouver, Canada) and "We Bring the Sacrifice of Praise" (composed by Kirk Dearman at the Shady Grove Church in Texas). A short voice-over by the worship leader as the music transitioned between the last two songs of the medley, which was the first spoken element on the recording, expressed standard Praise &

---

108. Prior studies of Promise Keepers have tended to interpret the organization and its events in terms of ethics, social context, and social dynamics. They have not looked at the rallies as liturgical events. See L. Dean Allen, *Rise Up, O Men of God: The Men and Religion Forward Movement and Promise Keepers* (Macon, GA: Mercer University Press, 2002); and John P. Bartkowski, *The Promise Keepers: Servants, Soldiers, and Godly Men* (New Brunswick, NJ: Rutgers University Press, 2004).

109. Allen, *Rise Up*, 196; Bartkowski, *Promise Keepers*, 4.

110. This information on the liturgical aspect of Promise Keepers was gained from an in-terview of Buddy Owens, a Maranatha! Music official who became central in the worship at these rallies. Buddy Owens, interview by Lester Ruth, September 10, 2018.

111. *Promise Keepers 93 Live*, recorded live in Boulder, Colorado (Laguna Hills, CA: Ma-ranatha! Music, 1993), cassette tape.

Figure 4.6. Joseph Garlington (on the left), a longtime leader in Praise & Worship, with Gary Mitrik, his prayer partner, at the Promise Keepers rally in Pittsburgh's Three Rivers Stadium, 1996

Worship theology: it noted that there was a propriety to lifting up a "sacrifice of praise" in God's house. Track two ("We've Come to Praise You")[112] on the recording picked up the same theological notion.

After the 1993 event, Maranatha! and Promise Keepers both began receiving letters from pastors asking what kind of worship had been experienced at that rally. The letters noted that the men who had attended wanted their home congregations to have something close to what had been experienced. Consequently, the role played by Maranatha! deepened when the organizations decided to hold a teaching seminar on Praise & Worship the Friday morning before the start of the rally at Texas Stadium in October 1994. All pastors and worship leaders who were going to attend the rally were also invited to attend the seminar, which was held at a nearby church. Owens spoke at this meeting, explaining the theology of what the worship organizers were doing in the rallies, since he was the one putting the worship music together. The response was so enthusiastic that, starting in 1995, organizers decided to hold a teaching seminar at every city in which there was a rally. Consequently, Promise Keepers became another disseminator of Praise & Worship's theology and practices, contributing to its spread.

112. A 1991 song from Amy Grant, Beverly Darnall, Gary Chapman, and John Darnall.

Among the theological points Owens taught was the core commitment of Praise & Worship: that is, praise leads to presence. He expressed it in this way: "In Psalm 22:3 David tells us that the Lord is enthroned on the praises of his people. In other words, the throne of God rests on our praises. . . . We come into his presence when we worship him."[113] By the time Owens was sharing this idea, his teaching would have gotten a hearty amen from worshipers across fifty years of Praise & Worship.

113. Buddy Owens, *The Way of a Worshiper: Discover the Secret to Friendship with God* (Lake Forest, CA: Purpose Driven, 2002), 42.

part 2

—

the history of contemporary worship

five

—

subterranean stirrings, pre-1965

For two thousand years it has been found that those who sought to do the will of God were progressive in their methods.

— *Torrey Johnson, president of Youth for Christ International*[1]

As we saw in part I, the "river" of Praise & Worship sprang from a clear theological source at an identifiable time. In January 1946 Pentecostal preacher Reg Layzell began to teach the promise of praise as a way of experiencing the presence of God. For Layzell it was a promise resting on God's faithfulness, and thus worshipers should praise whether or not they feel like it or are led to do it. Layzell's theology was one with a clear biblical framing: Psalm 22:3 and Hebrews 13:15 became the linchpins in Praise & Worship's nascent theology. Soon Layzell and this theology were linked with the 1948 revival known as the Latter Rain revival and its subsequent movement. This movement confirmed experientially for its participants the theological linkage of praise and divine presence. It also provided the platform for this theology's wider dissemination as congregations across the continent were swept up into the movement.

Theological developments from the late 1960s through the 1970s provided a deepened reframing of Praise & Worship, especially in linking it with one

1. Torrey Johnson as quoted in Mel Larson, *Youth for Christ* (Grand Rapids: Zondervan, 1947), 130.

or the other of the two tabernacles seen in the Old Testament. Regardless of whether the tabernacle of Moses or of David was emphasized, these developments produced an increased emphasis on praise as musically expressed, a growing distinction between praise and worship as corporate acts, and a clearer sense of the exalted role of musicians to facilitate an experience of God's presence in a time of sung Praise & Worship. Adherents began to promulgate and teach this maturing form of Praise & Worship, and an increasing number of congregations from across Pentecostalism—and also, through the Charismatic movement especially, non-Pentecostal parishes— adopted it. Praise & Worship was increasing in the number of its "currents" and gaining momentum.

By the late 1980s Praise & Worship's theology had gained a stable—but not static—form, one able to undergird it as a clear, distinct way of worship. The number of practitioners swelled. A supporting infrastructure was in place. Outlets for teaching and learning abounded. Racial, ethnic, and denominational boundaries had been breached. The river was swollen, sweeping much of global Pentecostalism and even evangelicalism into it. Innumerable worshipers and their leaders affirmed with one voice, "If we praise him, God will come."

But Praise & Worship was not the only liturgical development in the second half of the twentieth century. There was another river in which people advocated a different idea—namely, "If we change it (meaning worship), they (meaning other people) will come." If the theology of Praise & Worship began with defining the dynamic connection between people and God, the second river—let us call it the river of Contemporary Worship, since those who advocated it were the ones who popularized this term[2]—focused on the practicalities of people-to-people concerns. Specifically, the theological idea of Contemporary Worship was a certain mindset of striving for effective outreach by Christians to others. Thus, Contemporary Worship's compelling theological drives were, on the one hand, seeking to be faithful to a sense of evangelistic mission and, on the other, anxiety that one's current worship practices were not contributing to maximum faithfulness toward this mission. In sum, because Christians have a responsibility to fulfill their mission, worship should be changed if it is not effective in reaching and transforming people. (Evangelicals who accepted this theology would speak of this transformation as "converting" or "saving" people.)[3] In this view, worship practices in which

2. As a technical term, "contemporary worship" only arose in the late 1960s, as will be discussed in chap. 6.
3. Note that here and elsewhere in the book we use the term "evangelical" without any sort of political connotation. By using "evangelical," we only wish to highlight the spiritual, doctrinal, and ecclesiastical dimensions of a certain kind of Christianity.

people cannot or do not want to participate are also suspect and thus ripe for change. Therefore, stated negatively, the theological waters of Contemporary Worship were driven by disquiet or dis-ease; stated positively, they were moved by the desire to be apostolic in a God-given purpose.

The differences between the two bodies of thought worked themselves out in a variety of ways. One of the most striking was in what the two groups of adherents believed the Bible principally provided for the church with respect to guiding worship. As we have seen, adherents of Praise & Worship relied on the Bible to provide a biblical theology of worship with specifically detailed practices. In contrast, proponents of Contemporary Worship saw the Bible as first of all giving a message of salvation from God for people[4] and, secondarily, granting Christians freedom to find the most effective methods of communicating this message with contemporary people. Thus, Contemporary Worship has been less dependent on certain key verses. No single verse has played quite the same role as Psalm 22:3 did in the history of Praise & Worship. If there has been a pivotal proof text in Contemporary Worship's history, a biblical touchstone quoted by many of its adherents, that verse would be 1 Corinthians 9:22b: "To all people I have become all things in order that by all means I might save some" (authors' translation). For those who quoted it, this verse rooted an evangelistic purpose for worship in the Scriptures.

The simplicity of this liturgical vision—an intentional pragmatism to determine what "works" with people—has meant its adherents generally have not spent as much time as theologians in Praise & Worship ruminating on and developing theology. (Reminder to reader: whenever we use the term "liturgical" in this book, we simply mean something worship-related.) The main ideas in Contemporary Worship have not been as much developed as they have been repeated. Instead, the effort has been put into ongoing assessment of people and into the creativity to generate new means and methods. This attentiveness to people in their differences and this ingenuity to creatively adapt to them are implicit in the 1 Corinthians 9:22b passage in its broader context, in which the apostle Paul spoke of adapting to be able to reach both Jews and Gentiles. This second, more pragmatic approach has seen fewer theological developments because its adherents poured their energy into interpreting people and dreaming of ways to overcome the gap to reach them. Those that have come

4. Of course, as Pentecostals, all the original adherents to Praise & Worship also shared this root evangelical sensibility of the need to preach salvation and convert people. The difference was not in the absence of this commitment but in their not allowing it to overwhelm or subvert their biblical theology of Praise & Worship and its practices. Indeed, they saw no conflict between an evangelistic sensibility and Praise & Worship because, when God is present, God is present to save.

arrived less frequently than they did in Praise & Worship, especially in Praise & Worship's early decades.

Theological Summary: A Practical River

Because Contemporary Worship's theology has had a stability in its core sentiments from its historical inception, we can summarize these sentiments already so as to provide a contrast with Praise & Worship. We have previously alluded to one sentiment—namely, a key purpose of corporate worship is to communicate to people and to do so well. Thus, Contemporary Worship's theologians tended to be greatly concerned with the intelligibility of language, in both its literal and figurative senses. Of course, intelligibility is in the ear of the receiver, not in the mouth of the speaker, so these proponents have sought ways of speaking that have more impact on and reception by hearers. That search often has included a concern for easy-to-understand English, which is the literal dimension of this sentiment. The quest for intelligibility has understood "language" figuratively too. In this second dimension, Contemporary Worship theologians have often portrayed worship music as a kind of language and have described its ability to communicate. Consequently, some of the most striking liturgical innovations have been musical, as these theologians have hunted for the music that will speak to the people of their time.

Closely connected to this sensibility about communication has been a sensibility that worship has an evangelistic purpose. In Contemporary Worship there has been a porousness between corporate worship and evangelism. Simply put, adherents of Contemporary Worship have argued that those who plan and lead worship need to be concerned not only for deeply committed Christians but also for hearers whose spiritual conditions are less than ideal. Those who have advocated for Contemporary Worship therefore have assumed that worship assemblies are composed of individuals who are in varying spiritual states before God. Although worship must speak to all these people, the concern for fulfilling the church's gospel mission has tended to steer attention to those in lesser spiritual states, however those individuals are labeled.

The focus on language and its successful communication has also meant that Contemporary Worship's advocates usually have made a distinction between the form of a message and its content. Just as in everyday conversation where someone who speaks a language can find multiple ways (the form) to say something (the message), these theologians see worship as able to assume lots of different forms when presenting the unchanging message of the gospel.

That ability to separate form and content has enabled these proponents to be suspicious of forms inherited from the past and to have a predilection for novelty in the search for what is needed to overcome the perceived gaps between God's message, worship, and contemporary people. They have presumed that the forms—the details and outward practice of worship—can be adapted extensively and repeatedly. Indeed, whenever they have realized that the new measure of today is likely to be the inherited form of tomorrow, they have advocated for continual creativity. To be stagnant, in this view, is to undercut fulfilling worship's evangelistic purpose.

Thus, in its various historical iterations, the theological method of Contemporary Worship has had a degree of liturgical iconoclasm. Suspicion of liturgical inheritances has given it a predilection for novelty and a presumption that accessibility, relevance, and, above all, effective impact are the measures of worship faithful to God. A theological corollary has been an emphasis on human agency in the creation of worship forms. This theology saw people in the church as responsible for finding the measure to reach the lapsed and lost. God was not seen as passive, however, in that God respects wise, creative choices and blesses them with success.

How is this divine blessing of success known? Here theologians of this practical river usually have relied upon numbers. Increased numbers—whether of new converts, new members, or even attendance—provide validation for what should be considered faithful measures. This sense of numerical increase seems to be drawn from a general sense in the New Testament of expansion in which the early church increases in size and breadth. Beyond such biblical rooting, however, adherents of Contemporary Worship have shown their historical context in that major post-Enlightenment innovations like democracy and capitalism also use increasing numbers to indicate success.

Thus, in contrast to Praise & Worship, which flowed with the momentum of seeking God's presence, liturgical pragmatism gained its momentum from the goal of using the most effective means possible in worship. Less overtly concerned with the promise of God's presence, proponents of Contemporary Worship were mesmerized by an apostolic adaptability to become all things to all people in order to win the most people possible. Therefore, if Praise & Worship and Contemporary Worship are compared at the level of root concern, it becomes clear that they flowed under the impulse of different theological ideas. For Praise & Worship, the essential issue was gift—specifically, how God had given a restoration of praise to enjoy his presence and renew the church. For Contemporary Worship, the principal matter was a gap—namely, how the church could bridge the chasm that existed between worship and people so people could experience the grace of God.

Headwaters: A Longer Historical Pedigree

Beyond theological differences, the two approaches differed also in terms of historical development, especially with respect to origins. Whereas the praise-to-presence theology of Praise & Worship erupted onto the scene in the late 1940s with a clear headwater in Reg Layzell, the gap theology of Contemporary Worship bubbled up here and there during that same post–World War II period from subterranean stirrings that had been a recurring feature of American Protestant worship for 150 years. The initial impulse toward Contemporary Worship began long ago as several of the gap theology's central tenets guided several upstart churches of the early United States republic. Before the middle of the nineteenth century, popular publications were promulgating these ideas. By the end of the nineteenth century other proponents had fine-tuned them into new systems of worship. And, in the early twentieth century, cutting-edge churches were putting the ideas into practice by developing large-scale worship in some of the first megachurches. Indeed, liturgical historians have pointed out how a liturgically pragmatic way of thinking has been a perpetual force influencing much of North American worship.[5] Therefore, the bubbling-up in the 1940s might have been new in terms of the particular forms that it took, but it was not new with respect to the underlying theological perspective.

Because the 1940s bubbling-up of this liturgically pragmatic theology did not have as distinct an origin as did the theology of Praise & Worship, Contemporary Worship also has not had as clear an identification with a single movement as early Praise & Worship did with the Latter Rain movement. Liturgical pragmatism since the 1940s has had many adherents from a variety of movements, denominations, and theological camps. Its advocates have included evangelicals and mainliners; both theological conservatives and theological liberals have engaged in Contemporary Worship (although evangelicals and conservatives seem to have found more reasons to pursue it). Consequently, the late-twentieth-century emergence of overcoming-the-gap thinking has not had a single primary means of promulgation, since it was not as clearly connected to a single movement in its early stages as was Praise & Worship. Instead of imagining a single, clear spring serving as a headwater (e.g., Reg Layzell and the Latter Rain movement), think of several subtle outlets for subterranean groundwater.

As just noted, the historical background to the pragmatism seen in this gap-solving approach of Contemporary Worship extends to the earliest years of

---

5. See James F. White, *Protestant Worship: Traditions in Transition* (Louisville: Westminster John Knox, 1989), esp. 185–91; and James F. White, *Christian Worship in North America: A Retrospective, 1955–1995* (Collegeville, MN: Liturgical Press, 1997), 160.

the United States as a nation. The first decades after the American Revolution provided an encouraging context for upstart religious movements. The fluid religious environment and geographic expansion allowed heretofore small denominations like Methodists and Baptists, which had been on the margins of religious life before the American Revolution, to gain strength and grow numerically.[6] Part of this growth was due to the liturgical innovations that had naturally arisen in their midst. These movements quickly institutionalized these innovations and used them for evangelistic purposes.

Take, for example, the emergence of protracted meetings that came to be known as "camp meetings." The original camp meetings were a natural development from already-existing multiple-day meetings held by several churches, including Baptist, Methodist, and Presbyterian congregations.[7] Quickly, however, these meetings gained their own branding as "camp meetings" and were promoted as effective means of evangelizing through worship. Methodist bishop Francis Asbury, for example, called for their widespread use as early as 1802, saying that camp meetings "have never been tried without success. To collect such a number of God's people together to pray, and the ministers to preach, and the longer they stay, generally the better—this is field fighting, this is fishing with a large net."[8] Asbury's call was readily heeded. In 1800 Methodists held no camp meetings by that name, but within a few years they were a fixture of Methodist practice. By 1811 an estimated four hundred to five hundred camp meetings were held annually with an estimated one million participants.[9] Finding a camp meeting at that time would have been relatively easy, since these camp meetings stretched from Canada to Mississippi.

What was seen in camp meetings generally was replicated in a variety of specific new measures by which intentional, overt evangelism was done in worship, usually on a small scale as in the origins of altar calls in the 1790s. Whatever the particular practice, what is useful for our narrative is the theology implicit in Asbury's positive appraisal of the numerical success of "fishing with a large net." What is implicit here Asbury made explicit elsewhere: since conversion is a work of God, success is a sign of God's handiwork. God

6. For an overview of this history, see Nathan O. Hatch, *The Democratization of American Christianity* (New Haven: Yale University Press, 1989).

7. See Lester Ruth, *A Little Heaven Below: Worship at Early Methodist Quarterly Meetings* (Nashville: Kingswood Books, 2000), 183–208; and Leigh E. Schmidt, *Holy Fairs: Scottish Communions and American Revivals in the Early Modern Period* (Princeton: Princeton University Press, 1989).

8. Elmer T. Clark, ed., *The Journal and Letters of Francis Asbury* (Nashville: Abingdon, 1958), 3:251.

9. John H. Wigger, *Taking Heaven by Storm: Methodism and the Rise of Popular Christianity in America* (Oxford: Oxford University Press, 1998), 97.

respected the creative innovation of camp meetings and was blessing them with success. This sense of divine blessing causing camp meetings' success was also explicitly expressed by another Methodist, a contemporary of Asbury, who included camp meetings in a list of "means of grace."[10] The label "means of grace," an important technical term in early Methodism, indicated that Methodists understood camp meetings as one of the normal, regular ways God graced and blessed people. In this theology, liturgical pragmatism was not opposed to a liturgically active God, notwithstanding an awareness that humans had created and promoted the worship innovation.

Thirty years after Asbury's promotion of camp meetings, the theologizing of the gap-solving approach took a major step forward when Charles Finney, a Presbyterian preacher, gave a series of Friday night lectures beginning in the winter of 1834 and published in 1835 as *Lectures on Revivals of Religion*. In these lectures, Finney argued for the adoption of a series of liturgical innovations he called "new measures."[11] These measures were not really new in terms of Finney having created them; he had not. Rather, what he advocated were many of the worship-related innovations that had arisen earlier in the century. What made them new was their novelty to the readers whom Finney hoped to convince to adopt them. The publication of Finney's lectures, which proved to be very influential, was a significant development in liturgical pragmatism's theologizing because it pulled prior theological assumptions together and presented them in a systematic, compelling way.[12] In Finney's lectures (especially Lecture XIV, "Measures to Promote Revival"), the forerunners of Contemporary Worship found a sustained theological rationale justifying new ways of worshiping in order to maximize worship's evangelistic effectiveness with people. Finney was concerned deeply about the gap he saw between old forms of worship and the people he wished to evangelize. He strove to bridge it.

Finney expressed most of the critical aspects of the theology of this pragmatic approach.[13] The use of worship for evangelistic purposes was found in Finney's insistence that the salvation of souls is the goal of all practices of Christian ministry. To address how worship could best fulfill that purpose, Finney argued that in the time after Christ's coming God had done away with

10. Ruth, *Little Heaven Below*, 227.

11. The best recent treatment of Finney is Ted A. Smith, *The New Measures: A Theological History of Democratic Practice* (Cambridge: Cambridge University Press, 2007). See also Chae-Dong Han, "Tradition and Reform in the Frontier Worship Tradition: A New Understanding of Charles G. Finney as Liturgical Reformer" (PhD diss., Drew University, 2004).

12. White, *Protestant Worship*, 176.

13. Our summary of Finney is dependent on Smith's helpful review of the lectures. To support the points made in this paragraph, see Smith, *New Measures*, 45–56.

the prior ceremonial system and had not instituted anything in its place. This perspective made Finney suspicious of inherited liturgical forms, especially if they were proving ineffective with contemporary people. In this way Finney separated the content of worship—the gospel of Christ, which he considered nonnegotiable—from the form of worship, which was changeable.

No historical pedigree of practice—whether in Bible history or church tradition—was needed to validate the use of a worship measure. The one thing necessary was effectiveness in converting the most people possible. That effectiveness was what validated a worship measure. Indeed, Finney portrayed liturgical history as a constant series of new measures, highlighting how even the contemporary music of his day had been a novelty at one time. Thus, he leaned into the necessity of continual adaptation of worship forms, highlighting the need for wise, active human decision making and agency. Meanwhile he also insisted that all positive results, any success in saving souls, was the result of God's action and graciousness. God blessed the choice of the right measures for the right time and place in the same way that God might bless the practices of good farming. But, as Ted Smith has succinctly explained (unpacking Finney's thought), "Different circumstances require different measures, as a person had to farm one way in Connecticut and another way in northern New York."[14]

One particularly instructive section from Finney's Lecture XIV highlights the core of his overcoming-the-gap theology of worship:

> The Gospel was then preached as the appointed means of promoting religion; and it was left to the discretion of the church to determine, from time to time, what measures shall be adopted, and what forms pursued, in giving the gospel its power. . . . Their [the apostles'] commission was "Go and preach the gospel, and disciple all nations." It [the commission] did not prescribe any forms. It did not admit any. No person can pretend to get any set of forms or particular directions as to measures, out of this commission. Do it—the best way you can—ask wisdom from God—use the faculties he has given you—seek the direction of the Holy Ghost—go forward and do it. This was their commission. And their [the apostles'] object was to make known the gospel in the most effectual way, to make the truth stand out strikingly, so as to obtain the attention and secure the obedience of the greatest number possible. No person can find any form of doing this laid down in the Bible. It is preaching the gospel that stands out prominent there as the great thing. The form is left out of the question.[15]

14. Smith, *New Measures*, 54.
15. Charles G. Finney, *Lectures on Revivals of Religion* (New York: Leavitt, Lord, 1835), 232–33. Notice that Finney does not say that Scripture provides no direction whatsoever on worship. The direction provided by the Scriptures is that the Bible abstains from mandating

In this passage, Finney highlights many of the core thoughts that practitioners of Contemporary Worship have restated over the years. The irony is that Finney's new measures eventually became old measures. What had been shockingly new at the beginning of the century—novel ways of preaching and praying, styles of singing, church architecture, lay exhorters, among other practices—had turned into standard procedure by the time he died in 1875.[16]

Remember that Finney himself was not much of an innovator in terms of creating new forms of worship. That role was taken up by one of his devotees in the second half of the nineteenth century, Catherine Booth, a cofounder of the Salvation Army. Booth and her husband, William, came from Methodist origins. In 1865 they cooperated to start a ministry in England called the East London Christian Mission. In 1878 this mission was renamed the Salvation Army. Two years later overseas activities began, including ministry in the United States.

Catherine Booth's defenses of the necessity for liturgical innovation provide some of the best summaries within the history of liturgical thinking that sought to use worship evangelistically, and thus they deserve our attention. Catherine Booth is known as "the Mother of the Salvation Army," but she could just as well be known as "the Thinker of the Salvation Army" or "the Theologian of Contemporary Worship." In several presentations published during the Salvation Army's early years, Booth zealously laid out a theological rationale for an approach to evangelistic worship that emptied worship of all pretense and presumption. Booth advocated for popular approaches to worship that would appeal and work with the masses of the people.

It is clear that Booth and her husband were familiar with Finney's work—his lectures were required reading when they started a training school[17]—yet Catherine Booth also went beyond her American predecessor. She did so by combining (1) notions of apostolic adaptability from 1 Corinthians 9:22, (2) a vision of a humble Christ, (3) her sense of the pressing need to bridge the gap between the church and the people of her day, and (4) a willingness to intentionally update worship practices. The result in theory and practice was an intense form of Christianity (one historian has called it "red-hot

specific forms for Christian worship but does mandate zealous evangelism. This approach, it appears to us, was a form of liturgical biblicism, albeit in an interpretation of what the Bible did not say rather than in the use of the Bible to detail a plan for Christian worship. Thus, we do not agree with James F. White (*Protestant Worship*, 176–77), who suggested Finney was solely a pragmatist and not a biblicist. In contrast, we suggest that Finney's pragmatism was his liturgical biblicism.

16. Smith, *New Measures*, 9.

17. Diane Winston, *Red-Hot and Righteous: The Urban Religion of the Salvation Army* (Cambridge, MA: Harvard University Press, 1999), 20.

and righteous")[18] that at the time numerically succeeded in its evangelistic efforts.

Booth's sense of the gap between people and the standard forms of worship in the Victorian era was acute. One 1879 publication expresses her call to arms: "It is a fact, that the masses of the people have come to associate ideas of stiffness, formality, and uninteresting routine with our church and chapel worship, and if we are to be co-workers with God for them, we must move out of our jog-trot places and become all things to them in order to win them."[19] Booth's allusion to 1 Corinthians 9:22 (where she writes "become all things to them in order to win them") highlights the compelling role this verse played in her thoughts about how this gap might be bridged. For her, to be a co-worker with God for the sake of the unreached and bored-with-church people meant abiding by the only "law" laid down in the New Testament: that is, the law of adaptation (or expediency) found first and foremost in the 1 Corinthians passage. Consequently, this passage became one of her favorite, most-often-referenced scriptural citations.[20] In this way, Booth followed Finney's lead in seeing liturgical pragmatism as a form of liturgical biblicism. She thus agreed with former Free Church theologians in seeing the Scriptures as key for shaping worship, but rather than find specific details about how to conduct worship, as many of them had, she agreed with Finney that the compelling instruction the Bible does provide concerns the goal of worship: successful evangelism.

Moreover, she rooted the idea of adaptation's necessity not only in a specific biblical text but also in the nature of God's redemptive work. The apostle had expressed this principle in 1 Corinthians because it was intrinsic to the divine provision for salvation. "Adaptation is the great thing we ought to consider," Booth argued. "If one method or agent fails, we should try another—God does so. How He tries by various methods and strokes of providence to bring men to Himself. . . . And as He works, so He calls us to work with Him."[21] Indeed, she saw this law of adaptation expressly in the ministry of Jesus Christ, who, acting on existing natural law, did not choose refined theological divines for his evangelistic work (according to Booth, it would have required a miracle for them to be effective!) but average fishermen to connect with average people.[22]

18. Winston, *Red-Hot and Righteous*, 20.
19. Catherine Mumford Booth, *Papers on Practical Religion* (London: Partridge, 1879), 141.
20. Compare, for example, Catherine Mumford Booth, *Papers on Aggressive Christianity* (London: Salvation Army, 1880), esp. 41, 50–51.
21. Booth, *Papers on Practical Religion*, 140.
22. Booth, *Papers on Practical Religion*, 141.

For Booth, this law of adaptability applied not only to evangelistic activity generally but also to worship specifically. Defying anyone to show her otherwise from the New Testament, she denounced "quiet, proper, decorous services" and stated bluntly that "we cannot get the order of a single service" from that same New Testament.[23] Surely the problem she perceived with "decorous services" was their ineffectiveness, assessed numerically. Indeed, she once insisted that churches should be evaluated on the same principles as businesses. The question should be the same for both: do the measures they use produce results? Booth grounded this numerical pragmatism in the law of adaptation. First noting that she could not see any reason to keep religious establishments going without reference to results, she then exulted in the liberty to do whatever was needed to produce results: "Jesus Christ left us free as air as to modes and measures, that we may provide that kind of organization most suited to the necessities of the age. There is not a bit of 'red-tapeism' in the whole of the New Testament."[24]

No one in the late nineteenth or early twentieth centuries would have found any red tape in the worship practices of the early Salvation Army. Whether in England or in the United States, its ministers ("officers" is the correct Salvation Army term) took advantage of being "free as air" with respect to the how, when, and where of worshiping and evangelizing. In the streets of New York, for instance, the Salvation Army's success rested on attracting crowds who confused its activities with a circus, a variety show, or minstrels. The organization's internal magazine, the *War Cry*, regularly published testimonies from participants who said Army meetings were even better than those secular venues.[25]

For early Salvation Army leaders, music became a focus of adaptation. The *War Cry* regularly ran contests asking readers to turn tunes from familiar songs into hymns by putting new Christian lyrics to the music. Efforts went beyond new songs to the manner of making music too. Because lively music attracted a crowd and brass music, in particular, was a favorite of people at the time, William Booth helped spur an interest in developing brass bands in local congregations ("corps"). In actual practice, instrumentation could vary quite a bit according to what a congregation's members could play. Fiddles, guitars, violins, and flutes all found a place. Indeed, William Booth was willing

23. Booth, *Papers on Aggressive Christianity*, 51.
24. Catherine Mumford Booth, *The Salvation Army in Relation to Church and State* (London: Partridge, 1879), 46–47, 51.
25. Winston, *Red-Hot and Righteous*, 17, 24. Winston generally provides a useful description of Army activities, although her focus is on street evangelism, not worship services per se. But the porousness of all early Army activities makes her descriptions apt nonetheless.

to allow almost any instrument except for organs and harmoniums (a kind of pump organ). Why were those two excluded? They sounded too much like regular church.[26]

A daughter of a Salvation Army sergeant major (roughly equivalent to the top lay official in a local congregation) would become the public face for a new level of creative worship ministry in the early twentieth century. The daughter, Aimee Kennedy, spent her turn-of-the-century childhood in Ontario, Canada, engaging in her favorite role-playing game, "Salvation Army," surely influenced by the example of her mother, Mildred, the sergeant major.[27] By the 1920s that young Canadian girl had become Aimee Semple McPherson, often known simply as "Sister Aimee," a famed Pentecostal evangelist, the founding pastor of a Los Angeles megachurch named Angelus Temple, and the leader of a new denomination (the International Church of the Foursquare Gospel).

One might say that you can take the woman out of the Army, but you cannot take the Army out of the woman. And so, in her dynamic ministry, McPherson continued the pragmatic theologizing and innovating that had their origins over a century earlier. She thus became the public face of a new impulse for liturgical creativity to bridge the gap between worship and people in the first quarter of the twentieth century. In the process, she gave an early example of what liturgical pragmatism could look like in a large-scale congregational setting.

McPherson had become concerned about the gap she saw in standard church practices early in her career. She explained her theological unease in her 1927 autobiography: "The methods so often used to impart religion were too archaic, too sedate and too lifeless ever to capture the interest of the throngs."[28] Continuing her autobiographical reflection, she explained her goal in worship leadership: "I developed methods which have brought hundreds of thousands to meetings who otherwise would never have come."[29] Even in these two short sentences, long-standing sentiments of the theology of this pragmatic approach are easily seen: a porousness between worship and evangelism, a suspicion of inherited forms of worship, the use of "measures" to label acts of worship, the need for human agency to find the correct measures, and effectiveness seen in increased numbers as a sign of validation. Elsewhere she would use liturgical pragmatism's standard dichotomy between worship form and content to assure

---

26. Winston, *Red-Hot and Righteous*, 18, 246.

27. Matthew Avery Sutton, *Aimee Semple McPherson and the Resurrection of Christian America* (Cambridge, MA: Harvard University Press, 2007), 9, 64, 70. See also Linda M. Ambrose, "Aimee Semple McPherson: Gender Theory, Worship, and the Arts," *Pneuma* 39, nos. 1–2 (2017): 110.

28. Aimee Semple McPherson, *In the Service of the King: The Story of My Life* (New York: Boni and Liveright, 1927), 152. See also Sutton, *Aimee Semple McPherson*, 76.

29. McPherson, *In the Service*, 152.

others she had not forfeited what was truly essential. "Religion," she began, "to thrive in the present day, must utilize present-day methods. The methods change with the years, but the religion remains always the same."[30]

The most creative of McPherson's new methods were her illustrated sermons. Using church members working in the film industry of nearby Hollywood and McPherson's own acting skills, these sermons on Sunday nights were hugely popular dramatic presentations of Christian themes.[31] Elaborate sets occupied the large platform at Angelus Temple. Costumes gave new identities to McPherson and others who joined her on stage. Props to accentuate the drama and drive home the main metaphor captured the attention of the congregation. The music alone could be mesmerizing, contributing much to the sense of spectacle, as one journalist noted: "It [McPherson's church] has a brass band bigger and louder than Sousa's, an organ worthy of any movie cathedral, a female choir bigger and more beautiful than the Metropolitan chorus, a costume wardrobe comparable to Ziegfeld's."[32] Notwithstanding the elaborateness of such pageantry, McPherson had a christological rationale for her illustrated sermons, as she explained in one of the most famous, a sermon titled "Arrested for Speeding" that made the point that her audience was in danger of speeding to hell. Dressed in a police uniform with an officer's motorcycle on stage, she sermonized, "If Christ were alive today, I think he'd preach modern parables about oil wells and airplanes, the things you and I understand."[33] Asbury, Finney, Booth, and countless other advocates of a pragmatic approach would have agreed.[34]

A New Gap to Consider: The Youth

Aimee Semple McPherson was born in 1890 and died in 1944. Over approximately the same time as her span of life, a cultural development occurred

30. McPherson, *In the Service*, 211.
31. Illustrated sermons had a connection to the Salvation Army, too, in that Catherine Booth's daughter and granddaughter made use of them. See Ambrose, "Aimee Semple McPherson," 110.
32. Morrow Mayo, quoted in Sutton, *Aimee Semple McPherson*, 70.
33. Quoted in Sutton, *Aimee Semple McPherson*, 72.
34. A contemporary to McPherson using the same pragmatic approach was Paul Rader, a pastor who pursued an aggressive spirit of innovation in the Chicago Gospel Tabernacle. For Rader, a cold formality was not only evangelistically ineffective but was associated with modernism and theological liberalism. Rader was ready to use any and every method in order to get the gospel heard. See Mark Rogers, "End Times Innovator: Paul Rader and Evangelical Missions," *International Bulletin of Missionary Research* 37, no. 1 (January 2013): 17–24. We also thank Larry Eskridge for allowing us to see his unpublished thesis, titled "Only Believe: Paul Rader and the Chicago Gospel Tabernacle, 1922–1933" (master's thesis, University of Maryland, 1985). See also James L. Snyder, *Paul Rader: Portrait of an Evangelist (1879–1938)* (Ocala, FL: Fellowship Ministries: 2003), 6, 66.

that would significantly influence liturgical pragmatism in the years after her death—namely, widespread understanding of a "generation" as a cohort determined by age. This sense of "generation," formally defined by sociologists but eventually spreading as a common notion outside that academic guild, grouped people born within a certain time frame as a cohort with similar experiences and perspectives.[35] In other words, as a general framework for understanding society, North Americans had begun to group themselves based on when they were born. As one historian stated, this developing sense of generation implied that society was "divided into compartments or worlds defined by age."[36]

Theologians of Contemporary Worship likewise picked up on this approach to generation and incorporated it into their contemplation of a gap between worship and people. As we have seen, these sorts of gap thinkers have always looked for how the church's worship was ineffective and why it was so. Thus, these bridge-the-liturgical-gap thinkers have had a propensity to look at people and to consider them closely. This spreading sense of generation gave these thinkers a new lens through which to contemplate what the problem might be: the church's worship was ineffective because it did not connect with a certain generation defined by age. This line of thought became a recurring refrain after the mid-twentieth century.

What contemplating specific generations with respect to worship meant for liturgical pragmatism was the rise of age-based targeting to find a way to eradicate the gap. The problem was no longer conceived as just a gap between the church and people in general—whether the "lost" or the unchurched or the bored—it could now be thought of as an age-related gap. For the history of Contemporary Worship, this approach that sought to connect worship with specific generations had a major impact and was a major development. Consequently, in the mid-twentieth century the subterranean waters of the river that became Contemporary Worship bubbled up again but in a new form: ways of worship aimed at youth as the critical generation.

That pragmatic Christian thinkers would focus on youth was not surprising: the early sociologists who developed the notion of "generation" had shared the same focus. For example, Karl Mannheim, who wrote the seminal essay on the topic, had described generational location as involving certain

35. Jane Pilcher has pointed out that the sociologists who originally articulated this view actually used "generation" where other sociologists speak of "cohorts": "as people within a delineated population who experience the same significant event within a given period of time." See Jane Pilcher, "Mannheim's Sociology of Generations: An Undervalued Legacy," *The British Journal of Sociology* 45, no. 3 (September 1994): 483.

36. Robert Wohl, *The Generation of 1914* (Cambridge, MA: Harvard University Press, 1979), 204.

definite modes of behavior, feeling, and thought and highlighted the time of youth as the key period in which social generations are formed.[37] These sociologists were reflecting a sense that had grown in the late nineteenth century of "generation" meaning someone of the same age. As the nineteenth century came to a close, the term "generation" increasingly evoked a sense of a dichotomy between the older generation (i.e., adults) and the generation neither adults nor children (i.e., youth). This sense of a binary between adulthood and youth grew as industrialization enabled more people to experience a stage of life between the end of childhood and the commencement of adult roles in work and marriage.[38]

Several developments in the first half of the twentieth century increased this sense of a distinct generation known as youth. One took place within academia, as psychologists joined sociologists in writing about a youth as a distinct type of human. In this respect, one of the most influential psychological works in the first half of the century was G. Stanley Hall's two-volume work titled *Adolescence* in which Hall explored the distinctive psychology of youth in relation to a range of issues like physiology, sex, crime, religion, and education.[39]

Beyond academic discussions like Hall's, actual developments within education increased the sense of youth as a separate group. Key among these was the increasing rate of attendance in high school. By 1940, for the first time ever, a majority of fourteen- to eighteen-year-olds in the United States attended high school. This sort of age-based segregation for large segments of time created a fertile environment in which a youth culture could develop, complete with its own sense of values, styles, and even language.[40]

World War II itself would contribute to a sense of youth as a separate group. Although the financial hardships of the Great Depression in the early 1930s had eroded youth's influence as a distinct economic market, widespread employment of youth by businesses during the war restored to many young people a sense of empowerment that came from having income to spend. By one estimate, about three million young people aged fourteen to seventeen—about one out of three—had full- or part-time work by 1945.[41]

37. Pilcher, "Mannheim's Sociology," 483. Note that Karl Mannheim, the sociologist whose essay "The Problem of Generations" was the seminal sociological treatment of generations, published this essay in 1923, the same year Aimee Semple McPherson dedicated Angelus Temple.

38. Wohl, *Generation of 1914*, 204, 206.

39. G. Stanley Hall, *Adolescence: Its Psychology and Its Relations to Physiology, Anthropology, Sociology, Sex, Crime, Religion and Education* (New York: Appleton, 1916).

40. Thomas E. Bergler, *The Juvenilization of American Christianity* (Grand Rapids: Eerdmans, 2012), 44. Cf. Thomas Hine, *The Rise and Fall of the American Teenager* (New York: Perennial, 2000), 243.

41. Hine, *Rise and Fall*, 228.

Moreover, military draft policies during the war reinforced the importance and attractiveness of high school attendance for young men in the United States, because high school students received an automatic deferment from being drafted to serve in the military. Thus, graduating high school and turning eighteen became critical markers for social transition and helped define those without them as a separate group.[42] Not surprisingly, the 1940s saw the growing use of what would become a distinctive term for members of this group, regardless of gender: teenager.[43] Liturgical pragmatists, always attentive to whatever shifts in society might be creating a gap between people and Christianity, soon began to home in on teenagers' youth subculture with its distinctive qualities.

Mid-century liturgical pragmatists were not the only ones to do so—advertisers in the business world also began to target youth as a separate market. Arising around the beginning of the twentieth century, youth-specific marketing, especially from the 1920s onward, helped solidify in the general societal consciousness the idea that youth were a discrete group. This youth-specific marketing, too, served as a model for Christians wanting to provide youth-specific worship. The level and intensity of youth targeting in business and church would roughly mirror each other from the 1920s forward. Initial attempts in both spheres in the 1920s grew in force and focus in the 1940s and beyond, as did liturgical targeting of teenagers.[44] While youth marketing before World War II had been ad hoc in nature and narrow in its scope, the years after the war ended in 1945 saw a coherent teenage market established.[45] An enthusiasm for youth marketing became one of the key trends for American businesses in that period.[46]

Targeted marketing within the business world was itself a historical development. Before the end of the nineteenth century, a domestic market of consumers was "fragmented among hundreds of localities," as one historian described the situation, because there were no good transportation or communication infrastructures spanning the country.[47] The rise of such infrastructures allowed true mass markets to emerge in which a product could be

42. Hine, *Rise and Fall*, 228.
43. Bergler, *Juvenilization*, 45; Ian Brailsford, "Ripe for Harvest: American Youth Marketing, 1945–70" (PhD diss., University of Auckland, 1999), 4.
44. For historical background on early advertising to youth, see Stanley C. Hollander and Richard Germain, *Was There a Pepsi Generation before Pepsi Discovered It? Youth-Based Segmentation in Marketing* (Lincolnwood, IL: NTC Business, 1992), 11–26.
45. Brailsford, "Ripe for Harvest," 7.
46. Brailsford, "Ripe for Harvest," 2.
47. Richard S. Tedlow, *New and Improved: The Story of Mass Marketing in America* (New York: Basic Books, 1990), 5. See pp. 4–8 in Tedlow's book for a description of the general

advertised and marketed widely. The early Ford Motor Company followed this approach with its Model T car, which was mass produced in only one color, distributed across the nation, and marketed as suitable for everyone. For automobiles, a new phase of marketing arrived in the 1920s, however, when General Motors began developing different cars for different audiences. Distinct customers, whether defined by actual demographic differences or by psychological perceptions, could look for a car make (e.g., Cadillac or Buick) developed for them.[48]

Liturgical targeting for youth in the mid-twentieth century mirrored this trend. Rather than thinking that one expression of the gospel and way of worship was fitting for all, those who engaged in liturgical pragmatism began to seek ways to reshape worship and language to be fitting and appealing to different groups. Gaining initial momentum with the targeting of youth in the mid-century, this impulse would end up characterizing the push for Contemporary Worship by the end of the twentieth century. Those pushing for Contemporary Worship wanted the church's worship to be divided by make and model, becoming all things to all people so as to win some.

Ironically, some of the earliest attempts at youth-specific worship came from those who were not belligerently iconoclastic about inherited forms of worship. Instead of wholesale changes (as would be advocated, as we will soon see, by a subsequent group of zealous pragmatists), those who made the first overtures toward youth took small steps. A group of businessmen in Kansas City, Missouri, for example, took out a newspaper advertisement on April 3, 1926, the Saturday morning before Easter Sunday that year.[49] The ad was not tied to any specific congregation, nor did it promise any changes in congregational worship at all—but it did encourage youth to consider Jesus Christ as someone to whom youth could relate: "Christ typifies youth. He lived intensely. He died a young man. Maybe He knows your problems. Be a sport and give Him a chance. He will not take the fun out of life."[50]

Others soon moved to a logical next step: tailoring services for youth. Many churches were already in a way doing this, customizing by means of Sunday school assemblies that were part of graded (i.e., age-determined) Sunday school programs.[51] Indeed, one pragmatist, trying to help congregations fill

---

historical development of mass marketing. Cf. Hollander and Germain, *Was There a Pepsi Generation?*, 1–2.

48. Tedlow, *New and Improved*, 7.

49. See "A Jazz Appeal to 'Flaming Youth,'" *Literary Digest*, April 24, 1926, 32.

50. "Jazz Appeal," 32.

51. See Matthew Lawrence Pierce, "Redeeming Performance? The Question of Liturgical Audience," *Liturgy* 28, no. 1 (2013): 56–57. See also chap. 4 in L. Edward Phillips, *The Purpose, Pattern, and Character of Worship* (Nashville: Abingdon, 2020), 67–98.

their pews, encouraged pastors to consider the appeal of worship "adapted to young people." The lack of such adaptation, he continued, might explain why youth sometimes preferred Sunday schools and their assemblies rather than the main service.[52]

A stream of books meant to provide resources for youth-oriented worship began to appear over the next several decades. For example, Laura Armstrong Athearn, who had earlier contributed to a hymnal geared for youth,[53] published a 1931 book whose goal was to "present worship for youth in theory and practice so that the experience of worship may be known and shared."[54] Athearn addressed the problem that needed to be addressed as one rooted in the language of Christian experience: "The vocabulary of religious experience is fast becoming a dead language, and so youth to-day have no adequate means for expressing their religious aspirations and their emotional prompting."[55] A broader lack of understanding complicated the problem in her estimation. "Current practices in worship," she complained, were problematic because youth were neither "aware of the significance" of worship's form nor "adjusted to its possibilities."[56]

Notwithstanding the pointedness of her critique, Athearn's solutions seem mild, especially when compared to more aggressive approaches soon to come from some evangelicals. She directed most of her suggestions toward ways to increase youths' ability to appreciate and understand the form of worship. The goal was to appreciate worship's fine aesthetic quality and therefore supply resources that might enhance that quality and its appreciation. Athearn's approach was not an isolated one. Her book was joined by others in the same period, largely from authors in mainstream denominations and from those denominations' publishing houses. The Methodist Book Concern, in particular, seems to have been a regular contributor to this genre of literature.[57]

Such literature reflected a more general emphasis in worship-related books of the period. As historian David Bains has noted, the 1920s and 1930s were a period in which aesthetic or "psychological" concerns guided mainline

52. Ernest Eugene Elliott, *How to Fill the Pews* (Cincinnati: Standard, 1917), 261.

53. H. Augustine Smith, ed., *The New Hymnal for American Youth* (New York: Appleton-Century, 1930), xiv.

54. Laura Armstrong Athearn, *Christian Worship for American Youth* (New York: Century, 1931), vii.

55. Athearn, *Christian Worship*, 4.

56. Athearn, *Christian Worship*, 14.

57. For example, see Marie Cole Powell, *Guiding the Experience of Worship* (New York: Methodist Book Concern, 1935); and a series of such books from Alice Anderson Bays like *Worship Programs and Stories for Young People* (Nashville: Cokesbury, 1938).

Protestants.[58] Those writing in the period believed that congregational worship was best evaluated by looking at how it fostered the experience of individual worshipers. Worship was an art, they thought, and thus this approach valued what was considered aesthetically beautiful and artful so as to lead to elevated experience. Consequently, Athearn and those who shared her mindset were not classic liturgical pragmatists like Booth and McPherson, especially with respect to the music in worship. At points Athearn and like-minded comrades might dabble a toe in the river, but they never took the full dive into it. For them the problem lay not in current worship music itself, especially music that they would consider aesthetically excellent, but in forming youth to be able to appreciate it. "Cheap-tuned" religious songs and instruments like the saxophone, flute, or drum were specifically rejected because their use in other settings could cause young worshipers to be distracted in prayer or upward religious aspirations. On the other hand, instruments like the pipe organ, harp, or violin Athearn considered "especially suited to the expression of reverence and praise."[59]

If there was a problem with Athearn's approach, it was that the emerging youth culture was developing its own musical sound, and the instruments more likely to be associated with that sound were saxophones and drums, not organs and harps. While Athearn's church might not have been trying to fill that gap with youth, many secular marketers were. Even as the 1930s Great Depression caused a decline in the markets for many musical recordings, a young demographic kept strong a demand for "hot dance" albums. When in 1934 the electronics company RCA began selling inexpensive attachments to radios that could play records, youth drawn to swing music accounted for 40 percent of sales.[60] Consequently, where Athearn was unwilling to go in terms of changing the forms of worship, others would be. Even as rather tame books on connecting youth and worship issued from mainline sources, some evangelical leaders were strategizing for more aggressive musical and worship adaptations in order to reach youth.

Aggressive Christian Targeting of Youth

A more aggressive approach toward reaching youth motivated these evangelical leaders not simply because they thought attracting young people would

58. David Ralph Bains, "The Liturgical Impulse in Mid-Twentieth-Century American Mainline Protestantism" (PhD diss., Harvard University, 1999), 36.
59. Athearn, *Christian Worship*, 166.
60. Hollander and Germain, *Was There a Pepsi Generation?*, 70.

be a nice thing to do. Instead, they were channeling a larger societal angst about a perceived crisis in civilization itself, one understood to be wrapped up in the lives and destiny of youth themselves. The 1930s and 1940s had been a cosmically stressful time as the financial disaster of the Great Depression spilled over into the bloodbath of World War II that then evolved into ongoing fear of the Cold War with its prospect of nuclear conflict. If "youth are the future," as the popular saying went,[61] then the hope of having any future at all—not to mention a decent one—in the face of such sequential calamities rested on reaching and transforming youth.

Thomas Bergler describes the intimate links made at the time: "The battle for the future of civilization became quite literally the battle for the souls and bodies of youth. One reason young people acquired such symbolic power during the crisis years was that the potential, peril, and confusion of adolescence seemed to parallel the distress of American civilization."[62] While these concerns were shared widely by North American Christians, evangelicals had a knack for succinctly summarizing them in compelling sound bites. Torrey Johnson, who emerged in the 1940s as one of the key liturgical pragmatists, sounded such alarms, noting on one occasion, "As our youth goes, so go our countries. If Communism, materialism or wide indifference capture our youth, we shall go down the road to Fascism."[63] On another occasion, he warned that "if we have another lost generation, . . . America is sunk."[64]

The popular mindset held that such a future was a distinct possibility, given that the same collective mindset thought many youth were on a path to destruction. Just in the first half of 1943 alone, there had been 1,200 magazine articles on juvenile delinquency.[65] The view during the war years had been particularly dismal as fathers were overseas fighting, mothers were holding down jobs, and youth—at least the ones without jobs—were feared to have too much unsupervised time without parental guidance.[66] Adding to the worries were the government-sponsored youth canteens in areas with military bases and defense industries. Since they encouraged dancing and mixed-sex socializing, these canteens were viewed as morally questionable by some. Even in

---

61. Robert Wohl traces linking the future with youth back to the development of Enlightenment philosophy itself and especially the French upheavals of the late eighteenth and early nineteenth centuries. See *Generation of 1914*, 204.

62. Bergler, *Juvenilization*, 23.

63. Quoted in Larson, *Youth for Christ*, 134.

64. Quoted in Bergler, *Juvenilization*, 30.

65. Grace Palladino, *Teenagers: An American History* (New York: Basic Books, 1996), 81.

66. Hine, *Rise and Fall*, 241–42.

places without a nearby canteen, many adults were mystified and threatened by the growth of a separate youth culture generally.[67]

Not surprisingly, the mid-century period was a time when American church leaders began new youth organizations or reorganized their existing ones to revitalize them.[68] Evangelicals joined the trend, founding multiple organizations including Young Life, InterVarsity Christian Fellowship, the Fellowship of Christian Athletes, and one especially important to the history of liturgical pragmatism: Youth for Christ. Among the various endeavors across mainline and evangelical circles, some of the most creative thinking about how to bridge the gap and connect to youth would come from leaders in these evangelical parachurch organizations. Their sense of compulsion to reach youth innovatively teased the boundaries of hyperbole as, for example, when Jim Rayburn, the founder of Young Life, said to "consider it a sin to bore kids, especially with the Gospel." On another occasion, Rayburn expressed his fear of allowing new converts to join the "mainline religious establishment" lest it be "the kiss of death to any excitement a new believer may be experiencing."[69]

Rayburn was not the only evangelical seeking ways to bring accessible bridges to youth. Those who sought to connect with youth in terms of forms of worship tended to emphasize similar measures: performing music in a way that would be enticing to youth, including using new songs, new arrangements, and new instrumentation; putting on lively programs; using radio; providing testimonials from kids' peers as well as from prominent figures whom kids would want to emulate; and tailoring language to be understandable to the younger generation. Perhaps the first was Percy Crawford, a Canadian-born evangelist, who began holding weekly evangelistic services for youth in Philadelphia in the summer of 1931. By October of that same year, these services were being broadcast by radio under the name "The Young People's Church of the Air." Much of their appeal came from the lively music, inspired by popular music and led by Ruth Crawford, Percy's wife. The program's music featured 150 persons and included an orchestra, a brass ensemble, and smaller voice ensembles and soloists.[70] Within a decade Percy Crawford's on-air "church"

67. Hine, *Rise and Fall*, 242.

68. For an overview, see Bergler, *Juvenilization*, 25.

69. Quoted in Gretchen Schoon Tanis, *Making Jesus Attractive: The Ministry and Message of Young Life* (Eugene, OR: Pickwick, 2016), 102, 90–91. See also Char Meredith, *It's a Sin to Bore a Kid: The Story of Young Life* (Waco: Word, 1978), 53.

70. William Robert Bishop, "Christian Youth Musicals: 1967–1975" (DMA diss., New Orleans Baptist Theological Seminary, 2015), 29. See also Dan D. Crawford, *A Thirst for Souls: The Life of Evangelist Percy B. Crawford (1902–1960)* (Selinsgrove, PA: Susquehanna University Press, 2010), 168–69. Recordings of select radio broadcasts can be found at "Radio

was being broadcast on four hundred stations; by 1949 it had migrated to network television as "Youth on the March."

Listening to one of Crawford's broadcasts would have been much like listening to a secular musical broadcast of the time, albeit one with an evangelistic purpose.[71] For example, the musical core of the April 30, 1944, broadcast featured a male quartet, a brass quartet, and other vocal and instrumental ensembles playing religious songs, each section introduced by a male emcee. The program included testimonials, a short message, and an invitation, too, giving it an evangelistic focus.[72]

Among those influenced by Crawford was Jack Wyrtzen, a former dance band trombonist and insurance salesperson. Wyrtzen took Crawford's notion of youth targeting through radio and combined it with large-scale, weekly rallies on Saturday nights in the heart of New York City, first in a church located in Times Square, then in Carnegie Hall, and finally in Madison Square Garden as the number of participants grew.[73] The hallmark of Wyrtzen's approach was up-tempo, lively music and youth testimonies.[74] His first Saturday night rally took place in late October 1941 and incorporated a slogan, "Youth for Christ." Wyrtzen printed a songbook to accompany his evangelistic activities: *Word of Life Chorus Melodies*.[75] The collection's opening song, "Isn't It Grand to Be a Christian," set the evangelistic approach for the whole collection, which showcased Jesus and his saving work for the individual.

Whether in music or more generally, Percy Crawford's and Wyrtzen's efforts proved an inspiration to evangelical leaders in other cities. Many began to

Broadcasts," *Percy B. Crawford (1902–1960)* (website), accessed February 5, 2021, http://percy crawford.com/radio-broadcasts/. Ruth and Percy Crawford also compiled and published an accompanying hymnbook, titled *The Young People's Church of the Air Hymn Book* (Wheaton: Van Kampen, n.d.). Printed to showcase songs that had appealed to the youth of the day, this hymnbook consisting of 177 pieces featuring an evangelistic focus as well as an individual, subjective singer's response to Jesus. Most were four-part Western hymns; there were some choruses.

71. For a point of reference, listen to this broadcast of Glenn Miller from October 7, 1938: "Glenn Miller: NBC Radio Broadcast 1938 (1940)," YouTube video, posted by "Ralf Siebert," January 5, 2014, 29:42, https://www.youtube.com/watch?v=Z2-nBHPmBqM&feature=youtu.be &ab_channel=RalfSiebert.

72. To see a description of congregational worship during this period, see Julia Rady-Shaw, "Religion during the Second World War," accessed February 5, 2021, https://wartimecanada.ca /essay/worshipping/religion-during-second-world-war.

73. See Forrest Forbes, *God Hath Chosen: The Story of Jack Wyrtzen and the Word of Life Hour*, reprinted in *The Youth for Christ Movement and Its Pioneers*, ed. Joel A. Carpenter (New York: Garland, 1988), 54–60; and Larson, *Youth for Christ*, 19.

74. Jeff Heffley, *God Goes to High School* (Waco: Word, 1970), 20.

75. Jack Wyrtzen, Carlton Booth, and Norman J. Clayton, comps., *Word of Life Chorus Melodies: For Your Young People's Meeting, Conference, Youth Rally and Sunday School* (Malverne, NY: Gospel Songs, 1947). The songs were in a four-part Western hymn format.

model programs directly after Wyrtzen's efforts, including the use of the phrase "Youth for Christ." First Philadelphia, then Detroit, Indianapolis, St. Louis, and Minneapolis all had evangelicals willing to copy the template Wyrtzen used. Two men in Chicago soon jumped in, planning their first rally for May 1944. These two men—Robert Cook and, especially, Torrey Johnson—and their Youth for Christ rallies in Chicago shortly played a pivotal role in leading Youth for Christ into formal organization and guiding it as a widespread enterprise cultivating youth-oriented innovations.

By the mid-1940s Johnson and Cook had each served over a decade in evangelical churches and schools in the Chicago area, during which time the two men had established ties to each other

Figure 5.1. Jack Wyrtzen's 1947 songbook

by joint work on church staffs and even by family relationships. (Their wives were sisters.) They shared a common dedication to evangelism and a desire for creativity to find the most effective means to carry out that mission. Following the example of an event Wyrtzen had organized on New York's Hudson River, Johnson organized moonlight cruises in 1943 on Lake Michigan adjacent to Chicago. Some 2,200 people joined the first cruise, during which a service was held on the ship. The first cruise was so popular that Johnson scheduled another for the same summer, making sure to include a prelaunch evangelistic service for those who lined the docks to watch the boats. The service on board the ship was sent by shortwave to a radio station that then broadcast it with a delay. The delighted participants thus were able to hear how they sounded on the radio.[76]

Emboldened by this popular success and imitating the example of Saturday night Youth for Christ rallies in other big cities, Johnson and Cook scheduled the first Youth for Christ rally for Chicago on May 27, 1944. They launched their plans boldly, signing a twenty-one-week contract for that city's Orchestra Hall, which sat three thousand people. They also jumped confidently into the

76. Mel Larson, *Young Man on Fire: The Story of Torrey Johnson and Youth for Christ* (Chicago: Youth Publications, 1945), 75–76.

well-populated historical waters of liturgical pragmatism, advertising this meeting as "geared to the times, but anchored to the Rock."[77] This jingle, which would become the catchphrase for the whole Youth for Christ movement, summarized one of the classic theological underpinnings of liturgical pragmatism's desire for innovation—namely, distinguishing the form of expressing the gospel from its content. The form was considered malleable in order to be fitting to contemporary people ("geared to the times") but the content ("anchored to the Rock") was not.

This form-content dichotomy was not the only way Johnson and Cook expressed pragmatism's recurring theological sentiments. Even though Johnson and Cook left no extensive treatise explaining systematically their theological rationale, what they did write and say in the 1940s shows them as another clear bubbling-up of the theology that would ultimately create Contemporary Worship later in the century. Consider, for example, Johnson's explanation of Youth for Christ's purpose, published in 1947:

> Youth for Christ must be of God. It has come in the most unusual way and is moving in the most unpredictable fashion. All we know is that God is in it and is blessing it to the salvation of many souls. We believe that it is God's answer to the sin and unbelief of the present hour. For two thousand years it has been found that those who sought to do the will of God were progressive in their methods. The Wesley brothers preached in church yards, standing on tombstones, on street corners, in houses, halls, and other places. D. L. Moody was very unorthodox; he rented circus tents and introduced the evangelistic song leader into church programs. He was accused of violating good taste when he used Sankey, Bliss and others. In line with that, and in looking at the use made by the Apostle Paul of all the means available in his day, Youth for Christ leaders seek the courage to enable them to blaze the trail and meet the need of reaching the crowd of our day.[78]

Within a few lines Johnson affirms worship's evangelistic purpose, indicates a suspicion of inherited forms by highlighting the need to be "progressive" with respect to method, affirms the necessity of continual updating of forms of worship and evangelism, affirms the necessity of human agency in this innovation even as God blesses the results, and even subtly affirms the sense that large numbers indicate that blessing. Johnson also includes an allusion to the keynote verse, 1 Corinthians 9:22, when he speaks of the apostolic use of "all the means available." Johnson's statement thus served as a digest of the

77. The advertisement can be seen in the last page of unnumbered photographic inserts before p. 33 in Torrey Johnson and Robert Cook, *Reaching Youth for Christ* (Chicago: Moody, 1944).

78. Larson, *Youth for Christ*, 130.

classic theology of liturgical pragmatism even as he was aware of this tradition, making reference to John and Charles Wesley, the eighteenth-century British originators of Methodism, and Dwight Moody, the nineteenth-century evangelist connected to Chicago.

While in this quotation Johnson does not reference the need for language intelligible to the targeted people (another of the classic theological sentiments), he was known for this emphasis on speaking in the vernacular, as pointed out by one Chicago reporter: "Young people of today want to hear the language of youth, down to earth and straightforward. Torrey Johnson has a philosophy of making it easy for people to come to church, and they're coming."[79] Indeed, Johnson and Cook's guide for holding Youth for Christ rallies specifically warned against speaking in theological language and advocated using "typical, wholesome, youth expressions."[80] Because of how well they distilled the theology and because of the role they would play in shaping the Youth for Christ movement, which itself would become an influential source of momentum in the liturgical pragmatism leading to Contemporary Worship, their work in Chicago provides a useful case study and deserves a close look.

What the two men's theology lacked in systematic, exhaustive articulation,[81] it made up for in zeal. That intensity was especially noticeable in their emphasis on prayer, easily seen both in their narration of their practices in Chicago and in how they taught others to start youth rallies. In their guide for holding rallies, titled *Reaching Youth for Christ*, their emphasis on prayer substituted for more thorough theological reflection and justification of their methods. Convinced of the apostolic propriety of creative evangelism, they seem to have assumed a basic formula: lots of prayer combined with numerical success equates with seeing the hand of God. Their early accounts of their first rallies thus show constant attention to the level of attendance and the numbers of conversions attributed to these meetings.

That zeal in prayer—and their theological commitments—carried over to the care with which Johnson and Cook planned and conducted their first rallies in the summer of 1944. Even as they were praying fervently that these

79. Larson, *Youth for Christ*, 98.
80. Johnson and Cook, *Reaching Youth for Christ*, 41.
81. Consider, for example, how they did not try to systematically justify with theology the targeting of youth. They assumed youth as a distinct generation defined by age and its own subculture and shared the wider concern about the future and its connection to youth. But even here, the dividing of people into subgroups could be seen as implicit in the 1 Cor. 9 passage. This passage, which speaks of Paul adapting himself and his ministry for various groups of people, rests upon the Jew-Greek dynamic so critical in the New Testament and especially in Paul's writings.

rallies would be a true spiritual work of God, the men aimed for excellence in their scheduled speakers and musicians. They wanted youth to be able to say, "The quality of this program is as good as anything the world has to offer."[82] Designed to be winsomely attractive from the very beginning, the first rally boasted Billy Graham as its main speaker and incorporated for the music two grand pianos, a four-manual organ, an all-girl choir, George Beverly Shea doing solo singing, and Cook leading congregational singing. Achieving a compelling excellence in music was a particular concern, since Johnson and Cook were convinced that listening to good music on the radio had raised the level of what young people would be satisfied with. They noted, "They [teenagers] want the best. . . . Radio has spoiled things for the careless gospel musician. . . . Dare to offer them something shoddy, and they'll shun your meeting."[83]

Radio not only had an indirect impact on these rallies by shaping teenagers' sense of acceptable music but also had a direct effect on how the youth experienced the meetings. From the very beginning Johnson and Cook worked hard to make sure there was a radio broadcast of the meeting. They desired the radio outlet to help the youth at the rally feel like they were "part of something big, and alive, and vital."[84] Their poor opinion about regular church meetings, including worship services, lay just beneath the surface of this aspiration. Their ad for the twenty-second rally on October 21, 1944, expressed their latent iconoclastic suspicion in a leading question to their youth target: "So you thought all religious meetings were stuffy?"[85] Presuming a positive answer to this query, the ad promised a rally that would be the exact opposite.

82. Johnson and Cook, *Reaching Youth for Christ*, 23.
83. Johnson and Cook, *Reaching Youth for Christ*, 36.
84. Johnson and Cook, *Reaching Youth for Christ*, 37.
85. The advertisement can be seen in the last page of unnumbered photographic inserts before p. 33 in Johnson and Cook, *Reaching Youth for Christ*. Of course, some today might question whether it is appropriate to look at these evangelistic rallies as evidence of worship-related changes, especially since Johnson and Cook clearly expressed that their meetings were not worship per se, notwithstanding the implied conflation in the ad itself. We are convinced that it is legitimate to look at these rallies as connected to larger trends related to worship for the following reasons: The spirit of pragmatism and even the specific practices adopted have, from time to time, characterized worship services elsewhere. The boundaries between different kinds of meetings conducted by evangelicals can be quite porous (see Pierce, *Redeeming Performance*, and Phillips, *Purpose, Pattern, and Character*). In addition, as reported by some later Youth for Christ participants, some young people attended these rallies to substitute for what they considered the uninspiring worship of their home church (see R. Bruce Horner, "The Function of Music in the Youth for Christ Program" [MME thesis, Indiana University, 1970], 176). Finally, as perceptively noted by composer Ralph Carmichael, who was a key figure in the history of Youth for Christ, people often want to replicate in their ongoing worship the practices—especially the music—by which they first came to faith (see Horner, "Function of Music," 226).

This twenty-second rally in Chicago was designed to be a "Victory Rally" in which the dynamics of their regular weekly rallies were expanded and intensified. If the previous rallies in Orchestra Hall had implemented the men's pragmatic theology, then the Victory Rally was an explosive expansion of the same sentiments. So that the experience would be dynamic, the planners organized a 2,500-voice choir, a huge Salvation Army band pulled from all Chicago's area corps, and testimonies from speakers who included award-winning athletes, heads of large business corporations, and war heroes.[86]

Building on the immediate success of Youth for Christ rallies in Chicago and elsewhere, the leaders in the various cities soon pulled together in 1945 to solidify their movement into a formal organization under the name Youth for Christ International. Johnson and Cook respectively became the first two presidents of the organization, Johnson taking the lead in 1945 and Cook in 1948. In retrospect their selection seems obvious, given the success of the Chicago meetings and how they had already written a how-to guide for successful rallies in fall 1944 (the previously mentioned *Reaching Youth for Christ*). Within a year this book had purportedly sold fifteen thousand copies.[87] The two men's theology and the now-standard Youth for Christ practices proliferated quickly: what was estimated to be nine hundred rallies in mid-1946 had grown to one thousand local Youth for Christ organizations by 1947.[88] Part of the growth was surely attributable to the quality of the leaders involved. For example, the organization hired Billy Graham as one of its first evangelists to visit the rallies and preach.[89] Singer George Beverly Shea, who would join Graham in a long, fruitful, and famous evangelistic ministry apart from Youth for Christ, was also regularly employed. Whether with or without the Graham-Shea team, however, Youth for Christ continued to grow after the 1940s even as it had to continue to update its measures and practices. Never

---

86. Larson, *Young Man on Fire*, 84. Chicago's second Victory Rally in 1945 was even more expansive, with a three-hundred-piece band, a choir of five thousand, several well-known gospel singers (including George Beverly Shea), four hundred marching nurses, missionary volunteers in national costumes, and Billy Graham as the keynote preacher. See Joel Carpenter, "Geared to the Times, but Anchored to the Rock," *Christianity Today* 29, no. 16 (November 8, 1985): 44. For a description of early Youth for Christ activities generally, see Bergler, *Juvenilization*, 49–54.

87. Larson, *Young Man on Fire*, 88.

88. Bergler, *Juvenilization*, 30; Carpenter, "Geared to the Times," 44; Larson, *Youth for Christ*, 21–22.

89. Historian Grant Wacker has pointed out the natural affinity between the theology of Youth for Christ and Billy Graham. Wacker notes how Graham's studies in anthropology as an undergraduate at Wheaton College created a broadness in Graham and gave him a sense of the need for timeliness and fittingness. See Grant Wacker, *America's Pastor: Billy Graham and the Shaping of a Nation* (Cambridge, MA: Belknap, 2014), 53.

losing its focus on successfully reaching youth, the organization nonetheless needed to adapt as the details of youth culture continued to change.[90]

Youth: A Moving Target

In the years after the 1940s the sense of teenagers as a separate group with a separate culture continued to grow.[91] Thus, it was not considered outlandish when a 1961 article in a popular national magazine, *Newsweek*, labeled them "Fun Worshippers" and, based on a sociological study by a Pennsylvania State University professor, described their culture as "essentially the culture of a leisure class."[92] The figures quoted in the article seemed to support the conclusion: youth in the United States consumed more than ten billion dollars a year, including seventy-five million on records (and twenty-five million on deodorants). The sociological study upon which the popular article was based noted how, given the amount of spending by youth, "the values of teen-age culture become a matter of concern for the advertising industry. What teen-agers like and want, what they think is important."[93] The study also described how a distinctive language of teenagers helped reinforce a barrier between their subculture and others.[94]

To the casual reader the *Newsweek* article insinuated that these youth would have been a hard "market" for promotion of religion or other serious topics since teenagers were "more concerned with pimples than politics, virginity than divinity."[95] Indeed, the Pennsylvania State sociologist contrasted how advertisers and mass media could "flatter and cajole" youth whereas other adults, including ministers, had to "discipline, restrict, or deny" youth.[96]

90. For an overview of Youth for Christ's history, see Bergler, *Juvenilization*, 198–205; and Thomas E. Bergler, "'I Found My Thrill': The Youth for Christ Movement and American Congregational Singing, 1940–1970," in *Wonderful Words of Life: Hymns in American Protestant History & Theology*, ed. Richard J. Mouw and Mark A. Noll (Grand Rapids: Eerdmans, 2004), 123–49.

91. For general histories, see Palladino, *Teenagers*, esp. 117–89; and Hine, *Rise and Fall*, 232–46.

92. "The Fun Worshippers," *Newsweek* 58, no. 24 (December 11, 1961): 88.

93. Jessie Bernard, "Teen-Age Culture: An Overview," *Annals of the American Academy of Political and Social Science* 338, no. 1 (November 1961): 4. To be fair to this scholarly article, its author did note that this separate culture did not encompass all young Americans, since teenage culture was a product of affluence and thus as teenagers grew older more youth of a lower socioeconomic status had to drop out.

94. Bernard, "Teen-Age Culture," 5. Some of the distinctive phrases mentioned in the article made their way into wider usage (e.g., Mickey Mouse, wheels, roomy, clod, dressed up) while others did not (tweedy, tweeded down, whip, zowies).

95. "Fun Worshippers," 88.

96. Bernard, "Teen-Age Culture," 4.

While perhaps the sociologist was generally accurate, nonetheless there were ministers in the 1950s and early 1960s who did more than discipline, restrict, or deny youth with respect to worship. In both evangelicalism and mainline denominations, innovators continued to creatively search for expressions in worship that would bridge the gap to youth. It was a continual search because, even if a youth subculture existed, the tastes of this subculture perpetually evolved. Although the search might have been hard, there were still ministers eager to find what youth liked and wanted, what they thought was important.

Among these searchers, not surprisingly, were new leaders within Youth for Christ. Some of their innovations included the starting of "Bible clubs" at schools. These clubs first launched in the late 1940s, but they developed more strongly in the 1950s. In essence they were like miniature rallies involving many of the same practices as the regular rallies: lively singing, pointed prayer, student testimonies, guest preachers, and special musical performances.[97] Conducted on a much smaller scale than the weekly rallies, these clubs were one step closer to the dynamics of congregational worship.

Meanwhile, Youth for Christ organizers continued to conduct their large-scale rallies.[98] Yet here there was a growing concern among some Youth for Christ leaders. Not only had the overall number of rallies not increased since the mid-1950s—a bad sign when increasing numbers are necessary in your theology—but leaders began to question the basic appeal of rallies. Thus, some leaders became much less apologetic about using entertainment. One leader encouraged local rally directors in 1961, "Don't be afraid to 'entertain' and give teens what they want."[99] Youth for Christ resources, however, did not always follow the same advice. The songbook released in 1960, for instance, *Youth for Christ Songs and Choruses*, was mainly a rehash of the older revival music pervasive in the previous 1948 songbook, with the addition of a few newer gospel songs and choruses.[100] Some local directors took mat-

97. Bergler, *Juvenilization*, 151.

98. See this detailed schedule of a 1960s-era rally in Horner, "Function of Music," 14–15: 7:15 p.m. musical warm-up; 7:30 theme by choir; 7:32 organ bridge to welcome; 7:34 organ bridge to chorale; 7:37 organ bridge to singing vocal group; curtain; 7:43 organ bridge to skit; 7:48 organ bridge to audience singing; curtain; 7:52 organ bridge to choir number; 7:55 organ bridge to interview, scripture, and prayer; 8:00 singing vocal group; 8:03 offering and offertory; curtain; 8:10 announcements; 8:14 audience singing; curtain; 8:17 sung vocal solo; 8:25 acknowledgment of soloists and introduction to main speaker; 8:28 message; organ bridge to invitation; wrap-up; benediction; organ bridge to postlude. Although this is the schedule for a rally at a national convention of Youth for Christ, Horner stated that its organization and sequence were similar to well-planned local rallies he had attended since the early 1960s.

99. Quoted in Bergler, "'I Found My Thrill,'" 143–44.

100. Bergler, "'I Found My Thrill,'" 144. Note that the compilers of the 1960 songbook were Carl Bihl and Thurlow Spurr.

ters into their own hands, choosing to adopt music in their rallies to match popular sounds. For example, around 1963 the director in Fresno, California, searched for musicians who could replicate the folk or folk-rock sound of secular groups.[101] This director was discovering how liturgical pragmatism must perennially rebuild the bridge to span the gap to the targeted group and its culture. Although the dedication to be contemporary can remain firm, the particular methods to make the connection must shift even as the targeted subculture changes. There can be no static answer to the question of what will appeal to people.

Leaders in Youth for Christ were not the only evangelicals in the period who sought to connect to youth by using music alluring to them. Perhaps it was easier for evangelicals like the Youth for Christ leaders, who sought this appeal in settings outside of congregational worship. For instance, Percy Crawford, who had pioneered "The Young People's Church of the Air" radio broadcast in the 1930s, started a new music-based ministry called Youtherama in 1956. Crawford's new venture featured a full orchestra and youth choir doing popular and gospel music. Woven in and around the music were dramas and skits and sometimes guest speakers or Christian celebrities. Crawford would finish the meeting with an invitation for those who wanted to make a religious decision.[102]

A new musical sound also began to leak into church sanctuaries through the efforts of other enterprising evangelicals. One opening for such music took the form of traveling singing groups that were composed of youth and made use of nontraditional sounds when performing in churches. Two of the best-known groups were started by musicians with Youth for Christ backgrounds: Thurlow Spurr and Cam Floria. Spurr, who had experience leading music at Youth for Christ meetings at the local and national levels, in 1959 created a group called The Spurrlows. A few years after this group's creation, Floria, a Youth for Christ music leader in Portland, Oregon, formed a similar group in 1963 known as The Continentals. Both groups—and others like them—played an important role in making evangelical congregations more accepting of music with popular roots. That was not an easy task, given the discomfort and combativeness some evangelical churches expressed regarding popular music.[103] Wholesomeness and musical excellence seem to have helped change

101. Bergler, "'I Found My Thrill,'" 144. In a 1969 interview this director, Larry Ballenger, mentioned groups like The Association and Simon and Garfunkel, projecting these later groups back into the earlier period. See Horner, "Function of Music," 137.

102. Bishop, "Christian Youth Musicals," 30. See Crawford, *Thirst for Souls*, 252–55.

103. For more information, see Anna E. Nekola, "Between This World and the Next: The Musical 'Worship Wars' and Evangelical Ideology in the United States, 1960–2005" (PhD diss., University of Wisconsin–Madison, 2009).

people's impressions, as noted by music historian William Bishop: "Both groups showcased smiling, clean-cut young people performing a well-polished program of original religious folk songs, familiar hymns, and popular youth choruses—all with a mild folk-flavor that was exciting but not overly radical."[104]

Perhaps it was just a matter of time before new sounds began to emerge from church-based choirs. Although Baptist churches had been establishing increasing numbers of youth choirs since the late 1940s, for the most part their available music repertoire was the same as that of adult choirs. By the early 1960s many music ministers in these congregations found the numbers of youth singers shrinking, because the young people were unexcited about singing the same music as their parents and in the same way. Folk and rock music were more popular and were easily accessible through the radio and records. Music ministers who experimented with more popular music styles sometimes managed to reverse the downward trend.

For example, Billy Ray Hearn, a music minister at a Baptist church in southern Georgia, began adding secular folk songs to his youth choir's repertoire in 1960, especially in the form of smaller ensembles made up of these young singers. Hearn, who never totally dropped formal choir anthems and hymns from his youth choir's singing, nevertheless embraced the sound of groups like the Kingston Trio and used this folk sound with his church's teenagers. His experimentation reversed the numerical decline in his choir and it grew from twenty members to eighty, leading to both a few recordings and eventual touring.[105] His congregation's initial suspicion dissipated in the face of a dramatic increase in the number of youth participating. Hearn himself would move on to an influential role at the large evangelical publisher Word, where he was instrumental in the creation of Myrrh Records.

A few youth-oriented worship endeavors soon joined these initial bubbling-ups in evangelical youth ministries. Combined, these early outbreaks started to form something with shape, movement, and momentum. One of the most striking examples was the commissioning of a jazz setting for morning prayer

104. Bishop, "Christian Youth Musicals," 32.
105. Bishop, "Christian Youth Musicals," 39, 56–57. For Hearn's own explanation, see Billy Ray Hearn, "Billy Ray Hearn," interview (video), National Association of Music Merchants, July 13, 2013, https://www.namm.org/library/oral-history/billy-ray-hearn. Musical innovation in choir cantatas was not limited to youth experimentation. Composer John W. Peterson, influenced by Broadway musicals, began to incorporate some of these stylistic elements into his cantatas from 1957 onward. His work was some of the first to contain a "hint" of a pop-music style marketed to evangelical congregations. See Bishop, "Christian Youth Musicals," 36. Of course, such developments were not limited to North America. Geoffrey Beaumont and the 20th Century Church Light Music Group in the United Kingdom began composing new hymn tunes using folk and popular styles in the 1950s.

in the 1959 national Methodist youth conference at Purdue University in La-
fayette, Indiana. Attendance was so high that the services had to be moved
to a larger venue. The jazz setting was recorded on an album and for NBC
TV. Evening programs with jazz, dance, and drama supplemented morning
prayer. The Wednesday night program featured the well-known Dave Brubeck
Quartet accompanying a program of readings, dance, and songs by Odetta, a
popular African American vocalist. Notwithstanding these efforts' popularity with the youth attending, others complained—sometimes with a racist
undertone—about Methodist sacrilege.[106]

While Methodists were being innovative in occasional, large-scale meetings,
other mainline ministries were trying more regular, sustained youth-targeted
worship.[107] Episcopalians in a Honolulu suburb, for example, had created
a youth-only service in 1956 called Halepule Opio (Hawaiian for "House
of Prayer for Youth"). Called "virtually autonomous," the congregation
consisted of 180 twelve- to eighteen-year-olds in 1963, and members of the
congregation filled all the leadership positions except for that of presiding
minister.[108] In the same period, some college campus ministries had begun to
try novel approaches in their chapel services in order to connect with students.
Thus, by 1965 the chapel services at the Massachusetts Institute of Technology included everything from jazz Masses to a dance by a college student in a
leotard. Malcolm Boyd, an Episcopal "chaplain-at-large" to college students,
often started his prayer services with readings from his own one-act plays
about racial conflict or from Edward Albee, a playwright known for laying
bare the desperation of contemporary life.[109]

A more lasting impact on youth-targeted worship, however, was achieved
by a single song, "He's Everything to Me," from the movie *The Restless Ones*,
also released in 1965. The song was composed by Ralph Carmichael, another
musician with long ties to Youth for Christ. By the early 1960s Carmichael
had migrated from focusing his creativity on Christian musicals of the late
1940s to become a composer with sway in secular music. But doors opened
again for him in the 1960s to compose for Christians. He was invited to score
The Restless Ones, a Billy Graham Evangelistic Association movie about

106. Bergler, *Juvenilization*, 85–86.

107. Methodist authors provided some instruction for musical and liturgical innovation on
a small scale. For example, the *Handbook of the Methodist Youth Fellowship* had made some
allowance for use of folk or Black songbooks in local Methodist youth groups (*Handbook of
the Methodist Youth Fellowship* [Nashville: Methodist Publishing House, 1953], 61, 355–56).
Methodists also continued their earlier practice of youth-specific worship resource books with
Helen F. Couch and Sam S. Barefield's *Worship Sourcebook for Youth* (Nashville: Abingdon, 1962).

108. "Church for Teen-Agers," *Time* 82, no. 23 (December 6, 1963): 57.

109. "Helping Students Make the Spiritual Passage," *Time* 86, no. 14 (October 1, 1965): 85.

teenagers, about the same time that he discovered his teenage daughter was sneaking out to the family car at night to listen to pop-rock music on the radio. Consequently, he decided to write the score for this movie in a soft-rock style.[110] With his daughter in mind—and other teenagers with similar tastes—Carmichael composed a movie score edgy enough that it would have been rejected if the association had had enough money to purchase a new score.[111]

To have cut Carmichael's music from the movie would have been a grave error, however, judging by the numerical success of the movie and even of the single song "He's Everything to Me." Within eighteen months of its release, the movie had had nine hundred showings to a total of over three million people.[112] Moreover, by 1986 "He's Everything to Me" had been printed over thirteen million times, translated into twelve languages, and recorded more than 250 times.[113] As importantly, the scene in which the song occurred was probably how many evangelical teens were first exposed to guitar-led worship.[114] In the movie, a small male ensemble consisting of two acoustic guitars, a banjo, and an upright bass leads the song while around thirty youth gather informally around a fire on a beach on a quiet evening.

While this scene was novel in 1965, something like it would be replicated innumerable times in real life in subsequent years, as a small river of Contemporary Worship began to flow. Instead of an occasional bubbling-up of theological pragmatism around worship, a steady stream of worship innovations centered on congregational services and promoted by the name "Contemporary Worship" began to capture the imagination of evangelical and mainline congregations alike by the late 1960s. These "Contemporary" services—sometimes geared toward youth and sometimes not—not only involved inventiveness with new styles of music but also emphasized an updating of language and attentiveness to the pressing concerns of the people targeted. What had been ad hoc attempts to bridge the gap with liturgically disenfranchised people turned into a regular season of creativity to solve a perceived crisis in the church's worship.

110. To hear the story in his own words, see Ralph Carmichael, "Part 1. Ralph Talks about His Influence on Christian Music," interview, YouTube video, posted by "RalphCarmichael," December 7, 2012, 5:49, https://www.youtube.com/watch?v=57KGv1gPgIY&list=RD57KGv1gPgIY&index=1. Billy Graham had called on Carmichael before to score movies for his association.

111. As told by Carmichael in Horner, "Function of Music," 220. See also Bergler, "'I Found My Thrill,'" 126.

112. Bishop, "Christian Youth Musicals," 178.

113. Ralph Carmichael, *He's Everything to Me* (Waco: Word, 1986), 128.

114. Bishop, "Christian Youth Musicals," 179. To see this scene, go to "He's Everything to Me," YouTube video, posted by "maz59," September 24, 2010, 1:44, https://www.youtube.com/watch?v=0S5AknvJAUU.

six

---

the first wave of contemporary worship, 1965–85

Our ultimate aim is, as the apostle Paul says, "That I might by all means win some." And we say that you have to be winsome to win some.

—*Phil Palermo, member of the Palermo Brothers evangelistic singing team*[1]

July 7, 1968, was a lovely summer day in northern Indiana. Visibility was over ten miles and the high temperature was in the low eighties. In one of that state's quaint towns, a twenty-five-year-old master's student named Bruce Horner set up his reel-to-reel tape recorder to begin collecting the interviews that would provide the core of information for the thesis he wanted to write.[2] Horner was studying music education at Indiana University. The location was Winona Lake, a small town with a large place in American evangelical history. In the early twentieth century the town had hosted Chautauqua conferences (a

1. July 7, 1968, interview with Phil Palermo, as recorded in R. Bruce Horner, "The Function of Music in the Youth for Christ Program" (MME thesis, Indiana University 1970), 182.
2. We are indebted to personal correspondence with Sallie Horner, Bruce Horner's widow, for information about the background to this thesis. Sallie Horner, email message to Lester Ruth, June 22, 2020. We are also indebted to Thomas Bergler for providing us with a copy of Horner's thesis.

summer-based, adult-oriented event combining education, entertainment, and religious exercises, popular during the late nineteenth and early twentieth centuries) and Bible conferences. The famed evangelist Billy Sunday had had long associations with the town. In 1945 the meeting that founded the parachurch organization Youth for Christ had been held in Winona Lake. That organization had helped to shape Horner's own Christian journey, and it was Youth for Christ's annual convention that drew him to northern Indiana that day in the summer of 1968. Horner was about to interview some of the most prominent evangelical musicians and composers in the United States—many associated with Youth for Christ—to gain the raw material to write about the function of music in the organization. He would return the following July for the same purpose, supplementing these face-to-face interviews with telephone interviews and surveys returned from almost 60 percent of the local chapters of Youth for Christ. By 1970 Horner's thesis was completed. Youth for Christ, whose leadership had helped facilitate Horner's connection to some of the interviewees, was pleased enough to support distributing over two hundred copies.

Indeed, what Horner accomplished was not only a narrow look into the role of music in one organization but also an initial snapshot of the place music would have in a groundswell of liturgical creativity beginning in the late 1960s, not only in evangelicalism but more broadly across North American Protestantism. What had been subterranean stirrings in previous years would, after 1965, become a clear "river" of liturgical innovation aiming to bridge the gap between the church's worship and the people absent from that worship.

Through Horner's interviews, we can clearly see the important visibility that popular forms of music would indeed have in bridging that gap. However, the novelties in this first surge of Contemporary Worship would not be limited to music alone. To erase the gap, churches would pursue changes in language, electronic multimedia, space and architecture, worshipers' use of their bodies, visual art forms, preaching, and the manner and level of worshipers' participation. The new forms of worship that emerged were often called "Contemporary Worship," the first real use of the phrase as a technical term.

The breadth of change was matched by the breadth of churches seeking to change. This first wave of liturgical experimentation was not occupied just by theologically conservative evangelicals seeking to make new converts. Moderate and even liberal mainline Christians, driven by a general anxiety about people's disinterest in and boredom with church, jumped into the pursuit of measures that would make worship more exciting, interesting, and relevant to the pressing concerns of the day. By the late 1960s mainline Christians—and their organizations—had declared the liturgical gap to be so large that there was a "crisis" in worship.

And this crisis was not just with youth or young adults. Churches in this first wave of Contemporary Worship sought more generally to attract people back to worship. Indeed, the base of this crisis deepened as the 1970s brought a growing awareness of a loss of general membership, a decline that sank into the consciousness of mainline denominations. Church officials—as well as pastors and lay leaders—began to see the gap not only in a broad conceptual way, but also physically in their increasingly empty pews.

This numerical decline was not universal, however. The period from 1965 to 1985 witnessed the rise of some innovative pastors and congregations who spearheaded new ways to engage people, attract them to worship, and cultivate positive Christian experiences. These innovators would begin to produce ways to make their success known, teaching their methods and perspectives to others who wished to replicate their achievements.

Reinforcing these entrepreneurial pastors was the rise of the Church Growth movement in the 1970s and early 1980s. The Church Growth movement brought a new intensity to investigating America's unchurched and describing the obstacles that undercut their successful attraction to and inclusion in congregations. (The origins of the Church Growth movement will be described below.) While not initially overtly concerned about liturgical matters, Church Growth proponents soon began articulating their own sense of the gap that existed between people and traditional worship. Thus, this movement brought a more systematic, scientific, and numbers-driven approach to the gap anxiety that had been circulating since the 1960s.

Whether or not this period's liturgical innovators were evangelicals, youth-oriented, members of mainline denominations, or Church Growth proponents, all those who sought to find an effective, meaningful liturgical bridge spoke in ways reminiscent of the theological commitments of prior liturgical innovators. At stake was faithfulness to what they perceived as the mission of the church. They shared a fear that established forms of worship failed to allow the church to fulfill that mission and spread the message God had given it. Change was needed. To use the words of one of Bruce Horner's interviewees, the effectively worshiping church needed to become "winsome to win some."[3]

Evangelical Theology and the Composing of Youth Musicals

Horner's thesis not only showed how popular forms of music would be critical in the changes of the late 1960s; it also showed how widespread the pragmatic theology of Contemporary Worship was among key evangelical

3. Quoted in Horner, "Function of Music," 182.

musicians and composers at the time. Horner's interviewees, including some of the most important evangelical composers of the period, expressed ideas and sentiments that had characterized the subterranean stirrings described in chapter 5. A different time and a growing openness allowed this theology to create new forms that would have lasting impact on the shape of worship at the end of the twentieth century.

Two things were clear in Horner's research: evangelicals wanted to evangelize and they wanted to do it well. In the context of his inquiry into the work of Youth for Christ, Horner found that evangelizing *well* meant evangelizing *effectively*—specifically, reaching teenagers effectively. The concern about not achieving that end was real to his interviewees and survey respondents. Behind their specific angst laid a growing cultural sense that a "generation gap" existed at the time. Not only among evangelicals but among Americans generally there was a heightened fear of losing touch with youth and failing to communicate with them. In the broader culture, the term "generation gap" exploded in use after 1965, reflecting a consciousness that gripped the continent. Indeed, a 1969 book titled simply *The Gap* needed no other explanation for what it was about: it concerned the gap existing between older and younger adults.[4]

Horner's research sought to discover what that gap meant in terms of music, youth, and the Christian mission of evangelizing as understood throughout Youth for Christ. The responses he collected showed that the original drive of the organization had not changed: for example, 94 percent of the surveys returned to Horner insisted that the music used to reach youth must be "in tune with the times."[5] About that opinion there was widespread agreement. The struggle came in knowing what music "in tune with the times" sounded like. Some of Horner's interviewees complained that past forms of popular music from the 1940s through the early 1960s, music that was still used in some Youth for Christ events, no longer spoke to the youth of the late 1960s. Horner's respondents spent much time discussing which form of popular music (folk, folk-rock, or rock) was needed to effectively reach youth.

Despite their differences concerning which particular style of contemporary music they advocated, Horner's interviewees were more unified in certain core theological convictions, opinions that aligned them with the long history of theologizing leading to Contemporary Worship. One example was the repeated stressing of the need for understandable communication. Specifically,

4. Richard Lorber and Ernest Fladell, *The Gap* (New York: Signet, 1969). Lorber and Fladell were a nephew and uncle combination who explored living in each other's worlds.
5. Horner, "Function of Music," 42.

many interviewees grounded the need for using popular forms of music in the metaphor of music as a kind of language that could speak to people or not. Choose the right kind of music and one can communicate intelligibly; choose poorly and the gospel message will not be heard. Kurt Kaiser, for example, drew a parallel between the unintelligibility and unattractiveness of archaic English (the "'thee's' and 'thou's' and the 'thence's' and 'thither's'") and music that was not current in the listening and hearing habits of youth.[6] Other interviewees emphasized other aspects of seeing music as a language: archaic imagery should be eliminated; the sound can communicate emotions and affections; or, more poetically, music is the "language of the soul."[7]

To justify the freedom to find music that would speak to contemporary youth, Horner's interviewees also referenced the long-standing dichotomy between the form of communication and the content of the gospel. Kurt Kaiser thus argued, "Even though the message of Christ is the same, the method must change to be contemporary."[8] The director for the Lehigh Valley (Pennsylvania) Youth for Christ used the form-content divide to specifically argue for freedom: "The music is still a method. It is not the gospel. And when we realize that it is a method we will be much in freedom to use any style of music we want in order to communicate."[9] Thurlow Spurr, aware of how many objected to the use of popular forms of music and claimed they were inherently immoral, contended that the divide between communication's form and its content meant that music, regardless of its style, was amoral.[10] For Spurr morality was relevant only when looking at the purpose for which music was used. That view left Spurr furious with those who clung to past, ineffective forms as if those forms were God-given; he fumed that God "didn't leave us here to follow something down to its ugly death or its last drop of blood."

In Spurr's opinion, everyone should aim for this purpose: try to effectively communicate the gospel at the level of youth. Spurr's scriptural exemplar for that sort of effective flexibility was the apostle Paul. Citing 1 Corinthians 9:22, Spurr described Paul as someone willing to get on a group's "wave length." Such apostolic adaptability, he argued, was "the very essence of Christianity."[11]

One of Horner's most significant interviewees was Ralph Carmichael, the composer of "He's Everything to Me," the important song discussed in

6. Quoted in Horner, "Function of Music," 171–72.
7. Quoted in Horner, "Function of Music," 144, 177, 181.
8. Quoted in Horner, "Function of Music," 172.
9. Quoted in Horner, "Function of Music," 146.
10. To understand the background for Spurr's defensiveness, see Anna E. Nekola, "Between This World and the Next: The Musical 'Worship Wars' and Evangelical Ideology in the United States, 1960–2005" (PhD diss., University of Wisconsin–Madison, 2009).
11. Horner, "Function of Music," 197.

chapter 5. Not only did Carmichael have a long Youth
for Christ connection (dating
back to the late 1940s) but,
twenty years later, he had
emerged at the forefront of a
surge of evangelical composers seeking to write music appealing to people with modern listening tastes. As one
fellow musician, Cam Flo-
ria, put it, Carmichael was
"the Father of Contemporary
Christian music and there's
no way to describe the influence that he's had on all of
us and on the whole music
scene."[12] William Bishop, a
music historian, summarizes
his role similarly: "By the late
1960s and into the 1970s Car-

Figure 6.1. Ralph Carmichael

michael was . . . [the Christian music industry's] de facto leader, trendsetter,
visionary, and spokesperson."[13]

It had taken Carmichael much work and perseverance to reach that pinnacle
of influence. After a promising creative start with Christians in the late 1940s,
Carmichael's willingness to push the boundaries of musical creativeness grew
distasteful to many Christians and their publishers in the 1950s and early
1960s. Although some (like Billy Graham) remained supportive, Carmichael
turned his attention to composing and arranging secular music in this period,
which he did with widespread acclaim. At heart, however, Carmichael continued to want to make Christian music, especially music for youth.

12. From a 2015 interview by music historian William Bishop. See William Robert Bishop,
"Christian Youth Musicals: 1967–1975" (DMA diss., New Orleans Baptist Theological Seminary, 2015), 169.
13. Bishop, "Christian Youth Musicals," 171. The best sources to understand Carmichael's
early career are pp. 171–82 in Bishop's dissertation and Carmichael's autobiography, *He's
Everything to Me* (Waco: Word, 1986). For another useful source on Carmichael's influence,
see Thomas E. Bergler, "'I Found My Thrill': The Youth for Christ Movement and American
Congregational Singing, 1940–1970," in *Wonderful Words of Life: Hymns in American Protestant History & Theology*, ed. Richard J. Mouw and Mark A. Noll (Grand Rapids: Eerdmans,
2004), 123–49.

By the early 1960s Carmichael had discovered a solution that would enable him to continue to experiment with new styles of Christian music: he would establish his own music publishing company. Consequently, he approached the leadership at Word Music and proposed that they form a new music company together, Lexicon Music. Each party would own a 50 percent interest in the new company, Carmichael creating the music and Word distributing it. Word agreed and within a few years Carmichael added a record label, Light, through which he could offer albums featuring music with a new sound.

Bishop summarizes Carmichael's strategic setup: "By 1968 Ralph Carmichael had all the ingredients for a church music revolution: he had total freedom to create, publish, and distribute his experimental music via his own Lexicon Music/Light Records and its distribution deal with Word Music, he had re-established himself as the foremost composer and arranger in Christian music, and, most importantly, he had a vision to share the gospel to teens through their own style of pop music."[14] Moreover, among evangelical liturgical innovators in the late 1960s, Carmichael seemingly had the most fully developed theology behind this vision.

Regardless of whether it was the most developed, Carmichael's theology was perhaps the best documented. In addition to conducting the long 1969 interview with Carmichael, Horner also transcribed and included in his thesis a 1967 speech that Carmichael had given at a Youth for Christ convention.[15] Furthermore, from the late 1960s through the 1980s the composer was often interviewed and quoted.[16] Moreover, Carmichael's 1986 autobiography, which included a speech he gave in 1985 called "Music as Ministry Vehicle," provides a useful concluding summary of his thought for the period.[17] All these sources show a consistency and continuity in his theology for the period. They also reveal yet another articulation of themes that have characterized Contemporary Worship, seen both in Carmichael's contemporaries like Kaiser and Spurr and in earlier evangelicals.

Two general perceptions framed Carmichael's thoughts during the 1965–85 period. One was a root concern that there was in fact a real gap between people and Christian music. Throughout his theologizing during this period, he never dropped this concern and, indeed, sometimes began at just that point. For example, in his 1967 speech, Carmichael started by saying how a "credibility

14. Bishop, "Christian Youth Musicals," 182.
15. For the interview, see Horner, "Function of Music," 146–55; for the 1967 speech transcription, see pp. 217–30.
16. For a useful anthology of such quotations, see appendix E in Bishop, "Christian Youth Musicals," 489–507.
17. Carmichael, *He's Everything to Me*, esp. 183–89.

gap in religious music" had concerned him repeatedly since he was a child. He had never understood why Christian people would want to listen to one kind of music—often "popular" music—outside of religious settings but limit themselves once they gathered as the church.[18]

Carmichael believed the problem of a gap between people and worship would never be completely settled or solved since people and culture continually changed. Thus, Carmichael saw a need to perpetually innovate, an opinion that was the second of the general perceptions framing his thought. Perpetual innovation was not scary to Carmichael. In a move reminiscent of Finney's argument that "new measures" of the past often become the widely accepted "normal" of the current time, Carmichael pointed to past novelties that were no longer considered novel.[19] The suggestion was that Christians could eventually accept popular music for religious purposes. But Carmichael pushed beyond accepting a single updating of music. For him, the church should always be reappraising where people were in terms of their music in order to be faithful to the mission God had given it. Thus, he complained about Youth for Christ pioneers who had been aggressive in their use of new music in the 1940s but had grown static and cautious since then.[20] Only two things did not change, according to Carmichael: God's provision for redemption through Jesus Christ and the human need for this salvation. Beyond those two things, as Carmichael declared in 1985, "all else changes, even music—or perhaps *especially* music. . . . We must never stop learning and creating, striving and experimenting, in our efforts to be effective communicators of the gospel through music."[21]

From these two general perceptions (that there is a gap and that continuing creativity is needed to bridge the gap), Carmichael argued for a theology of liturgical innovation that shared three classic elements often repeated by other liturgical pragmatists: a split between form and content, the need for intelligibility of language in expressing the gospel, and the optimism that numerical success indicates what is faithful adaptation.

A form-content split was behind Carmichael's belief (mentioned above) about the only two invariable things being God's provision for salvation and the human need of salvation. Carmichael held that the proclamation of these

18. Horner, "Function of Music," 218. See also Nina N. Ball, "The Carmichael Touch," *Christian Life* (February 1971): 59, quoted in Bishop, "Christian Youth Musicals," 504–5.

19. Horner, "Function of Music," 219.

20. Horner, "Function of Music," 221.

21. Carmichael, *He's Everything to Me*, 188. See also John Gillies, "What's So Sacred about Music?," *Church Musician*, May 1974, 51; Ralph Carmichael, "Interview: Ralph Carmichael," *Creator*, July 1980, 18; and Bishop, "Christian Youth Musicals," 499, 502, 504.

two things is the core of the gospel message. How that message is communicated is the form. In effect, Carmichael was repeating in his own way that sensibility common to prior advocates of liturgical pragmatism: the gospel is distinct from any particular form that might communicate it.

Carmichael did not have to convince his evangelical audiences that this split existed, and so his speeches and interviews insinuated it rather than argued it at length. What Carmichael did promote forcefully was a more contentious point: all forms are morally neutral and thus potentially usable for proclaiming the gospel. It was at this point that Carmichael ran into the conservatism of some fellow evangelicals, who were suspicious of new forms based on popular culture and predisposed in their cautiousness to label pop forms as evil or "carnal." This view Carmichael addressed directly at various times: "Things in themselves are not evil. It's only what they're used for that makes them good or evil," or "Music is not carnal in any shape or form. There is no thing that is carnal. Man's nature is carnal."[22] The next logical steps in this theology were easy ones for Carmichael to take. If all forms are morally neutral, in that their morality depends on their ultimate use, then any form can potentially be used to communicate the content of the gospel. And if all forms are potentially available, the right choice is the one that communicates best, as he said in 1967: "I think that, as Christians, if we're going to use a vehicle, a tool, it should be the sharpest, most effective tool that we can find."[23] In Carmichael's mind, "the sharpest, most effective" musical tool was some form of popular music. Through his work Carmichael helped transmit an acceptance of the moral neutrality of music to evangelical congregations. That acceptance was the key that allowed these churches to adopt the new Christian music based in popular forms.[24]

Carmichael repeatedly expressed the link between effective communication and popular music by speaking of music as a kind of language: for instance, "To me, music is a language. It's nothing more and it's nothing less."[25] Although this metaphorical description of music in linguistic terms was not exceptional in the perspective of liturgical pragmatism leading to Contemporary Worship, Carmichael put his own spin on it by stressing the

22. Horner, "Function of Music," 152, 226.
23. Horner, "Function of Music," 218. For Carmichael, effectiveness in communication was not only connected to the form or style of music but also to the quality or excellence of its performance. At one point in his 1967 speech, he sought to shame his listeners by telling a story of the quest for excellence in a prune commercial's music he had helped make. Surely, Carmichael argued, the gospel is a more important "product" to be "sold" than prunes. See Horner, "Function of Music," 225.
24. Bishop, "Christian Youth Musicals," 364.
25. Quoted in Horner, "Function of Music," 148.

need for music to be in the "vernacular" of youth. The term was a recurring one as he spoke about the type of music needed to bridge the gap with youth and convey the gospel effectively to them.

Indeed, to speak of music in the "vernacular" was how Carmichael typically expressed the quality of Christian music that was intelligible to youth. For example, in the liner notes to a 1966 album, Carmichael expressed his intent: "I wanted to do an album for today . . . in the vernacular of today." In his 1967 speech to Youth for Christ, he declared, "With the kids today it's [popular music is] the gut-real vernacular." In the 1969 interview with Bruce Horner, Carmichael applauded how new Bible translations had "arrived at a vernacular that kids can understand," highlighting how the same needed to be done with music. Describing one of his newly written youth musicals (*Natural High*) in 1971, he noted how it was "communication music for a new day, in their [youth's] language, their vernacular." A 1980 interview gave the composer the chance to argue that the musical vernacular should be embraced, not resisted: "If the vernacular changes in which we are 'proclaiming,' then it's foolish to fight it." At the end of the 1965–85 period, Carmichael was still sounding the same note, linking a metaphorical musical vernacular to a literal linguistic vernacular: "The message we have to share is timeless and unchanging, but if we are to communicate it to a changing world, the medium must be constantly changing. There are new concepts in rhythm, pitch, harmonization, and phrasing, as well as state-of-the-art technology in sound reproduction, not to mention the constant evolution in lyrical vernacular. All of these make it imperative to be acutely aware of these changes in our search for ways and means to stay relevant."[26]

When Carmichael spoke of music as a language that needs to be in the "vernacular" of contemporary people, his concern was about the intelligibility of the music to those people. To make this point, he liked to use an analogy comparing the intelligibility of the Bible and the intelligibility of music: both need to be in an actual contemporary vernacular, he argued, so that people can understand them. Just as the church does not make Africans learn Latin to hear the gospel, and just as it does not make American Christians learn Hebrew or Greek to read the Bible in its original languages, and just as we applaud when new versions of the Bible leave behind the archaic expressions

26. The 1966 liner notes were to *The Restless Ones and Other Ralph Carmichael Songs*, as quoted in Bishop, "Christian Youth Musicals," 181; the quotation from the 1967 speech can be found in Horner, "Function of Music," 229; the excerpt from the 1969 interview with Bruce Horner can likewise be found in the same source on p. 148; the 1971 description of *Natural High* can be found in Ball, "Carmichael Touch," 57, quoted in Bishop, "Christian Youth Musicals," 197; the 1980 quotation was in Carmichael, "Interview: Ralph Carmichael," 18; and the 1985 speech is reproduced in Carmichael, *He's Everything to Me*, 188.

of the King James Version, Carmichael reiterated that the church in the same way should put its music into popular forms to use the understandable musical vernacular of people today.[27] In the three minutes or so that it takes to play a song, he argued, the church does not have time to try music education to get a youth to appreciate a nonpopular form of music. What is better, he continued, is to "speak in a musical language" youth can understand.[28]

Carmichael's emphasis on a musical vernacular was a compelling rhetorical point. By tying use of the vernacular in proclaiming the gospel and in the Bible to having music in the vernacular, he was tapping into long-standing, unassailable Protestant sensibilities. His evangelical listeners especially would have accepted without question the propriety of having the Bible in an understandable form, and they would have insisted that worship be in the language of the people. Consequently, by speaking of the necessity for a musical vernacular, Carmichael was connecting his argument for updating music to foundational Protestant assumptions about Scripture and worship.

In this commitment to making music intelligible to contemporary people, Carmichael felt supported by no less a figure than Billy Graham, the preeminent evangelist of the era, who sent him a letter in April 1974. Carmichael deeply valued this letter that Graham wrote to encourage him in his composing work. Graham framed his approval of Carmichael's efforts in terms of seeking an effective language: "A communication medium is chosen on how well it reaches an audience. In sharing Christ and the gospel, it is natural that the contemporary sound, with its freshness and spontaneity, has become a popular medium, reaching beyond the influence of traditional methods. Christian composers have proven that you can be musically relevant to contemporary society and yet have gospel content which the Holy Spirit can employ."[29]

Carmichael's commitment to musical adaptability was not a matter of pure pragmatism but was actually rooted in deep theological principles he derived from the Bible, especially the New Testament. However, rather than reference the entirety of Scripture and pile up specific biblical citations for what he was advocating—methods more common to theologians of Praise &

27. See Horner, "Function of Music," 149, 223–25.

28. Horner, "Function of Music," 148. Compare the assessment of historian Michael Hamilton to the social value of music for those coming of age at that time: "For this generation music is at the very center of self-understanding. Music for baby boomers is the mediator of emotions, the carrier of dreams, and the marker of social location." Put more simply, music communicated. Michael S. Hamilton, "The Triumph of the Praise Songs: How Guitars Beat Out the Organ in the Worship Wars," *Christianity Today* 43, no. 8 (July 12, 1999): 30.

29. Quoted in Carmichael, *He's Everything to Me*, 159. See also p. 183. Historian Grant Wacker attributes Graham's attitudes in this respect to his undergraduate studies in anthropology. See Grant Wacker, *America's Pastor: Billy Graham and the Shaping of a Nation* (Cambridge, MA: Belknap, 2014), 53.

Worship—Carmichael liked to reference certain scripturally based images to undergird fundamental points he was trying to make compelling. For example, the breadth of Christ's saving work—involving our souls, minds, and bodies—established the breadth of Christ's lordship. That lordship is over the entirety of a person, including culture and creativity.[30] Thus, Christian musicians have a responsibility as stewards to use well their ability to make music, both for the praise of God and for communicating the gospel.[31] Carmichael envisioned this stewardship of music making broadly, not narrowly, since "all melody, harmony, pitch, and rhythm" belong to God.[32]

In addition to this glory-based image of Jesus Christ, Carmichael could also use a vision of Christ as suffering savior to support his approach to Christian music. Noting how others had accused him and other progressive evangelical composers of sacrificing themselves on the "altar of communication," Carmichael was willing to accept the accuracy of the charge. That willingness came from understanding the redemptive, sacrificial sufferings of Christ as a communication of God's grace to the world: "Well, Christ did some sacrificing, I think, on the altar of communication too. He went so far to get bloodied up, lose His life, be spit upon and cursed, and went through the soul-shattering experience of bearing the vile sin of the whole world. That's going to quite a length in order to communicate His love to the world."[33]

By pointing to the extent of Christ's sufferings, Carmichael was picking up New Testament ideas relating to Jesus's greater concern for others than for himself. Although Carmichael did not emphasize the connection, it is not hard to see that same self-emptying concern in how Carmichael described his own attraction to the type of music he was writing for others. Simply put, he acknowledged that the popular music he was writing to communicate with youth was not his own preferred musical style and that he did not particularly like it, stating bluntly on one occasion, "Personally, I don't like the new forms of music," and on another, "My personal taste in music cannot be allowed to motivate what I write. . . . I frankly dislike the new trend in music because I'm forty and my music is not today's music."[34] Although Carmichael seems not to have quoted 1 Corinthians 9:22 specifically, this concern for others rather than himself fitted a certain apostolic sensibility of adapting to become someone—in this case, a composer of

30. Carmichael, *He's Everything to Me*, 184.
31. Carmichael, *He's Everything to Me*, 185.
32. Carmichael, *He's Everything to Me*, 64.
33. Quoted in Horner, "Function of Music," 148.
34. Quoted in Horner, "Function of Music," 148, 224. See also Carmichael, "Interview: Ralph Carmichael," 18.

popular music—for the sake of others in order to carry on the redeeming mission of God.[35]

Carmichael's theologizing was not done merely in the abstract but with one hand on a keyboard and the other holding a pen to music staff paper. He and like-minded evangelical composers turned their talents to writing new music for the church, especially its youth. From the late 1960s through the mid-1970s, perhaps the most creative—and most influential—outlet for these talents was a genre known as the Christian youth musical. Historian William Bishop's definitive study of this genre highlights many of these musicals' common features: solo and chorus musical numbers, choreography, lighting, and a religious plot dwelling on a problem relatable to youth, all staged by the youth in a church.[36] The first such musical was titled *Good News*, coproduced and compiled by Eddie Lunn Jr. and Bob Oldenburg, and performed at a Baptist camp in June 1967.[37] The genre quickly became popular. It reached a high-water mark from 1970 to 1972, when around a dozen new musicals were released in each year. Overall, Bishop identifies seventy-nine distinct musicals composed between 1967 and 1975. After 1975, churches and composers quickly lost interest and moved on to other projects.

Within this genre, Carmichael had a leading role. As Bishop has noted, nearly everyone involved in the creation of these musicals "worked for him, was inspired by him, or was working in competition with him."[38] Indeed, in conjunction with Kurt Kaiser as a cocomposer, Carmichael contributed some of the best-known musicals: 1969's *Tell It Like It Is*; 1970's *Natural High*; and 1973's *I'm Here, God's Here, Now We Can Start*. Moreover, his company, Lexicon Music, published some of the other widely used musicals, especially those from the wife-husband team of Carol and Jimmy Owens.[39]

35. For examples of Carmichael's work, see "Ralph Carmichael Singers," YouTube video, posted by "Dick Bolks," January 31, 2013, 3:07, https://www.youtube.com/watch?v=20blU4 -E3zQ&feature=youtu.be&ab_channel=DickBolks; "I Looked for Love—Ralph Carmichael (Full Album)," YouTube video, posted by "CCM International," May 24, 2017, 33:07, https://www .youtube.com/watch?v=D2tds5QxhH4&feature=youtu.be&ab_channel=CCMInternational; and "Young—Ralph Carmichael and the Young People [1971]," YouTube video, posted by "Kurt Clark," September 30, 2015, 31:56, https://www.youtube.com/watch?v=VT817uYDkFA&feat ure=youtu.be&ab_channel=KurtClark.

36. See Bishop, "Christian Youth Musicals," 4–5.

37. Bishop, "Christian Youth Musicals," 60.

38. Bishop, "Christian Youth Musicals," 169.

39. The musicals by Carol and Jimmy Owens published by Lexicon Music were *Come Together* (1972) and *If My People* (1974). Bishop ("Christian Youth Musicals," 349) notes that the topic of worship was rarely addressed in the whole genre and, when it was, it usually came from composers with a Pentecostal background, especially Carol and Jimmy Owens. This couple were members of Jack Hayford's Church on the Way in California and were influenced by his approach to Praise & Worship (see chap. 3). This influence would explain the statement in their

These musicals, written for the ears of music-listening youth, influenced the worship of evangelical churches—youth and adults alike—in several respects. One of the most striking influences was the introduction of a wider range of musical instruments into church sanctuaries. Evangelical congregations became familiar with seeing the components of a pop band (acoustic and electric guitars, electric bass, and drum kit) and other instruments (brass instruments, woodwinds, and strings) in their holy space and hearing them used for religious purposes. Congregations, too, grew used to seeing these instruments arranged into a distinct kind of ensemble, the band.[40] Youth musicals also played a role in increasing technological dependence in church music making. If a congregation did not have enough sufficiently skilled instrumentalists to handle the accompaniment required by the musical score, it could use an instrumental accompaniment track recorded by professional studio musicians.[41]

Whether they employed live or recorded music, these musicals moved many evangelical congregations toward more popular forms of music in worship. William Bishop summarizes how they set the scene for later developments: "They were the first form of contemporary, pop-styled music to be used in many churches and paved the way for later developments like Praise and Worship, adult choir musicals, and Contemporary Christian Music. CYMs [Christian youth musicals] also brought the guitar, bass, and drum set into churches. This, perhaps more than anything else, is the main musical legacy of CYMs: today's church music could not exist in its current form if not for the introduction and normalization of rhythm instruments."[42] In other words, Christian youth musicals made it easier for evangelical congregations to jump into Contemporary Worship as it developed after 1975.[43]

Moreover, these musicals contributed specific songs that became mainstays of congregational singing in worship for many years. Two of the most obvious examples are Carol Owens's song "Freely, Freely" from *Come Together* and Kurt Kaiser's number "Pass It On (It Only Takes a Spark)" from *Tell It Like It Is*. These songs were soon included in songbooks and even hymnals—and certainly circulated freely in oral form. Consequently, they were quickly detached from their origins in youth musicals and became part of the mix of new songs circulating among worshiping congregations.

---

musical, *Come Together*, that "There's power in praise." See Jimmy Owens and Carol Owens, *Come Together: A Musical Experience in Love* (Waco: Lexicon Music, 1972), 30.

40. Bishop, "Christian Youth Musicals," 380.

41. Bishop, "Christian Youth Musicals," 394.

42. Bishop, "Christian Youth Musicals," 404.

43. Of course, these musicals were not the only means by which popular music became familiar to evangelical churches. Explo '72, the large youth-targeting evangelism and music event in Dallas in 1972, as well as the rise of other Christian music festivals are examples of other means.

Ever the entrepreneur, Carmichael himself worked hard to make available the new songs he and others had written. From the late 1960s into the 1970s, he published several anthologies of songs through Lexicon Music, either in the form of paperback songbooks (such as *He's Everything to Me Plus 53* [1969] and *He's Everything to Me Plus 153* [1974]) or in the form of a more conventional hardback hymnal suitable for pew racks (*The New Church Hymnal* [1976]). While the songbooks aimed for a youth audience (guitar chords were provided for the songs), *The New Church Hymnal* had the look and feel of a congregation's main Sunday morning hymnal. This resource helped mainstream new songs more widely. In addition to including his own songs in *The New Church Hymnal*, Carmichael included songs from others, most notably Kurt Kaiser, Carol and Jimmy Owens, Andraé Crouch, and Larry Norman. He also included two songs by musicians associated with Maranatha! Music and Calvary Chapel (Terrye Coelho's "Father I Adore You" and Karen Lafferty's "Seek Ye First").

Mainline Exasperation in a New Age

By the late 1960s it was not just evangelical musicians who were concerned about a gap between worship and people and, for those anxious about a gap, it was not just a disconnection with youth that propelled the anxiety. Consider, for example, this broad 1969 appraisal of the status of Christian worship:

> In our time, Christian worship has become more and more problematical. Faithful members find it empty or impotent. Marginal members find it phony. . . . Why is this so? As culture changes, the Church preserves forms which emerged during previous periods of creativity. The Church retains the forms intact but the different cultural context blurs or hides the original meaning. Oddly enough, the more obscure the forms are, the more sacred they tend to become. Eventually the cultural lag is so great that there is a credibility gap and people either say that the Spirit does not speak or they say that He speaks to someone else.[44]

The commentator, an English professor, offered his scathing, general evaluation of worship in order to applaud a creative, multimedia service at the Episcopal campus ministry at the University of Michigan, but his sentiment was widely shared by many mainline Christians and even by some evangelicals.

44. Tony Stoneburner, "Emotional Resonance and Life Change in Worship," in *Multi-media Worship: A Model and Nine Viewpoints*, ed. Myron B. Bloy Jr. (New York: Seabury, 1969), 133. Stoneburner was a poet and longtime professor at Denison University in Ohio.

Angst like this professor's was present in a wide swath of congregations, pastors, professors, and even denominational and ecumenical structures.

By the late 1960s there was a surge in literature calling for liturgical change, seeking to address the gap between worship and "modern man," and providing resources and encouragement for those experimenting with ways of worship that bridged that gap. At the same time there was a swell in the number of experimental services, often called by a term that soon gained a technical meaning: "Contemporary Worship." Echoing the sentiments of the professor quoted above, early adherents of "Contemporary Worship" thought the problem involved more than being out of touch with youth or young adults, even though both groups were included in the disenfranchised. These adherents also believed that the solution to the gap involved more than upgrading the music to more popular forms. What was needed was an overhaul of worship to span the chasm that the modern era had inserted between worship and contemporary people.

Those worried about the gap often framed the issue in terms of a "crisis in worship," one so widespread that it was a global pandemic. For instance, when the World Council of Churches assembled in Sweden in 1968, the worship section used crisis language to speak of the challenge that secularization had brought to the church's worship. More-conservative members of the section complained that worship had already become too secularized, while others argued that the secularization of society meant it was urgent to still take "the risk of indigenization," adapting worship even more in language, music, ceremonies, and symbols so these elements would better fit contemporary people.[45]

A similar gap-induced distress gripped North American denominations. For example, the first ever national meeting on worship in the newly created United Methodist Church (created in a 1968 merger) dedicated its four-day assembly to the same theme: the crisis in worship. The keynote address by the bishop who chaired the denomination's Commission on Worship unfolded the problem directly: scientific progress had created a divide between people and the church, including its worship. After several days of plenary presentations and small-group discussions, a report stated that the nearly two thousand lay and clergy participants had settled on two things: there was not a single source for the worship gap and there would be no single solution. To the participants, the problem seemed endemic to the times: "The church has clung to tradition and ancient customs which have become meaningless to many persons."[46]

45. See Norman Goodall, ed., *The Uppsala Report 1968: Official Report of the Fourth Assembly of the World Council of Churches Uppsala, July 4–20, 1968* (Geneva: World Council of Churches, 1968), 74–84.
46. "2,000 Discuss 'Crisis in Worship,'" *Interpreter* 13 (1969): 38.

Beyond acknowledging the church's conservatism and the resultant gap, mainline commentators offered a variety of explanations for what had created the fissure between worship and contemporary people. Many pointed to broad cultural or societal changes, perhaps connected to recent scientific advances. One Episcopalian, seeking to address a specific "crisis in the language of prayer," noted, "We seem to have come to one of those times—an end of an era. Rapid and deep cultural changes in our time are creating a new world necessitating new people to live in it."[47] Another Episcopalian agreed, connecting the radical change to the period's "technological revolution." This revolution, he continued, had brought to the mid-1960s "the fastest, deepest, and most extensive cultural change the world has known."[48]

If technology was creating a new world inhabited by a new kind of person, multiple flashpoints of conflict in the 1960s—an unpopular war in Vietnam, an ongoing Cold War with communism, protests of various kinds, changing gender roles and race relations, and political assassinations, among other things—created a sense of societal flux that accentuated technological and scientific changes. According to some, the period's dis-ease was being felt particularly by youth and young adults. As one influential Lutheran pastor described in a book straightforwardly titled *Worship in Crisis*, the younger generation dealt with a world of "urgent hope and dire disaster." According to this author, worship by a younger generation had to include the tension of hope born from scientific advancement and of disaster arising from continual conflict.[49]

Moreover, others pointed to the rise of new theologies and the tumult that they brought to how traditional ways of worship were valued (or not valued). New ideas about God—including whether God was even alive or dead—caused some to view traditional images of and language about God as stale, tired, and outdated.[50] The whole mindset of traditional worship did not fit those exploring the boundaries of new theologies, including some of the fundamental presumptions about the divine-human relationship. One well-known biblical scholar reflected on the period's liturgical/theological turmoil: "The crisis arose partly because the secular version of the gospel called into question the relevance of worship in its traditional forms, and partly because the concept of transcendence and the 'numinous' has been challenged in recent

47. Daniel B. Stevick, *Language in Worship: Reflections on a Crisis* (New York: Seabury, 1970), 3.

48. Myron B. Bloy Jr., *The Crisis of Cultural Change: A Christian Viewpoint* (New York: Seabury, 1965), 9, 11.

49. Henry E. Horn, *Worship in Crisis* (Philadelphia: Fortress, 1972), 17.

50. Stoneburner, "Emotional Resonance," 134.

time."[51] Observing the effects of technological advances, social turmoil, and nouveau theologies, some traditional worshipers wondered if anything was still sacred in worship. For an increasing number of people in the late 1960s, the answer was "No, thank God."

Someone at the time who would have agreed with that answer was one of the most widely read authors in Canada, Pierre Berton. Not a writer on religion per se, Berton was surprised in 1963 when the Anglican Church of Canada asked him to come study the church's situation and write a critique. He accepted the invitation. The result was a 1965 book, *The Comfortable Pew*, which soon broke all existing sales records for books in Canada.[52] The success in Canada brought a release of the book in the United States in the same year.

Berton's book was a blistering indictment of mainline Protestantism, including its worship. (The Anglicans had agreed to his request to consider all the major Protestant denominations.) His appraisal of the typical Sunday morning was straightforward in its two basic assertions: worship was out of touch with people and worship was completely and utterly boring to people. The standard service was so dull, Berton suggested, that no one cared whether it was true or right.[53]

His critique went into specifics. The liturgy generally? "Dull and old-fashioned." The terms and phrases? "A general fossilization of language." The words? "Archaic." The sermons? "Cliché-ridden and irrelevant to the times." The organ music? "Square." The songs? "Banal hymns." Leaders' use of their voices? "Funereal." And the assembled church? "Spiritless." Berton was sure that these were perceptions widely held and experienced, especially among the young.[54] To cross-check his own appraisal, Berton asked an acquaintance, a mother in her early forties, to sample a range of a dozen churches over as many weeks. Her written report almost made Berton sound like someone enamored of traditional worship:

> Most of all I failed to find an air of enthusiasm and vigour in the churches I attended. There is a dead-wood feeling about the whole service; an automatic and indifferent response on the part of the congregation, and an almost apologetic

51. Ralph P. Martin, *The Worship of God: Some Theological, Pastoral, and Practical Reflections* (Grand Rapids: Eerdmans, 1982), 16.

52. Pierre Berton, *The Comfortable Pew: A Critical Look at Christianity and the Religious Establishment in the New Age* (Philadelphia: Lippincott, 1965), viii.

53. Compare Berton's evaluation to that of a Methodist official: "Much worship is as dull as getting in an elevator, watching the doors close, then getting out without going anywhere." See David James Randolph, *God's Party: A Guide to New Forms of Worship* (Nashville: Abingdon, 1975), 67.

54. Berton, *Comfortable Pew*, 90–92.

attitude in the delivery of the milk-and-water sermons on the part of the minister. . . . In the last several months not one sermon has even touched on any
of today's pressing, conscience-pricking social problems. . . . The ministers
have preached in circles, in platitudes, and in clichés. . . . I found it trouble
that children are small shadows who slip quietly into pews and just as quietly
fidget, kneel, and grope in complicated prayer books. At a given signal, they
file out uninterestedly. . . . The services I attended would have been unbearably
flat without the relief of choir music. Hymn-singing, however, might as well
be dispensed with. Hardly any of the congregation made any attempts at all
to sing the tuneless dirges that are supposed to reflect Christian joy and love.[55]

Berton offered an explanation for why he thought the church's worship
was so boring and out of touch. The reason was the same malady that possessed early Western missionaries who had taken the gospel to new people
but had also enforced a certain culture in its adoption. Churches today may
decry this previous error, Berton pronounced, but they fail to realize they are
making the same mistakes of inflexibility and the "refusal to adapt to native
conditions."[56] Coupled with this inflexibility and refusal to adapt were a
whole series of underlying problems in the mainline churches of the 1960s:
presumptuousness, pride, a lack of humility, and a reliance on wealth and
status.[57] In his opinion, the result was a grievous gap between the church—
including its worship—and modern people.

Berton believed this gap was not new; it had been growing since the rise
of the scientific age in the nineteenth century. He suggested, however, that
an acceleration of the rift was occurring at his time because of recent advancements in electronic technology, especially television. In his opinion,
congregations needed to embrace such new technology "to breathe fresh
vitality into a message that has lost much of its sting through familiarity."[58]
To support his point, Berton referenced another Canadian, someone who
was just beginning to make a splash as *the* evaluator and philosopher of new
electronic media: Marshall McLuhan. Appropriating McLuhan, Berton accepted that television was more than just a medium of expression because
it had become one of the "great facts of the New Age" that was changing
who people were. Since television had changed people, the church had to
master it in order to survive.[59]

55. Quoted in Berton, *Comfortable Pew*, 95–96. Specifically, the unnamed woman was commenting on Anglican churches she had visited.
56. Berton, *Comfortable Pew*, 87.
57. Berton, *Comfortable Pew*, 116–17.
58. Berton, *Comfortable Pew*, 103.
59. Berton, *Comfortable Pew*, 105.

Berton might have been one of the first of the period's commentators on mainline worship to reference McLuhan, but he was certainly not the last. McLuhan, a professor at the University of Toronto, quickly gained widespread prominence—even the popular magazine *Vogue* printed an early article about him—after the publication of his best-known book, *Understanding Media*, in 1964.[60] For a time his influence seemed everywhere, including among those advocating for changes in worship. Indeed, his thoughts were so widely circulated and referenced that a certain perspective could be labeled "McLuhanesque" and no one wondered what was meant.[61] As a cultural force, McLuhan shaped the discussion about new electronic media, perhaps by providing language for the inklings people were already having about a new world saturated with this media. Indeed, McLuhan's most famous one-liner—"the medium is the message"—still resonates today, even if we have forgotten its source. Less remembered is his witty counterpart to this one-liner, "the medium is the *massage*," by which McLuhan meant that the new media was reshaping (i.e., massaging) the people who used the media and thus the world they lived in. This message-massage combination influenced proponents for liturgical change in two ways. One was to point out descriptively how using out-of-date media in worship communicated a message to people—specifically, a wrong message that the church was out of contact with modern people. The other was to suggest prescriptively the remedy by which this gap could be overcome—namely, adopting up-to-date media. Since people were already formed to understand new media by participating in culture generally, modern media in worship would be effective in communicating with modern people.

Pierre Berton imbibed both ideas. On the one hand, he complained about a church whose media of liturgical communication was worse than antiquated, a situation derived from the church's intransigent conservatism. In his view, the church had an obsession with preserving "certain jargons, myths, and mysteries," delivered in outdated modes, "in the belief that by so doing it will also preserve itself." Stick to that approach, Berton warned, and the church would indeed preserve itself "as a fly is preserved in amber, or a corpse in glacial ice, or a fossil embedded in imperishable granite."[62]

On the other hand, Berton hoped for a church that would be willing to experiment and be daring in re-creating its worship. He wished for a church

60. "People Are Talking About: Marshall McLuhan," *Vogue* 148, no. 1 (July 1, 1966): 60–61.

61. For an example, see the editor's comment in Stoneburner, "Emotional Resonance," 133. Consider also the impact when McLuhan-derived categories can be used to frame an entire scholarly article on liturgy. See Thomas F. O'Meara, "Liturgy Hot and Cool," *Worship* 42, no. 4 (April 1968): 215–22.

62. Berton, *Comfortable Pew*, 106.

driven by the purpose of picking up new ways of communicating effectively in a new age. However, he feared his hope would be a perpetually frustrated one, given how conservative he thought mainline churches were.[63]

This prophet of pessimism spoke too soon.

Liturgical Experimentation and the Rise of Contemporary Worship

Even while Berton was finishing the final edits of his damning critique, a period of liturgical experimentation was breaking out among many enterprising mainline Christians—and even some evangelical Christians—who had caught a vision of finding new liturgical means to connect with people. This experimentation lasted for about ten years, starting around 1965 and petering out in the mid-1970s. During this period many pastors, leaders, congregations, and denominations engaged in wholesale experimenting in worship to find ways to connect with disenfranchised people, to be relevant to these people's concerns, and to worship God in harmony with their modern worldview. The experimentation would address many of the problematic areas Berton had highlighted in his book: language, music, the other arts, social issues, preaching, the people's participation, fellowship and belonging, and technology. Even though the overtness of the experimentation faded away in the mid-1970s, many of the practices explored in this period would continue to have an ongoing effect, even if it went unrecognized.

For North American mainline Christianity, this period of experimentation was the first significant, widespread springing forth of Contemporary Worship, even if later forms would take a different outward shape. Nonetheless, through the underlying theology there was a continuity between these early experiments in Contemporary Worship and its widespread adoption later. Moreover, this period of experimentation was the first time that the phrase "Contemporary Worship" became a technical term among mainline worshipers, a usage that has never ended.

Although there was some mainline worship experimentation directed to youth before 1965, as we saw in chapter 5, the mid-decade point seems to be when there was a rush of new efforts. Thus, James F. White, a young worship historian (he was in his early thirties at the time) and professor at the United Methodist–related Perkins School of Theology in Dallas placed the impetus for change in the mid-1960s.[64] Not only was White relying on press accounts of

63. Berton, *Comfortable Pew*, 105.
64. James F. White, *New Forms of Worship* (Nashville: Abingdon, 1971), 7, 15.

change, but he was speaking from his own experience, as we shall see. Similarly, Donald Hustad, a Baptist music professor writing in 1981, named the late 1960s as the time when worship experimentation blossomed among both mainline and evangelical congregations.[65] Indeed, Henry Horn, an influential pastor and prior chairperson of the Lutheran Commission on Liturgy, presumed (disapprovingly) by the early 1970s that the push for liturgical change was so widespread it had become a "fad." He called it the "of course movement," because when any sort of change was suggested people simply said "of course."[66]

The new forms of worship developed by experimenters went by several names. Not surprisingly, "experimental worship" was one of the most common. The term highlighted the innovative process itself and the boldness that lay behind it. In a period bursting with scientific advancements, it seemed appropriate to have "experimental worship" or an "experimental service."[67] The other widespread term was "contemporary worship." The latter term quickly became commonplace in this period and was often used to note opposition to what had preceded it—that is, "traditional worship." If "experimental" stressed the process, then "contemporary" named the goal: worship that had overcome the liturgical chasm and was fitting for contemporary people. Like many expressions, the term apparently arose naturally but soon gained a technical meaning. Churches began to advertise their "contemporary services," assuming people would have an idea what that meant (and would be attracted by it).[68] At the time, people tended to use "experimental worship" and "contemporary worship" as synonyms, as happened in a conference on worship conducted by the United States Navy Chaplain Corps or in books aimed at providing resources to local congregations that wanted to explore new liturgical practices.[69]

65. Donald P. Hustad, *Jubilate! Church Music in the Evangelical Tradition* (Carol Stream, IL: Hope, 1981), 332.

66. Horn, *Worship in Crisis*, 7, 20. Horn acknowledged that he had borrowed the label from renowned Orthodox liturgical theologian Alexander Schmemann. That Horn had in mind the sort of gap-solving liturgical experimentation discussed in this section can be seen by comparing his book to an earlier article: Henry E. Horn, "Experimentation and the Congregation," *Religion in Life* 39, no. 1 (Spring 1970): 8–17.

67. This term was used at least by 1962. See "News of the Brotherhood," *Christian* 100, no. 11 (March 18, 1962): 20. Note that "experimental" was also a liturgical term that circulated among Roman Catholics. See Robert F. Hoey, ed., *The Experimental Liturgy Book* (New York: Herder & Herder, 1969).

68. The term had a porousness in the sense that it could be used more generally to describe new liturgical resources, not just a specific kind of service identified by style. For instance, drawing on the former sense, the Inter-Lutheran Commission released at that time a series of new resources for which "Contemporary Worship" was the series name.

69. United States Navy Chaplain Corps, *The Layman as a Leader of Worship* (Washington, DC: US Government Printing Office, 1969), 8; James L. Christensen, *New Ways to Worship: More Contemporary Worship Services* (Old Tappan, NJ: Revell, 1973), 14–15.

One of the participants in the Navy-sponsored conference was James F. White, the Methodist professor mentioned earlier. His participation was fitting. Not only was he one of the rising significant voices in Methodist worship, but he himself was also plunging headfirst into the period's Contemporary Worship. From the late 1960s into the early 1970s, he may have been the most published sympathetic thinker reflecting on Contemporary Worship. White worked out his perspectives in two different settings of liturgical experimenting.[70]

In his writing, White is vehement that there was a gap between the worship of mainline Christians and many people, especially those born in the late 1930s and afterward. The significance of being born in the late 1930s or later was that these people had grown up in a world with televisions. Those born earlier had lived for a while without the ever-present TV.[71] Thus, White repeatedly framed the

Supplied by Martin White and used by permission of Ellen Toliver

Figure 6.2. James F. White in the early 1970s

70. Between 1967 and 1976, White published three books on the subject as well as numerous articles. See James F. White, *The Worldliness of Worship* (New York: Oxford University Press, 1967); White, *New Forms of Worship*; and James F. White, *Christian Worship in Transition* (Nashville: Abingdon, 1976). He also wrote numerous articles and essays on that period's Contemporary Worship. See especially James F. White, "Worship in an Age of Immediacy," *Christian Century* 75 (February 21, 1968): 227–30, reprinted as "Worship in the Age of Marshall McLuhan," in James F. White, *Christian Worship in North America: A Retrospective, 1955–1995* (Collegeville, MN: Liturgical Press, 1997), 135–41. Other relevant articles include James F. White, "Characteristics of Effective Christian Worship," *Studia Liturgica* 8, no. 4 (1971–72): 195–206; and James F. White, "Worship and Culture: Mirror or Beacon?," *Theological Studies* 35, no. 2 (June 1974): 288–301. Moreover, White's theological reflections and liturgical work in the period have been examined recently and insightfully. See R. Matthew Sigler, *Methodist Worship: Mediating the Wesleyan Liturgical Heritage* (New York: Routledge, 2019), 150–57; and R. Matthew Sigler, "James F. White, Grady Hardin, and Methodist 'Contemporary' Worship in the 1970s," in *Essays on the History of Contemporary Praise and Worship*, ed. Lester Ruth (Eugene, OR: Pickwick, 2020), 13–33. Sigler's work is especially helpful for seeing the development in White's thought and practices across time.

71. Note that White was born in 1932 and was only a few years older than those in the TV generation.

gap between worship and people in terms of generations shaped by different technologies. As these younger folk were coming of age in the 1960s, society was slipping, in White's opinion, from a "radio era" to a time in which television was the dominant mode of communication. The result was a communications revolution parallel to the development of the printing press. Just as the printing press reshaped worship from its medieval form to the word- and text-centered forms of the Protestant Reformation, so White expected the TV-induced communications revolution to reshape worship again.[72]

Unfortunately, White thought, much of Protestant worship was still stuck in forms more in tune with prior forms of communication than with the new TV era. The result was a crisis, as he expressed in 1968: "We face today a crisis in Protestant worship, one that seems certain to increase in intensity in the years ahead. The crisis is created by the alienation of the usual forms of worship from the modern world's means of perception."[73] Consequently, White went to church on Sunday morning and expected to find yawns, because he knew young adults and youth were bored by the "unrelieved dullness."[74] At one point he himself even confessed to being bored by this "dullest hour of the week."[75]

In framing the gap between people and worship as a crisis born from shifts in communication, White showed the influence that the work of Marshall McLuhan had had on him. Indeed, White quoted and cited McLuhan repeatedly, acknowledging at one point that, although McLuhan had not created the communications revolution, he was describing it better than anyone else.[76] White accepted McLuhan's descriptive analysis of the situation, applying it to worship: "The chief problem, then, is that the medium is wrong and, consequently, so is the message. Worship in the mainline adult churches is a diet of words spooned out to us by the minister."[77] White also relied on the *massaging* dimension of media, agreeing that the TV generation had different forms of perception requiring "direct participation in the event" that reading did not

72. White, *New Forms of Worship*, 28–30.

73. White, "Worship in an Age of Immediacy," 227; White, "Worship in the Age of Marshall McLuhan," 135. For all citations of this piece from White, whether here or in subsequent notes, we will give both references to this twice-published work.

74. White, "Worship and Culture," 299.

75. White, "Worship in an Age of Immediacy," 228; White, "Worship in the Age of Marshall McLuhan," 136–37. On several occasions White made references to Pierre Berton's book, *The Comfortable Pew*. See White, *The Worldliness of Worship*, 43; and White, *New Forms of Worship*, 100.

76. White, "Worship in an Age of Immediacy," 227; White, "Worship in the Age of Marshall McLuhan," 135.

77. White, "Worship in an Age of Immediacy," 228; White, "Worship in the Age of Marshall McLuhan," 137.

provide. Applied to worship, this TV-formed mode of perception produced worshipers who wanted sight, touch, and hearing integrated.[78] Television, too, produced a desire for color, not to mention the capacity for a nonlinear structure in which multiple things can happen simultaneously and still be understood.[79]

James F. White's theologizing about the necessity for experimenting through Contemporary Worship manifested several similarities to that of other Contemporary Worship theologians, both at the time and previously. Highlighting effective communication as one of worship's purposes, for example, aligned with others' emphasis on the intelligibility of language. (Although White included the updating of language from archaic English as one of the goals to be pursued in new forms of worship, he spoke infrequently about "language" per se, wanting to avoid creating a presumption that worship was exclusively about the verbal.)[80] White also synced with the general impulse in this theological perspective to shape worship with a close eye on the people you wanted to reach, stating at the time, "We need to relate to people as they are, not just as we imagine them to be" and suggesting that congregations should hire sociological consultants for that purpose.[81] This emphasis on analyzing people and then finding the right forms to communicate well in worship implies the importance of human agency in developing the context-influenced shape of worship, another of liturgical pragmatism's common theological emphases.

Thus, like other theologians of Contemporary Worship, White felt that such an analysis of people should determine the particular form of worship, a freedom allowed because of the distinction between the forms of worship and the biblical content that must be expressed in worship.[82] The distinction between form and content could exist, White argued, because "theologically the communications medium is largely neutral"[83] and "forms of communication are theologically ambiguous."[84] Forms should fit the people. In contrast, the content of worship was dependent upon the story of God's dealings remembered in Scripture.

Distinguishing between worship's forms and its contents allowed White—as it had others—to contend zealously for a liturgical adaptability based on

78. White, *New Forms of Worship*, 29–30.
79. White, *New Forms of Worship*, 23, 136.
80. White, *New Forms of Worship*, 195.
81. White, "Worship in an Age of Immediacy," 229–30; White, "Worship in the Age of Marshall McLuhan," 140.
82. See White, *Christian Worship in Transition*, 14–15.
83. White, *Christian Worship in Transition*, 15.
84. White, *New Forms of Worship*, 35.

1 Corinthians 9:22. In a business-related image that would have made Salvation Army founder Catherine Booth proud (see chap. 5), White proclaimed in 1971 his sense of an apostolic mission:

> The splintering of society means that to be true and relevant to people as they now are, we will need to be all things to all people. In the past we have offered what businessmen call a manufacturing mentality. We produced a product and then looked for someone to take it. Now, instead, we need a marketing mentality. Businesses operating on a manufacturing mentality are not apt to survive since their competitors can produce something that people really want. Yet such has been the mentality of the church. A marketing mentality searches for what people want and need and then resolves to satisfy that need. Our pastoral norm emphasizes the need to recognize the great variety of persons in the church today and their varying conditions of life. This almost automatically demands a greater number of choices of types of worship.[85]

White closed on an ominous note for change-rejecting Christians, reminding his readers that, if the Ford Motor Company had not changed its original policy to produce cars in one color only, it would not have remained in business.

As White implemented his vision for worship fitting for a new era, he found two ongoing outlets for his experimental creativity: the chapel services at his school (Perkins School of Theology in Dallas) and a newly created contemporary service at his home church, Highland Park United Methodist Church (located across a parking lot from Perkins School of Theology). In each, he worked with others to plan services that transformed McLuhan's abstract descriptions of a TV generation into concrete liturgical practices. The goal was to provide Contemporary Worship (that term was used at Highland Park) services that were more than passive, one-dimensional listening on the part of worshipers. To that end, White and his colleagues sought to plan highly active, participatory services with a variety of immersive dimensions: sight, touch, hearing, color, decoration (including balloons and banners), sacraments as robust "sign-acts," creative preaching, electronic audio and visual media, movement, innovative arrangement of the space and furnishings, and different ways for the congregation to participate.[86] In one service, for example, a standard order of worship was straightforwardly observed in the midst of an audio loop of sounds from everyday life while random slides

---

85. White, *New Forms of Worship*, 33.
86. For descriptions of services and the general approach, see Sigler, *Methodist Worship*, 152–53; and especially Sigler, "James F. White, Grady Hardin." For White's own discussion of the different dimensions that could be adapted, see *New Forms of Worship*, 80–148.

of scenes outside the sanctuary were projected all around the worshipers. In one Communion service White preached in a rented janitor's uniform, speaking on how sharing the bread related communicants to all people. Another Communion service was observed in total silence: worshipers had the text for the service but it was led entirely through movement, gestures, posture, expressions, and objects. On another occasion, the service consisted entirely of songs from the Broadway musical *Godspell*.[87]

The specific dimensions of experience engaged could vary from service to service, but some things remained standard: the planners' commitment to addressing relevant issues, the use of updated English, and the use of an eclectic range of music (often popular). Also consistent behind all White's experimenting was his extensive, deep understanding of worship history and ecumenical liturgical theology, sources that provided guiding norms for his creativity and innovations.[88]

Besides James White in Dallas, there were many other mainline apologists for early experimenting in Contemporary Worship during the same period of time. This initial outburst encompassed a spectrum of churches, denominations, settings, and promoters. Even if no one matched White's extensive theological and pastoral reflection on the need for these early forms of Contemporary Worship, nonetheless there was no slippage in the zeal with which others promoted and experimented. That was true even if mainline apologists never emphasized the evangelical sense of adapting worship for the sake of getting people saved. Nonetheless, there was an urgency throughout all the mainline voices about a critical gap that existed between people and worship. Everyone agreed that people should be in worship. Therefore, churches must adapt to get, keep, motivate, and deepen people for the church, its membership, and its

87. Sigler, *Methodist Worship*, 152–53; White, *New Forms of Worship*, 119, 112–13; Sigler, "James F. White, Grady Hardin," 23.

88. Thus James White did not approach a contemporary service as a blank slate. His works in the period show the influence that liturgical history, classic liturgical theology, and the emerging ecumenical Liturgical movement had on his creativity and innovation. In other words, using a concept he himself applied to his Methodist tradition's founder (John Wesley), he was more of a "pragmatic traditionalist" than a liturgically iconoclastic, traditional pragmatist who felt no restraints whatsoever from history or from the broader church (see James F. White, *Protestant Worship: Traditions in Transition* [Louisville: Westminster John Knox, 1989], 151). Indeed, over the years it was these guiding dimensions that continued to shape White more and more as he sought to apply history, theology, and pastoral sensibilities to new forms of worship for his denomination. He would become one of the main shapers of the new official rites of United Methodism. Although it is little realized today, some of White's experiments for increasing participation in worship and Communion in this period later became part of that denomination's Word and Table I service. See Sigler, *Methodist Worship*, 152.

mission in the world.[89] Vanderbilt professor John Killinger vividly described his despondency over the gap between this goal and reality:

> We live in a Peter Max world of exciting colors and configurations. We listen to music that is produced both electronically and atonally. We read novelists who write cryptically and suggestively, so that we are forced to puzzle over their meanings or else despair of their having any meaning. We produce and watch television shows and movies that are so weird or imaginative as to defy our intelligence and appeal only to our emotions. But for some reason we have not brought our everyday way of life into the sanctuary of the church. We have a syncopated, rock-and-roll, electronic consciousness for most of the week and a funereal, four-four attitude toward Sunday morning. And what it means is that Sunday morning is where least is happening in our lives.[90]

Killinger's solution was a vision in which Sunday morning would become where the most was happening in people's lives. His solution was worship that made more dynamic use of the body, dance, drama, story, language, music, preaching, time, and space.

Killinger's list provides a summary of the sorts of liturgical dimensions that mainline experimenters often emphasized. For example, James Christensen, an experimenting pastor who published two resource volumes on Contemporary Worship, summarized the hodgepodge of typical aspects found in his contemporary services: modern ballads, varied instruments, light, color, all kinds of arts, movements, dance, recorded music, films, picture projections, clapping, Scriptures and prayers using words in current usage, varied sermon methods, and popular music.[91] The goal was contemporary services

89. In its own way, the emphasis on *aggiornamento* ("openness" in Italian—that is, open conversation with the modern world) in the Second Vatican Council, including its liturgical reforms, was a Roman Catholic struggle with the same situation. See John W. O'Malley, *What Happened at Vatican II* (Cambridge, MA: Belknap, 2008), 36–43. The impact of these reforms and discussions could be quite striking, as Mark Massa has noted: "For the first time in their history, ordinary Catholics now addressed how 'relevant' their religious symbols and worship should be" (Mark Massa, *The American Catholic Revolution: How the Sixties Changed the Church Forever* [Oxford: Oxford University Press, 2010], 7). For the relevant conciliar statements, see Annibale Bugnini, *The Reform of the Liturgy 1948–1975*, trans. Matthew J. O'Connell (Collegeville, MN: Liturgical Press, 1990), 42–43. Some of the significant liturgical voices within Roman Catholicism at the time wondered if "modern man" was still capable of liturgical worship. See especially Romano Guardini, "A Letter from Romano Guardini," *Herder Correspondence* 1 (1964): 24–26. For an Eastern Orthodox reflection on the question of worship in a "secular age," see Alexander Schmemann, "Worship in a Secular Age," *St. Vladimir's Theological Quarterly* 16, no. 1 (1972): 3–16.

90. John Killinger, *Leave It to the Spirit: Commitment and Freedom in the New Liturgy* (New York: Harper & Row, 1971), 7. Peter Max was a popular artist in the 1960s known for the use of bright, bold colors.

91. James L. Christensen, *Contemporary Worship Services: A Sourcebook* (Old Tappan, NJ: Revell, 1971), 11.

that were more participatory, celebratory, communal, mystical, mobile, and variable.[92] Methodists and Presbyterians published similar descriptions with similar lists and goals.[93]

In virtually all the new services put together by those experimenting with early Contemporary Worship and throughout their lists of possibilities, there were three standard traits and a common goal. The first trait was an updating of English from the archaic forms derived from the King James Version. This change was foundational, matching the time period's general trend in the explosion of new versions of the Bible and the push for updated language in all text-based liturgies in Western Christianity.[94] Contemporary Worship's propensity for the colloquial matched a shift occurring more broadly in culture concerning what was heard as true, authentic speech.[95] The second standard trait was a care to make the content of the services relevant to people's concerns and lives. In that tumultuous time in history, there was no patience for the irrelevant. The third trait was the use of music drawn from some sort of popular music. The specific form of music varied: an early interest in jazz gave way to folk, pop, or rock-based forms of music making.[96] Perhaps the difficulty of finding qualified jazz musicians in rank-and-file congregations and the difficulty of corporately singing this form explain the shift.

The common goal involved making the worship service fitting for contemporary people. That was what made worship itself "contemporary" in

92. Christensen, *New Ways to Worship*, 14–15.

93. See Randolph, *God's Party*, and the whole theme issue of *Presbyterian Life* magazine for October 15, 1971. Perhaps the furthest extent of the innovations was the rise of clowning as part of Protestant worship, a development of the same time period. In particular, Floyd Shaffer, a Lutheran minister, was an influential groundbreaker in this sort of liturgical ministry. See Floyd Shaffer and Penne Sewall, *Clown Ministry: A How-To Manual and Dozens of Skits for Service & Worship* (Loveland, CO: Group Books, 1984), 12; and Floyd Shaffer, *If I Were a Clown* (Minneapolis: Augsburg, 1984). For another early example, see Janet Litherland, *The Clown Ministry Handbook* (Colorado Springs: Meriwether, 1982).

94. See Lim Swee Hong and Lester Ruth, *Lovin' on Jesus: A Concise History of Contemporary Worship* (Nashville: Abingdon, 2017), 106–8; Stevick, *Language in Worship*; and Peter C. Finn and James M. Schellman, eds., *Shaping English Liturgy* (Washington, DC: Pastoral Press, 1990).

95. See John McWhorter, *Doing Our Own Thing: The Degradation of Language and Music and Why We Should, Like, Care* (New York: Gotham, 2003).

96. At the time many commentators highlighted the groundbreaking role of Geoffrey Beaumont (a priest in the Church of England and musical composer) and the 20th Century Church Light Music Group, especially through a piece titled *A Twentieth Century Folk Mass*, published in 1956. The recording was released in 1957. For early attestations of jazz, see the account of the New York Annual Conference of the Methodist Church in "Cool Creed," *Time* 86, no. 2 (July 9, 1965): 48; and the account of a Massachusetts campus ministry in "Helping Students Make the Spiritual Passage," *Time* 86, no. 14 (October 1, 1965): 85. In the 1960s folk masses became more popular among Roman Catholics too.

the most fundamental sense. Contemporary Worship in the late 1960s and early 1970s sought to fully gain the people's investment, interest, and active participation.

Because people varied from place to place, it should be no surprise that particular examples of Contemporary Worship in the period showed their own variety and nuances.[97] At First Presbyterian Church of Hollywood, for example, the services evolved from the efforts of Don Williams, one of the pastors, to reach the young adults he saw in the streets around the church. Listening to and studying them, Williams quickly latched on to the importance of music in their world, noting, "Here I began to feel the full weight of the cultural revolution, and here I found a great secret: music is the key to this generation because music is the one place in the mass media where kids editorialize to kids."[98] Williams began to weave popular music into the Sunday evening services at his church, including his preaching, as when he interlaced a sermon with Bob Dylan lyrics.[99]

Eventually, Williams led the church to change from a strategy of bringing folks into the church building to a strategy of going outside the sanctuary walls to take the gospel into the streets. He found the rationale for his let's-go-to-the-world approach in Paul's first letter to the Corinthians: "But how shall we go? Our clue comes from the Apostle Paul [1 Cor. 9:22] who became all things to all men in order to win some. The form of our approach must have a contemporary cultural identification, while the content must remain unchanging."[100] Subsequently, the church opened a coffeehouse, formed a musical group using folk-rock music, and began offering concerts in a variety of public locations, including the beach and the well-known Pasadena Civic Auditorium. Finally, in 1970, the church created two ongoing services featuring contemporary music, movement, and other standard elements of new experimentation.[101]

On the other side of the country, at Mount Vernon Place Methodist Church in Washington, DC, congregational leaders were struggling with declining attendance at the evening service, on the one hand, and a "cry of desperation" from young adults and teenagers for something different, on the other.

---

97. While the examples provided here are from mainline contexts, for evangelical examples see the series of three articles by Edward E. Plowman and Ray C. Steadman: "The Minister's Workshop: Let's Put Life in Church Services," *Christianity Today*, March 26, 1971; April 23, 1971; May 21, 1971.

98. Don Williams, *Call to the Streets* (Minneapolis: Augsburg, 1972), 23.

99. Williams, *Call to the Streets*, 27.

100. Williams, *Call to the Streets*, 30. Compared to many of his contemporaneous mainline counterparts, Williams was more overtly evangelical in his piety and theology.

101. Williams, *Call to the Streets*, 71–72.

Their response was Church-O-Theque, which debuted in 1966.[102] On paper the service often looked like a traditional one: the order of worship was still strongly text-based and paralleled that of the congregation's other services. It was in the music, in the use of multiple media, and in how the service was led that Church-O-Theque was different. Eschewing jazz-based experiments seen elsewhere because of the difficulty in getting congregants to sing, the church musicians composed entirely new tunes in a "disco-cinematic" style for three hymn texts selected by the preacher. These were led by a small band that usually consisted of an electric guitar, an electric bass, drums, and an organ, along with a small vocal team. Service planners also included in the service some type of media that went beyond "normal" expectations: a film or filmstrip, a recording, dance, a dramatic piece, or a dialogue. On occasion, the service became edgy. Leaders reported that one of the most effective calls to worship was the one led by college cheerleaders to the tune of Notre Dame's fight song.[103]

Experimentation in Contemporary Worship went beyond parish settings. Campus ministries at universities and colleges were often at the forefront of experimentation. Perhaps the best-documented case involved the Episcopal campus ministry at the University of Michigan, mentioned earlier. A full-length book, *Multi-media Worship*, described the sort of services held there. A standard Eucharistic order was adapted to include a folk trio, contemporary hymns, secular pop music (the Beatles seem to have been a particular favorite in this location), electronic visual media, newly composed musical settings for critical liturgical texts, and even dramatic presentations. On the specific occasion fully documented in the book, a mime troupe acted out the trial of some Vietnam War protesters.[104]

A different sort of campus setting for Contemporary Worship could be found at the United States Air Force Academy near Colorado Springs. In the mid-1970s contemporary services began to be offered there, with updated music and a liturgical dance group. This move at the Air Force Academy paralleled experimentation being done by Air Force chaplains at a variety of bases around the world, including Lackland Air Force Base in Texas, the site for basic training of new inductees. There a survey of trainees indicated that nearly four out of five had recently dropped out of an "institutional church" because they found the services boring and the sermons irrelevant. To tackle these complaints, chaplains began using contemporary music played by

102. Floyd E. Werle, "Church-O-Theque," *Music Ministry* 9, no. 6 (February 1968): 2–9.
103. Werle, "Church-O-Theque," 6.
104. Myron B. Bloy Jr., ed., *Multi-media Worship: A Model and Nine Viewpoints* (New York: Seabury, 1969), 18–50.

talented musicians in their ranks and began carefully crafting entire services around a coherent, relevant theme. These practices and more found their way onto other bases.[105]

Not surprisingly, given the growing interest in Contemporary Worship, this same time period saw a stream of resources published on new ways of worship. Some were mainly descriptive (James White's *New Forms of Worship* is an example) while others provided texts and services intended for immediate use (James Christensen's two books, *Contemporary Worship Services* and *New Ways to Worship*, are examples). Some came from individuals whereas others were denominationally sponsored and published. There was no dearth of available materials. A 1973 bibliography of materials related to Contemporary Worship ran for fifteen pages, including four pages on nonmusical art forms (vestments, posters, photography, art and architecture, drama, and dance) and more than five pages on sources for music (scores, albums, etc.).[106] Occasional conferences supplemented published resources. At a 1973 conference sponsored by various Lutheran bodies, eighteen hundred participants heard James White give a lecture called "Worship in Our Changing Culture" and chose from fifty-one workshops on topics such as dramatic presentations, films, puppetry, multimedia, and folk singing.[107]

With this seeming flood of congregations, people, and resources involved in developing Contemporary Worship by the early 1970s, what happened? Why did this initial rush to experiment and bridge the liturgical gap seem to dissipate in the years following?

In several respects it only *seemed* to evaporate. Even as early as 1976, James White noted how many aspects of experimental worship had become so standard, permanent, and "routinized" it hardly appeared appropriate to call them experimental any more.[108] His Baptist counterpart, Donald Hustad, provided a list of what he saw as the permanent changes: (1) much more congregational, lay participation in things like calls to worship, Scripture readings, and prayers; (2) contemporary, updated English; (3) expressions of Christian fellowship between worshipers; (4) a greater variety of musical styles, often within a single service; and (5) more functional designs in the space and room furnishings. (Indeed, these qualities migrated throughout

105. John E. Groh, *Air Force Chaplains, 1971–1980,* vol. 4 of *Air Force Chaplains* (Washington, DC: Office, Chief of Air Force Chaplains, 1986), 94–96, 349–60, 378–81.

106. Don M. Wardlaw, "Come to Our Liturgical Storehouse," in *Ventures in Worship,* ed. David James Randolph (Nashville: Abingdon, 1973), 3:209–23.

107. Mandus A. Egge, "A Lutheran Conference on Worship," *Studia Liturgica* 9, no. 3 (1973): 158–60.

108. White, *Christian Worship in Transition,* 131.

Used by permission of Donald C. Cousins

Figure 6.3. Drama in a service put on by Son City, an evangelical, youth-targeting ministry in the Chicago area, in the late 1970s

much of Protestant worship, Contemporary or otherwise.) Hustad also noted, however, that many of the "revolutionary communicative methods" in "preaching-singing-praying" had just about disappeared.[109] White agreed, noting how electronic media was not nearly as important or widespread as he had thought it would be just a few years earlier.[110]

Another development White and Hustad could have pointed to was the mainstreaming of new songs from this period. Songs written in a new style became increasingly available to congregations in the old-style format of hymnals. Ralph Carmichael's 1976 edited work, *The New Church Hymnal*, was one example. It was joined by others, including Word Music's *The Hymnal for Worship & Celebration* and multiple denominational hymnals.[111]

In addition, in some places early mainline Contemporary Worship continued after the mid-1970s. Thus, Zwingli United Church of Christ celebrated its

109. Hustad, *Jubilate!*, 332–33.

110. White, *Christian Worship in Transition*, 131. Immediately after this observation, White also commented (pp. 132–42) on how the constant experimentation had been labor intensive, not to mention that some had discovered they were not all that creative while others had "inflicted" experimentation on their congregations with little concern for parishioners. White would eventually prove right about electronic media, but it would take twenty more years. See Lim and Ruth, *Lovin' on Jesus*, 46–51.

111. Tom Fettke, ed., *The Hymnal for Worship & Celebration* (Waco: Word Music, 1986). Note how this hymnal's design provided the possibility of using song medleys reminiscent of those used in Praise & Worship. In this way, this hymnal anticipated the confluence that would eventually fuse Praise & Worship and Contemporary Worship by the end of the century.

one thousandth Contemporary Worship service in Souderton, Pennsylvania (a suburb of Philadelphia), on January 15, 1989.[112] Its service had begun in the late 1960s when the pastor felt that "there was a need for a more involving, contemporary style that spoke more clearly to the people." Other churches continued to have the occasional service targeted to a particular segment of the congregation (often youth), while some large congregations continued to have multiple services differentiated by style, setting, and time.[113]

In other places, early mainline Contemporary Worship began anew in the late 1970s and early 1980s. Among a dedicated group of Missouri Synod Lutheran pastors and musicians, for example, there was a small rush to develop contemporary services featuring contemporary worship music beyond their denominational hymnal. The motivation was these leaders' frustration that the new, official denominational resources exacerbated the gap between the unchurched (and non-Lutherans) with traditional Lutheran ways of worshiping. One of these early initiators expressed a desire to be able to "speak" in worship in ways that connected with these people: "[We need] to design some kind of worship so we can reach them—we need to speak their heart language."[114]

Notwithstanding these ongoing and new expressions of Contemporary Worship, the period after the mid-1970s became, as we have called it elsewhere, "a period of incubation" awaiting a later flood of mainline and evangelical adoption of contemporary services.[115] The Contemporary Worship that had broken to the surface through youth musicals and mainline contemporary services went underground again for a time. But the waters were not still. Waiting for a time to rage to the surface once again, they continued to circulate and bubble with new developments, gaining momentum in the process.

Incubation: Contemplating Growth and Decline

"Worship is boring." Despite nearly ten years of mainline and evangelical experimentation in Contemporary Worship, that assessment was still being asserted in the mid-1970s. Consider, for example, this 1974 indictment from a mainline pastor who hoped to stir things up with his new book: "Many churches are so dignified they're dull! The music is dull, the messages are dull,

---

112. "Zwingli Marks 1000th Innovative Worship," *News Herald* (Perkasie, PA), January 11, 1989.

113. White, *Christian Worship in Transition*, 133–34.

114. Samuel Eatherton, "The Introduction of Contemporary Worship Music into the Lutheran Church–Missouri Synod," *Concordia Historical Institute Quarterly* 92, no. 2 (Summer 2019): 30.

115. Lim and Ruth, *Lovin' on Jesus*, 9.

the architecture is dull; there is no excitement in the air! The worship service might be described as sleepy, quietly meditative and a perfectly tranquilizing arrangement—guaranteed to produce yawning and boredom."[116] The pastor, who had a strong mainline pedigree (he was affiliated with the Reformed Church in America and was a graduate of Hope College and Western Theological Seminary), targeted boring worship as one of the top eleven things that would erode a congregation's ability to grow. Many who read this pastor's book thought he ought to truly know what could cause or stifle growth because he, Robert Schuller, was the founding pastor of a tremendously growing church in Orange County, California, originally named Garden Grove Community Church. Schuller and this congregation, which he had founded in 1955, had already become fixtures in the national consciousness by the early 1970s through Schuller's innovative ministry, his popular books, the weekly telecast of the congregation's worship under the name "The Hour of Power," and articles about the church in popular magazines.[117] (When the church's new sanctuary opened in 1980, the congregation changed its name to the Crystal Cathedral to match the space.)[118]

Schuller was more than just another example of someone complaining about boring mainline worship: he was a key figure in the period of incubation for Contemporary Worship following the 1970s. Although the worship at his church would not fit most people's image of "Contemporary Worship"— there was a choir and organ, Schuller wore a robe, and hymns were sung— nonetheless Schuller's work fed the underground circulation of waters in Contemporary Worship. Part of his influence came through his teaching, both in his Institute for Successful Church Leadership and in his 1974 book, *Your Church Has Real Possibilities!* Many of the pastors whose ministries would provide the megachurch models for Contemporary Worship in the late 1980s either came through this institute, were inspired by this book, or both (see chap. 7). Since the book was a distillation of Schuller's lectures in the institute, it did not matter which. (Indeed, since Charles Blake of West Angeles Church of God in Christ was a participant in the first class of the institute in 1969, Schuller also influenced a key church in Praise & Worship. See chap. 4 for Blake's congregation's history.)[119]

116. Robert H. Schuller, *Your Church Has Real Possibilities!* (Glendale, CA: Regal, 1974), 39.

117. For example, see "Drive-In Devotion," *Time* 90, no. 18 (November 3, 1967): 83–84.

118. For an excellent historical overview of Schuller and this church, see Mark T. Mulder and Gerardo Martí, *The Glass Church: Robert H. Schuller, the Crystal Cathedral, and the Strain of Megachurch Ministry* (New Brunswick, NJ: Rutgers University Press, 2020).

119. Robert H. Schuller, *My Journey: From an Iowa Farm to a Cathedral of Dreams* (San Francisco: HarperSanFrancisco, 2001), 292.

Moreover, Schuller's leadership approach as an evangelizing pastor provided a template that was followed by others as they launched new churches that would feature Contemporary Worship. The influence of Schuller and his congregation was not in providing a type of service that others imitated as much as it was in shaping the entirety of congregational life, including worship, for the purpose of attracting the outsider and the unchurched, all with an optimism that an entrepreneurial pastor could develop this effort into a large congregation. New congregations, whose Contemporary Worship in the next period would indeed provide a model that others did try to emulate, thus began by following Garden Grove's pattern of forgoing denominational affiliation in the name in favor of the less off-putting label "community church" (for example, Willow Creek Community Church). Or they emulated Schuller's initial step to begin his congregation— that is, door-to-door visits to ask the unchurched what they would like to find in a church (two pastors who followed this strategy were Bill Hybels at Willow Creek and Rick Warren at Saddleback Valley Community Church).

Moreover, Schuller was loosely affiliated with the nascent Church Growth movement, an emerging network that promoted missiological theories to assess the social dynamics behind why some evangelistic works grew numerically and others did not. Not only had Schuller on his own landed on many of the practices and perspectives advocated by Church Growth theorists, but the phenomenal growth of his congregation meant it served as a kind of poster child that could be referenced by early Church Growth proponents.[120] Schuller's church even hosted early meetings of Church Growth theorists applying their thought to an American context.[121] The Church Growth movement would prove important in the history of Contemporary Worship, as the movement increasingly questioned whether congregations could grow if they did not provide liturgical options beyond a dull, traditional service that was detached from popular culture. In other words, this movement would become the new proclaimer of a substantial gap between worship and people. This note of concern would help keep the waters circulating in the period of incubation for Contemporary Worship between the mid-1970s and mid-1980s. In short, Robert Schuller was the nexus of a series of discussions about congregational growth and decline that would set the stage for the next surge of Contemporary Worship in the late 1980s.

Although Schuller rarely addressed worship directly or extensively, his thought about ministry and church life matched many of the classic theological

120. See, for example, the foreword to Schuller's 1974 book, *Your Church Has Real Possibilities!*, in which C. Peter Wagner links Garden Grove Community Church to the Church Growth movement.

121. Mulder and Martí, *Glass Church*, 135.

themes that had characterized the theology of Contemporary Worship. For instance, an emphasis on human agency and freedom to adapt the forms of church life, including worship, was implicit in his entrepreneurial mindset. That emphasis was evident in his use of business techniques and categories to consider his congregation's ministry. In other liturgical pragmatists we have seen a similar approach (e.g., Catherine Booth or James White), but Schuller carried the appropriation to a higher level by a lengthier analogy. Chapter 2 in his 1974 book, for example, is called "Seven Principles of Successful Retailing."[122] In this chapter, he argues that excellent, inspiring worship is part of a good "inventory"—that is, church programming. These general "principles" were meant to guide successful pastoral entrepreneurs in making good choices for a successful "return" in their particular contexts. Implicit throughout the discussion was the freedom of human agency in worship to find the most successful methods.

The drive to be successful came from Schuller's notion of a local congregation as an evangelizing mission first and a parish church second. This notion, too, was in continuity with the standard theology of Contemporary Worship. The issue concerned a congregation's essential purpose: was it to take care of itself or was it to take the gospel to others? For Schuller, choosing the latter option could lead to growth: "We are a mission first and a church second. . . . I believe any church can grow if it is willing to die as a church and be born again as a mission."[123]

This prioritizing of mission naturally led to the search for the most effective way to accomplish the church's biblical mission. The answer for effectiveness, as we have often seen, was sought not by looking at details in the New Testament but by close attentiveness to the Californians Schuller's missional church was trying to reach. Couching his efforts in business concepts, Schuller sought customer satisfaction and relied on customer polling, even regarding the congregation's worship life. This was how he began his Orange County ministry in 1955. Realizing that there were few regular members of his denomination in the area where he was starting a church (unlike Methodists or Presbyterians), Schuller rang the doorbells of more than three thousand homes his first year. If the respondent was already an active member of a church, he moved on. If the person was not, Schuller asked some critical questions: What would you look for in a church? What would attract you and your family to a church? With that information he began his work.[124] Customer satisfaction and polling was

---

122. Schuller, *Your Church Has Real Possibilities!*, 19–29.

123. Robert Schuller, "Hard Questions for Robert Schuller about Sin and Self-esteem," interview by V. Gilbert Beers, Kenneth S. Kantzer, and David F. Wells, *Christianity Today* 28, no. 11 (August 10, 1984): 16.

124. Schuller, *My Journey*, 220.

how the ministry continued too. A constant feedback loop from attendees—a "relentless attentiveness to the potential patron"—allowed the church staff to respond and improve the worship experience, among other aspects of congregational life.[125] A striving for excellence in worship became a standard part of this ongoing quest to provide a satisfying liturgical experience.

This attentiveness to those Schuller was trying to reach and evangelize determined the language that was used at Garden Grove—yet another point of connection to the regular themes historically associated with the pragmatic approach. Thinking that some classic Christian terms caused an unnecessary stumbling block, Schuller quit using them. For example, at the suggestion of Doris Day, a famous mid-century actress and singer, he quit using the term "lost" to refer to those who had no faith.[126] Positively, he sought to translate the gospel into terms that met the needs he saw in those he was trying to reach. Specifically, seeking to address the emotional hungers and desire for dignity he saw in others, Schuller stressed self-esteem and "possibility thinking" through God.[127]

Schuller sought validation of his approach in numbers, another way in which his approach linked to Contemporary Worship. Indeed, the method he taught to others involved setting specific numerical goals and then using creativity to find a way to reach them. Force yourself to set a church attendance goal, Schuller advised, and "you will be forced to think of possible ways to raise the attendance."[128] Even though in this advice he was not thinking of liturgical creativity per se but of other ministry activity (programming, relations, advertising, and door-to-door calling), there was nothing in his teaching to prevent his students from applying the advice to forms of worship themselves. Indeed, everything in Schuller's approach seemed to applaud doing so. This perception and approach to ministry was what Schuller instilled in his students and what they replicated in their own ways and contexts. Through these students, Schuller's pragmatic paradigm helped lead to a new wave of Contemporary Worship.

Schuller was confident that his perception and approach were thoroughly biblical and apostolic. Once, when challenged about whether he was indeed following the apostle Paul's methods, he responded, "Am I not? Paul used many methods. He said, 'I am made all things to all men that I might by all

---

125. Mulder and Martí, *Glass Church*, 18–19.
126. Schuller, *My Journey*, 318. See also Schuller, "Hard Questions for Robert Schuller," 17.
127. Schuller, "Hard Questions for Robert Schuller," 18–20. "Possibility thinking" was a theme Schuller was famous for during his ministry. Although Schuller was often criticized for this approach, one prominent theologian (Richard Mouw) told Schuller he was one of the key contextualizers of theology in North America. See Mulder and Martí, *Glass Church*, 72.
128. Schuller, *Your Church Has Real Possibilities!*, 80.

means save some.'" Once again 1 Corinthians 9:22 provided the key text upon which liturgical pragmatism rested.

If Schuller as a mainline pastor was rejoicing in his church's increasing numbers in the 1970s, in contrast there were other mainline leaders who were growing aware of their own congregations' decline. Even as Schuller peddled possibility, many other mainline pastors piddled around in the probability that they were involved in something whose influence and numbers would likely continue to wane over time. The 1970s was a time when studies began to be published that documented the numerical decline across mainline denominations. These studies, complete with graphs showing downward arrows for a multitude of mainline denominations, were sobering and staggering in their implications. If the trend continued on its present course, the numbers seemed to say, the future of mainline Christianity was in trouble. That perception— true or not—became part of the stirrings in the stream of Contemporary Worship in its period of incubation post-1975. It would also be a part of the mix motivating the next wave of Contemporary Worship in the late 1980s, as congregations looked to contemporary services as a way to attract people they did not already have.

Amazingly, however, using *specific* declining numbers to argue for the necessity of Contemporary Worship was rarely done in the first wave of the late 1960s. James White was exceptional in that regard, tying to increasing attendance a motivation to experiment.[129] Perhaps, for most, the general sense of a gap between people and worship was strong enough motivation to experiment. Perhaps other mainline worshipers had a vague sense of the slippage of their beloved congregations and denominations, but did not connect that sense to how they worshiped.

Regardless of any connection to Contemporary Worship, a watershed 1972 book, Dean M. Kelley's *Why Conservative Churches Are Growing*, made awareness of numeric decline widespread.[130] Seeking to address the question implied in the book's title, Kelley, who was on staff at the National Council of Churches, began on a warning note for mainline Christians: a two-century trend of increase had reversed in the 1960s. He based the assertion on decreased numbers in at least ten of the largest denominations in the United States. After pointing out this drastic, dramatic situation, Kelley immediately followed up with graphs for multiple denominations.[131] Kelley's numerical

129. White, *New Forms of Worship*, 16–17.
130. Dean M. Kelley, *Why Conservative Churches Are Growing: A Study in Sociology of Religion* (New York: Harper & Row, 1972).
131. Kelley, *Why Conservative Churches Are Growing*, 1–8. Kelley spent little time discussing the connection of this numerical decline to churches' liturgical life, only noting at one point (p. 13)

documentation would have smashed any vague sense of slippage. (By the way, Kelley decided that the reason conservative churches—and not mainline churches—were increasing was that the former made more demands on their members in terms of doctrine and behavior.)

Kelley's book was only the first in a series of studies documenting mainline numerical decline. Charts with declining arrows became fixtures in mainline consciousness. By the late 1970s at least three mainline denominations (the United Methodist Church, the United Church of Christ, and the United Presbyterians) had commissioned their own major studies. In 1979 a grant-funded, data-driven sociological study of nearly four hundred pages, involving contributions from both academic and church researchers, was published, along with a shorter, more popular volume based on the large study.[132] The title of the shorter book summarized the question pressing on mainline minds: *Where Have All Our People Gone?* Behind the question lay the angst of mainline churches feeling like they had awoken to find themselves in a precipitous demise. The book noted how "membership decline for most mainline denominations, in the past decade, had been unexpected, unprecedented, and most upsetting."[133]

The sense of anxiety over this question continued to escalate, it seems. A 1982 article in the popular periodical *Christianity Today* began with the most distressing of scholarly prognostications about sheer survival of mainline denominations: "Extrapolating from present trends it is not unlikely that by the beginning of the 21st century most of what are presently considered the mainline Protestant denominations in America . . . will either have ceased to exist or ceased to claim any distinctively Christian character for themselves."[134] Mainline Christians surely wondered where they could turn for hope and solutions.

The very next article in the same 1982 issue of *Christianity Today* highlighted the movement to which many were turning for hope and solutions:

---

that the solutions he had heard proposed included "a more contemporary liturgy," "making fuller use of the arts," and "greater empathy with the youth culture."

132. The larger study was Dean R. Hoge and David A. Roozen, eds., *Understanding Church Growth and Decline, 1950–1978* (New York: Pilgrim, 1979); the shorter was Carl S. Dudley, *Where Have All Our People Gone? New Choices for Old Churches* (New York: Pilgrim, 1979).

133. Dudley, *Where Have All Our People Gone?*, x. Note that this book considered worship as one of several "programmatic areas" that could have an impact on including the "outsider." Specifically, Dudley (pp. 67–71) noted that feelings about worship were consistently among the most significant factors associated with growth or decline.

134. Walter A. Elwell, "How to Deal with Decline: Options for Mainline Denominations," *Christianity Today* 26, no. 5 (March 5, 1982): 36.

the Church Growth movement.[135] This movement was a school of missiological cal thought that had originally been developed mid-century to explain why some mission work prospered and other work was unsuccessful. In the early 1970s its proponents began to apply it to a North American context. Driven by sociological analysis and a concern for numbers and data, it offered a systematic way for denominational leaders and ministers to address how to develop churches in their multiple dimensions. Initially, congregational worship was mentioned only in passing in early Church Growth materials, although certainly a concern for worship was inherent and implicit in the movement's inclusive approach to congregational assessment. By the early 1980s that peripheral concern had become explicit in the works of a few Church Growth authors. This liturgical focus would continue to grow and Church Growth proponents would eventually tie a focus on worship to generational concerns, the advantage of multiple services differentiated stylistically, and, eventually, a clear advocacy for a more "indigenous" form of worship—that is, Contemporary Worship. In this way the Church Growth movement would become a major gravitational pull accelerating the pace of Contemporary Worship's adoption. As more denominations turned to Church Growth for answers, the Church Growth movement was focusing ever more on worship, especially Contemporary Worship, as a critical part of those answers.

Mainline denominations had started to become aware of Church Growth and increasingly turned to this movement even before it had begun to spend much time discussing liturgical issues. Leading Church Growth theorists had contributed to the large 1979 study mentioned above, for instance.[136] That same year a report of the Evangelism Working Group of the National Council of Churches noted how the Church Growth approach was "sweeping the mainline denominations" as "grass-roots pressure" about membership decline had brought about the hiring of new denominational staff who promoted this approach even as existing evangelism staffers had begun to learn it.[137] Such learning opportunities were easy to find because, reportedly, Church Growth seminars could be found from Alaska to Florida by 1980.[138]

The fact that a Church Growth approach was being applied to North America was a secondary development in the history of the movement and not a part

135. Specifically, the article was Arthur P. Johnson, "Church Growth Gets a Shot in the Arm," *Christianity Today* 26, no. 5 (March 5, 1982): 40–41.

136. Specifically, C. Peter Wagner and Lyle E. Schaller.

137. Alfred C. Krass, "What the Mainline Denominations Are Doing in Evangelism," *Christian Century* 96, no. 16 (May 2, 1979): 493.

138. Donald A. McGavran and George G. Hunter III, *Church Growth: Strategies That Work* (Nashville: Abingdon, 1980), 13.

of the initial motivations of its founder.[139] Donald McGavran, a mid-century missionary to India, was the recognized originator of Church Growth theory. While in India, McGavran had become mesmerized by the different evangelistic success varying missionary efforts produced. He began to focus the bulk of his work on cultural impediments to Christian conversion or, put more simply, the cultural and societal causes and barriers to conversion and, therefore, church growth. Concerned with helping others become more effective missionaries, McGavran easily turned his descriptive work into prescriptive notions as he began to publish in the mid-1950s. In the early 1960s he returned to the United States in order to teach, first moving to Oregon and then, more significantly, to Pasadena, California, in 1965 to become the founding dean of a school dedicated to missions and evangelism at Fuller Theological Seminary. In 1970 he published his definitive work, *Understanding Church Growth*. Throughout all this early work, his focus was on missionary work outside North America.

Starting in 1972, however, the Church Growth school of thought turned its attention to the United States. In that year McGavran and another Fuller professor, C. Peter Wagner, taught Americans this theory for use in their own contexts in a pilot course held at Pasadena's Lake Avenue Congregational Church.[140] One of the participants in that first class, Win Arn, was so impacted he left his current job to found the Institute for American Church Growth, from which he would generate a steady stream of teaching materials including seminars, workshops, pastors' conferences, films, and the first magazine devoted to American Church Growth.[141] The year 1972 also saw the first publication in a long line of books dedicated to applying Church Growth thought to North America.[142] In 1975 Fuller began offering Church Growth

---

139. A useful historical overview can be found in Gary L. McIntosh, "Introduction: Why Church Growth Can't Be Ignored," in *Evaluating the Church Growth Movement*, ed. Elmer Towns and Gary L. McIntosh (Grand Rapids: Zondervan, 2004), 7–28. Glenn Stallsmith applies this overview to a discussion of how the movement began to shape North American worship in "The Path to a Second Service: Mainline Decline, Church Growth, and Apostolic Leadership," in *Essays on the History of Contemporary Praise and Worship*, ed. Lester Ruth (Eugene, OR: Pickwick, 2020), 55–73. Our discussion of Church Growth's history is dependent on these two sources.

140. C. Peter Wagner, *Your Church Can Grow: Seven Vital Signs of a Healthy Congregation* (Ventura, CA: Regal, 1976), 15.

141. McIntosh, "Introduction," 17. McIntosh (p. 19) helpfully provides a schema for the multiple outlets for early Church Growth thought.

142. Paul Benjamin, *The Growing Congregation* (Lincoln: Lincoln Christian College Press, 1972). Other significant books of the 1970s include Donald A. McGavran and Win Arn, *How to Grow a Church: Conversations about Church Growth* (Ventura, CA: Regal, 1973); Wagner, *Your Church Can Grow* (1976); Donald A. McGavran and Winfield C. Arn, *Ten Steps for Church Growth* (New York: Harper & Row, 1977); and Winfield C. Arn, ed., *The Pastor's Church Growth Handbook: America's Leading Authorities on Church Growth Share the Keys to Building a Dynamic Church* (Pasadena, CA: Church Growth, 1979).

conferences to its students in the doctor of ministry program. By 1985 the program had trained over a thousand pastors in Church Growth.[143] The core of this growing body of teaching was, as Glenn Stallsmith has described it, "a commitment to contextualization—that is, the lowering of communication barriers—that resulted in an emphasis on forming homogenous congregations": that is, congregations gathered and grown on cultural similarities.[144]

This foundational commitment to contextualization came from one of the centerpieces of the movement's theoretical framework: the homogeneous unit principle. By this principle, the movement described the role of culture and natural social networks in how people became Christians. Simply put, people "like to become Christian in their own social groupings, without crossing barriers." Prescriptively, that meant, McGavran asserted, that "we must make sure that we ask people to become Christians where they don't have to cross barriers of language and culture and class and wealth and style of life."[145] Specifically, with reference to effective proclamation and hearing of the gospel, the Word is not given a fair hearing unless listeners can hear it in their own "heart language" without annoying "friction" or "static" caused by sharing it in the wrong language or cultural form—that is, in a language or form alien or unknown to the intended listeners.[146] In the case of North American congregations, Church Growth theorists saw these congregations too easily falling into unfortunate "maladies" that prevented them from being able to attract people and grow. These "illnesses" included "people-blindness" (when church members do not recognize the significant differences that separate people into subcultures and thus presume that the inherent subculture embodied in one's own congregation is able to attract everyone) and "koinonitis" (when church members become so concerned with themselves that they forget that there are others outside their congregation and outside the Christian faith).[147]

Throughout the 1970s, Church Growth literature amazingly paid little attention to worship per se. When it did, the comments were very generic:

143. McIntosh, "Introduction," 17.

144. Stallsmith, "Path to a Second Service," 58–59.

145. Quoted in McGavran and Arn, *How to Grow a Church*, 45. This principle was critiqued then and has continued to be critiqued since on a variety of grounds, including theological and scriptural grounds. For an extensive early defense of the theory on social-psychological, theological, and scriptural grounds, see C. Peter Wagner, *Our Kind of People* (Atlanta: John Knox, 1979).

146. McGavran and Arn, *Ten Steps for Church Growth*, 53–54.

147. C. Peter Wagner, "Church Growth Research: The Paradigm and Its Applications," in *Understanding Church Growth and Decline, 1950–1978*, ed. Dean R. Hoge and David A. Roozen (New York: Pilgrim, 1979), 284–85. Note the use of a wellness analogy behind Wagner's approach: growth is a sign of health and decline is not. The analogy, in terms of speaking of "healthy congregations," was common.

suggestions that worship needed to be more of a fun celebration, must be well designed, and ought to provide a strong sense of having actually met God.[148] However, it was just a matter of time before Church Growth advocates turned to the sanctuary, since these theorists themselves were expansive in the scope they used to assess congregational dynamics. When they did turn their eye to worship services, they did so in a way that picked up on some older trends like using "language" metaphors for worship. But, using their more systematic scheme for cultural assessment, they intensified the discussion of inculturation or indigeneity with respect to worship and its forms. Church Growth proponents writing on worship began with an assumption that worship forms were heavily stamped by the culture of each respective worshiping community. Consequently, they evaluated whether these enculturated forms presented obstacles to those who did not already belong to that community. Often, they saw a cultural gap: in too many cases, the current form of worship constituted an obstacle to effective outreach.

George Hunter III, a United Methodist denominational official, seems to have been the first Church Growth advocate to look at worship more thoroughly by making it a regular part of his writings in the early 1980s. Hunter, the former professor of evangelism at Perkins School of Theology (and a colleague of James F. White), published in 1980 both a specific guide for United Methodist congregations, *Finding the Way Forward*, and a book aimed for a more general audience, *Church Growth: Strategies That Work*, coauthored with Donald McGavran.[149] In both books, Hunter worried that many existing worship forms presented unnecessary obstacles to attracting people and introducing them to Christian faith. In the book coauthored with McGavran, for example, Hunter argued that over time most denominations settled into cultural forms of "dignified" worship that only fitted a small part of the broader community. Thus, "liturgical style" was one of the difficulties that could inhibit church growth, especially in a new church plant. Those starting new congregations therefore had to be careful not to exhibit "cultural imperialism" by importing "culturally foreign music and worship" into settings where those were foreign. The principle was clear: "Worship must be expressed in the 'heart language' of the target subculture if its members are really to see it, to appropriate it, and to be involved in it."[150]

148. Wagner, *Your Church Can Grow*, 97–100. Wagner argued that small churches face a series of obstacles to achieving these dynamics.

149. George G. Hunter III, *Finding the Way Forward* (Nashville: Discipleship Resources, 1980); McGavran and Hunter, *Church Growth*.

150. McGavran and Hunter, *Church Growth*, 107–8. Although the book did not attribute these specific thoughts to Hunter, the lack of a similar discussion in prior materials authored

Similarly, in *Finding the Way Forward*, Hunter emphasized the value of "indigenous music," along with a fitting liturgy and preaching, in order to have worship that is "alive" in the "idiom, rhythms, instrumentation, and the 'heart-language' of the culture."[151] Accompanying Hunter's text were discussion worksheets authored by Ron Crandall, who was Hunter's colleague at the United Methodist General Board of Discipleship. These worksheets helped a congregational committee ask questions to get at this fittingness. The committee was instructed to ask those it was hoping to attract, "Did our 'style' of worship . . . appeal to you and meet your needs, or are you looking for something else?" The questions for new members (and for the committee members themselves) were similar: "What aspects of our worship are most difficult for visitors and/or 'unchurched' persons to understand, follow, or participate in? What parts of our worship are most rewarding and inspirational to new persons and the 'unchurched'?"[152]

To answer such questions, Hunter and Church Growth advocates of the early 1980s had only hints of a specific liturgical vision that they could offer to congregations that wanted a definitive liturgical approach that could bring growth. Hunter was indeed certain that a congregation's main worship service was a kind of "shop window" through which visitors made up their mind about that church as a whole. On that general principle he was settled, yet the specifics were less clear. He wondered, "What makes for the kind of worship that clearly and attractively presents the church's wares? What makes corporate worship potentially contagious for the new person entering in?" He acknowledged the fuzziness of the picture, stating, "We do not know nearly as much about this as we want to."[153] Shortly, however—in fact, in the late 1980s—a specific image would come into focus and there would be a clear answer: Contemporary Worship. By the mid-1980s, the period of incubation was almost over. There would be a second wave of the Contemporary Worship river in the years following.

---

by McGavran and the parallel to other things written by Hunter make us think he authored these thoughts.

151. Hunter, *Finding the Way Forward*, 29. For a similar early, short treatment in which "indigenous worship" is synonymous with "indigenous music," see Herb Miller, *Fishing on the Asphalt: Effective Evangelism in Mainline Denominations* (St. Louis: Bethany, 1983), 108–10.

152. [Ron Crandall], "Session III-A Providing Ports of Entry for New People," in *Finding the Way Forward Session Worksheets* (Nashville: Discipleship Resources, 1980), 1–2. These worksheets were part of a whole education and research kit that congregations used to apply Church Growth theory. Ron Crandall, interview by Lester Ruth, December 11, 2017; Ron Crandall, email message to Lester Ruth, November 20, 2017.

153. Hunter, *Finding the Way Forward*, 27–28.

seven

—

the second wave of contemporary worship, 1985–mid-1990s

We were all looking for ways of reaching people. We all had a passion for doing something that would reach people. And I think that this [starting a contemporary service] was one specific thing [to do].

—Gary Formby, early United Methodist promoter of Contemporary Worship, Alabama[1]

"The guitar preacher." That was Gary Formby's nickname while serving as a chaplain in the Alabama National Guard during Operation Desert Storm, the United States–led international military effort in early 1991 to reclaim Kuwait from an Iraqi invasion. Formby, who had been serving as a Methodist pastor before being called up for active duty as a member of the National Guard, found that his skill on the guitar was helpful as he led worship for coalition soldiers in the Middle East. The guitar was easy to carry around the desert, and it brought joy to the soldiers as they sang far from home.

1. Gary Formby, interview by Lester Ruth, July 3, 2014. The information on Gary Formby and his ministry as a pastor and district superintendent was gained in two interviews with Lester Ruth on June 26, 2014, and July 3, 2014. The connection between the name of Formby's church and the name of one of this book's authors is entirely coincidental (providential?).

Once the war was over, Formby carried this memory back with him to northern Alabama. Soon he was serving at Lester Memorial United Methodist Church in Oneonta, Alabama. There his experience and musical skill joined with his own evangelistic impulses as well as the desires of some of his parishioners for something liturgically different from the church's traditional service. The result was a "contemporary celebration service" that featured—according to the advertisements distributed throughout Oneonta's restaurants—extensive use of modern praise choruses projected on a screen; new musical instruments like guitars, keyboards, and drums; very casual dress; an informal worship center rather than a formal sanctuary; a great deal of flexibility and spontaneity; and "prayers of the heart."[2] (Formby would continue as one of the service's guitarists.) The advertisements clearly sought to increase the appeal of the congregation's worship, informing the prospective visitor "you will have a choice"—that is, between Lester Memorial's traditional, "time-honored" worship service and the new contemporary service. This new service launched in early 1994.

One of the diners who picked up this advertisement and was intrigued by it was the United Methodist bishop for northern Alabama, Robert Eugene Fannin. Taking a break from a business meeting at the nearby denominational campground with his cabinet of district superintendents, Bishop Fannin was in town to eat. Formby's initiative stuck with him and within a few years the bishop tapped Formby to become a district superintendent with the expressed intent of helping other Methodist congregations in northern Alabama start contemporary services. The bishop was interested in reaching out to areas that Methodism was not reaching at the time and he saw Contemporary Worship as a way to do that. And, in this way, a simple experience with a guitar in the desert of Saudi Arabia helped propel the start of numerous contemporary services in United Methodism.

Formby's and Lester Memorial's story was not an entirely exceptional one, notwithstanding the connection to a war in the Middle East. Around the beginning of the 1990s, there was an increasing groundswell of interest in Contemporary Worship among mainline Christians like Methodists and mainstream evangelicals like Baptists. By the mid-1990s this groundswell had become a second wave of Contemporary Worship as congregation after congregation sought to reach new people, make new Christians, and expand their churches.

By the mid-1990s, increasing numbers of proponents with a growing body of resources were advocating for Contemporary Worship as the way to achieve

2. "Three Churches Try Out Contemporary Worship," *Circuit Rider* 18, no. 10 (December 1994/January 1995): 14.

these ends. Timothy Wright, a Lutheran pastor at one influential congregation, stated the appeal succinctly: "Contemporary worship is today's method for reaching new people. . . . Creative, contemporary styles of worship are essential if we want to reach new generations for Jesus Christ. The decision to offer new, contemporary services is not so much a worship issue as an evangelistic one."[3] While in actuality a variety of motivations moved congregations to adopt Contemporary Worship—not the least of which were the past experiences and current desires of their own members—this appeal to successful outreach was a dominant note sounded by mainline and evangelical voices alike.

Wright spoke not only with a sense of urgency but also with optimism: Wright's congregation, Community Church of Joy, was one of the leading Lutheran congregations to model how Contemporary Worship adaptability could lead to evangelistic success with increasing numbers of people. This Arizona congregation itself was one of a number of churches lifted up as exemplars for how to do Contemporary Worship and how it could lead to faithful achievement of a church's evangelistic mission. These congregations were innovative in their approach to being a church, including in worship. Rick Warren, the founding pastor of another one of these churches in Southern California, Saddleback Valley Community Church, thus called them "CAMEO churches" because they used a "Contemporary Approach to Ministry, Evangelism, and Organization."[4]

In a variety of ways these exemplary churches influenced smaller congregations toward Contemporary Worship. Their pastors wrote books and articles exploring the why and how of this alternative way of worship. Their innovative congregations hosted conferences, held workshops, and produced resources to show others how to move toward Contemporary Worship. Their campuses served as pilgrimage sites: leaders desiring to see something new traveled to them. And their stories of numerical success were reprinted in national newspapers, magazines, and books. Looking at CAMEO churches allowed medium-sized and small congregations and their leaders to dream and aspire.

Behind it all lay the long-held theological commitments of liturgical pragmatism. Priority was given to the church's New Testament–based mission to evangelize, especially as commanded in the Great Commission and as seen in the apostle Paul. This Bible-derived call to make new Christian disciples

3. Timothy Wright, A Community of Joy: How to Create Contemporary Worship (Nashville: Abingdon, 1994), 54, 56.

4. Rick (Richard Duane) Warren, "New Churches for a New Generation: Church Planting to Reach Baby Boomers; A Case Study; The Saddleback Valley Community Church" (DMin thesis, Fuller Theological Seminary, 1993), 368.

was the consuming drive behind CAMEO churches' activities, especially their advocacy of Contemporary Worship. Rick Warren summarized the connection to the New Testament in his doctoral thesis:

> The basic principle behind CAMEO churches is not new. In fact, it is as old as the New Testament. The apostle Paul stated it in 1 Corinthians 9:22–23 ". . . I become all things to all men so that by all possible means I might save some. I do this for the sake of the gospel . . ." Paul wisely adapted his approach to whatever situation he found himself in. Even though the message was the same, he often presented it in different ways depending on the culture. This is the strategy of CAMEO churches. Because CAMEO churches are willing to step out in faith and risk trying new approaches to ministry, evangelism, and organization, I believe they will be on the cutting edge of church growth in the 1990s.[5]

Not surprisingly, these sorts of churches were the favorites of the Church Growth movement itself, which by the late 1980s could point to them as effective examples of adapting worship to bring down unnecessary cultural barriers and provide a more accessible way for people to join and participate in church. Congregations like Community Church of Joy and Saddleback Valley Community Church provided a specific vision for a new, "contemporary" approach to worship that supplanted the movement's previous appeal, a rather generic call for something new in worship. Tapping into the continuing angst of mainline congregations about declining numbers, the Church Growth movement could thus point to the worship of CAMEO churches as an example of what a truly innovative, "indigenous" liturgy looked like at the end of the twentieth century, one drawn from the wells of popular culture.

The CAMEO churches provided a vision for Contemporary Worship that gained widespread acceptance. Contemporary Worship's incubation was over. The "river" was ready to rage.

The Church Growth Movement's Advocacy for Contemporary Worship

By the latter half of the 1980s the popular branch of the Church Growth movement was a well-established feature in the ecclesiastical landscape, affecting both mainline and evangelical constituencies.[6] A steady line of books (some

---

5. Warren, "New Churches for a New Generation," 386–87.
6. This notion of a "popular branch" of the movement as contrasted to a "classical" or more academically oriented branch is drawn from Gary L. McIntosh, "Introduction: Why Church Growth Can't Be Ignored," in *Evaluating the Church Growth Movement*, ed. Elmer Towns and

addressing specific denominational or congregational contexts, e.g., Baptists or small churches, but most not) fed the hunger of those wishing to know more about how to grow their congregations.[7] Some denominational publishing houses published series of titles featuring a Church Growth approach to congregational life. Magazines and newsletters, like Herb Miller's *Net Results*, supplemented the books. The 1990s opened up web-based approaches, as in the six online discussion forums—including one on Contemporary Worship— sponsored by the Easum, Bandy & Associates consulting group. William "Bill" Easum and Thomas "Tom" Bandy were only two of numerous Church Growth consultants, some of whom had been in business since the 1970s. Such consultants developed teaching materials, held workshops, did direct consultations, and reached tens of thousands of people over time. The work of George Barna, a market researcher who studied North American Christianity, and Lyle Schaller, an urban planner turned church consultant undergirded the efforts of those writing from a clear Church Growth perspective. Barna's and Schaller's figures and insights permeated Church Growth writing from the mid-1980s onward.

The size and scope of the popular branch of the Church Growth movement were important for the second wave of Contemporary Worship because this movement provided a steady, transdenominational backdrop advocating liturgical innovation throughout this period. Shifting from their earlier, more general call for something more dynamic and interesting in worship, Church Growth voices increasingly and specifically promoted band-based Contemporary Worship as the necessary step for congregational health and faithfulness. Unlike the first wave of Contemporary Worship in the late 1960s and early 1970s, this second wave therefore gained strength and permanency in part because the Church Growth movement was an undergirding advocate for it.

As we saw in the emergence of the Church Growth movement in the 1965–85 time period, these later advocates rooted their approach in particular theological commitments that were a variation on long-held sensibilities of liturgical pragmatism. By the late 1980s these commitments would lead to Contemporary Worship as we know it in a series of logical steps and sequenced advocacy.

Gary L. McIntosh (Grand Rapids: Zondervan, 2004), 16–20. McIntosh (p. 21) notes a diluting of the original Church Growth theory by the late 1990s as its early theorists died or retired and "Church Growth" began to be applied by publishers to anything vaguely speaking of growing a church. Our discussion that follows attempts to draw from standard, classic expressions of Church Growth thought.

7. Some of the most prolific, well-known authors included C. Peter Wagner, Herb Miller, George G. Hunter III, William M. Easum, and Win Arn.

The utterly foundational commitment was the belief that the church exists to fulfill its New Testament mission: proclaim the gospel and thus evangelize all people. That is *the* purpose of the contemporary church. Whatever else the church might be called or led to do, seeking to fulfill the Great Commission—the concluding instruction of Christ to the disciples in Matthew 28:18–20—in imitation of the efforts of the early church seen in the New Testament was the reason God had called the church into existence. Therefore, to veer from that purpose was to be unfaithful to God. Moreover, to be deficient in seeking this purpose meant not only unfaithfulness before God but also, not surprisingly, putting individual congregations at risk. As William Easum expressed it in a "basic law" of congregational life, "Churches grow when they intentionally reach out to people instead of concentrating on their institutional needs; churches die when they concentrate on their own needs."[8]

With so much at stake, it was natural for Church Growth advocates to search for the most effective ways to fulfill that purpose. The commitment to the "what"—evangelization—led to a seeking of the "how"—the best means—to fulfill the church's purpose. As it was with Church Growth's originator, Donald McGavran, so it was with Church Growth proponents at the end of the century: the desire to be faithful and as successful as possible in fulfilling the Christ-given commission led to the sociological evaluation of the methods of evangelism that worked. So wedded were the "what" and "how" in this Church Growth approach that the "hows" could be justified in terms of general New Testament principles and thereby gained a theological character.

These later Church Growth voices accepted as a fundamental theoretical premise McGavran's early, key emphasis that people are more likely to become Christians if they do not have to cross racial, linguistic, or class barriers to do so. This perception thus led to an appreciation for assessing cultural differences, perspectives, and expressions. Church Growth authors took McGavran's central emphasis (the homogeneous unit principle) and applied it both specifically with reference to becoming a Christian through conversion and generically about becoming an active member of a congregation. In their generic application these authors thus argued that people are more likely to join a congregation and become part of a Christian community if they do not have to cross any unnecessary cultural obstacles to do so.

There was therefore a twofold result to this principle: The first result was that a Church Growth perspective inherently saw being a Christian as a deeply social experience. The second was an elasticity in how popular Church Growth thought could be applied. Evangelical Christians comfortable with

8. William M. Easum, *The Church Growth Handbook* (Nashville: Abingdon, 1990), 16.

notions of conversion and commitment to Jesus Christ could utilize Church
Growth insights; so could mainline types more comfortable with a noncrisis
approach that spoke of including people in Christian community and the
path of discipleship.

Driven by the purpose of the church's evangelistic mission and guided by
a sense that appraisal of cultural ease of access was critical in pursuing that
purpose, Church Growth advocates by the late 1980s stressed worship's role in
fulfilling that purpose. Simply put, they ascertained that a worship service was
where the unconverted/unchurched/nonmember (the specific term depended on
the user's level of comfort with traditional evangelical sensibilities) mainly heard
the gospel. To stress worship's evangelistic role was a long-standing pragmatic
sensibility, as we have seen, but the Church Growth movement gave it a new
technical label: worship was a primary "port of entry." Baptist Church Growth
author James Emery White stated the evangelistic role for worship as a given
from the Bible: "To summarize, worship and church growth are biblically joined;
worship is often the barrier which keeps nonchurched persons from involvement
in the life of the church; worship is the 'front door' of the church, the first impression and introduction of the life of the church to people exploring church and
the Christian faith as an option for their lives; and finally, worship is the single
most dominant reason for the initial choice of involvement in a particular local
church."[9] Others agreed and used this biblical connection—clearly seen in the
experience of countless congregations—to rebut those who wanted to argue that
worship's purpose is not evangelistic. Even if theoretically worship's purpose
is not evangelistic, George Hunter III queried in his 1996 book titled *Church
for the Unchurched*, what do congregations do with the "pre-Christians" who
show up on Sunday morning to see if there is anything in Christianity for them?[10]

Given worship's importance as a make-or-break port of entry for the non-
Christian or nonmember, Church Growth thinkers stressed the importance
of the communicative function of worship services. Communication involved
not only how the content of the service spoke of the Gospel, but how the
form or "style" of the service itself was a message to the non-Christian or
nonmember visitor, even at the subconscious level. Donald McGavran himself
made this point, arguing that the gospel needs to be wrapped in the cultural
forms of the people the church hopes to present it to.

The goal was presenting a "naturalness of Christian life and worship,
witness and learning" to the targeted cultural group, leading to a kind of
"unconscious witness." Therefore, a thorough appraisal of every dimension

9. James Emery White, *Opening the Front Door: Worship and Church Growth* (Nashville:
Convention, 1992), 21.

10. George G. Hunter III, *Church for the Unchurched* (Nashville: Abingdon, 1996), 76.

of a worship service to make sure it was fitting to the targeted culture was necessary, as Hunter argued in 1987: churches wanting to attract new people must use a "style" of clothing, architecture, music, worship setting, and liturgy with which the subculture can resonate. Simply put, a worship service in all its dimensions must be in the "heart language" of the targeted group.[11]

Although the Church Growth authors of the period never used the term, they continually insinuated that a worship service was a kind of "icon" offering a vision of whether it was possible for Christianity to be found in every cultural subgroup. Actual diversity in worship style was a test for whether the catholic nature of the church could really be experienced by everyone. Thus, Sunday morning was when potential members decided whether being a Christian was possible for them specifically. As Church Growth advocates began to suggest that churches desiring to grow should target North Americans who were attracted to forms of popular culture, these advocates therefore thought it critical to highlight emerging examples of Contemporary Worship as evidence that it was possible for Christianity and its worship of God to exist in a "pop" form too.

Undergirding Church Growth authors' optimism that worship could indeed be iconic for all people—including those immersed in popular American culture—was that long-standing vision exemplified in Paul for the apostolic propriety of adaptation. Time and time again these authors referenced 1 Corinthians 9:22 as the biblical support for adapting worship to a specifically targeted subculture. For one author this adaptability was the biblical way to be relevant to "today's society."[12] For another it was the standard pattern for the first-century church and, if needed in a contemporary situation, even the justification for crafting an entire service for the unchurched or non-Christians.[13] George Hunter referenced the verse while discussing the commonality among three things: how through the incarnation Jesus self-emptied himself into a specific Galilean culture, how Paul pursued measures to become an effective evangelist among the Gentiles, and how a modern church should take care to develop an indigenous strategy for its target group.[14]

This regular appeal to Paul's example summarized in 1 Corinthians 9:22 led to a regular stressing of human agency in liturgical creativity and innovation.

---

11. George G. Hunter III, *To Spread the Power: Church Growth in the Wesleyan Spirit* (Nashville: Abingdon, 1987), 170. The quotation from McGavran can be found on p. 158 of Hunter's book. Hunter is quoting from the 1980 revised edition of McGavran's *Understanding Church Growth*.

12. Leith Anderson, *Dying for Change* (Minneapolis: Bethany House, 1990), 165.

13. White, *Opening the Front Door*, 24, 39–41.

14. Hunter, *To Spread the Power*, 159–60.

The referencing of Paul—and even Jesus—gave such agency a theological propriety in a Church Growth worldview. Theological integrity did not necessarily attach to any specific liturgical form, notwithstanding its historical pedigree. Rather, this integrity attached to a minister's willingness to adapt and find a way with the people to whom the gospel, the church, and Christian worship were being offered. Since God wants the church to grow—as a chapter title in *The Church Growth Handbook* (1990) asserted—it fell to pastors to be a certain kind of strong, daring leader.[15] In the years ahead, lifting up Contemporary Worship in growing churches led by innovative pastors became a positive model for what vital, faithful pastoral leadership looked like. Conversely, although it was never stated quite this bluntly, the failure to implement a contemporary service could insinuate that a church had poor, unfaithful pastoral leadership.

Part of strong pastoral leadership at that time, the Church Growth literature said, was recognizing the problematic nature of worship forms cemented in previous times and cultures. There was a gap, this literature said, between the people of today and the worship of yesteryear: "An amazing phenomenon in the twentieth-century church is that we are still stuck in forms of worship and ministry which are more culturally appropriate to the nineteenth century. The robes, the pipe organ, the hymnals, the order of worship, and the nature and place of the sermon are all vestiges of nineteenth-century culture."[16] The unfortunate result was an experience of worship seen as boring, lifeless, and, even worse, off-putting for so many contemporary people. As the 1980s rolled over into the 1990s, the solution became ever more apparent: Contemporary Worship.

As we have seen, highlighting such a problematic gap was nothing new in this way of thinking. What was original was that Church Growth proponents were attaching the problem to numbers, which was the first of several logical and sequential steps toward direct Church Growth advocacy of Contemporary Worship by the 1990s. The literature that highlighted the existence of the gap associated with more traditional worship inevitably included a nod to the decreasing numbers indicated in measures of North American church attendance and membership. The implication was less than subtle: rigid attachment to old forms of worship was tantamount to chaining oneself to a sinking ship. Conversely, the wisdom of pursuing more lively worship was confirmed by increasing numbers. One author summarized this contrast in

15. Easum, *Church Growth Handbook*, 55–56. Cf. Glenn Stallsmith, "The Path to a Second Service: Mainline Decline, Church Growth, and Apostolic Leadership," in *Essays on the History of Contemporary Praise and Worship*, ed. Lester Ruth (Eugene, OR: Pickwick, 2020), 66–69.

16. Robert E. Logan, *Beyond Church Growth* (Grand Rapids: Revell, 1989), 60.

1990, citing recently conducted surveys: "A positive, uplifting worship service ranks among the top six reasons why people say they join growing congregations (on a list of forty-eight). Another study reports that 82.7 percent of new members in all congregations rate the quality of the worship service as an important reason for joining. In still another study, 64 percent of the church dropouts declared that the 'worship service is not meaningful' was a major cause."[17]

Such numerically specific appeals for richer worship supplemented general appeals for more exciting, lively, and fast-moving worship—appeals made by both Black and White Church Growth authors.[18] Given such numerical validation of worship's importance in expanding a church in terms of new Christians and new members, it was only a matter of time before these authors moved from discussing worship in passing as one of several critical issues to dedicating whole works to the subject. Shorter articles giving advice on how to increase attendance by more lively worship[19] were followed by entire books, the first of which had appeared by the early 1990s.[20]

The next logical, sequential step in Church Growth thinkers' promotion of Contemporary Worship was an increasing advocacy for adding second services to a single congregation's menu of services. The promotion of second services was not entirely new; it had been mentioned in earlier Church Growth literature.[21] The earlier promotion of second services was loosely connected to differentiating style: A second service ought to provide the more general, uplifting sort of worship experience that the early Church Growth literature thought would be appealing to new people. But the promotion also emphasized

17. Herb Miller, *The Vital Congregation* (Nashville: Abingdon, 1990), 29. Miller was citing studies conducted by the American Lutheran Church and the Disciples of Christ.

18. Compare, for example, Herb Miller, *How to Build a Magnetic Church* (Nashville: Abingdon, 1987), 45–56; and Carlyle Fielding Stewart, *African American Church Growth: 12 Principles of Prophetic Ministry* (Nashville: Abingdon, 1994), 55–56. For another illustrative example of promoting worship with increased exuberance but without specific advocacy of a contemporary style, see Lyle E. Schaller, "Where Is the Excitement? Or Why Do First-Time Visitors Return?," *Net Results*, September 1987, 7–8, 10.

19. For examples, see John P. Jewell Jr., "Ten Ways to Increase Your Church Attendance," *Net Results*, April 1984, 1–2; C. Frank Speight, "How to Increase Average Morning Worship Attendance," *Net Results*, December 1986, 1–2; Joe A. Harding, "Increase Worship Attendance by Ten Percent!," *Net Results*, February 1987, 9; Lyle E. Schaller, "What Does the Frequency of Attendance Tell You?," *Net Results*, January 1989, 4–5. See also Lyle E. Schaller, *44 Ways to Increase Church Attendance* (Nashville: Abingdon, 1988).

20. James Emery White's *Opening the Front Door: Worship and Church Growth* appears to have been the first. White was the leadership consultant for preaching and worship for the Southern Baptist Convention's Sunday School Board.

21. See Stallsmith, "Path to a Second Service," 59–60. For a specific earlier example, see Lyle E. Schaller, "One Worship Service or Two?," *Parish Paper* 9, no. 8 (February 1980): 1–2.

straightforward matters like convenience and choice. Simply put, people who wanted a more convenient time for worship would be drawn to churches offering more options for service starting times.[22] Some authors liked to attach numbers to the prospect of growing by adding a second service. Herb Miller offered such hope openly in 1990 in a straightforward cause-and-effect formula: "Adding a second worship service usually increases total attendance by five to fifteen percent. A simple principle stands behind that universal statistic: Offer more options, and you get larger responses."[23]

A sharper promotion of second services differentiated by a clearer connection to a contemporary style came with the next sequential step in Contemporary Worship promotion—namely, tying second services to a specifically named target audience. At this point the Church Growth literature began to show signs of generational thinking: baby boomers were usually suggested as the generation that churches desiring to grow should target.[24] The literature's fascination with baby boomers reflected the growing emphasis on the boomer generation in popular culture at the time, perhaps culminating for the church in sociologist Wade Clark Roof's book, *A Generation of Seekers*, in 1993.[25]

In 1990 James Emery White's entire book on worship and Church Growth stated matter-of-factly the emerging consensus of opinion based on congregational experience: for most growing churches in the period, the targeted group was unchurched baby boomers.[26] It became standard among Church Growth promoters at the time to separate North Americans into large generational groups, providing descriptions of what each generation was like, what its members' concerns and perspectives were, and what would appeal to them in terms of ministry.[27] The details included aspects of worship. One schema contrasted baby boomers to "pre-boomers," linking to the former praise songs, "how-to" sermons, multiple people praying, guitars and drums, and

22. For examples, see Easum, *Church Growth Handbook*, 33, 51–52; and Glen J. Stewart, "Thirteen Reasons for Adding Another Worship Service," *Net Results*, January 1989, 1–3.

23. Miller, *Vital Congregation*, 38.

24. As commonplace as this generational targeting was, it was not the only option. This period also saw the rise of ministries aiming for a country-and-western subculture, leading to the rise of "cowboy church." See Marie W. Dallam, *Cowboy Christians* (Oxford: Oxford University Press, 2018), 76–77, 80–84. Such targeting has also been done in non-White ministry. For example, see Stacey B. Jones, *(i)Pastor Hip-Hop: Bridging the Gap between Hip-Hop and the Christian Faith Community* (n.p.: One Communications, 2020); and Tryenyse Jones, interview by Lester Ruth, December 29, 2014.

25. Wade Clark Roof, *A Generation of Seekers: The Spiritual Journeys of the Baby Boom Generation* (San Francisco: HarperSanFrancisco, 1993).

26. White, *Opening the Front Door*, 29.

27. For examples from the late 1980s and early 1990s, see Robert L. Bast, *Attracting New Members* (New York: Reformed Church in America; Monrovia, CA: Church Growth, 1988), 29–34; Logan, *Beyond Church Growth*, 60–61; and Anderson, *Dying for Change*, 62–127.

more congregational participation. In contrast, according to this portrayal, older adults preferred quietness, hymns, expository sermons, pastoral prayers, organs and pianos, and less congregational participation.[28] Such portrayals created an enduring impression that different worship styles were linked to different age groups, an assumption seen throughout much of the second wave of Contemporary Worship in the 1990s.

Once society had been subdivided for ministry-targeting purposes into large generational groups and the liturgical preferences named for each group, the next logical step in Church Growth advocacy of Contemporary Worship to reach baby boomers was inevitably the promotion of this way of worship by the label "Contemporary Worship." Thus, for example, the same author who had complained that so many churches remained stuck in nineteenth-century forms of worship (see earlier discussion) could offer a remedy: add a new, second service of Contemporary Worship to provide an alternative to traditional services (which only appealed to older adults anyway).[29] Such promotion of Contemporary Worship by name would become ever more commonplace throughout the 1990s.

As seen in the example of generational preferences above, the vision for Contemporary Worship typically highlighted multiple liturgical dynamics like general feel and atmosphere, manner and goal of preaching, manner and type of prayer, song repertoire, musical instruments, and opportunity for participation of the worshiping congregation. To institute a contemporary service for baby boomers did not mean changing just one thing; rather, it was an overhaul of the entire liturgical experience.

But of these various dimensions, one stood out as particularly important: music. Part of that importance was due to the perception of how much of a service was musical. According to one statistic that circulated among Church Growth authors, 40 percent of a service was music.[30] But not just any music would do. Because baby boomers' sense of identity and belonging were linked to music, finding the music that attracted them was critical. As social historian Michael Hamilton put it in a much-read article in 1999, praise songs triumphed over hymns, and guitars beat out organs, because for baby boomers, "When one chooses a musical style today, one is making a statement

---

28. Leith Anderson, *A Church for the 21st Century: Bringing Change to Your Church to Meet the Challenges of a Changing Society* (Minneapolis: Bethany House, 1992), 159–60. Anderson also listed the preferences of baby busters, the generation coming after baby boomers.

29. Logan, *Beyond Church Growth*, 61–64.

30. The earliest use of the statistic we found was in Kennon L. Callahan, *Twelve Keys to an Effective Church: Strategic Planning for Mission* (San Francisco: Harper & Row, 1983), 27. See also Miller, *How to Build a Magnetic Church*, 53; Easum, *Church Growth Handbook*, 47; and White, *Opening the Front Door*, 82.

about whom one identifies with, what one's values are, and ultimately, who one is."[31] Not surprisingly, 1990s-era prescriptions for Contemporary Worship were clear: style of music was the most critical decision to be made and, to target boomers, middle-of-the-road rock was the most successful choice, since it was that generation's "traditional music."[32]

With this sort of prescriptive advocacy and, as we shall see, the success of certain large, exemplary churches (the CAMEO churches mentioned at the beginning of the chapter), music became as important in Contemporary Worship as it had been in Praise & Worship. However, the importance emerged for completely different reasons. Whereas music was how Praise & Worship had developed the means by which lengthy congregational praising brought an experience of the presence of God, early advocates of Contemporary Worship stressed the stylistic dimensions of various kinds of music for a different goal—that is, a musical style's ability to attract a targeted group and enable members of that group to feel at home in a worship service. Moreover, because of the different reasons music was important, the two rivers highlighted different aspects of music. Praise & Worship advocates spoke about musical techniques to bring about a good sense of flow to facilitate discerning God's manifest presence. In contrast, Contemporary Worship promoters among Church Growth thinkers focused on the stylistic qualities of a kind of music and how those were experienced by people belonging to the targeted subculture.

Church Growth advocacy of Contemporary Worship was not purely theoretical. To have merely theorized about how doing Contemporary Worship would be effective in reaching new people would have been contrary to the Church Growth method itself. From its beginnings, Church Growth thought had pursued the examination of actual cases where growth was taking place, assessing the social, cultural, and experiential dynamics of why that growth was occurring and then extrapolating principles and practices for wider implementation elsewhere. In the case of Contemporary Worship, this method meant highlighting the number of churches exploding numerically by worshiping in a contemporary style. As noted above, Rick Warren had called these CAMEO churches. George Hunter III used a more scripturally

31. Michael S. Hamilton, "The Triumph of the Praise Songs: How Guitars Beat Out the Organ in the Worship Wars," *Christianity Today* 43, no. 8 (July 12, 1999): 30.

32. White, *Opening the Front Door*, 85. On the criticalness of music, see Easum, *Church Growth Handbook*, 47; and Charles Arn, *How to Start a New Service: Your Church Can Reach New People* (Grand Rapids: Baker, 1997), 123, 166. Compare Rick Warren, *The Purpose Driven Church: Growth without Compromising Your Message & Mission* (Grand Rapids: Zondervan, 1995), 280. Warren was a practitioner of Church Growth thought.

grounded, historically evocative term: in 1996 he referred to them as "apostolic congregations."[33] Their importance in the religious landscape could not have been greater for Hunter. Given the growing gap between unchurched people influenced by a secular culture and traditional churches still doing church as if an earlier Christendom was still the norm, the "real future of Christianity" itself was linked in Hunter's mind with the model of these "pioneering local churches."[34] Specifically, "apostolic congregations" were willing to make bold adaptations in language, music, and the style of the target population's culture; they did so to obey the Great Commission by making outreach their first priority.[35] It was this commitment to adaptability that made these congregations apostolic, Hunter explained:

> The "apostolic congregations" that are emerging over the land are more different from the traditional churches on this point [adaptability] than any other. As once the apostle Paul was willing to "become all things to all people that [he] might by all means save some," so we are observing the emergence of entire congregations who are willing to be culturally flexible in order to reach people. These churches are dramatizing a truth that missionaries have known for decades. . . . When a church employs the language, music, style, architecture, art forms, and other forms of the target population's culture, Christianity then has a fair chance to become contagious within their ranks. But when the church's communication forms are alien to the host population, they may never perceive that Christianity's God is for people like them.[36]

Not surprisingly, of the nine exemplary congregations that Hunter documented in his 1996 book, all were using Contemporary Worship in at least some of their weekend services.[37] For Hunter and others, to worship in a contemporary style had become the pathway to being apostolic in the 1990s.

A Headliner Role for CAMEO Churches

Although Rick Warren and George Hunter III had used different terms for the churches spearheading Contemporary Worship, they agreed on the origins and growing numbers of these congregations. While they gave different guesses about the total numbers by the mid-1990s (Warren estimated around one

33. Hunter, *Church for the Unchurched*, 12.
34. Hunter, *Church for the Unchurched*, 19–20.
35. Hunter, *Church for the Unchurched*, 29, 32.
36. Hunter, *Church for the Unchurched*, 58.
37. Stallsmith, "Path to a Second Service," 61.

thousand while Hunter merely said hundreds), both saw them as the cutting edge of the future. And both men saw these churches as having a similar past and location. Hunter's portrayal that "this breed of church was reborn in the US in the 1970s, began spreading in the 1980s, and is now found in virtually every city in North America in the 1990s" was roughly matched by Warren's thought that most had been established since 1980 and that there was "at least one example in most metropolitan areas."[38]

Both men also concurred on the significance of these congregations. If for Hunter these congregations were "pioneering local churches," Warren held them in no less esteem: he was convinced that they were "a new movement of God springing up in America."[39] Setting this theological interpretation of significance aside, what is clear from the history is that this sort of church played a critical role starting in the late 1980s in modeling and promoting Contemporary Worship for other congregations. In particular several specific churches, including Warren's own Saddleback Valley Community Church, became models of how to do a contemporary style of worship as well as training centers teaching updated approaches to church life and ministry, including worship. This teaching function, often centered in conferences and workshops the churches sponsored, was supplemented by the literature that the staff of these congregations produced. Books, articles, tapes and CDs, and videos enabled others to see, hear, and contemplate what Contemporary Worship looked like.

Both the example provided by these numerically growing congregations— such growth being linked to a contemporary style of worship—and the resources they produced made the second wave of Contemporary Worship different from the early wave of the 1960s and 1970s. In an ecclesiastical atmosphere desperate for good news, being able to see the fabulously positive numerical results of having Contemporary Worship gave this second wave the momentum to achieve a breadth of adoption and stability of continuation that the earlier wave did not have. Simply put, Warren's CAMEO churches became the headliners in a new story of hope and possibility for other congregations, a narrative tied to 1990s-era Contemporary Worship.

Despite their multiple points of agreement, Hunter did something that Warren did not do: study several specific congregations.[40] Surveying the range

---

38. Compare Hunter, *Church for the Unchurched*, 12, to Warren, "New Churches," 368.

39. Warren, "New Churches," 368.

40. Of course, since Warren's discussion occurred within his doctor of ministry thesis focused on his own congregation, he had no reason to do so. Hunter was not the only Church Growth author at the time to provide book-length case studies of innovative churches. See Elmer L. Towns, *An Inside Look at 10 of Today's Most Innovative Churches: What They're Doing, How They're Doing It & How You Can Apply Their Ideas in Your Church* (Ventura, CA: Regal, 1990); and C. Peter Wagner, ed., *The New Apostolic Churches: Rediscovering the New*

of possibilities offered by the hundreds of "apostolic congregations," Hunter identified nine cases that he thought were particularly instructive. As mentioned previously, all nine had Contemporary Worship in at least part of their weekend spectrum of services.[41] However, as the 1990s progressed, four of these nine churches would turn out to be instrumental in the history of Contemporary Worship: Willow Creek Community Church in South Barrington, Illinois (a Chicago suburb), with pastor Bill Hybels; Saddleback Valley Community Church, originally started in Laguna Hills, California (in southern Orange County), with Rick Warren; Community Church of Joy in Glendale, Arizona (a Phoenix suburb), with Walt Kallestad; and Ginghamsburg United Methodist Church in Tipp City, Ohio (a Dayton suburb), with Mike Slaughter. Although they were not the only cutting-edge churches influencing others in favor of Contemporary Worship, these four were the most prominent in terms of media attention, teaching impact, and number of instructional resources produced.[42]

These four congregations and their pastors shared multiple similarities. All the pastors themselves were baby boomers: Walt Kallestad was the oldest (born in the late 1940s) and Rick Warren was the youngest (born in 1954). They all began ministries in their "apostolic congregations" within the same general time period. Willow Creek emerged out of an evangelistic youth ministry Hybels and others had been doing in the Chicago area; it held its first service in October 1975.[43] Walt Kallestad became the pastor

Testament Model of Leadership and Why It Is God's Desire for the Church Today (Ventura, CA: Regal, 1998). Willow Creek Community Church was the only church to be considered in all three books (Hunter, Towns, and Wagner).

41. Interestingly, in the two works in which the Hunter and Warren highlighted their "apostolic congregations" or CAMEO churches, neither used the term "megachurch" to identify these congregations, even though the term would surely have fit many of the churches they were describing, especially Hunter's nine specific examples. Perhaps they preferred terms that focused attention on a theological appraisal (Hunter's notion of "apostolic") or on the methods used by the congregation (Warren's highlighting of the "Contemporary Approach" in the acronym CAMEO).

42. Another possibility would have been Eastside Foursquare Church in Kirkland, Washington, under the leadership of Doug Murren. It is not clear why Hunter did not include Murren as part of his study. Murren's church had a similar historical trajectory to the churches Hunter included and fit Hunter's description of what an exemplary congregation looked like. Moreover, Murren was an acquaintance of many of the pastors whom Hunter featured and was part of the existing networks connecting these sorts of churches. For the history of Contemporary Worship, Murren is important for authoring an early, full-length monograph on targeting baby boomers (*The Baby Boomerang: Catching Baby Boomers as They Return to Church* [Ventura, CA: Regal, 1990]) and for being featured on an instructional videocassette (VHS), *How to Design Contemporary Worship Services* (Ventura, CA: Global Net Productions, 1994). See also Doug Murren, *Developing an Outreach-Focused Church* (Pasadena, CA: Charles E. Fuller Institute, 1993), 4 videocassettes (VHS).

43. See Don Cousins, *Tomorrow's Church . . . Today!* (Elk Grove Village, IL: Kukla, 1979), 17–18; and Todd E. Johnson, "Disconnected Rituals: The Origins of the Seeker Service

of his already-existing Lutheran congregation in 1978. Mike Slaughter was placed by his bishop in the Ginghamsburg church in 1979. Rick Warren began Saddleback on Easter 1980 as a new church plant sponsored by the Southern Baptist Convention.

Many of the same background influences shaped these pastors and bonded them in common networks and perspectives. For example, Robert Schuller at Garden Grove Community Church (see chap. 6) was a strong guiding force for all four. For both Bill Hybels and Rick Warren, reading Schuller's 1974 book, *Your Church Has Real Possibilities!*, soon after its release crystalized what a congregational ministry aiming for the unchurched could look like.[44] At Willow Creek the book became required reading for all the early staff members.[45] These pastors, too, had connections to Schuller's Institute for Successful Church Leadership, as learners, teachers, or both. Hybels attended just weeks before launching Willow Creek. So impressed was he that the following year he brought twenty-five Willow Creek staff people with him. (Schuller's public recognition of Hybels on this occasion made a strong impact on these staff members.)[46] Warren attended in his last year of seminary (1979) and Kallestad in the mid-1970s, the latter possibly influenced by his own senior pastor at the time, Merv Thompson at Prince of Peace Lutheran Church in Burnsville, Minnesota. Thompson had attended the institute in 1971 and returned home to start an outdoor service in imitation of Schuller's California practice (though in summertime only, owing to Minnesota weather).[47] Kallestad and Hybels, at least, were later invited to be speakers at the institute.[48]

Movement," in *The Conviction of Things Not Seen: Worship and Ministry in the 21st Century*, ed. Todd E. Johnson (Grand Rapids: Brazos, 2002), 53–66.

44. Lynne Hybels and Bill Hybels, *Rediscovering Church: The Story and Vision of Willow Creek Community Church* (Grand Rapids: Zondervan, 1995), 51; Warren, *Purpose Driven Church*, 190.

45. Rory Noland, interview by Lim Swee Hong and Lester Ruth, July 27, 2020.

46. Gregory A. Pritchard, *Willow Creek Seeker Services: Evaluating a New Way of Doing Church* (Grand Rapids: Baker, 1996), 54. Pritchard based the book on his 1994 sociology dissertation, titled "The Strategy of Willow Creek Community Church: A Study in the Sociology of Religion" (PhD diss., Northwestern University, 1994).

47. For Warren, see John Curran Hardin, "Retailing Religion: Business Promotionalism in American Christian Churches in the Twentieth Century" (PhD diss., University of Maryland, 2011), 438; for Kallestad's attendance, see Walt Kallestad, *Entertainment Evangelism: Taking the Church Public* (Nashville: Abingdon, 1996), 121. The information on Merv Thompson and Prince of Peace came from Handt Hanson, interview by Lester Ruth, December 28, 2014, and Handt Hanson, email message to Lester Ruth, July 7, 2020. In the early 1970s Thompson had hired Kallestad, a new college graduate, as a youth worker.

48. Mark T. Mulder and Gerardo Martí, *The Glass Church: Robert H. Schuller, the Crystal Cathedral, and the Strain of Megachurch Ministry* (New Brunswick, NJ: Rutgers University Press, 2020), 134; Pritchard, "Strategy of Willow Creek," 200.

Schuller's relationship with the four pastors was not merely formal. Schuller offered to help outline and coauthor a book with Kallestad. He invited Slaughter to participate in the formation of a new organization.[49] Schuller's friendships with and mentoring of Bill Hybels and Rick Warren seem to have been especially close—on one occasion Schuller remarked that the two were his most famous students and that they had outrun him in creating successful churches.[50] On another occasion, Schuller said he believed Hybels had been the one to take the Church Growth principles Schuller had encouraged and refine and maximize them "to the ultimate length of their potential."[51]

Similarly, these pastors shared a common influence from the Church Growth movement. For example, Warren's reading of Donald McGavran while still a college student resulted in his shift from the desire to pastor an already-established church to the desire to plant a growing church that would reach non-Christians. Warren would later claim to have read seventy-five books on Church Growth and to have attended every Church Growth conference and seminar he could find. Indeed, using a method reminiscent of this movement, in seminary he did an independent study of the one hundred largest churches in the United States.[52] Warren graduated from Fuller Theological Seminary as a doctor of ministry in 1993; renowned Church Growth expert C. Peter Wagner had served as his thesis advisor. A year earlier, Walt Kallestad had graduated with the same degree from the same school, having studied with Church Growth faculty; he quoted other Church Growth authors in his thesis.[53] Though Mike Slaughter did not earn a degree from Fuller, he attended seminars there in his early years of ministry; he was also influenced by George Hunter III, whose book *The Contagious Congregation* Slaughter had his church's leadership read in the first year he was at Ginghamsburg.[54]

The pastors, too, shared participation in meetings and organizations that gathered like-minded pastors of larger, growing churches. Especially important was the Leadership Network, which a Texas businessman, Bob Buford,

49. Walther Paul Kallestad, "Entertainment Evangelism" (DMin thesis, Fuller Theological Seminary, 1992), 59–60; Michael Slaughter, *Spiritual Entrepreneurs: 6 Principles for Risking Renewal* (Nashville: Abingdon, 1994), 137. Slaughter's book was previously published as *Beyond Playing Church: A Christ-Centered Environment for Church Renewal* (Anderson, IN: Bristol House, 1994).

50. Mulder and Martí, *Glass Church*, 135.

51. Pritchard, *Willow Creek Seeker Services*, 56. Two specific examples of influence can be seen in the "community church" names and in the use of door-to-door surveying before launching the congregations.

52. Warren, *Purpose Driven Church*, 29–30; Warren, "New Churches," 2.

53. Kallestad, "Entertainment Evangelism" (DMin thesis).

54. Slaughter, *Spiritual Entrepreneurs*, 108, 117.

had started in 1984 with a mission to "identify, connect, and help high-capacity Christian leaders multiply their impact." Participants primarily were senior pastors of churches with more than a thousand members. Buford wanted to foster a continuous "stream of innovation" with these sorts of pastors by providing networking opportunities, allowing them to share ideas and support each other.[55] The Leadership Network also served these sorts of pastors by introducing them to thinkers and writers who would challenge them by expanding their frameworks for thinking about their work. Such contributors included Everett Rogers, a groundbreaking theorist in the diffusion of innovations; George Barna, a market researcher focusing on Americans and their religious beliefs and behaviors; Lyle Schaller, perhaps the most traveled church consultant of the time and someone who brought an emphasis on demographics and structures from his background as an urban planner; and Peter Drucker, an academic specialist in business management.[56] Hybels, Warren, Kallestad, and Slaughter all participated in Leadership Network meetings; Hybels and Warren had a particularly strong influence in the network.

For one example of the Leadership Network's role in shaping these pastors, consider the impact of Drucker's approach to management on the pastors. They and their staffs had read Drucker before they had met him in the Leadership Network.[57] They also quoted him at critical points in their writing.[58] At least two of the pastors (Hybels and Warren) had a poster in their office that featured Drucker's essential questions: "What is our business? Who is our customer? What does our customer value?"[59] Their public statements, too, confirmed the importance of Drucker's influence. Endorsements by

55. Bob Buford, *Drucker & Me: What a Texas Entrepreneur Learned from the Father of Modern Management* (Brentwood, TN: Worthy, 2014), 92. Buford would also provide the grant money for another organization that Leith Anderson spearheaded, the Teaching Church Network. Rather than focusing on conferences and meetings, this second network linked pastors in a mentoring network. It operated from 1994 to 1997. Paul Borden, interview by Lester Ruth, August 17, 2020.

56. Drucker was instrumental in helping Buford develop the idea for the organization. Information on the Leadership Network and participation in it came from the following sources, in addition to Buford's book *Drucker & Me*: Warren Bird, email message to Lester Ruth, August 23, 2020; Dave Travis, email message to Lester Ruth, August 25, 2020; and Tom Tumblin, interview by Lester Ruth, August 14, 2020.

57. Kimon Howland Sargeant, *Seeker Churches: Promoting Traditional Religion in a Nontraditional Way* (New Brunswick, NJ: Rutgers University Press, 2000), 198. Cf. Buford, *Drucker & Me*, 93.

58. For an example, see Kallestad, "Entertainment Evangelism" (DMin thesis), 45. In this passage in his thesis, Kallestad immediately followed the Drucker quotation with a quotation from George Barna.

59. R. Gustav Niebuhr, "The Minister as Marketer: Learning from Business," *New York Times*, April 18, 1995, A20; Hardin, "Retailing Religion," 446.

both Hybels and Warren for Bob Buford's book *Drucker & Me* highlighted Drucker's role in their lives and ministries: for Bill Hybels "being mentored by Peter Drucker was one of God's great gifts to my ministry," while Rick Warren described Peter Drucker and Bob Buford as "two of my best friends."

The impact of the Leadership Network and interaction with Peter Drucker was to reinforce the pragmatic liturgical worldview held by these pastors.[60] Specifically, what the network and its speakers did was fortify an aggressive attentiveness to average people as they actually were and to how they really experienced Christian worship. This attentiveness to actual people harmonized well with what the pastors had imbibed from Church Growth sources, not to mention Robert Schuller. Consequently—and not surprisingly—the liturgical theology expressed by Hybels, Warren, Kallestad, and Slaughter showed much commonality and placed them squarely in the flow of liturgical pragmatism that led to Contemporary Worship.

Indeed, in comparison to the long history of liturgically pragmatic theologizing, there was little that was novel in the thoughts of these four influential pastors. All the classic themes of this liturgical approach were there, beginning with the priority of the Great Commission given by Jesus to the church and the resulting importance of active evangelizing. These four pastors were not only evangelical in theology and spirituality; they were also at heart evangelists, a vocation that they built into their visions for their churches. Hybels, Kallestad, and Slaughter would have agreed with how Rick Warren summarized a New Testament ecclesiology: "A Great Commitment to the Great Commandment (i.e., the commandment to love God in worship and neighbor in service) and Great Commission will create a Great Church."[61]

As an ecclesiology, this commitment to evangelism meant that all four pastors saw the church as essentially a missionary enterprise to seek and evangelize the lost and unchurched. That was the church's fundamental purpose. Thus, the first two of Willow Creek's founding "philosophical principles" would have applied equally to the other churches: "1. All people matter to God; therefore, they

60. In addition, the prior experience in creative youth and college ministries that some of these pastors had should not be discounted. As previously mentioned, Hybels's work at Willow Creek was an extension of his immediately prior experience in the youth ministry named Son City. Kallestad was deeply influenced by an evangelistic, pietistic form of Lutheranism in Minnesota and the surrounding areas. He was active, for example, in innovative, traveling college-based singing groups in the late 1960s and early 1970s. See Jonathan D. Anderson, *Fifty Thousand Evangelists: Lutheran Youth in the Jesus Revolution* (privately published, 2019), 25–28. As Kallestad's associate pastor, Timothy Wright, told us, "Everything we were doing at [Community Church of] Joy, I learned as a kid." Wright said Kallestad had had the same experience. Timothy Wright, interview by Lester Ruth, February 6, 2015.

61. Warren, "New Churches," 26.

must matter to us. 2. Lost people need to be sought out and found."[62] To veer from that mission was to risk proving unfaithful to God's call to the church and to violate the example of Christ himself—since, as Slaughter put it, "the agenda of Jesus is . . . the needs of the unchurched."[63] With an evangelizing concern for the lost and unchurched at the center of a biblical understanding of the church, it was only natural to make worship a critical part of how churches could fulfill this God-given calling. The imperative and opportunity were very clear to Walt Kallestad: "Sunday morning is the time for congregations to bring in the 60 percent to 90 percent unchurched, unreached population. Sunday morning is a prime time to seek and to save the lost. . . . Christians should design Sunday nights for themselves and turn the morning over to evangelistic outreach."[64]

Kallestad was quite sure, however, that most churches were failing in this mission. His judgment was clear: "It is time for radical reform of Sunday mornings."[65] Hybels, Warren, and Slaughter all agreed with Kallestad. This iconoclastic reading of the current state of worship, affirming the existence of a severe gap between people and traditional worship, was another way the four pastors' theology fit the classic theological emphases of liturgical pragmatism. Indeed, they saw an iconoclastic bent as necessary to staying faithful in every age. Evangelistically effective church life, they believed, is built on perpetual change and adaptation of the means by which the church proclaims the gospel. Indeed, innovation is necessary for every new move of God, since "every great awakening through nearly two thousand years of church history has employed different techniques."[66] To seek effective innovation is biblically allowable since what the New Testament gave the church was broad principles—like the command to reach out with the most effective means—not the particular means themselves.[67] In fact, Slaughter applied this

---

62. Barbara Stewart, ed., *Willow Creek Community Church: Church Leader's Handbook* (South Barrington, IL: Willow Creek Community Church, 1991), 20.

63. Slaughter, *Spiritual Entrepreneurs*, 68.

64. Walther P. Kallestad, "Entertainment Evangelism," *The Lutheran*, May 23, 1990, 17. Kallestad was writing at a time and in a context when Sunday evening services were very common in Protestant churches, perhaps even near universal. It was his way of placing an evangelizing service within the larger context of discipling those who were Christians. Each of the other three churches likewise envisioned evangelistically successful worship within a larger complex of congregational programming to disciple continually maturing Christians.

65. Kallestad, "Entertainment Evangelism," *The Lutheran*, 17.

66. Slaughter, *Spiritual Entrepreneurs*, 17. Compare Kirbyjon Caldwell and Walt Kallestad, *Entrepreneurial Faith: Launching Bold Initiatives to Expand God's Kingdom* (Colorado Springs: WaterBrook, 2004), 33–37, in which Jesus himself is portrayed as the ultimate entrepreneur. Caldwell and Kallestad's collaborative book extends the image of pastoral entrepreneurship to actual non-worship-related entrepreneurial activities supported by a church.

67. For an interesting discussion of biblical "principles" and their universality in contrast to particular means or methods, see Warren, "New Churches," 10–13.

iconoclastic stance to earlier forms of Contemporary Worship, chastising churches in the 1990s that wanted to add a contemporary service but actually had in mind moving "forward into the 1970s."[68] Such a service would not be truly effective, he argued, because it was not truly contemporary.

Of course, this deep suspicion of inherited forms of worship was not new, as we have seen. But what these four pastors—and other like-minded pastors—brought to the search for effective innovation in worship was an overtly entrepreneurial perspective drawn from the world of business as they used business-related language and metaphors. Several of the key influences on their thought and approach to ministry—for instance, Robert Schuller, George Barna, and Peter Drucker—reinforced this economic framing of liturgical iconoclasm. The use of market research (by Hybels and Warren), the description of a pastor as an "entrepreneur" (Slaughter), and the search for entertainment in worship because it worked with audiences (Kallestad) were ways in which a business orientation was brought to the matter of shaping congregational worship. The business world provided the images, metaphors, terms, and measures to these pastors' liturgical approach.

As we have seen with prior liturgical pragmatists, a divide between the content of the gospel and the form in which it was communicated provided the basis on which these four pastors could argue for innovation in worship. Hybels, Warren, and Slaughter would have affirmed how Kallestad appraised the current situation, the need for change, and the propriety of innovation: "What was relevant in the 16th century in terms of the medium of the day is not relevant today. Certainly the changeless message remains the same. It is a matter of stylistic changes, not substance changes."[69]

Moreover, the four pastors expressed this content-form split in terms of language, both literal and metaphorical. Of the four, Kallestad provided the most complete list of literal and metaphorical aspects of language that needed to be evaluated for effectiveness in communicating to the targeted audience: spoken elements, tone of voice, gestures, mannerisms, physical expressions, music, seating arrangements, lighting, sound, room arrangement, and wardrobe.[70] The similarity of contemporary services in all four churches shows that all four worked with similar checklists of "languages" that needed to be considered to develop worship that would bridge the gap with their target audiences.

Finally, the divide between form and content supported the emphasis all four pastors placed on the importance of human agency in finding the means

68. Michael Slaughter, *Out on the Edge: A Wake-Up Call for Church Leaders on the Edge of the Media Revolution* (Nashville: Abingdon, 1998), 58.
69. Kallestad, "Entertainment Evangelism," *The Lutheran*, 17.
70. Kallestad, "Entertainment Evangelism" (DMin thesis), 65.

that God would bless with numerical success. Of the four, Warren argued the theological point the most succinctly: "I believe church growth is a choice. A church must choose to grow or not to grow. Many churches have deliberately chosen not to grow. They make that choice in a variety of ways: by the programs they offer, by the amount of time and energy they invest in evangelism, and by the size of the building they build."[71] In contrast to non-growing churches, Hybels, Kallestad, and Slaughter joined Warren in intentionally choosing to grow by finding the liturgical means by which they could effectively reach a growing number of people. Such growth could be seen as being in agreement with the New Testament. There Jesus instructed his followers to spread the gospel, there the images about evangelism and church life created a sense of expansion, and there the early church itself grew numerically.[72]

The scriptural hub in the four pastors' theologizing about using Contemporary Worship was the standard verse: 1 Corinthians 9:22. Each used the verse at a critical point to provide the essential scriptural support for what they sought to do liturgically. For Hybels, the verse provided the rationale for his efforts to identify with the non-Christian people he sought to evangelize, by adopting their language, clothing, customs, and lifestyle so as to make himself a more "credible witness" to them.[73] In Hybels's estimation, "Common sense, street smarts, business savvy and Biblical teaching would all agree"[74]—that is to say, the Bible verse confirmed his practical, business-oriented approach to ministry. Warren used the verse to argue for an apostolic approach of allowing the target to determine the best way to evangelize. The apostle Paul had adapted his approach to be able to speak to Jews at one point and Gentiles at another, and Warren was sure that if Paul were to come to Southern California, he would learn to communicate in Southern California terms.[75] Slaughter similarly found the verse to be the biblical justification for the need to read the culture of a targeted group and then adjust to this culture in one's ministry, including in worship.[76] Kallestad perhaps highlighted the verse the most, at one point making it the signature verse for a whole book and on another occasion noting how flexibility in communicating could characterize the ministry of Jesus himself: "If Jesus were here today walking the face of the earth, he would

71. Warren, "New Churches," 346–47.

72. For the most thorough theological discussion of the propriety of assessing numerical growth as a measure of faithfulness among the four pastors, see Warren, "New Churches," 340–52.

73. Pritchard, *Willow Creek Seeker Services*, 122; Pritchard, "Strategy of Willow Creek," 405.

74. Quoted in Pritchard, "Strategy of Willow Creek," 691.

75. Warren, *Purpose Driven Church*, 171. See also Rick Warren, "Becoming a Purpose Driven Church (an Interview with Rick Warren, Part 1)," by Jon Walker, *Pastors.com*, November 3, 2015, http://pastors.com/becoming-a-purpose-driven-church-interview-with-rick-warren-part -1/. This 2015 posting is a re-presentation of a 2002 interview.

76. Slaughter, *Out on the Edge*, 30.

without a doubt use the No. 1 medium of the day to tell his story. Jesus would become all things to all people to save some. He would use entertainment."[77]

Faithfulness to an apostolic approach could find no more critical rooting than in Paul and Jesus. Whether with this keynote verse or with the other aspects of their theologizing, as compared to other pragmatists, there was indeed little uniqueness in the way these four pastors articulated the classic theological themes of Contemporary Worship. Their contribution came not in newness of thought but in their ability to use these classic themes to devise a rigorous approach to the entirety of congregational life and programming, including worship. It was an approach driven by targeting specific types of people and an approach that provided a model that other congregations would see and seek to appropriate.

What was clear was that these four congregations and their pastors were not literally trying to become all things for all people. Each made clear, precise decisions about whom they were trying to reach. Peter Drucker's question (Who is our customer?) was something each had pondered and answered. Moreover, another of Drucker's questions (What do these customers value?) was translated by each congregation into a systematic shaping of the entire worship experience, starting with a worshiper's initial drive up to the church campus and not stopping until after that person's departure. During the service itself and its content, each congregation sought to establish relevance to a targeted person's "felt needs." In these ways the four congregations not only sought to "lower barriers" for intelligibility and accessibility (a rather passive way to consider the Church Growth movement's homogeneous unit principle), but they also aggressively desired to build bridges over the gap assumed between more traditional ways of worship and the targeted audience.

Indeed, Willow Creek and Saddleback each established a kind of marketing profile for the person they wished to reach. For Willow Creek, it was "Unchurched Harry and Mary," Chicago-area suburbanites between the ages of twenty-five and forty-five—college-educated white-collar workers and independent thinkers. If Harry and Mary had prior church experience, it was unsatisfactory.[78] Saddleback targeted "Saddleback Sam and Samantha,"

---

77. For the signature verse, see the unnumbered page ahead of the table of contents in Kallestad's book, *Entertainment Evangelism*. For the application to Jesus, see Kallestad's *Lutheran* article, "Entertainment Evangelism." Compare a similar use and highlighting by Kallestad's associate pastor, Timothy Wright, in "Making the Gospel Accessible through Worship," in *Contemporary Worship: A Sourcebook for Spirited-Traditional, Praise and Seeker Services*, ed. Tim and Jan Wright (Nashville: Abingdon, 1997), 20; and Wright, *Community of Joy*, 51.

78. One of Willow Creek's pastors published an entire book on this profile: Lee Strobel, *Inside the Mind of Unchurched Harry & Mary: How to Reach Friends and Family Who Avoid God and the Church* (Grand Rapids: Zondervan, 1993).

baby boomers who had imbibed typical Southern California values and life-style and thus have distinct cultural preferences like informality in behavior, casualness in clothing, and a preference for large groups rather than small ones for first contact.[79]

In these four CAMEO churches—and others like them—what did a commitment to become "all things" for the target audience produce in terms of congregational worship? Simply put, this theological commitment led to Contemporary Worship as we have known it over the past several decades.[80] If you had walked into any of these four churches around 1990, you would have recognized the basic dynamics of a contemporary service as found in most mainline or evangelical congregations since then. A commitment to intelligibility of language (in the literal sense) meant that everything was in contemporary, colloquial English. A commitment to understandable metaphorical language meant that all the other details of the service could also be "read" by contemporary people: the pace and timing, the space inside and out, the decorations, the lighting, the seating, and the hospitality. A dedication to relevance meant that the content of the service, especially the sermon, dealt with issues that participants recognized as their own pressing concerns. The atmosphere was informal, in both dress and behavior. That was true for both the congregation and the worship leaders. People could feel free to express themselves physically, too, by clapping or raising hands. Production values, if we can call them that, were high, characterized by a striving for excellence. That included the use of electronic technology like projection, whose importance would only grow throughout the 1990s.

Contemporary music—its sound, song repertoire, instrumentation, and performance practices—was an especially critical part of the services in these congregations. The platform up front was primarily musician space, and extended periods of singing were standard. Church leadership carefully assessed what was the heart music of the target audience and aimed to reproduce that style of music in church services. Nothing was left to chance with respect to

79. Warren names this target audience in his 1993 thesis (Warren, "New Churches," 24–26; see also Warren, *Purpose Driven Church*, 169–72). The baby boomer identification was much more present in Warren's thesis, where it can be found prominently in the title and abstract, whereas Warren's best-selling book mutes the generational identification. This muting was one of multiple ways in which Warren transitioned his thesis for a broader readership. Even when generational thinking targeting baby boomers was not prominently displayed in churches' publications, it could still shape them. For example, Timothy Wright told us (Wright, interview) that he began reading every book on baby boomers he could find after initially encountering Paul Light's 1988 book titled *Baby Boomers*.

80. Cf. Lim Swee Hong and Lester Ruth, *Lovin' on Jesus: A Concise History of Contemporary Worship* (Nashville: Abingdon, 2017), 2–7.

the music because—as Rick Warren once explained—for a purpose-driven church, music "may also be *the* most influential factor in determining who your church reaches for Christ and whether or not your church grows."[81]

The commonalities between these four CAMEO churches did not mean there were no differences. Willow Creek, for example, emphasized "seeker" terminology to designate its target audience and thus made a sharp distinction between weekend services targeting Unchurched Harry and Mary, which were not called "worship" services, and midweek services, which were intended to be the worship opportunities for believers.[82] In its weekend seeker services, Willow Creek expected little, if any, participation by those attending. These seeker services, too, became known for the life situation dramas that established the connection of relevance for the seekers in attendance.

A Saddleback distinctive was how the leaders there developed their own formula for sequencing the songs in a service so as to establish an appealing, purpose-driven, and collaborative flow. An acronym used in public teaching, IMPACT, gave the order: the sequence called for progressing from songs that inspire movement to praise to adoration to commitment to a song to tie it all together.[83] The *I*, *M*, *P*, and *T* songs were all upbeat. The *A* and *C* songs were slower and more contemplative.[84] Internally, leaders had a shortcut way of expressing the flow that focused on worshipers' involvement and connection: the songs moved from a "hand clapper" (an upbeat song about God) to a "hand holder" (a song that brought a sense of commonality to the assembly engaging in dialogue with God) to a "hand raiser" (a more intimate song addressing God directly) to another "hand holder" at the end of the service.[85]

The uniqueness of Community Church of Joy was in the range of services that it conducted on a weekend, each aiming for its own target audience and each at a particular level along the scale from traditional to contemporary. The Saturday evening service was "Contemporary Country." Sunday morning began with "Spirited Traditional," which was the service most likely to use denominational worship liturgies. The next three services (the "Contemporary Blend," the "New Contemporary," and the "Modern Contemporary") increasingly moved away from anything considered traditional, especially with respect to music.[86]

81. Warren, *Purpose Driven Church*, 280.

82. Rick Warren at one time made a similar distinction, although it was less prominent and less stressed in his public materials. See his doctoral thesis: Warren, "New Churches," 276.

83. Rick Muchow, email message to Lester Ruth, May 9, 2015.

84. Warren, *Purpose Driven Church*, 287.

85. Rick Muchow, interview by Lim Swee Hong and Lester Ruth, April 30, 2015.

86. See Kallestad, *Entertainment Evangelism*, 71–73. For a near-contemporaneous description, along with a contrast to practices at Willow Creek and other churches in the 1990s, see

Used by permission of Timothy Wright

Figure 7.1. A service at Community Church of Joy, a Lutheran congregation in Arizona

The distinctive stamp of Ginghamsburg United Methodist Church was a strong emphasis on electronic media and "multisensory" worship. A move to a new facility with increased technology in 1994—along with some serendipitous exposure to media use elsewhere—prompted the church to stress technology in its worship planning and leading.[87] Soon staff members were publishing books and resources based on their own experiences, works that showed others how to employ multisensory multimedia to tell a good story.[88]

If the Church Growth movement provided a constant backdrop in this period of constant advocacy for Contemporary Worship, then CAMEO churches provided successful models and resources for other congregations that might want to adopt Contemporary Worship. Unlike the first wave of Contemporary Worship in the late 1960s and early 1970s, the second wave had headlining, landmark congregations whose public profile, numerical success, and resources made them exemplars for others. These four congregations— and others like them—thus made it easy for Contemporary Worship to spread and become a fixture in mainline and evangelical congregations by the mid-1990s.

Lester Ruth, "*Lex Agendi, Lex Orandi*: Toward an Understanding of Seeker Services as a New Kind of Liturgy," *Worship* 70, no. 5 (September 1996): 386–405.

87. Slaughter, *Out on the Edge*, 47, 121; Kim Miller and Dan Bracken, interview by Lester Ruth, February 5, 2016.

88. See Len Wilson and Michael Slaughter, *Using Media in Your Message* (Tipp City, OH: Ginghamsburg Communications, 1996), videocassette (VHS); Kim Miller, *Handbook for Multisensory Worship* (Nashville: Abingdon, 1999); and Len Wilson, *The Wired Church: Making Media Ministry* (Nashville: Abingdon, 1999).

The CAMEO churches indeed had quite a public profile, especially Willow Creek Community Church and Saddleback Valley Community Church. Willow Creek caught the initial focus of national media. Starting in the late 1980s, periodicals as varied as *Woman's Day* and *U.S. Catholic* ran articles on Willow Creek.[89] Willow Creek's exceptional increase in weekly attendance through the 1980s—reportedly from 2,057 in 1980 to 12,002 in 1989—and vigorous seeker approach to ministry made for good headlines and interesting reading, but it was not the only one of the four churches to garner national and regional attention.[90] After the publication of Rick Warren's *The Purpose Driven Church* in 1995, which has been called the "best-selling church-growth manual in the history of the genre,"[91] Saddleback, too, became very well known. Indeed, by the turn of the century, one author was calling these churches' respective pastors, Bill Hybels and Rick Warren, the "Roger Bannisters of the church world."[92] (Roger Bannister set records by becoming the first person to run a mile in under four minutes.)

Notwithstanding the varying levels of national prominence experienced by Willow Creek, Saddleback, Community Church of Joy, and Ginghamsburg, all four served as producers and promoters of resources that would teach others how to do Contemporary Worship. What Community Church of Joy and Ginghamsburg lost in national attention, they gained by denominational links to Lutherans and Methodists respectively, including to their denominational publishing houses. All four churches sponsored conferences—sometimes on church leadership and sometimes specifically on worship—that taught both a missional mindset and the specifics of doing Contemporary Worship. At Willow Creek, for example, conference participants got to watch one of the congregation's weekend seeker services while Hybels and Nancy Beach, the church's programming director, provided commentary on the service and dissected it for the understanding of these participants.[93]

In addition to holding conferences, these churches developed resources that promoted Contemporary Worship, explaining why a congregation might want

89. Susan Headden, "Worshiping God," *Woman's Day* 55–56, no. 14 (October 13, 1992): 114–15, 118, 186–87; Robert J. McClory, "Why Did the Catholic Cross the Road?," *U.S. Catholic* 56, no. 1 (January 1991): 6–12. The back cover of Prichard's *Willow Creek Seeker Services* mentions articles in the *New York Times*, *Time* magazine, *Fortune*, the *Wall Street Journal*, and *Christianity Today*.

90. For attendance numbers, see Towns, *Inside Look*, 263. For an example of a national article that featured other CAMEO churches, see Charles Trueheart, "Welcome to the Next Church," *Atlantic Monthly* (August 1996): 37–58.

91. Justin G. Wilford, *Sacred Subdivisions: The Postsuburban Transformation of American Evangelicalism* (New York: New York University Press, 2012), 2.

92. James Emery White, *Rethinking the Church: A Challenge to Creative Redesign in an Age of Transition*, rev. ed. (Grand Rapids: Baker Books, 2003), 15.

93. Noland, interview.

to worship in that way and how to do it successfully. From the four churches came books, essays, chapters, and articles. Songbooks and CDs supplemented the prose materials. To help other churches visualize what Contemporary Worship looked like they produced videos (distributed on videocassette), sometimes of services themselves, sometimes of teaching to support this worship style, and sometimes both. The most aggressive channeling of resources was the development of the Willow Creek Association in 1992, which dedicated a separate staff to gather up the Willow Creek congregation's dissemination efforts, thereby freeing the pastoral staff from what had become a massive responsibility. By 1998, Hybels reported, the association had three thousand member churches representing seventy denominations and twenty-four countries, served by forty staff persons in the United States. The association also managed the website for Willow Creek Resources, which (as reported in 1998) had ten thousand pages of weekend service elements (message transcripts, drama sketches, music, etc.) dating back to 1990.[94]

Through all these measures, Willow Creek and the other CAMEO churches or "apostolic congregations" popularized Church Growth theory and theology, repackaging them in a very understandable and accessible way. This reframing included attaching the theology and its advocacy for Contemporary Worship to examples of growth and success that were compelling and attractive to smaller churches. The CAMEO churches' effectiveness in spreading the vision for Contemporary Worship would become ever more evident as the 1990s unfolded and an increasing number of mainline and evangelical congregations started contemporary services.

A Raging River of Contemporary Worship

Picture this worship scene from the mid-1990s: a guitar-playing worship leader guides the service, supported by a keyboard and rhythm section. Everyone sports casual dress; an atmosphere of informality saturates the air. The leaders, free to change the service to fit the atmosphere in the room, use spontaneity in a celebratory mode. These same leaders search the depths of their hearts to pray extemporaneously. While the lyrics of contemporary songs are projected on screens, the congregation stands and sings with a wonderful gusto.

Was this Willow Creek Community Church? Saddleback Valley Community Church? Another one of the CAMEO churches discussed above? Yes, possibly. But remember Pastor Gary Formby and Lester Memorial United

94. Bill Hybels, "Willow Creek Community Church and the Willow Creek Association," in *The New Apostolic Churches*, ed. C. Peter Wagner (Ventura, CA: Regal, 1998), 85–87.

Methodist Church in Oneonta, Alabama, from the beginning of this chapter. This scene is also a description of the 1994 worship in this small-town Methodist church during its newly created contemporary service. Lester Memorial was not alone. What this congregation had done was being replicated in an increasing number of congregations as Contemporary Worship became a raging river sweeping through small towns, county seats, and major urban areas in both mainline and evangelical congregations. A second wave of Contemporary Worship was at hand.

For example, by one estimate there were only fifteen Lutheran congregations in 1985 doing worship in a way that went beyond the format in Lutheran hymnals. By this same estimate there were at least three thousand (out of a total of twenty thousand) doing so by the end of 1994.[95] The same source estimated that from 1988 to 1991 about a thousand Lutheran congregations had taken up contemporary songs and instruments. This number made news in the *Wall Street Journal*.[96]

Other numerical evidence supports an expanding presence of Contemporary Worship in other denominations. In the denominational breakdown for the first royalty payout period (in 1989) of Christian Copyright Licensing International, which was the company whose licensing arrangements were facilitating widespread use of new songs, the Southern Baptist Convention was the only denomination from among the major mainline or evangelical denominations with a high ranking. In contrast, by 1996, the United Methodist, Missouri Synod Lutheran, Presbyterian Church (U.S.A.), and Evangelical Lutheran Church in America denominations had all risen in relative rank to be among denominations with the strongest positions on the list, evidenced in the number of congregations of each reporting for that period.[97]

Similarly, since publishers and editors keep an eye on what the "hot" topics are and where the trending interests of readers lie, a growing number of denominationally affiliated publications in the 1990s confirm the growth of this second wave of Contemporary Worship. The Lutheran Church–Missouri Synod publishing house, Concordia, launched the decade with a 1991 book titled *Courageous Churches*, which contained a chapter on new forms of worship and asked pastors and congregations in a concluding chapter whether

95. David S. Luecke, *The Other Story of Lutherans at Worship: Reclaiming Our Heritage of Diversity* (Tempe, AZ: Fellowship Ministries, 1995), 2. See also pp. 19–20 for additional statistics on adoption.

96. R. Gustav Niebuhr, "So It Isn't 'Rock of Ages,' It Is Rock, and Many Love It," *Wall Street Journal*, December 19, 1991, A1. For these numbers of Lutheran adoption of Contemporary Worship, the source was David Anderson of Fellowship Ministries, an Arizona-based ministry cultivating Contemporary Worship practices among Lutherans.

97. This appraisal is based on unpublished lists supplied to us by CCLI in 2004.

they too could be courageous.[98] That same year the Christian Reformed Church's magazine on music and liturgy, *Reformed Worship*, dedicated a whole issue to the topic, including photographs of two congregations—one in the United States and one in Canada—that had already taken the plunge into adopting more contemporary forms of worship. The opening essay, by a member of the editorial staff, noted the heightened interest in and anxiety over the issue: "There is probably no issue within Reformed churches at this point that is charged with more emotion than the debate over which direction the style of worship and music ought to go."[99] Notwithstanding the tension, by 1996 the Christian Reformed Church's publishing wing had published a how-to guide titled *So You've Been Asked to Develop a Worship Team.*[100]

Other denominations pursued the same readership interested in Contemporary Worship. From the Division for Congregational Ministries of the Evangelical Lutheran Church in America came practical resources in 1994 on starting new services for outreach (with a particular interest in Contemporary Worship) and in 1997 on evaluating contemporary music for worship. Both came from that denomination's publishing house, Augsburg Fortress.[101] Similarly, magazines coming from its Division for Congregational Ministries, the *Evangelizing Congregation*, and *Voice for Congregational Life* regularly carried materials on Contemporary Worship in issues throughout the 1990s. A graph in a 1997 issue of the latter magazine, for instance, showed how Evangelical Lutheran congregations in six out of seven geographic contexts had growth in average worship attendance from 1990 to 1994 if they had "alternative" worship, whereas congregations without "alternative" worship endured decline in all seven contexts.[102]

Other denominational agencies and publishing houses promoting Contemporary Worship and showing congregations how to do it included, at least, the Southern Baptist Convention and the Christian Church (Disciples of Christ).[103]

98. Paul T. Heinecke, Kent R. Hunter, and David S. Luecke, *Courageous Churches: Refusing Decline, Inviting Growth* (St. Louis: Concordia, 1991). See also David S. Luecke, *Evangelical Style and Lutheran Substance: Facing America's Mission Challenge* (St. Louis: Concordia, 1988).

99. Dave Vanderwel, "The Issue You Thought You'd Never See," *Reformed Worship* 20 (June 1991): 2.

100. Robert R. Castle, *So You've Been Asked to Develop a Worship Team* (Grand Rapids: CRC Publications, 1996).

101. Donald M. Brandt, *Worship and Outreach: New Services for New People* (Minneapolis: Augsburg Fortress, 1994); Dori Erwin Collins and Scott C. Weidler, *Sound Decisions: Evaluating Contemporary Music for Lutheran Worship* (Minneapolis: Augsburg Fortress, 1997).

102. "'Alternative' Worship and Worship Attendance in the ELCA," *Voice for Congregational Life* 9, no. 2 (Spring 1997): 20.

103. Respectively, White, *Opening the Front Door*; and Tim Carson and Kathy Carson, *So You're Thinking about Contemporary Worship* (St. Louis: Chalice, 1997).

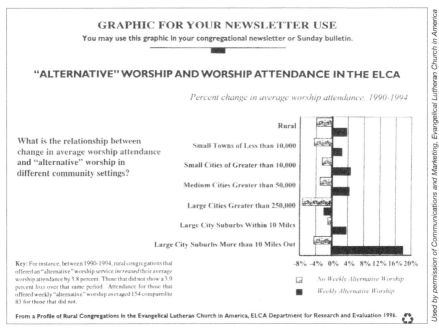

Figure 7.2. A 1997 chart from an Evangelical Lutheran Church in America magazine

Perhaps the most aggressive denominationally affiliated publisher of Contemporary Worship materials in the 1990s was the United Methodist Publishing House. Under its Abingdon Press imprint this publisher released more books with the terms "contemporary" and "worship" in the title than any other publisher in the period, including what seems to have been the first book in this second wave of Contemporary Worship with that term in its title: Timothy Wright's 1994 *A Community of Joy: How to Create Contemporary Worship*. (Wright was the associate pastor of the Lutheran congregation Community Church of Joy, whose senior pastor was Walt Kallestad.) By the next year Abingdon had printed a step-by-step guide for congregations wanting to start a contemporary service, complete with videocassette and songbook.[104]

Between the publications of these first two resources, the United Methodist Publishing House focused an entire issue of its clergy magazine, *Circuit Rider*, on Contemporary Worship. The issue highlighted several early adopters, including Lester Memorial United Methodist Church.[105] It also included

104. Cathy Townley and Mike Graham, *Come Celebrate! A Guide for Planning Contemporary Worship* (Nashville: Abingdon, 1995).

105. "The Pastor Wears Tennis Shoes," *Circuit Rider* 18, no. 10 (December 1994/January 1995): 14.

an interview with Kirbyjon Caldwell, a United Methodist pastor, which highlighted the themes that reflected the spirit of mainline and evangelical adoption of Contemporary Worship in the period. Caldwell described the approach in his own Houston congregation: "We can no longer assume that Christianity is the only game in town. So we need to be more assertive and aggressive, more relevant and more pragmatic. . . . [Our] worship service is user friendly. They [the unchurched] don't need a dictionary to figure out what is happening. . . . It addresses their needs, hopes, and hurts. . . . [A congregation's goal should be] developing and presenting music that meets the needs of the people right now."[106]

If Caldwell's appeal seems reminiscent of the perspective of Church Growth advocates and the pastors of the CAMEO churches reviewed above, this should be no surprise, since Caldwell was the pastor of one of United Methodism's own CAMEO megachurches. The Church Growth movement and the iconic status of CAMEO churches undergirded a promotion of Contemporary Worship in the 1990s and provided models for Contemporary Worship that a growing number of rank-and-file mainline and evangelical congregations imitated from the late 1980s forward. In-house denominational promotion—stronger in some denominations and weaker in others—helped provide momentum for Contemporary Worship in addition to that provided by the Church Growth movement and CAMEO churches. Throughout this promotion were the root characteristics of this worship-related pragmatism, the characteristics it had retained from its beginnings: a sense of a gap between worship and people, a desire to reach real people not being currently reached by the church, and a compulsion to use Contemporary Worship to do so.

But even as Contemporary Worship began to expand in the 1990s there were differences in how rank-and-file congregations implemented Contemporary Worship, at least in comparison to large CAMEO churches. Music making, while excellent in many larger congregations, tended to be hit or miss in medium and small congregations because they often had to simplify the ensemble of instruments and rely on musicians of varying talent. In addition, the motivations many North American churches expressed for adopting Contemporary Worship were both more simple and more complex than those of the CAMEO churches. Their motivations were simpler in that the leaders in favor of adoption rarely articulated the level of cultural analysis using Church Growth theory or the thorough profiling of a target audience found in the leading CAMEO churches. But many congregations' attraction to

---

106. Neil M. Alexander, "Breaking the 'Rules' of Worship: Conversations with Two Pastors," *Circuit Rider* 18, no. 10 (December 1994/January 1995): 16.

Contemporary Worship was also more complex in that they sometimes found that the strongest impulse toward it was the repressed desires and experiences of their already-active members. In other words, the journey to and practice of Contemporary Worship in rank-and-file congregations were both similar to and different from those expressed by its main theoretical proponents and large-scale practitioners.

An underlying concern about a continuing decline in congregational attendance or membership numbers should not be discounted, however, as a pervasive backdrop for the period. If we can mix metaphors, this numerical decline was the elephant in the river, at least for mainline denominations. As one United Methodist official stated, explaining the appeal of Contemporary Worship, "The decline in United Methodist membership is causing anxiety among pastors, musicians and worship leaders. . . . They do not feel as though they are reaching out effectively [and so] they want a new way to appeal to new people."[107] A Lutheran layperson stated this angst even more bluntly, describing his congregation's reason for adopting Contemporary Worship: "We realized that, unless we changed worship, we were going to die."[108]

This sort of anxiety was not decreasing but, instead, was being heightened by denominational failures to meet growth goals. Perhaps the most spectacular case was the 1984 meeting of the legislative body for the United Methodist church, which set a goal of growing to twenty million members by 1992—a target that would have meant nearly doubling membership in eight years. Not only did the goal prove unobtainable, but a few years after the goal was set, one United Methodist bishop wrote a book whose title—borrowing the first line of a Charles Wesley hymn—contemplated a more ruinous outcome: *And Are We Yet Alive?* The answer, seemingly, was no, since the first chapter was ominously labeled "Sick unto Death."[109] Two other Methodists, hoping nonetheless to revive lagging spirits by casting a new vision, summarized the despair that easily overwhelmed some mainline congregations: "For too long too many congregations have suffered from a myopic image of death and decline, which has destroyed their vision, emasculated their power, and thwarted the efforts of deeply dedicated believers who have tried to rise above

107. "Church Speaker Urges Pastors to Respect All Worship Services," *Tyler Courier-Times* (Tyler, TX), May 19, 1995, p. 1, sec. 5.

108. Stephen Ellingson, *The Megachurch and the Mainline: Remaking Religious Tradition in the Twenty-First Century* (Chicago: University of Chicago Press, 2007), 116.

109. Richard B. Wilke, *And Are We Yet Alive? The Future of the United Methodist Church* (Nashville: Abingdon, 1986). Note that Wilke would provide one of the printed endorsements for Rick Warren's *The Purpose Driven Church*.

this paralyzing concept."[110] For many congregations in the 1990s that wanted to shake off this pall, the answer was found, at least in part, in adopting Contemporary Worship.[111]

However, the desire to find an effective way to reach people was not the only motivation that drove the adoption of Contemporary Worship in mainline and evangelical congregations in the 1990s. In almost three dozen interviews we conducted with early adopters across a range of denominations, ethnicities, and geographic regions in both Canada and the United States, these persons reported a variety of reasons why they tried a contemporary service.[112] Indeed, some indicated that the ability to reach and attract people was a compelling force for Contemporary Worship, but they rarely articulated the highly developed theological motivations expressed by Church Growth advocates or by our exemplary large church pastors. The key verse, 1 Corinthians 9:22, was very seldom mentioned. Any sophisticated targeting of specific subcultures tended to be reduced to a basic idea: having a contemporary service would attract people who did not already attend their services.

The specific group of targeted people varied among the early adopters. Some mentioned that the contemporary service had been started to attract baby boomers. That sentiment was neither universal nor standard, however. Other congregations did it to retain their youth or even to engage their children. Others wanted a contemporary service to appeal to college students in the area. One mainline congregation started the service to attract inactive members who had once belonged to some other kind of mainline church. At

110. Joe A. Harding and Ralph W. Mohney, *Vision 2000: Planning for Ministry into the Next Century* (Nashville: Discipleship Resources, 1991), vi. Mohney's work at the time was particularly useful in providing examples of liturgical innovation in vibrant United Methodist congregations. Working with his wife, he wrote two volumes of case studies of churches exhibiting vitality. See Ralph W. Mohney and Nell W. Mohney, *Parable Churches: Stories of United Methodism's Ten Fastest Growing Churches* (Nashville: Discipleship Resources, 1989); and Ralph W. Mohney and Nell W. Mohney, *Churches of Vision: Stories from the Five Jurisdictions of United Methodism* (Nashville: Discipleship Resources, 1990).

111. Whether there was actual widespread decline was not the issue. The perception of being in decline and the resulting anxiety were the critical things. For a contemporaneous numbers-driven assessment of denominational growth and decline, see David A. Roozen and C. Kirk Hadaway, eds., *Church & Denominational Growth: What Does (and Does Not) Cause Growth or Decline* (Nashville: Abingdon, 1993). For reappraisals of whether there was actually decline and whether it was critical, see Robert Bacher and Kenneth Inskeep, *Chasing Down a Rumor: The Death of Mainline Denominations* (Minneapolis: Augsburg Fortress, 2005); and Ted A. Campbell, *The Sky Is Falling, the Church Is Dying, and Other False Alarms* (Nashville: Abingdon, 2015).

112. Unless we are referencing a specific congregation or providing a direct quotation of one of the interviewees, we will not cite individual interviews in the following section for the sake of space. Our description will be a synthesis of insights we gained from these interviews. The interviews are listed in the bibliography at the end of the book.

least one congregation found that a contemporary service helped to bring back its own inactive members.[113] Early adopters with a more evangelical bent could speak of trying to reach the unsaved or unchurched by presenting the gospel, while others spoke more generically of just trying to attract one group or another.

The desire to reach others was not the only motivation mentioned, however. Many of the early adopters described how their congregations ventured into the waters of Contemporary Worship because of the desires and aspirations of their already-existing members for a different experience in worship. Sometimes the latent impulse came from laypeople, and sometimes it came from pastors who wanted something different in worship for themselves. In some mainline and evangelical congregations, therefore, the gap between worship and people was not external but internal: active members craved something different liturgically.

The origins and details of these desires and aspirations varied. Some worshipers wanted the freedom to be more physically demonstrative in worship. Others preferred the informality and casualness of Contemporary Worship. Still others wanted songs that allowed for a greater degree of emotional expression than people were experiencing while singing hymns to organs and pianos. Some laity called for a new service with a new style of worship because they were tired of being unable to use their own musical skills. Some, too, had long submerged their own preference for music based on popular forms, hoping for a day when band-based music could be heard Sunday to Sunday.

Some worshipers had recently discovered this kind of music. For example, Pastor Silverio Sanchez Sr., soon after he began leading a new, Spanish-speaking United Methodist congregation near Houston, first heard a contemporary style of worship music while attending a conference in Reynosa, Mexico, in 1991. Within a very short time, he had hired one of the band members from that conference to come start a comparable band in his church plant. Iglesia Metodista Unida San Marcos in Baytown, Texas, thus became the first Hispanic church of any sort in that area with Contemporary Worship. Soon it was attracting both Baptists and Pentecostals, who came to see what Contemporary Worship was and whether they wanted it for their own congregations. While Sanchez was pleased to find that Contemporary Worship appealed to a younger generation, he had also discovered that this new, upbeat music touched him deeply, too, as a more direct and prayerful way of worshiping God.[114]

113. Joyce Fry, interview by Lester Ruth, July 14, 2014.
114. Silverio Sanchez Sr., interview by Lester Ruth, May 25, 2015.

For many, the desire for Contemporary Worship came from past experiences that had primed them for it. For example, memories of 1970s-era youth musicals and cantatas, the occasional youth service, or experiences in youth or college campus ministries left some worshipers desiring something other than a traditional service. For some, this desire was accented by attending concerts featuring Christian music that sounded like some form of popular music. Those with charismatic experiences of the Holy Spirit often hungered for something different too (see chap. 3). For others, past experiences in church-sponsored spiritual renewal events like Cursillo, Walk to Emmaus, or Lay Witness Missions—events that cultivated deep experiences tied to simple choruses led by guitars or other instruments—created the longing for something other than organ-led worship. In this way, some denominations had unintentionally created their own internal drive toward Contemporary Worship.

Other congregations ventured toward Contemporary Worship more because of a circumstance of location or occasion. The pastor of Christ Lutheran Church, a Missouri Synod congregation in Anderson, Indiana, found that the town's musical "patron saints," Sandi Patty and Bill and Gloria Gaither, provided the backdrop for ministry in that locale. Patty and the Gaithers were famous, groundbreaking contemporary Christian artists and songwriters. Their presence created a desire for contemporary worship music within the inhabitants of Anderson, which the pastor filled by starting a second, more contemporary service.[115] A large United Methodist church in Texas added a contemporary service, despite a lack of interest on the part of the senior pastor, because the director of the church's endowment (a baby boomer) wanted it.[116] The music director at a Baptist church in Virginia was able to move his congregation in a more contemporary direction after the church installed screens and began using projection to show song lyrics. The screens enabled the musician to introduce music that was not found in the hymnals.[117] A United Methodist church in Louisiana added a contemporary service after it lost one prominent family by failing to have Contemporary Worship. The church determined not to lose any more members for this reason, and asked its choir director, who had an Assemblies of God background, to lead the new service.[118]

If the motivations for starting a contemporary service were myriad, so were the ways in which mainline and evangelical congregations went about starting

115. Tom Eggold, interview by Lester Ruth, June 30, 2014.
116. Mark Fleming, interview by Lester Ruth, May 25, 2015.
117. Art Werner, interview by Lester Ruth, May 14, 2014.
118. Craig Gilbert, interview by Lester Ruth, May 27, 2015.

one. One of the most common methods was to start an entirely new service at a different time than the main worship service and sometimes in a different space. Sometimes choices about timing and location were made to decrease the sense of any threat or competition to those protective of a congregation's prior service (or services). In some congregations this separate time and space became permanent, whereas in others the contemporary service moved to a more prominent time slot as its attendance grew. Still other congregations took the approach of transforming one of their already-existing services into a more contemporary service. This could be done quickly or slowly. Sometimes the result was a completely transformed service, and sometimes it was a "blended" service mixing traditional and contemporary elements.[119]

Churches that adopted Contemporary Worship also had a variety of experiences in terms of its overall effect on the life of the congregation. Sometimes the adoption of Contemporary Worship led to a complete metamorphosis of a congregation, remaking it in the mold of a CAMEO church. Some of these churches achieved megachurch status. More typically, however, a church ended up with a menu of different styles of services, often using the labels "contemporary" and "traditional," which could be offered to both nonmembers and members.[120] Finally, new church plants often adopted Contemporary Worship as the preferred mode of worship from the start.

As was the case with Lester Memorial United Methodist Church, the accounts of mainline and evangelical churches that were early adopters of Contemporary Worship emphasize, not surprisingly, the important role of new musical instruments, a new song repertoire, and, in many cases, having lengthy periods of congregational singing at the beginning of the service. In imitation of what they saw elsewhere, these congregations usually placed the musicians front and center in the liturgical space, giving them a clear prominence while

---

119. The well-known worship speaker and author Robert Webber popularized the notion of "blended worship" in the 1990s. For more information on Webber, see Jonathan A. Powers, "Robert Webber: Preserving Traditional Worship through Contemporary Styles," in *Essays on the History of Contemporary Praise and Worship*, ed. Lester Ruth (Eugene, OR: Pickwick, 2020), 95–115.

120. Ethnomusicologist Deborah Justice argues that having this spectrum under the labels "contemporary" and "traditional" allows such congregations to feel that they are embracing diversity—a positive value in today's culture—while also maintaining internally a fair degree of similarity in the macro-level approach to worship. See Deborah R. Justice, "The Curious Longevity of the Traditional–Contemporary Divide: Mainline Musical Choices in Post–Worship War America," *Liturgy* 32, no. 1 (2017): 20–21; Deborah R. Justice, "Sonic Change, Social Change, Sacred Change: Music and the Reconfiguration of American Christianity" (PhD diss., Indiana University, 2012), 322–36; Deborah R. Justice, "Mainline Protestantism and Contemporary versus Traditional Worship Music," in *The Oxford Handbook of Music and World Christianities*, ed. Suzel Ana Reily and Jonathan Dueck (Oxford: Oxford University Press, 2016), 487–512.

leading worship. In some services worshipers were physically expressive and generally a predilection for informality reigned. The services also included classic elements of the first wave of Contemporary Worship (in the 1960s): use of contemporary English and relevance to contemporary concerns of worshipers. For a time in the late 1990s and after, therefore, certain circles encouraged the use of life situation dramas or popular movie clips to make a visual connection with worshipers to enable them to see what the service's topic was about. Increasing levels of sophistication in the use of electronic technology enabled this latter practice, although a more common use of projection was for song lyrics.

Talking about Contemporary Worship as a certain "style" of worship—surely a term drawn from the broad cultural practice of talking about styles of music—was common among these early adopters. Doing so allowed them to focus on the outward, perceptible dynamics of this way of worship without dealing more substantially with the theological underpinnings, especially if these adopters were appropriating practices from the world of Praise & Worship. One early promoter of Contemporary Worship, for instance, valued the congregational singing of Praise & Worship for its strategic use rather than for its connection to biblical promises: "If you're an out-reaching congregation looking for an effective strategy to use in beginning worship when the service starts, try singing in the Praise & Worship style."[121]

As in this case, it was easy for early mainline and evangelical adopters of Contemporary Worship to occasionally use the term "Praise and Worship" since the already-developed infrastructure for Praise & Worship (see chap. 4) provided resources for early Contemporary Worship services. Songs from Maranatha! Music and Integrity's Hosanna! tapes, for example, were commonplace in contemporary services. (The fact that the term "Contemporary Worship" did not become commonplace until the mid-1990s prompted some early adopters to think they were doing "Praise & Worship" even though they were unaware of the latter's theology and spirituality.)

The fact that Maranatha! Music and Integrity's Hosanna! Music both had roots in the Pentecostal world of Praise & Worship was not important. As sociologist Stephen Ellingson has shown in a study of Lutheran churches in California (and as our interviewees confirmed), individual congregations

---

121. Duane E. VanderBrug, "Worship as Witness: Six Strategies for Using P&W in Your Worship," *Reformed Worship* 20 (June 1991): 22. See a similar sentiment in Steve Elzinga and Marie Elzinga, "Bridges to Praise: Three Songs in the Praise and Worship Style," *Reformed Worship* 20 (June 1991): 28. VanderBrug did write of a connection between congregational singing and God's presence, but it was a secondary emphasis.

mixed and matched materials and models from a variety of sources.[122] Appropriation of selected elements from one model or proponent was common, as was local adaptation in actual implementation. For example, congregations seeking to imitate Willow Creek's clear distinction between its weekend seeker-*driven* services and its midweek believers worship services often ended up with a once-a-week, seeker-*sensitive* service on the weekend.[123] Sometimes congregations appropriated some specific item or practice for a different purpose than the one for which it had originally been used or promoted, as when churches used Praise & Worship music for strategic evangelistic purposes.

Providing resources for Contemporary Worship was not limited to Maranatha! and Integrity. For instance, some of the early adopters of Contemporary Worship took pilgrimages to the well-known CAMEO churches and to other churches seen as being innovative in worship, sometimes after reading the materials written by those churches' pastors. Conferences and workshops, whether sponsored by individual churches or by denominational officials, provided additional opportunities for people to learn about Contemporary Worship and be encouraged to adopt it. For some, close geographic proximity to an even earlier innovator in worship provided the impetus and model to follow. For United Methodist pastor Joyce Fry, being close to Ginghamsburg United Methodist Church in Ohio and seeing how it had grown influenced her to lead her congregation to Contemporary Worship. Similarly, Emanuel Heyliger, a West Virginia Baptist pastor, learned a new way of worship from TD Jakes, who led a church very close by.[124]

National denominational offices and staff for worship contributed toward providing resources for the early adoption of Contemporary Worship in the 1990s too. As noted above, denominational magazines sometimes dedicated whole issues to the topic and increasingly addressed it throughout the 1990s. National offices and staff also sponsored conferences, wrote books, and authored short articles. Denominational publishing houses, too, responded to the growing desire by printing songbooks and releasing CDs of music. For one small-town United Methodist congregation in South Carolina, the latter were critical. Having no musicians to play for its newly created contemporary service, the congregation relied entirely on CDs it had purchased.[125] A very different kind of influence came from Kadasha, a traveling worship team

122. See Ellingson, *Megachurch and the Mainline*.
123. See Ruth, "*Lex Agendi, Lex Orandi*," 389–97.
124. Joyce Fry, interview; Emanuel Heyliger, interview by Lester Ruth, August 16, 2018. Jakes ministered in his native West Virginia before moving to Texas and becoming prominent as the pastor of The Potter's House, a megachurch.
125. Fred Buchanan, interview by Lester Ruth, June 3, 2014.

affiliated with the Southeastern Jurisdiction of the United Methodist Church and organized to model alternative worship for interested congregations.[126]

Perhaps the most subtle way national offices helped promote Contemporary Worship was in the editorial decisions by revision committees to include contemporary songs in new hymnals. In this way congregations became familiar with a new song style even before having to address the issue of an entirely different kind of service.[127] As one church musician discovered, his people thought a song in a hymnal was good, respectable, and palatable even if it was, in actuality, contemporary worship music. They trusted the book form of the hymnal.[128]

The significance of obtaining such trust should not be underestimated, since gaining acceptance for Contemporary Worship and its individual elements was in many instances contentious. For many, nothing about Contemporary Worship was good, respectable, or remotely palatable.[129] Tension often arose about Contemporary Worship, and many Christians discovered the literal rage involved in a raging river. The fighting occurred broadly, sweeping up congregations, Christian schools and seminaries, and even denominational offices with their staffs. Perhaps the opening salvo that launched the public dimension of the warring came in 1990 when a Lutheran theologian took a copy of Walt Kallestad's "Entertainment Evangelism" article and flung it from the pulpit of the chapel at St. Olaf College during a denominational "Call to Faithfulness" conference.[130]

The grounds upon which the wars raged included social identity, different sensibilities about aesthetics, fear of attracting people of a different class and race, and even feelings that popular culture–based forms of worship were not reverential enough or violated fundamentalist codes about involvement in the "world."[131] Fights over worship style could be drawn into larger denominational conflicts over other issues or into efforts to promote new, official denominational worship books and resources. With so many triggers for conflict and so many battlegrounds, the fighting was often passionate.

126. Jeff Crawford, interview by Lester Ruth, January 25, 2014. See also Chris Hughes and Jennifer McSwain, *The Kadasha Workbook: Experiential Worship for the Next Generation* (Franklin, TN: Providence House, 2001).

127. We are indebted to the insights of Adam Perez on this point.

128. Paul Detterman, interview by Lester Ruth, May 18, 2020.

129. See, for instance, A. Daniel Frankforter, *Stones for Bread: A Critique of Contemporary Worship* (Louisville: Westminster John Knox, 2001).

130. Ted Peters, "Worship Wars," *Dialog* 33, no. 3 (Summer 1994): 168.

131. See Anna E. Nekola, "Between This World and the Next: The Musical 'Worship Wars' and Evangelical Ideology in the United States, 1960–2005" (PhD diss., University of Wisconsin–Madison, 2009).

The tension was also theology based. David S. Luecke's retrospective offers perhaps the most insightful analysis on this point, highlighting how the warring camps often talked past each other because of differences in theological method. According to Luecke, those who rejected Church Growth theory—and by extension Contemporary Worship—did so by approaching theology (and worship) normatively, describing the church as it should be. The contrasting view, which also was Luecke's, was to begin sociologically with how the church and people actually were, utilizing the Bible to guide ministry with real people.[132] Working this out with respect to worship, Luecke argued that 1 Corinthians 9:19–23 was relevant to the differences in theological method: he suggested that Paul's statement showed the apostle being concerned with actual people and adjusting to them to present the gospel effectively. Luecke applied this reading of Paul's method to the fighting over worship, asking, "If the Apostle Paul were to enter the current debate between contemporary worship and classical liturgical worship, is there any doubt about the direction he would take?" Luecke did not directly answer his own question since, in his opinion, Paul's willingness to become "all things to all people" surely gave the obvious answer.[133]

Luecke's theological framing of the conflict reveals what he and other Contemporary Worship advocates heard when they were asked to reject Contemporary Worship. To repudiate Contemporary Worship was not merely to give up one's own preferences in worship; it was to forfeit a missional, pastoral concern for people as well as to forfeit New Testament apostolicity. In this way the worship wars were theological too. At their heart were indeed different visions about what a call to faithfulness entailed. Indeed, for many advocates of Contemporary Worship, their commitment to their theological vision drawn from the New Testament for evangelism and worship was what sustained them during the fighting.

Notwithstanding the tensions that arose, Contemporary Worship proliferated during the 1990s. Perhaps this spread heightened the contentiousness, because the scope and sweep of the change were intimidating to many. Nonetheless, with a desire to be faithful to the mission of God and for the other reasons discussed above, an increasing number of churches adopted contemporary elements and started contemporary services. By the latter half of the 1990s Contemporary Worship had become a raging river with increasing momentum and breadth.

132. David S. Luecke, *Apostolic Style and Lutheran Substance: Ten Years of Controversy over What Can Change* (Lima, OH: Fairway, 1999), 41.
133. Luecke, *Apostolic Style*, 56.

One 1997 book, Charles Arn's *How to Start a New Service*, illuminates the variety of approaches congregations across a range of regions and denominations were using to start new services. Arn, who was working from a Church Growth perspective, based his book on a series of nine two-year studies in the early 1990s of a range of churches that had started new services.[134] Arn's book sought to distill the practices from these churches as guidelines for others contemplating starting a new service. Applying a Church Growth principle that "new units equal new growth," Arn wanted to encourage more churches to start new services, suggesting at the beginning of his book that half of the 355,000 Protestant churches in Canada and the United States should consider adding a new service. If they did, Arn continued, eight out of ten of these congregations would see measurable increases in worship attendance, giving, and conversions.[135]

Arn's book was not a single-minded, narrow advocacy of Contemporary Worship per se. However, nothing in the guidelines deduced from the congregations he had studied argued against Contemporary Worship and, indeed, many of them led to it, especially given the times and how trendy adding a contemporary service was in the late 1990s. (Consider Arn's use of terms like "worship leaders" and "music teams," both of which were by this time technical terms within Contemporary Worship.)

One of the book's key principles was that leaders should be intentional in selecting the target group that a congregation wished to reach. Showing the complexity of possible targets, Arn's work demonstrated the variety of possibilities. One grid listed two possible spiritual conditions (Christian or seeker) matched with three different generational groupings (seniors, baby boomers, and baby busters), for a total of six separate potential target audiences. Defining possible cultural categories (e.g., ethnicity, prior liturgical experience, marital status, geographic influence) brought a further refinement to the targeting.[136] Such variety surely reflected the various approaches Arn had seen in his congregational studies.

Regardless of the selected target, the key was adapting the style of the service to fit the respective group. All the various liturgical dimensions, especially the music, needed to be indigenous to the target. Indeed, Arn's clear goal in the book was advocating the start of new services with a style different from what a congregation was already doing. As he straightforwardly stated at the

134. Charles Arn, email message to Lester Ruth, July 19, 2020. Charles Arn is the son of Win Arn, a key figure in the first generation of leaders in the popular Church Growth movement in North America.

135. Arn, *How to Start a New Service*, 14.

136. Arn, *How to Start a New Service*, 30, 106–16.

beginning of the book, whenever he said "new service" he actually meant "new *style* service."[137] The greatest growth came not merely from starting a new service—although the increased convenience of multiple times could be helpful—but from starting a new service with a different style. Arn argued for the importance of the right design of the service in terms reminiscent of Marshall McLuhan's in the 1960s (see chap. 6): "The sermon is not the message; the service is the message."[138]

For those with eyes to see, Arn's book also subtly provided a theological, biblical basis for emphasizing worship style as the key to evangelistic faithfulness. Highlighting how a new service would reach some new kinds of people, Arn said, "No single service can be all things to all people."[139] In the long history of biblical theologizing leading to Contemporary Worship, this sentence was perhaps the most creative, explicit application of the apostle Paul's sentiment in 1 Corinthians 9:22, moving it from a statement about individual ministry to a standard about congregational worship itself. But in one sense Arn was expressing nothing new: this application had been implicitly commonplace in the history leading to Contemporary Worship.

Arn's declaration can be used as a summary for the 1990s too. It provides a window into the motivation that brought a growing number of mainline and evangelical congregations to adopt Contemporary Worship. If no single service (including a traditional one) could be all things to all people and if a congregation wanted those other people, then there was a clear choice: start a service of Contemporary Worship to bridge the gap.

137. Arn, *How to Start a New Service*, 14.
138. Arn, *How to Start a New Service*, 153.
139. Arn, *How to Start a New Service*, 29–30.

part 3

the confluence of praise & worship and contemporary worship

eight

—

the new liturgical normal, late 1990s

Get past the glamorous, the slick, and the sensational to a relevance based on spiritual realities.

—Sally Morgenthaler, worship consultant[1]

By the mid-1990s both "rivers"—Praise & Worship and Contemporary Worship—were alive and roaring with activity. In an increasing number of Pentecostal, evangelical, and mainline congregations, worshipers engaged in practices that half a century earlier were largely unknown. These included informality, hands lifted in the air, projected lyrics, bands, drama and other arts, and times of congregational singing of choruses. All these liturgical elements and more could be seen in a surge of sanctuaries.

How the various congregations had gotten to this point varied. The underlying theological visions, drawn from the Bible, likewise varied. For some, the compelling motivation had been a promise connecting praise with an experience of the presence of God. For others, it had been to find a way to bridge the gap between an earlier, stale way of worship and people whom the

---

1. Sally Morgenthaler, *Worship Evangelism: Inviting Unbelievers into the Presence of God* (Grand Rapids: Zondervan, 1995), 170. Morgenthaler's book enjoyed strong sales in the 1990s. It was released early in both hardback and paperback editions. It was re-released with at least two cover changes as well as the addition of a study guide.

church wanted to reach. Whatever their theological origins, however, both rivers were in full flow by the mid-1990s.

Moreover, regardless of the original theological impetus, the geography of this decade was bringing about a confluence of the two rivers. Although the two names of this way of worship would continue to be used by different groups, the two rivers shared a supporting infrastructure that supplied this new way of worship with books, education, technology, songs, and musicians. In many respects, the two rivers became one by the late 1990s, one we will call Contemporary Praise & Worship in order to embrace the full breadth of the liturgical phenomenon.

In some instances there was even a merger of theologies. Perhaps the first—at least the clearest—indication of such a theological confluence was a 1995 book whose very title hinted at the fusion: *Worship Evangelism*. The book's author was Sally Morgenthaler, a worship leader for a new church plant in Colorado in an area largely unchurched. Morgenthaler had visited several of the CAMEO churches profiled in chapter 7 to see what others were doing to make worship an appealing experience for the unchurched, but she was not completely satisfied with what she saw in those churches and came away with a part of herself not engaged. Conversations with others and her own reflection on what she felt was missing led her to write her book.[2]

Morgenthaler openly accepted certain basic evangelical convictions held by those who advocated for Contemporary Worship. She spoke with a passion for the unchurched, the unsaved, and the seeker. She recognized that evangelism could take place in worship services. But her approach to how evangelism could best take place in worship was different from that usually found in Contemporary Worship advocates. Instead of arguing for a biblical freedom to find and adapt the most effective measures based on close cultural analysis of the targeted group, she instead embraced the biblical theology of Praise & Worship. Her articulation was classic. Quoting Psalm 22:3, she argued that praise was what God had chosen to be revealed through: "When we exalt God in our worship . . . God is made manifest among us."[3]

For Morgenthaler it was this divine manifestation that was the true evangelizing power in worship. Combined with parallel emphases on robust scriptural content and a vulnerability expressed in honest confession and lament, her focus on the centrality of praising gave what she saw as the proper fulfillment of a church worshiping in spirit and in truth. Her goal was to provide an alternative approach for evangelicals who had been sucked into a

2. Sally Morgenthaler, interview by Lester Ruth, September 29, 2020.

3. Morgenthaler, *Worship Evangelism*, 101. See also p. 289, where she frames Ps. 22:3 as part of a scriptural promise.

hyper-seeker-focused model involving "methodological abuse" with "certain market-driven approaches" taken to extremes. She perceived danger in an age of the "quick fix," resulting in many services in which "the very essence of worship has been quietly removed."[4] A better goal of evangelism, she insisted, was to produce more and better worshipers who possessed the same passionate longing for God as did David in the Bible.[5] For Morgenthaler, looking to David as the ultimate type for worship allowed the discussion to move well past an ultimately unfruitful focus on worship style.[6]

Morgenthaler's advocacy of both scriptural evangelistic concerns and a biblically derived theology of praise and presence placed her at the tip of the junction for Praise & Worship and Contemporary Worship. Her work alone did not cause this confluence, although it was probably the clearest example of it at the time.[7] Indeed, the book's popularity in the 1990s hints at the growing confluence and people's desire to make sense of the complexity of the liturgical situation.

Early Hints of a Confluence

Though Morgenthaler may have been the clearest example of a confluence, she was neither the only nor the first example of it. Indeed, at various points before the 1995 publication of Morgenthaler's book, the banks of the two rivers were often quite low. The divide between the two had never been absolute or complete. The two theologies—and the people who held and practiced them in congregational worship—could meet in a kind of floodplain between the two rivers.[8]

4. Morgenthaler, *Worship Evangelism*, 19, 23.
5. Morgenthaler, *Worship Evangelism*, 37, 39, 283.
6. Morgenthaler, *Worship Evangelism*, 283.
7. Her cited sources alone reflect the breadth of the two rivers. From the world of Praise & Worship she utilized Tommy Walker, Tom Kraeuter, Gerrit Gustafson, Tommy Coomes, Jack Hayford, Bob Fitts, LaMar Boschman, Bob Sorge, and Paul Baloche, among others. From the circles of Contemporary Worship, she utilized material from Willow Creek including material by Nancy Beach and Lee Strobel, Handt Hanson, George Barna, Elmer Towns, Lyle Schaller, Leith Anderson, and Doug Murren. For a similar, contemporaneous perspective to Morgenthaler's, see Jennifer Brody, "Trends and Truths in Worship: An Interview with Tom Coomes," *Psalmist* 8, no. 1 (January/February 1993): 15–16.
8. Even Chuck Smith Sr., the pastor of Calvary Chapel of Costa Mesa, who eschewed all forms of gimmickry in ministry, once mentioned in passing that the new music being developed at his church in the early 1970s allowed the church to fulfill 1 Cor. 9:22. See Chuck Smith and Hugh Steven, *The Reproducers: New Life for Thousands* (Philadelphia: Calvary Chapel of Philadelphia, 2011), 80. Smith and Steven originally published the book in 1972. Remember that this new Jesus People music was used in evening Bible studies and in special concerts, not on Sunday mornings.

John Wimber is one example of this meeting. With prior work in the Church Growth movement, Wimber had a pragmatic strand that he did not jettison as he became affiliated with the Praise & Worship of Calvary Chapels and Vineyard congregations.[9] Thus, in 1980 Wimber clearly identified his congregation's target "market" in a five-year plan: namely, young to middle-aged members of the "'Rock' generation."[10] To a national audience he could describe his congregation's mission in classic pragmatic terms: "We speak the language of these people. . . . We find ourselves communicating eternal truths in a contemporary style."[11] Part of that communication was the utilization of popular forms of music making, in some respects more like the approach of those in the river of Contemporary Worship than like that of many of his comrades in Praise & Worship at that time.

However, Wimber's bridge-the-gap thinking was occasionally matched by others involved in Praise & Worship. For example, the rock band Petra released a CD of worship songs in 1989, *Petra Praise*, after conversations with youth pastors had led band members to believe that many youth could not relate to standard Praise & Worship services.[12] The band's lead singer explained the album's background using long-standing logic more usually found among pragmatic evangelicals:

> We feel that youth as a whole are misunderstood more than any other group, and this is just as true in praise and worship. A lot of times we forget that our youth are a different generation. We forget that their musical tastes and ways of expressing themselves can be very different and very foreign to someone of another generation. I'm afraid we are not taking that into consideration in a lot

9. For Wimber's background in the Church Growth movement, see C. Peter Wagner, Win Arn, and Elmer Towns, eds., *Church Growth: State of the Art* (Wheaton: Tyndale, 1986), 275; C. Peter Wagner, *Your Church Can Grow: Seven Vital Signs of a Healthy Congregation* (Ventura, CA: Regal, 1976), 20; Donald A. McGavran and Winfield C. Arn, *Ten Steps for Church Growth* (New York: Harper & Row, 1977), 95; and John Wimber, "Zip to 3,000 in 5 Years," *Christian Life* 44, no. 6 (October 1982): 20. Wimber once spearheaded a strategy in his prior Friends congregation involving offering potty training seminars to young parents. See George G. Hunter III, *To Spread the Power: Church Growth in the Wesleyan Spirit* (Nashville: Abingdon, 1987), 146; and George G. Hunter III, *The Contagious Congregation: Frontiers in Evangelism and Church Growth* (Nashville: Abingdon, 1979), 123–24. The congregation was seeking to address the felt needs it had found by direct survey of the parents.

10. See Andy Park, Lester Ruth, and Cindy Rethmeier, *Worshiping with the Anaheim Vineyard: The Emergence of Contemporary Worship* (Grand Rapids: Eerdmans, 2017), 116–17.

11. Wimber, "Zip to 3,000," 22. Wimber seemingly had worked on inculcating this same pragmatism into Calvary Chapels via the Maranatha! Missions Development organization. See "Wanted: Men with Burning Hearts," *Last Times Magazine* 3, no. 1 (March/April 1980): 12–14, 16.

12. Petra, *Petra Praise: The Rock Cries Out* (New York: Word, 1989), CD. The group did not normally record worship-related albums.

of praise and worship in a lot of different churches. Unfortunately, our worship bores the kids and we lose them.[13]

Petra intended its album to be a sing-along tool for youth group meetings. For Petra, it seems, what youth heard on the radio and on rock albums—a common concern in Contemporary Worship but not as much in that period's form of Praise & Worship—shaped what this rock band wanted to promote.

The flow of influence could run in the other direction, too, as Pentecostal insights impacted evangelical and mainline congregations. For example, although published materials from Ginghamsburg United Methodist Church little reflected the influence, this congregation's worship leader was ruminating on a Davidic pattern of worship, attending LaMar Boschman's International Worship Institute training in Dallas, and getting the church to subscribe to *Psalmist* magazine.[14] Similarly, while pragmatic thinking continued to dominate Willow Creek Community Church's approach to its weekend seeker services, more Pentecostal and Charismatic forces were deepening the approach to its midweek worship services for believers, including visits by Tommy Walker and Darlene Zschech.[15] By 1992, Bill Hybels, Willow Creek's pastor, could thus speak about the desirability of pouring out one's heart in praise.[16] Another example of Pentecostal influencing of key evangelical congregations concerns Saddleback Valley Community Church. Before being hired as its worship leader in 1987, Rick Muchow had learned flow during congregational singing according to a distinct Pentecostal pattern: a journey into the holy of holies in the tabernacle of Moses, something he saw at a Hope Chapel in Southern California. Muchow brought this learning, along with influences from other churches, with him to Saddleback where, with Rick Warren, he transformed it into the approach described by the acronym

---

13. Jennifer Brody, "Making Praise Youth Can Relate To: An Interview with John Schlitt, the Lead Singer of Petra," *Psalmist* 7, no. 5 (October/November 1992): 7.

14. Randy Tate, email message to Lester Ruth, August 19, 2020; Tom Tumblin, interview by Lester Ruth, August 14, 2020.

15. Rory Noland, interview by Lim Swee Hong and Lester Ruth, July 27, 2020; Joe Horness, "Contemporary Music-Driven Worship," in *Exploring the Worship Spectrum: 6 Views*, ed. Paul A. Basden (Grand Rapids: Zondervan, 2004), 108; Joe Horness, email message to Lester Ruth, February 21, 2013; and Gregory A. Pritchard, "The Strategy of Willow Creek Community Church: A Study in the Sociology of Religion" (PhD diss., Northwestern University, 1994), 88. For an account of a retreat on worship that Bill Hybels led, see Lynne Hybels, "My Life—a Living Sacrifice," *Psalmist* 3, no. 3 (June/July 1988): 6–7.

16. See the post-service interview on Bill Hybels and Nancy Beach, *An Inside Look at the Willow Creek Worship Service: Building a New Community* (Grand Rapids: Zondervan, 1992), videocassette (VHS).

IMPACT (see chap. 7). It would be this latter form that Muchow and Warren modeled and taught widely.[17]

Indeed, not only were perspectives being shared between Praise & Worship and Contemporary Worship, but some individuals had already settled into a middle ground. Chuck Fromm, president of Maranatha! Music, was perhaps the most influential. While working for Maranatha! Music, Fromm had started a magazine, *Worship Times*, which initially was sent to subscribers in the company's early attempt at a song copyright clearinghouse, Music Net. The magazine's first issue was the Winter 1986 issue.[18] Fromm served as the magazine's first editor in chief, and his broad interests clearly shaped its content and mediating position. Fromm solicited a wide range of authors, including authors from evangelical and mainline backgrounds. While the classic praise-to-presence theology of Praise & Worship could be found within *Worship Times*, it was never the magazine's central focus and was not as strongly pushed as it was in other Praise & Worship circles. Over time, Fromm included materials from or about people as diverse as the leaders of Willow Creek Community Church, evangelical songwriter Bill Gaither, and Pentecostal pastor/songwriter Jack Hayford. The *Worship Times* print run was short, ending in 1989. In 1992, Fromm came back to periodical publication and launched *Worship Leader* magazine. With this new magazine Fromm again found a middle point between all the parties, printing materials relevant to the breadth of Praise & Worship and Contemporary Worship. Not surprisingly, parts of Sally Morgenthaler's book, *Worship Evangelism*, first appeared in an early issue of *Worship Leader*, and she was a regular contributor throughout the 1990s.[19]

Joining Fromm in a middle ground between Praise & Worship and Contemporary Worship was a close colleague, Robert Webber. Webber, the son of fundamentalist Baptist missionary parents to Africa, was a historical theology professor at Wheaton College who had found his way over time into the Episcopal Church and had begun to write on worship in the early 1980s.[20] Webber

---

17. Rick Muchow, interview by Lester Ruth, March 9, 2015; Rick Muchow, interview by Lim Swee Hong and Lester Ruth, April 30, 2015; Rick Muchow, email message to Lester Ruth, May 9, 2015.

18. For a picture of the first page of this issue, see Lim Swee Hong and Lester Ruth, *Lovin' on Jesus: A Concise History of Contemporary Worship* (Nashville: Abingdon, 2017).

19. Sally Morgenthaler, "Worship Evangelism: Bringing Down the Walls," *Worship Leader* 1, no. 6 (December 1993/January 1994): 20–23, 26, 28, 30–32. According to our interview with Morgenthaler, this article caught the attention of an editor at Zondervan, who contacted her about writing a book.

20. For background on Webber, see Jonathan A. Powers, "Robert Webber: Preserving Traditional Worship through Contemporary Styles," in *Essays on the History of Contemporary*

was a frequent contributor to *Worship Times*, serving for a time as its editor, and later had a regular column in *Worship Leader* magazine. In addition, Webber became one of the most traveled speakers on worship renewal in the 1990s. His broad interests and background—and ability to see developments historically—made him a chief interpreter of Praise & Worship to evangelical and mainline audiences, as when he contributed to the 1991 theme issue of *Reformed Worship*, the magazine of the Christian Reformed Church.[21] Thus, when Webber began to release his multivolume *Complete Library of Christian Worship* in 1993, articles on seeker services in Contemporary Worship sat next to articles on Praise & Worship (as well as on worship in the early church and Middle Ages). For his own part, Webber's distinction between a service's structure (order of worship), content, and style allowed him to affirm contemporary expressions in worship while still aiming for historically grounded structure and biblically based content.[22] In this way, Webber also served as a mediating force helping to create the geography for a confluence in the 1990s.

The Supportive Infrastructure

Middle-ground people like Chuck Fromm and Robert Webber thus helped to reinforce the confluence of Praise & Worship and Contemporary Worship. However, the ability of the two rivers to come together and become an ongoing reality also derived from a multifaceted infrastructure of support. Differences between the two lessened as a common body of resources taught the congregations, provided the technology, sold the songs, and trained the musicians who could lead this new way of worship regardless of whether the motivation was seeking God's presence or bridging the gap to a targeted subculture. Indeed, the parts of this infrastructure that sought to sell items were often unconcerned about what theology prompted their purchase.

In the early stages of the confluence, a key aspect of the merging was speakers who could address a wide breadth of congregations. Robert Webber, just mentioned, was one example; another was Buddy Owens, who taught in seminars connected to the cross-denominational Promise Keepers rallies (see chap. 4). Judson Cornwall was another. Cornwall, who was instrumental

---

Praise and Worship, ed. Lester Ruth (Eugene, OR: Pickwick, 2020), 95–115. For Webber's own story of liturgical migration, see Robert E. Webber, *Evangelicals on the Canterbury Trail: Why Evangelicals Are Attracted to the Liturgical Church* (Waco: Word, 1985).

21. Robert E. Webber, "Enter His Courts with Praise: A New Style of Worship Is Sweeping the Church," *Reformed Worship* 20 (1991): 9–12.

22. Powers, "Robert Webber," 98–109.

in developing a theology based on the tabernacle of Moses (see chap. 2), remained cautious about being too closely aligned with any single group or institution so that he could maintain the ability to speak in a variety of churches, including "traditional" ones. Similarly, Tom Kraeuter, after leaving his position as managing editor of *Psalmist* magazine at the end of 1992, intentionally followed Cornwall's lead to start a teaching ministry that could reach across a wide span of congregations.[23]

Supplementing such direct instruction was a growing body of materials providing instruction in Contemporary Praise & Worship. Such materials, targeting a broad audience, helped supply resources for the entire confluence and, sometimes, reflected the scope of participants in it. For example, Kraeuter's 1995 book *Things They Didn't Teach Me in Worship Leading School* included contributions from fifty experienced worship leaders. Kraeuter collected an ensemble of contributors from a variety of contexts including, among others, Presbyterian, Baptist, Assemblies of God, Pentecostal Assemblies of Canada, Vineyard Ministries International, Latter Rain, and Oral Roberts University. He even included an Australian church on the cusp of global recognition in the mid-1990s: the Hills Christian Life Centre (i.e., Hillsong Church).[24] This anthology fitted the general purpose of Kraeuter's multiple writings: provide wisdom on how to do Contemporary Praise & Worship well in a time of confluence.

In this regard Kraeuter's contributions reflect the general trend in the literature since the late 1990s. More and more the novelty of Contemporary Praise & Worship wore off and the level of unfamiliarity evaporated as the number of congregations practicing it increased dramatically. Thus, the resources moved from being primarily introductory or invitational to including more thorough instruction in the practices associated with this way of worship. Such a shift witnesses to the changing status of Contemporary Praise & Worship and testifies to its proliferation and permanence in North American congregations.

Developments in electronic technology for worship likewise provided an infrastructure that supported the entirety of Contemporary Praise & Worship. An attraction to technology had long been a characteristic of both Praise & Worship and Contemporary Worship. Both often used technology in their earlier periods for reasons tied to their respective theological commitments. Projection of song lyrics, for example, was desirable in Praise & Worship to free hands for raising and bodies for dancing as part of a Davidic pattern of

---

23. Tom Kraeuter, interview by Lester Ruth, September 30, 2019.

24. Tom Kraeuter, ed., *Things They Didn't Teach Me in Worship Leading School* (Lynnwood, WA: Emerald, 1995). See also Tom Kraeuter, ed., *More Things They Didn't Teach Me in Worship Leading School* (Lynnwood, WA: Emerald, 1998).

worship. Early practitioners of Contemporary Worship, too, often sought to use electronic media in order to bridge the gap to a generation formed by watching TV. Moreover, larger congregations, regardless of theological background, found sound amplification through microphones, speakers, and a soundboard necessary because of the size of their worship spaces.

Since the late 1980s, technology has attracted even greater attention from congregations, and more people have begun specializing in providing and staffing technological support for worship. Throughout the 1990s technology developed for congregations in either Praise & Worship or Contemporary Worship proliferated, along with increasing marketing, support, educational opportunities, and sophistication. The latter half of the 1990s saw such technology crossing important thresholds of affordability, thus making it more feasible for the growing range of congregations involved in Praise & Worship or Contemporary Worship. Simply put, from the late 1980s to the first few years after 2000, high-level technology went from being novel to being standard and expected. The pervasiveness of technology became one of the elements of infrastructure forming a bond between Praise & Worship and Contemporary Worship. Technology therefore became a standard feature in the confluence of the two.

Developing a technological infrastructure involved multiple dimensions.[25] Earlier attempts at magazines (*Clarity* and *Soundcheck*) gave way to magazines still in circulation (*Technologies for Worship* since 1992 and *Church Production* since 1999). Articles and advertisements in *Psalmist* magazine and *Worship Leader* magazine supplemented these tech-specific periodicals. The 1990s also saw the publication of standard reference books supporting technology, like Jon Eiche's *Guide to Sound Systems for Worship*.[26] For those wanting direct instruction, workshops, conferences, and consultants were increasingly available. By 1999, for example, the Inspiration Technology Conference offered 123 sessions in ten tracks: acoustics, audio, lighting, internet, video, music, broadcasting, computers, drama, and general administration.[27] The 1990s also saw an increasing computerization of the technology as overhead projectors and slide projectors gave way to computer-driven projectors using first Microsoft PowerPoint and then, by the late 1990s, the first software

25. See Lim and Ruth, *Lovin' on Jesus*, 44–51. The following issues of *Psalmist* magazine are also helpful for seeing early developments: December 1986/January 1987; August/September 1988; February/March 1990; August/September 1990; October/November 1990; December 1990/January 1991; February/March 1992; and June/July 1992.

26. Jon F. Eiche, *Guide to Sound Systems for Worship* (Milwaukee: Leonard, 1990).

27. Robert Phillips, "Changes in Technology," *Southwestern Journal of Theology*, 42, no. 3 (Summer 2000): 56.

designed specifically for projection during worship. Similarly, early versions of worship planning software gave way to more sophisticated versions.

Consequently, by the turn of the century, everyone involved in Contemporary Praise & Worship knew that it meant being invested in a technologically dependent way of worship. But everyone also knew there was a large marketing and support network to make it easier to access the technology. Indeed, in an ironic development, some of those whose liturgical heritage was in Praise & Worship—and thus were theoretically more concerned with the promise of experiencing God's presence through praise—had grown concerned about maintaining cutting-edge technology lest a gap be created with people used to state-of-the-art technology outside church.[28] In this case, technology had created a sharing of theological perspectives across the confluence.

Technology was not the only aspect of the undergirding infrastructure that saw increased commercialization. By the late 1990s a well-financed music industry had arisen among the people and processes that supplied churches with congregational songs. Contemporary Praise & Worship music was becoming big business as the companies that had been supplying music were purchased by even larger companies.[29] These acquisitions supplied new capital for song development and marketing. For congregations within the growing confluence of Contemporary Praise & Worship, the industrialization of this music meant there was a wealth of songs and music to draw from, easily found through a variety of outlets. Simply put, the same large companies that supported other styles of music in North America was now supporting the Contemporary Praise & Worship songs that congregations chose to sing on Sunday morning. A common repertoire of songs, mass-marketed and mass-mediated across the entire confluence, attested to the existence of this confluence and also strengthened its existence. Thus, this music industry, marshaling a large catalog of songs and offering them to an expanded range of marketing outlets, provided a critical aspect of the infrastructure that enabled and supplied the whole world of Contemporary Praise & Worship.[30]

28. Cf. Donnie Haulk, *God's Laws of Communication: Exploring the Physiology and Technology of Worship* (n.p.: AE Global Media, 2011), 49.

29. For details about these acquisitions, see Andrew Theodore Mall, "'The Stars Are Underground': Undergrounds, Mainstreams, and Christian Popular Music" (PhD diss., University of Chicago, 2012), 185–202; and, especially, Wen Reagan, "A Beautiful Noise: A History of Contemporary Worship Music in Modern America" (PhD diss., Duke University, 2015), 315–35. The companies that by acquisitions had bought into having a line of Contemporary Praise & Worship music did so because they were attracted by this line's profitability. The increasing profitability of worship music was another indication of the liturgical confluence's existence and growth.

30. This industry even made easier the introduction of songs from outside North America. For a particularly striking example in the late 1990s, see Monique M. Ingalls, "Transnational

Even the packaging of the music witnessed to the existence of the Contemporary Praise & Worship confluence and its desire for music. By the late 1990s compilation albums and songbooks began to appear, drawing from a range of music companies and collecting well-known songs under labels like "favorites," "hits," "classic," or "greatest." Both the compilation collections themselves and such labels hint at a substantial market for whom these songs were well known and well loved. The confluence was that market.

The actual sales of the early compilation albums attested to the size of this market/confluence. For example, the first *WOW Worship* CD, released on June 1, 1999, and offering "30 Powerful Worship Songs from Today's Top Artists," sold well enough to reach double platinum status (two million units) within two years. Availability in stores like Walmart facilitated such sales.[31] As successful as the three *Wow Worship* CDs (released in 1999, 2000, and 2001) were, the *Songs 4 Worship* series surpassed their numbers. This series, which was a collaborative effort between Integrity Music and Time Life Music, began in 2000. By 2008, the series had produced more than thirty albums featuring "The Greatest Praise & Worship Songs of All Time" and had sold more than twenty million units. These CDs, too, were available in secular outlets. They could also be purchased by mail order, online, or through a 1-800 telephone number.[32]

Of course, the infrastructure involved in creating and supplying the songs was only part of the musical infrastructure supporting the large confluence of Contemporary Praise & Worship. Congregations had to be able to easily use the songs in congregational worship. The existence of Christian Copyright Licensing International (see chap. 4), more commonly known as CCLI, provided the solution to that problem. By purchasing a license with an annual fee based on worship attendance, a congregation gained legal permission to use and copy a huge repertoire of songs. According to a 1997 advertisement, more than eighty thousand churches were using the license to copy more than one hundred thousand songs from more than two thousand publishers.[33] Each of these numbers corroborates the existence and scope of the confluence by the late 1990s, as does the fact that more than one hundred different ecclesiastical

Connections, Musical Meaning, and the 1990s 'British Invasion' of North American Evangelical Worship Music," in *The Oxford Handbook of Music and World Christianities*, ed. Suzel Ana Reily and Jonathan M. Dueck (Oxford: Oxford University Press, 2012), 425–48.

31. Holland Davis, interview by Lester Ruth, March 6, 2015. See also Reagan, "Beautiful Noise," 339–40.

32. Reagan, "Beautiful Noise," 340. To view a commercial for *Songs 4 Worship*, see "*Songs 4 Worship* Commercial," YouTube video, posted by "David MB," April 10, 2013, 2:00, https://www.youtube.com/watch?v=5bcwTvdMGrI.

33. *Worship Leader* 6, no. 2 (March/April 1997): 28.

affiliations were found in the denominational breakdown lists for various royalty payout periods during that time. Like the words in a children's Sunday school song, the confluence of Contemporary Praise & Worship was deep and wide by the late 1990s, if the various music-related numbers meant anything.

The fact that these numbers did indicate something substantial is supported by the development of programs in colleges and universities to educate worship leaders in the late 1990s. The creation of certificates and degrees for musical worship leaders indicates that the whole phenomenon of Contemporary Praise & Worship had ar-

Figure 8.1. A 1997 advertisement for Christian Copyright Licensing International in *Worship Leader* magazine

rived at a certain stage of development and permanence. The fact that a school would commit to a new program to train worship leaders showed that there was a substantial body of potential students to draw from, because programs needed enough students for them to be viable for an educational institution. These new programs also needed a substantial number of churches to which graduates could be sent, since potential students want to know there is a reasonable chance that employment will make their education costs worthwhile. The creation of the first programs—and the expanding number of them since the late 1990s—therefore attests to the expansion of Contemporary Praise & Worship by the end of the century. These programs, in addition, constituted the fourth element of the infrastructure supporting the confluence.

Regent University in Virginia Beach, Virginia, was one of the first schools to head in this direction by offering in 1997 a worship studies concentration in the master of arts in practical theology. The concentration was a collaborative effort between this school and Integrity Music, which provided instructors to teach the core worship courses in the concentration.[34] In 1998 Liberty University in Lynchburg, Virginia, likewise collaborated with Integrity Music to provide both a graduate certificate in worship and a concentration in worship studies within its master of arts in religion program.[35] Undergraduate programs soon followed. By 2000, Northwest Nazarene College in Nampa, Idaho, and Judson College in Elgin, Illinois, were advertising programs to appeal to worship leaders. Judson had introduced its program in 1999, partly because of the broad influence of Willow Creek Community Church, which was located ten miles to the east of Judson.[36]

By the year 2000, the rise of educational options for worship leaders was significant enough that *Worship Leader* magazine could run an article reviewing some of the choices, including the programs at Liberty and Regent.[37] As importantly, *Worship Leader* also had a steady stream of classified ads from churches seeking musicians who could lead Contemporary Praise & Worship. Hints of both of the two theologies surface in the ads. Thus, one Texas church in 1997 was seeking someone "with a passion for God and leading people into His presence" while an Illinois church wanted someone who could "lead innovative weekly worship to reach a new segment of the community."[38] The classified ads routinely expressed such sentiments, suggesting that such notions were widely understood and accepted. Strikingly, the ads reflected the breadth of churches—Baptist, community churches, Bible churches, Lutheran, Presbyterian, independent and non-denominational, and Reformed, among others—caught up in the confluence that was Contemporary Praise & Worship. The breadth and depth of the confluence meant that the first graduates of the first certificate and degree programs faced a promising field for employment.

34. Integrity had begun a trajectory of worship leader training in 1991 through its division known as Worship International. These collaborative efforts with universities were an outgrowth of that earlier emphasis. Integrity would also collaborate with University of Mobile (in Alabama) and The King's College and Seminary (associated with Jack Hayford in Van Nuys, California). Steve Bowersox, interview by Lester Ruth and Lim Swee Hong, July 21, 2020.

35. Jonathan Ottaway, "The Rise of the Worship Degree: Pedagogical Changes in the Preparation of Church Musicians," in *Essays on the History of Contemporary Praise and Worship*, ed. Lester Ruth (Eugene, OR: Pickwick, 2020), 162; Paul Harrison Randlett, "Training Worship Leaders through the Worship Wars: A Study of the Development of Liberty University's Undergraduate Music and Worship Leadership Degree Programs from 1971 to 2018" (PhD diss., Southern Baptist Theological Seminary, 2019), 196–211.

36. Ottaway, "Rise of the Worship Degree," 163.

37. Robb Redman, "Expanding Your Worship Worldview: Education and Training for Worship Leaders," *Worship Leader* 9, no. 3 (May/June 2000): 18–20, 22.

38. See *Worship Leader* 6, no. 1 (January/February 1997): 52; and *Worship Leader* 6, no. 2 (March/April 1997): 52.

The Future

In addition to prospects for employment, these same graduates faced a shared future. Walking across their respective graduation stages and taking their newly earned educational credentials in hand, they stepped into a future shared across the entire expanse of the new liturgical normal, Contemporary Praise & Worship.

One aspect of this future was the continued growth of Contemporary Praise & Worship. The most recent sociological analysis of congregational trends in the United States indicates that "informal and enthusiastic worship" and worship incorporating electronic technology have both increased since the late 1990s.[39] This analysis, based on four waves of the National Congregations Study (1998, 2006–7, 2012, and 2018–19),[40] shows a trend toward liturgical practices associated with Contemporary Praise & Worship across a range of groups and congregations. Indeed, some practices have increased tremendously since the late 1990s like the proportion of congregations using drums in worship (from about 20 percent in 1998 to 41 percent in 2018–19) or using projection on screens (from 12 percent in 1998 to 46 percent in 2018–19).

This shared future involved not only the continuation of trends since the late 1990s but also new impulses. Some of these new impulses had a retro feel to them, seeking to repurpose liturgical good from the past for worshipers in a new millennium. The years after 2000, for example, saw a push for the "emerging church," which was a desire to recapture the best of the past for a postmodern context. Others sought recovery on a more focused scale, as in the retuned hymn movement. This movement sought to take older hymn texts, especially from the classic period of English hymnody of the eighteenth century, and compose entirely new tunes for them, fitting the musical sensibilities of the current age.

Not all new impulses in Contemporary Praise & Worship looked to the past, however. The "British Invasion" of new songs in the late 1990s sparked a desire by musical executives to find a name to differentiate this new sound from that of earlier Praise & Worship songs. They coined a new label, "modern worship music," to be able to brand the new sound.[41] Despite the different

39. Joseph Roso, Anna Holleman, and Mark Chaves, "Changing Worship Practices in American Congregations," *Journal for the Scientific Study of Religion* 59, no. 4 (December 2020), https://doi.org/10.1111/jssr.12682.

40. For more information on this study, see "Welcome to the National Congregations Study," National Congregations Study home page (Duke University), accessed February 6, 2021, https://sites.duke.edu/ncsweb/.

41. Ingalls, "Transnational Connections," 442–43.

sonic quality of the new music, the underlying theology and spirituality had not changed.

The future brought some surprises too. Some of the influential CAMEO churches that had promoted an aggressive targeting of seekers in the 1980s and 1990s (see chap. 7) reassessed what they were doing liturgically. Both internal studies showing less-than-desired results in spiritual growth and new experiences brought about new perspectives about church ministry and worship, sometimes leading to dramatic changes. At Community Church of Joy, for example, visiting other churches led the senior minister to bemoan his earlier emphasis on worship entertainment as "a substitute for leading them [worshipers] into the presence of God."[42]

The first graduates of worship leader programs who strode across the stage and stepped into a shared future also have seen the rise of new centers of influence within Contemporary Praise & Worship. Some of these new centers—like Hillsong Church, Passion Conferences, Bethel Church, and the International House of Prayer with its approach to 24-7 prayer and worship—were just breaking onto people's consciousness as the new century began. Some people would have been aware of these new centers, but few might have guessed the level of eventual influence, especially musical influence, that would be wielded by such new centers or by ones with even more recent origins, like Elevation Church in Charlotte, North Carolina.

Those first graduates of the first worship leader degree programs, too, stepped into a future in which there was growing popular awareness of Contemporary Praise & Worship's pervasiveness and permanence. By 2011, for example, the editor of *Christianity Today* was suggesting that there was at least a "tense truce" in the worship wars as the desperate battles of previous years had waned.[43] The editor's comments came in a theme issue on the trajectory of worship. On the cover was a picture of a young worshiper, hands raised in the air and singing. Indeed, such an image has become ubiquitous on the covers of books about Pentecostals and evangelicals, even in instances where the book is not about their worship.[44] In other words, an image from Contemporary Praise & Worship has become the visual icon to represent huge numbers of Christians worldwide. Perhaps the most backhanded sign that

---

42. Walt Kallestad, "'Showtime!' No More: Could Our Church Shift from Performance to Mission?," *Leadership* 29, no. 4 (Fall 2008): 42. To find Willow Creek Community Church's self-study, see Greg L. Hawkins and Cally Parkinson, *Reveal: Where Are You?* (Barrington, IL: Willow Creek Resources, 2007).

43. Mark Galli, "The End of Worship Wars," *Christianity Today* 55, no. 3 (March 2011): 5.

44. For examples, see Lester Ruth, "Introduction: The Importance and History of Contemporary Praise & Worship," in *Essays on the History of Contemporary Praise and Worship*, ed. Lester Ruth (Eugene, OR: Pickwick, 2020), 1.

Contemporary Praise & Worship has become a widely recognized feature of worship in North America is the video parodies made of it like "meChurch," "Contemporvant," and "The Worship Song Song," videos made not by outsiders but by insiders wanting to poke fun at themselves.[45] Such parodies only work as parodies if people can recognize easily the forms they are trying to imitate. The fact that these short videos do work as funny parodies reflects how universal Contemporary Praise & Worship has become.

More serious and yet still a part of the shared future into which the first graduates stepped was a continuation of the biblical theologizing that had given momentum to both rivers from the beginning. Sometimes the theology was found in reprinting classic works like Bob Sorge's *Exploring Worship* (reprinted in 2004) or David Blomgren's *Restoring Praise & Worship to the Church* (reprinted in 2019).[46] Sometimes the theology was found in works from longtime worship leaders eager to make sure a new generation understood the biblical foundations for Contemporary Praise & Worship.[47] Sometimes the biblical theologies came from a new generation of worship leaders and pastors energized by the insights they drew from Scripture, and eager to pass them on as the way of vitality in the life of the church today.[48] And sometimes the theology came from some of the best-known worship leaders in all of current Contemporary Praise & Worship, struck by the power of reflecting on the words of Scripture.[49]

In the beginning was the Word of God—that is, the Bible. In this book, we have tried to tell two stories that have emphasized the priority of people grappling

45. See "meChurch | Igniter Media | Church Video," YouTube video, posted by "Igniter Media," July 31, 2006, 1:20, https://www.youtube.com/watch?v=cGEmlPjgjVI; "Contemporvant," YouTube video, posted by "Church Soundguy," November 16, 2011, 3:09, https://www.youtube.com/watch?v=giM04ESUiGw; "The Worship Song Song by Random Action Verb Worship," YouTube video, posted by "After School Program," March 15, 2020, 3:39, https://www.youtube.com/watch?v=fWicNLXxtj4.

46. Bob Sorge, *Exploring Worship: A Practical Guide to Praise & Worship* (Lee's Summit, MO: Oasis House, 2004); David K. Blomgren and Rodrigo Zablah, *Restoring Praise & Worship to the Church* (Shippensburg, PA: Destiny Image, 2019). The latter book has several new chapters.

47. For example, see Stephen R. Phifer, *Worship That Pleases God* (Victoria, BC: Trafford, 2005).

48. For a Praise & Worship example, see Cheryl Wilson-Bridges, *Deeper Praise: Music, Majesty, or Mayhem* (Lake Mary, FL: Creation House, 2016). For Contemporary Worship examples, see Olu Brown, *Zero to 80: Innovative Ideas for Planting and Accelerating Church Growth* (Atlanta: Impact, 2010); or F. Douglas Powe Jr., *New Wine, New Wineskins: How African American Congregations Can Reach New Generations* (Nashville: Abingdon, 2012).

49. Chris Tomlin and Darren Whitehead, *Holy Roar: 7 Words That Will Change the Way You Worship* (Brentwood, TN: Bowyer & Bow, 2017).

with this Bible in order to shape their approaches to congregational worship. This priority of struggling with the Bible applies both to time—when both stories begin—and to importance—being faithful to Scripture was the key force motivating the people involved in these stories. Thus, we have told the history of Contemporary Praise & Worship as a journey of theologizing beginning with the Bible.

Our approach has differed from other works on this topic. Previous books have explored this journey as a history of cultural or societal impulses, a history of songs and music making, a history of the music industry, a history of a so-called revivalistic order of worship finding a new home in megachurches, or even as a history of conflict in the worship wars. Each approach offers insight, but our focus on how these Christians wrestled with the foundational text of their religion, the Bible, allows us to see what the historical figures themselves considered to be the heart of the matter: being true to God by being true to the Scriptures.

Perhaps this approach has surprised you, the reader. Perhaps you came to this book expecting it to be one of the standard, previously told narratives, just with much more detail. Perhaps you were startled because you love one of the standard narratives and our approach thus seemed to ask you to reject your love. If you were shocked, we tender these final words to explain the propriety of emphasizing biblical theologizing as a critical window into this history. We see three elements in this propriety.

Emphasizing biblical theologizing enables a useful reconfiguration of the shape of the history. New historical figures rise to our attention and their significance becomes evident as we focus on the role of the Bible in this history. Similarly, it is possible to push the beginning points for this liturgical phenomenon earlier than most might expect since the connecting sinews are no longer obvious similarities in worship style but are shared biblical perspectives. In addition, new points of significant development become noticeable once we look for how the historical figures handled Scripture. Focusing on how they strove to articulate what they heard the Bible calling them to do shines the light on new turning points in history and enables us to see anew how this history unfolded. In short, when you emphasize biblical theologizing, a new history emerges with new headwaters, new people, new affiliations, and new time frames. If we emphasize biblical theologizing, then the sources offer a richer history that is truer to the actual complexity of Contemporary Praise & Worship's development.

Accentuating biblical theologizing is also appropriate and reasonable because the historical figures themselves were engaged in it with the zeal reserved for the most important matters. This importance is indicated by the large amounts of time many spent doing biblical theology and the amount of ink they spilled expressing their thoughts on worship and the Bible. Even historical figures for whom biblical theologizing did not occupy large amounts of time or ink still referenced the Bible at critical moments in their teaching or writing. Whether in extensive or short explanations, all the historical figures wanted to reach out and touch the Bible as foundational so that they felt assured that what they were advocating was biblical. Simply put, for all the figures included in this history, the Scriptures were *the* authoritative text as the revealed will of God. Therefore, seeing their liturgical approach as rooted in Scripture was important to them because they wanted to be obedient to God's will. Consequently, taking biblical theologizing into account must be important to anyone who wants to write their history fairly.

Finally, highlighting how historical figures grappled with the Bible is useful for placing the history of Contemporary Praise & Worship within the history of Protestant worship as a whole. Rather than assume that Contemporary Praise & Worship is completely new and disconnected from anything that has ever occurred in Protestantism (Who else has ever used fog machines in worship before, thuribles notwithstanding?), emphasizing biblical theologizing allows us to see this history as part of a long-standing approach in Protestantism called the Free Church tradition. Found across a variety of groups and denominations over the past five hundred years, the Free Church approach has emphasized the freedom to shape congregational worship exclusively on the basis of Scripture. The freedom *to* follow Scripture has been paralleled by a freedom *from* being strictly tied to inherited forms of worship.[50] Both aspects of this freedom can be found in the biblical theologizing of both Praise & Worship and Contemporary Worship. Thus, neither they nor the confluence they formed in the 1990s was an anomaly in the history of Protestant worship, even if some of the specific forms have seemed so.

Indeed, to tell the histories of Praise & Worship and Contemporary Worship as the stories of biblical theologizing is helpful to demonstrate that different approaches to Scripture can be found within the broad Free Church tradition.[51] Whereas theologizing in Praise & Worship stressed the Old Testa-

---

50. See Christopher J. Ellis, *Gathering: A Theology and Spirituality of Worship in Free Church Tradition* (London: SCM, 2004), 27–30, 75–81; and James F. White, *Protestant Worship: Traditions in Transition* (Louisville: Westminster John Knox, 1989), 80–81, 118–19. Strictly speaking, White (pp. 172, 177) would not see the pragmatic approach of Contemporary Worship as an example of Free Church liturgical biblicism, but rather as sheer pragmatism superseding biblicism. We disagree: we believe that the pragmatism behind Contemporary Worship was its own form of biblical theologizing.

51. See also Michael A. Farley, "What Is 'Biblical' Worship? Biblical Hermeneutics and Evangelical Theologies of Worship," *Journal of the Evangelical Theological Society* 51, no. 3 (September 2008): 591–613.

ment and especially the Psalms, relied on typologies such as the restoration of the tabernacle of David, and defined a detailed pattern of worship, in contrast the theologizing of Contemporary Worship was open-ended by being ambivalent about any specific form of worship as long as it could be used well for the church's evangelistic mission found in the New Testament. Thus, the two biblical theologies were different in character, as each expected to find different liturgical visions in the Bible. For Praise & Worship, what was found was a biblical promise of God's presence tied to specific practices, especially praise. For Contemporary Worship, what was seen in the Scriptures was a God-given evangelizing mission as the purpose of the church itself. The two theologies thus ended up being not competitive but complementary in the scriptural guidance they offered on worship. Their complementarity allowed each of them to contribute to a confluence in which the Protestant worship world still swims—that is, Contemporary Praise & Worship.

appendix

the two histories summarized in parallel columns

The River of Praise & Worship

Theological Conviction: God inhabits the praises of his people. This way of worship is a gift from God to renew the church.

1946–65
This "river" began with a Canadian Pentecostal, Reg Layzell, who was frustrated with his ministry and desired a new move of God. What he perceived as a revelation that praise is the biblical way to experience God's presence became the centerpiece of a compelling liturgical theology that prioritized praise and made it the necessary initial activity of a worshiping congregation. Soon this theology was linked to the Latter Rain movement, a Pentecostal revival that broke out in Canada in 1948. This movement provided the platform for widespread dissemination of Layzell's theology and also linked it to the movement's sense of a broader restoration of key biblical principles.

The River of Contemporary Worship

Theological Conviction: An unfortunate gap exists between worship and contemporary people. Faithful Christians must creatively strategize to overcome this gap.

Pre-1965
This "river" began in the early nineteenth century as a pragmatic, numbers-driven approach to worship innovation. It first appeared with Methodists and others concerned with successful evangelizing in the Second Great Awakening. Across the nineteenth century and into the early twentieth century, new impulses in this approach emerged as its advocates articulated their theological rationale and sought measures that would be effective with people. These adherents, too, began to argue that the Scriptures had left Christians free to pursue whatever means would prove most effective in doing what had been commanded in the New Testament: evangelize.

The River of Praise & Worship

The theology also became linked with—as well as helped shape—distinctive liturgical practices of the Pentecostals involved in the Latter Rain movement. Prioritizing praise resulted in prolonged periods of praising, seen as preparatory to all other worship-related activity. The movement under the Holy Spirit's guidance also began to produce new songs—particularly short, Scripture-based choruses, sometimes composed prophetically on the spur of the moment in corporate worship. The congregational voice in singing became critical. Pinnacles of corporate praising were those times when a swell of focused praise—sometimes spoken but usually sung, sometimes in English but often in tongues, sometimes in unison but more commonly in each individual's expression—would arise. Rather than experiencing this phenomenon as discordant, worshipers reveled in the spontaneous harmony of what they called the "heavenly choir."

1965–85

A second generation of leadership arose within the Pentecostal churches—often independent of denominational affiliation—associated with the Latter Rain movement. This leadership continued to spread the "restoration of the sacrifice of praise," as the theology was known. This leadership also accelerated the level of theological reflection on corporate praise, creating theological systems usually rooted in one of the two tabernacles found in the Old Testament: Mosaic and Davidic. The increasing theological sophistication highlighted the role of the church's musicians in Praise & Worship. This biblical highlighting of musicians morphed the earlier song leader into a "worship leader" who facilitated the encounter with the presence of God. Moreover, an increasing importance attached to David as prototypical worshiper led to a sense of a "Davidic way of worship" in which the Psalms provided biblical underscoring for a variety of physical expressions in worship.

As Praise & Worship continued to expand across a range of Pentecostals—and some evangelicals and charismatic mainline Christians—the range of expressions became more diverse, too, both among those who introduced band-based pop and folk

The River of Contemporary Worship

Just before the mid-twentieth century, this long-standing pragmatic sensibility reemerged—now tied to a new sense of generation (defined by age) and to a business model that called for targeted marketing to different ages, especially to youth.

The global turmoil of the mid-twentieth century intensified special concern for reaching youth, since society and churches generally thought that the future lay with this generation. Concerned Christians, especially leaders in several parachurch organizations, feared the loss of a generation of young people who found worship boring and out of touch. These leaders creatively targeted youth and the developing youth subculture by using music and other parts of worship to reach and attract them. As youth subculture continued to evolve into the 1960s, the particular liturgical expressions adopted had to evolve in order to stay attractive to those being targeted.

1965–85

The angst about the disconnection between people and the church's worship continued into the late 1960s, spreading to a range of people and churches. Among evangelical musicians, for example, a continuing concern about reaching youth motivated them to try new popular forms of music in their compositions. They wanted their songs to speak the "language" of young people. The result was nearly ten years of youth musicals that introduced new songs and musical instruments into many evangelical sanctuaries.

At the same time, mainline Christians saw a gap emerging between older forms of worship and modern people, especially as these people had been shaped by new media of communication such as the television. New media produced a new time that shaped a new people. Motivated by this vision, mainline congregations (and some evangelicals) began a period of liturgical experimentation emphasizing contemporary language, concerns, and music as well as seeking to make the worship experience less dependent on words alone and more participatory.

Even as this period of experimentation waned in the mid-1970s, mainline Christian grew more aware of the startling numerical decline that was beginning to overshadow

The River of Praise & Worship

forms of music making and among those who emphasized that God is enthroned on (not just inhabits) praise. This enthronement motif led to the sights and sounds of pageantry. Regardless of the specific expression used, the first outlets for widespread dissemination and teaching of Praise & Worship began to arise in this period.

Across the range of Christians practicing Praise & Worship, the writing of new songs for both praise and worship continued to gather momentum.

1985–95

With the underlying theological system and liturgical practices firmly in place, this period saw an explosion of teaching resources and opportunities to train musicians in the techniques required to help a congregation in Praise & Worship. Between theology and training, the role of a chief musician as worship leader became a well-established, recognized position. Worship leaders bore responsibility for a long period of congregational singing intended to facilitate the worshiper's experience of the presence of God.

The breadth of Praise & Worship increased as expansion occurred across a range of cultural, racial, and denominational contexts. Even as the theological core stayed stable, the sights and sounds of Praise & Worship diversified.

The swelling breadth of Praise & Worship was facilitated by the rise of key institutions that allowed congregations to become aware of and legally use the abundance of new Praise & Worship songs that had been written. In addition, a series of high-profile events raised the prominence of Praise & Worship even more, providing a launching point from which new adopters could join in.

The possibility of a new danger arose from Praise & Worship's own "success." The amazing breadth of congregations practicing and institutions supporting Praise & Worship could present Praise & Worship as a learned liturgical practice but with a decreasing focus on the original underlying theology connecting praise to God's presence.

The River of Contemporary Worship

their denominations. In the midst of these troubling reports about numbers, there were those who trumpeted a more optimistic note as they sought to show the way to church growth. The solution, from both enterprising pastors and a growing body of thought called "Church Growth," emphasized close attentiveness to the cultural dimensions of worship and the willingness to adapt worship in order to attract new people to the Christian faith.

1985–mid-1990s

The propensity toward attempting to bridge the perceived gap between worship and people received a jolt of energy from the Church Growth movement, which paid ever closer attention to worship issues and increasingly advocated starting new services with a distinct style. Much of this push came because of greater attention paid to the baby boomer generation and what its members found appealing in worship.

Reinforcing the Church Growth appeal were several large churches that were models for Contemporary Worship. Gaining prominence in the period, these churches not only confirmed to Church Growth advocates that worshiping in a contemporary way brought about growth, but they also modeled for smaller churches how to do Contemporary Worship. They supplemented this modeling with an abundance of resources and opportunities to learn Contemporary Worship. The combination of the Church Growth movement and these model churches provided an impetus for and backdrop to this second wave of Contemporary Worship that the first wave of the late 1960s did not have.

What the Church Growth movement advocated and what these large churches demonstrated found a ready audience in many mainline and mainstream evangelical congregations. Part of the appeal came from anxiety about ongoing numerical loss. Another part of the appeal, however, came from internal motivations, as many congregations found that their own members had been hungering for something new liturgically. Thus, by the mid-1990s many congregations were implementing Contemporary Worship, often by starting a second service in this distinctive style. By the mid-1990s, this river was raging too.

bibliography

A Note on the Bibliography

We believe the contribution of this book is not only the narratives we have told but also the wealth of materials we have used to tell these stories. Thus, we believe that the following bibliography is the most complete, helpful list of materials related to this liturgical phenomenon published to date. To help the reader see this abundance—and breadth—of sources, we have divided and subdivided this book's bibliography.

The main division is between primary and secondary materials. As we have organized the bibliography, the primary materials come from the people within the history whereas the secondary materials come from others, usually scholars, who are looking back and writing about the history.

We have subdivided the primary materials by organizing them by type, using five categories: interviews, email correspondence, periodicals, media, and books and chapters. While this subdivision may make it more burdensome to find the full citation for any one item, we believe the benefit is worth asking for a little extra effort from you, the reader. Specifically, we offer this arrangement of primary materials as a template for further research. The detail in this bibliography not only shows the types of materials that should be used but also names some of the less recognizable historical figures and some sources that possess critical information. In this way, we offer this bibliography as a call for further scholarly work on this important liturgical development of the late twentieth century.

Primary Material: Interviews

Anthony, Douglas, and Mary Lu Anthony. August 5, 2015; September 10, 2015.

Arreguin, Joey. March 10, 2015.

Barker, Jeff. June 14, 2013.

Bentley, Bob. June 27, 2014.

Bomer, Steve. January 9, 2014.

Borden, Paul. August 17, 2020.

Boschman, LaMar. August 3, 2017.

Bowersox, Steve. July 21, 2020.

Bracken, Dan. February 5, 2016.

Brodersen, Cheryl, Kathy Gilbert, and Kim Linn. March 10, 2015.

Brown, Bradley. July 2, 2014.

Brown, William H. (Bill). August 20, 2019.

Buchanan, Fred. June 3, 2014.

Cain, Kenneth. November 9, 2019.

Chironna, Mark. September 30, 2019.

Cooley, Lindell. July 6, 2015.

Crandall, Ron. December 11, 2017.

Crawford, Jeff. January 25, 2014.

Davis, Holland. March 6, 2015; August 24, 2018.

DeJarnett, Jim. July 26, 2020.

Detterman, Paul. May 18, 2020.

Dwyer, Bill, Jimmy Reyes, and Leroy Chavez. September 21, 2017.

Eggold, Tom. June 30, 2014.

Espinosa, Eddie. May 2, 2015.

Espinosa, Eddie, and Joey Arreguin. March 12, 2018.

Fischer, Sharon Gardner. March 7, 2015.

Fleming, Mark. May 25, 2015.

Formby, Gary. June 26, 2014; July 3, 2014.

Fry, Joyce. July 14, 2014.

Garlington, Joseph L. February 13, 2020.

Gilbert, Craig. May 27, 2015.

Gordon, Kayy. May 17, 2019.

Green, Charles. October 13, 2017; May 3, 2019.

Griffing, Barry, and David Fischer. May 25, 2017.

Griffing, Olen. October 10, 2017.

Griffing, Steve. October 13, 2017; February 13–15, 2018.

Gulliksen, Kenn. January 7, 2017.

Gulliksen, Kenn, and Joanie Gulliksen. May 27, 2017.

Hammack, Denise, and Doug Hammack. December 5, 2018.

Hanson, Handt. December 28, 2014.

Henderson, Patrick. November 8, 2018.

Herron, Mike. September 24, 2019.

Heyliger, Emanuel. August 16, 2018.

Huebert, Fran, and Dave Huebert. January 7, 2018.

Iverson, Dick. April 19, 2017.

Johnson, Bob. April 8, 2017.

Jones, Tryenyse. December 29, 2014.

Kanipe, Smoke. June 3, 2014.

Kauflin, Bob. October 17, 2019.

Kraeuter, Tom. September 30, 2019.

Kucera, Ralph. January 22, 2020.

Kung-Poon, Doris. March 8, 2018.

Langford, Andy. May 7, 2013.

Layzell, Hugh, Audrey Layzell, and James Layzell. January 8, 2018.

Maracle, Jonathan. October 28, 2019.

McAllister, Judith. June 7, 2018.

Miller, Kim, and Dan Bracken. February 5, 2016.

Miller, Robert. November 21, 2019.

Morgenthaler, Sally. September 29, 2020.

Muchow, Rick. March 9, 2015; April 30, 2015.

Murphy, Steve. April 13, 2015.

Noland, Rory. July 27, 2020.

Olson, Dave. December 27, 2014.

Owens, Buddy. September 10, 2018.

Owens, Jimmy, Carol Owens, Jamie Collins, and Dan Collins. September 21, 2017.

Peterson, Marion. February 20, 2018.

Phifer, Stephen R. December 12, 2017.

Rachinski, Howard. April 17, 2017.

Reed, Ted. January 6, 2015.

Sanchez, Silverio, Sr. May 25, 2015.

Scifres, Mary. March 8, 2015.

Stuckenberg, Karl. March 9, 2015.

Surrett, David. June 3, 2014.

Teal, Rodney A. June 12, 2018.

Teseniar, Chris. December 7, 2017.

Townley, Cathy. December 29, 2014.

Tsang, Herbert. March 8, 2018.

Tumblin, Tom. August 14, 2020.

Tuttle, Carl. February 1, 2013.

Vermilya, Emily. June 17, 2014.

Werner, Art. May 14, 2014.

Williams, Cindy. March 9, 2015.

Wiseman, Alan. December 20, 2019.

Wright, Timothy. February 6, 2015.

Yu, Sandy. September 16, 2017.

Zabel, Lyndy. December 31, 2014.

Primary Material: Email Correspondence

Arn, Charles. July 19, 2020.

Bird, Warren. August 23, 2020.

Cain, Faith. September 10, 2019.

Cain, Jon. November 25, 2019.

Crandall, Ron. November 20, 2017.

Ferguson, Beverly. March 2, 2020.

Gentile, Ernest B. September 16, 2019.

Hanson, Handt. July 7, 2020.

Horner, Sallie. June 22, 2020.

Horness, Joe. February 21, 2013.

Kucera, Ralph. January 13, 2020.

Muchow, Rick. May 9, 2015.

Rachinski, Howard. October 2, 2020.

Rising, Jon. November 21, 2019; December 6, 2019.

Tate, Randy. August 19, 2020.

Travis, Dave. August 25, 2020.

Primary Material: Periodicals

In studying the history of Contemporary Praise & Worship, the following are the most critical periodicals:

> *Charisma*
> *Charisma and Christian Life*
> *Christianity Today*
> *First Fruits*
> *Music Notes*
> *New Wine*
> *Psalmist*
> *Worship Leader*
> *Worship Times*

The individual articles cited can be found in the following list:

Alexander, Neil M. "Breaking the 'Rules' of Worship: Conversations with Two Pastors." *Circuit Rider* 18, no. 10 (December 1994/January 1995): 16–17.

"'Alternative' Worship and Worship Attendance in the ELCA." *Voice for Congregational Life* 9, no. 2 (Spring 1997): 20.

Ball, Nina N. "The Carmichael Touch." *Christian Life*, February 1971, 20–22, 57–60.

Bernard, Jessie. "Teen-Age Culture: An Overview." *Annals of the American Academy of Political and Social Science* 338, no. 1 (November 1961): 1–12.

Bickle, Mike. "The Secret Place: Revelation of the Throne." *Psalmist* 1, no. 7 (June/July 1986): 16–18, 27.

Brooks, Tom. "Inside Music: Practical Applications of Theory in Worship." *Psalmist* 1, no. 1 (1985): 14–15.

———. "An Interview with Tom Brooks." By Marcie Gold. *Psalmist* 8, no. 4 (July/August 1993): 18–21.

———. "Worship Forum: Spontaneity in Worship." *Worship Times* 1, no. 2 (Summer 1986): 4.

Caldwell, E. S. "Charles Green: Called to Win a Sinful City." *Charisma* 10 (February 1985): 54–57, 58, 60, 62–63.

Carmichael, Ralph. "Interview: Ralph Carmichael." *Creator*, July 1980, 12–19.

"Church for Teen-Agers." *Time* 82, no. 23 (December 6, 1963): 57.

"Church Speaker Urges Pastors to Respect All Worship Services." *Tyler Courier-Times* (Tyler, TX), May 19, 1995, p. 1, sec. 5.

"Cool Creed." *Time* 86, no. 2 (July 9, 1965): 48.

Coomes, Tom. "Trends and Truths in Worship: An Interview with Tom Coomes." By Jennifer Brody. *Psalmist* 8, no. 1 (January/February 1993): 14–17.

Cornwall, Judson. "Trend toward Praise & Worship." *Charisma* 11, no. 1 (August 1985): 22–26.

"Drive-In Devotion." *Time* 90, no. 18 (November 3, 1967): 83–84.

Egge, Mandus A. "A Lutheran Conference on Worship." *Studia Liturgica* 9, no. 3 (1973): 158–60.

Elwell, Walter A. "How to Deal with Decline: Options for Mainline Denominations." *Christianity Today* 26, no. 5 (March 5, 1982): 36–39.

Elzinga, Steve, and Marie Elzinga. "Bridges to Praise: Three Songs in the Praise and Worship Style." *Reformed Worship* 20 (June 1991): 28–32.

Espinosa, Eddie. "Worship in the 90's." *Psalmist* 6, no. 2 (April/May 1991): 20–24.

"Frontline Worship." *Psalmist* 8, no. 4 (July/ August 1993): 14–15.

Fulton, Bob. "The Genesis of Vineyard Kinships." *First Fruits*, February 1985, 6–7.

"The Fun Worshippers." *Newsweek* 58, no. 24 (December 11, 1961): 88.

Galli, Mark. "The End of Worship Wars." *Christianity Today* 55, no. 3 (March 2011): 5.

Gillies, John. "What's So Sacred about Music?" *Church Musician*, May 1974, 50–51.

[Griffing, Barry.] "Go Tell It on the Mountain: Music Ministry on the Move." *Music Notes* 2, no. 6 (December 1980): 1–2.

———. "New Products Review." *Music Notes* 4, no. 1 (Winter 1982): 3.

———. "The Praise Movement of the '80s: Past Roots, Present Problems, Future Promise." *Music Notes* 4, no. 1 (Winter 1982): 1–2.

———. "Seeing Regional Worship Conferences as Part of Your Music Ministry." *Music Notes* 3, no. 2 (April 1981): 1–2.

———. "Symposium '81 in Dallas: The Keynote Word Was 'Overflow.'" *Music Notes* 3, no. 4 (Fall 1981): 1.

———. "Symposium '81 in the Big 'D.'" *Music Notes* 3, no. 3 (June 1981): 1.

———. "Symposium '83: Excitement Mounts in Pasadena." *Music Notes* 5, no. 1 (Spring 1983): 1.

———. "ZionSong's First Year: Praise Him for His Mighty Acts." *Music Notes* 2, no. 6 (December 1980): 1.

———. "ZionSong Has Moved!" *Music Notes* 5, no. 2 (1983): 1.

Guardini, Romano. "A Letter from Romano Guardini." *Herder Correspondence* 1 (1964): 24–26.

Harding, Joe A. "Increase Worship Attendance by Ten Percent!" *Net Results*, February 1987, 9.

Headden, Susan. "Worshiping God." *Woman's Day* 55–56, no. 14 (October 13, 1992): 114–15, 118, 186–87.

"Helping Students Make the Spiritual Passage." *Time* 86, no. 14 (October 1, 1965): 85.

Horn, Henry E. "Experimentation and the Congregation." *Religion in Life* 39, no. 1 (Spring 1970): 8–17.

Howard, Jenny. "The Sleeping Giants." *Psalmist* 3, no. 6 (December 1988/January 1989): 7.

Hybels, Lynne. "My Life—a Living Sacrifice." *Psalmist* 3, no. 3 (June/July 1988): 6–7.

"A Jazz Appeal to 'Flaming Youth.'" *Literary Digest*, April 24, 1926, 32.

Jewell, John P., Jr. "Ten Ways to Increase Your Church Attendance." *Net Results*, April 1984, 1–2.

Johnson, Arthur P. "Church Growth Gets a Shot in the Arm." *Christianity Today* 26, no. 5 (March 5, 1982): 40–41.

Kallestad, Walther P. "Entertainment Evangelism." *The Lutheran*, May 23, 1990, 17.

———. "'Showtime!' No More: Could Our Church Shift from Performance to Mission?" *Leadership* 29, no. 4 (Fall 2008): 39–42.

Kiteley, Violet. "Remembering the Latter Rain." *Charisma*, 2000, https://www .charismamag.com/site-archives/24-un categorised/9494-remembering-the-latter -rain?fbclid=IwAR0dy_ujPVfxZDTuo SrWVdykypXKSpje3AKTbf-4tuDS1Bn Cf9MmZYzQW2k.

Kraeuter, Tom. "Music: Emotionalism or Real Spiritual Power?" *Psalmist* 2, no. 6 (December 1987/January 1988): 7.

Krass, Alfred C. "What the Mainline Denominations Are Doing in Evangelism." *Christian Century* 96, no. 16 (May 2, 1979): 490–96.

Mason, Bob. "I Inhabit Your Praises." *Psalmist* 2, no. 3 (April/May 1987): 20.

McClory, Robert J. "Why Did the Catholic Cross the Road?" *U.S. Catholic* 56, no. 1 (January 1991): 6–12.

Mira, Greg. "Spiritual Warfare through Worship." *Psalmist* 6, no. 6 (December 1991/ January 1992): 41–43.

Morgenthaler, Sally. "Worship Evangelism: Bringing Down the Walls." *Worship Leader* 1, no. 6 (December 1993/January 1994): 20–23, 26, 28, 30–32.

"News of the Brotherhood." *Christian* 100, no. 11 (March 18, 1962): 20.

Niebuhr, R. Gustav. "The Minister as Marketer: Learning from Business." *New York Times*, April 18, 1995, A20.

———. "So It Isn't 'Rock of Ages,' It Is Rock, and Many Love It." *Wall Street Journal*, December 19, 1991, A1, A4.

"Noteworthy News." *Psalmist* 1, no. 1 (1985): 20.

O'Meara, Thomas F. "Liturgy Hot and Cool." *Worship* 42, no. 4 (April 1968): 215–22.

"The Pastor Wears Tennis Shoes." *Circuit Rider* 18, no. 10 (December 1994/January 1995): 14.

"People Are Talking About: Marshall Mc-Luhan." *Vogue* 148, no. 1 (July 1, 1966): 60–61.

Peters, Ted. "Worship Wars." *Dialog* 33, no. 3 (Summer 1994): 166–73.

Phifer, Stephen R. "I Am a Worship Leader." *Psalmist* 1, no. 5 (February/March 1986): 26.

Phillips, Robert. "Changes in Technology." *Southwestern Journal of Theology* 42, no. 3 (Summer 2000): 56–71.

Plowman, Edward E. "The Minister's Workshop: Let's Put Life in Church Services." *Christianity Today* 15, no. 13 (March 26, 1971): 22–23.

———. "The Minister's Workshop: Let's Put Life in Church Services." *Christianity Today* 15, no. 15 (April 23, 1971): 31–32.

"Praise and Worship Resource Organizations." *Psalmist* 3, no. 4 (August/September 1988): 30–31.

Rachinski, Howard. "Christian Copyright Licensing, Inc.: One Solution." *Psalmist* 4, no. 1 (February/March 1989): 21.

———. "Relief for Your Copyright Headache." *Psalmist* 4, no. 1 (February/March 1989): 20–21, 27.

Redman, Robb. "Expanding Your Worship Worldview: Education and Training for Worship Leaders." *Worship Leader* 9, no. 3 (May/June 2000): 18–20, 22.

Schaller, Lyle E. "One Worship Service or Two?" *Parish Paper* 9, no. 8 (February 1980): 1–2.

———. "What Does the Frequency of Attendance Tell You?" *Net Results*, January 1989, 4–5.

———. "Where Is the Excitement? Or Why Do First-Time Visitors Return?" *Net Results*, September 1987, 7–8, 10.

Schlitt, John. "Making Praise Youth Can Relate To: An Interview with John Schlitt, the Lead Singer of Petra." By Jennifer Brody. *Psalmist* 7, no. 5 (October/November 1992): 4–8.

Schmemann, Alexander. "Worship in a Secular Age." *St. Vladimir's Theological Quarterly* 16, no. 1 (1972): 3–16.

Schuller, Robert. "Hard Questions for Robert Schuller about Sin and Self-Esteem." Interview by V. Gilbert Beers, Kenneth S. Kantzer, and David F. Wells. *Christianity Today* 28, no. 11 (August 10, 1984): 14–20.

Speight, C. Frank. "How to Increase Average Morning Worship Attendance." *Net Results*, December 1986, 1–2.

Spurr, Thurlow. "Praise: More Than 'Festival.' It's a Way of Life." *Charisma* 2, no. 6 (July/August 1977): 12–14, 26.

Steadman, Ray C. "The Minister's Workshop: Let's Put Life in Church Services." *Christianity Today* 15, no. 17 (May 21, 1971): 38–39.

Stewart, Glen J. "Thirteen Reasons for Adding Another Worship Service." *Net Results*, January 1989, 1–3.

Synan, Vinson. "Pentecostalism: Varieties and Contributions." *Pneuma* 9, no. 1 (Fall 1986): 31–49.

"Three Churches Try Out Contemporary Worship." *Circuit Rider* 18, no. 10 (December 1994/January 1995): 14–15.

Trueheart, Charles. "Welcome to the Next Church." *Atlantic Monthly*, August 1996, 37–58.

"2,000 Discuss 'Crisis in Worship.'" *Interpreter* 13 (1969): 38.

VanderBrug, Duane E. "Worship as Witness: Six Strategies for Using P&W in Your Worship." *Reformed Worship* 20 (June 1991): 20–22.

Vanderwel, Dave. "The Issue You Thought You'd Never See." *Reformed Worship* 20 (June 1991): 2.

"Wanted: Men with Burning Hearts." *Last Times Magazine* 3, no. 1 (March/April 1980): 12–14, 16.

Webber, Robert E. "Enter His Courts with Praise: A New Style of Worship Is Sweeping the Church." *Reformed Worship* 20 (1991): 9–12.

Werle, Floyd E. "Church-O-Theque." *Music Ministry* 9, no. 6 (February 1968): 2–9.

"What Others Say about Praise and Worship." *Charisma* 11, no. 1 (August 1985): 25.

White, James F. "Characteristics of Effective Christian Worship." *Studia Liturgica* 8, no. 4 (1971–72): 195–206.

———. "Worship and Culture: Mirror or Beacon?" *Theological Studies* 35, no. 2 (June 1974): 288–301.

———. "Worship in an Age of Immediacy." *Christian Century* 75 (February 21, 1968): 227–30. Reprinted as "Worship in the Age of Marshall McLuhan." In White, *Christian Worship in North America*, 135–41.

Wimber, John. "Worship: Intimacy with God." *Equipping the Saints* 1, no. 1 (January/February 1987): 4–5, 13.

———. "Zip to 3,000 in 5 Years." *Christian Life* 44, no. 6 (October 1982): 19–23.

Wohlgemuth, Paul W. "Praise Singing." *Hymn* 31, no. 1 (January 1987): 18–23.

"Worship Analysis." *Psalmist* 2, no. 5 (Fall 1987): 28.

"Zwingli Marks 1000th Innovative Worship." *News Herald* (Perkasie, PA), January 11, 1989.

Primary Material: Media

All the Earth Shall Worship: Worship Songs of the Vineyard. Mercy Records, 1982. 33⅓ rpm.

Clattenburg, Jeannie. *Chosen Generation*. Mission, KS: Tempo Records, 1977. 33⅓ rpm.

Gulliksen, Kenn. *Charity: Songs of Love to Jesus and the Family*. Irvine, CA: Maranatha! Music, 1974. 33⅓ rpm.

Hybels, Bill, and Nancy Beach. *An Inside Look at the Willow Creek Worship Service: Building a New Community*. Grand Rapids: Zondervan, 1992. Videocassette (VHS), 116 min.

Murren, Doug. *Developing an Outreach-Focused Church*. Pasadena, CA: Charles E. Fuller Institute, 1993. 4 videocassettes (VHS).

———. *How to Design Contemporary Worship Services*. Ventura, CA: Global Net Productions, 1994. Videocassette (VHS), 32 min.

Petra. *Petra Praise: The Rock Cries Out*. New York: Word, 1989. CD.

Promise Keepers 93 Live. Laguna Hills, CA: Maranatha! Music, 1993. Cassette tape.

Revival at Brownsville. Mobile, AL: Integrity Music, 1996. CD.

Sorge, Bob. *Piano Improvisation Techniques for Worship*. Canandaigua, NY: n.d. 2 videocassettes (VHS). Volume 1, 89 min.; volume 2, 95 min.

Vineyard Ministries International. *Worship Seminar*. Placentia, CA, 1984. 16 cassette tapes in 2 volumes featuring Steve Robbins, John Wimber, and Carl Tuttle.

Wilson, Len, and Michael Slaughter. *Using Media in Your Message*. Tipp City, OH: Ginghamsburg Communications, 1996. Videocassette (VHS), 20 min.

Primary Material: Books and Chapters

Allison, Lora. *Celebration: Banners, Dance and Holiness in Worship*. New Wilmington, DE: SonRise, 1987.

Anderson, Leith. *A Church for the 21st Century: Bringing Change to Your Church to Meet the Challenges of a Changing Society*. Minneapolis: Bethany House, 1992.

———. *Dying for Change*. Minneapolis: Bethany House, 1990.

Arn, Charles. *How to Start a New Service: Your Church Can Reach New People*. Grand Rapids: Baker, 1997.

Arn, Win, ed. *The Pastor's Church Growth Handbook: America's Leading Authorities on Church Growth Share the Keys to Building a Dynamic Church*. Pasadena, CA: Church Growth, 1979.

Ashton, Ruth Ann. *God's Presence through Music*. South Bend, IN: Lesea, 1993.

Assemblies of God, the 23rd General Council of the. *Minutes and Constitution with Bylaws Revised*. Seattle, September 9–14, 1949.

Athearn, Laura Armstrong. *Christian Worship for American Youth*. New York: Century, 1931.

Baker, E. Charlotte. *The Eye of the Needle and Other Prophetic Parables*. Hagerstown, MD: Parable, 1997.

———. *On Eagle's Wings: A Book on Praise and Worship*. Seattle: King's Temple, 1979. Republished, Shippensburg, PA: Destiny Image, 1990.

Barker, Ken, ed. *Songs for Praise & Worship*. Worship Planner Edition. Waco: Word Music, 1992.

Bast, Robert L. *Attracting New Members*. New York: Reformed Church in America; Monrovia, CA: Church Growth, 1988.

Bays, Alice Anderson. *Worship Programs and Stories for Young People*. Nashville: Cokesbury, 1938.

Beall, James L. *The Ministry of Worship and Praise*. Detroit: Bethesda Missionary Temple, n.d.

Beall, Myrtle Dorthea Monville. *A Hand on My Shoulder: God's Miraculous Touch on My Life*, edited by K. Joy Hughes Gruits. N.p.: Embrace His Call, 2014.

Benjamin, Paul. *The Growing Congregation*. Lincoln: Lincoln Christian College Press, 1972.

Bennett, Dennis J. *Nine O'Clock in the Morning*. Plainfield, NJ: Logos International, 1970.

Berton, Pierre. *The Comfortable Pew: A Critical Look at Christianity and the Religious Establishment in the New Age*. Philadelphia: Lippincott, 1965.

Bickle, Mike. *Growing in the Prophetic*. Lake Mary, FL: Creation House, 1996.

Billheimer, Paul E. *Destined for the Throne: A New Look at the Bride of Christ*. Fort Washington, PA: Christian Literature Crusade, 1975.

Bixler, R. Russell, ed. *The Spirit Is a-Movin': 16 Charismatic Descriptions of How, Where, and Why*. Carol Stream, IL: Creation House, 1974.

Blomgren, David K. *Prophetic Gatherings in the Church: The Laying on of Hands and Prophecy*. Portland, OR: Bible Temple, 1979.

———. *Restoring God's Glory: The Present Day Rise of David's Tabernacle*. Regina, SK: Maranatha Christian Centre, 1985.

———. *The Song of the Lord*. Portland, OR: Bible Temple, 1978.

Blomgren, David K., Dean Smith, and Douglas Christoffel, eds. *An Anthology of Articles on Restoring Praise & Worship to the Church*. Shippensburg, PA: Revival, 1989.

Blomgren, David K., and Rodrigo Zablah. *Restoring Praise & Worship to the Church*. Shippensburg, PA: Destiny Image, 2019.

Bloy, Myron B., Jr. *The Crisis of Cultural Change: A Christian Viewpoint*. New York: Seabury, 1965.

———, ed. *Multi-media Worship: A Model and Nine Viewpoints*. New York: Seabury, 1969.

Booth, Catherine Mumford. *Papers on Aggressive Christianity*. London: Salvation Army, 1880.

———. *Papers on Practical Religion*. London: Partridge, 1879.

———. *The Salvation Army in Relation to Church and State*. London: Partridge, 1879.

Boschman, LaMar. *A Passion for His Presence: Keys to Living in God's Presence*. Shippensburg, PA: Destiny Image, 1992.

———. *The Prophetic Song*. Shippensburg, PA: Revival, 1986.

———. *The Rebirth of Music: A Unique View of the Real Meaning and Purpose of Music*. Little Rock: Manasseh Books, 1980.

Brandt, Donald M. *Worship and Outreach: New Services for New People*. Minneapolis: Augsburg Fortress, 1994.

Brown, Olu. *Zero to 80: Innovative Ideas for Planting and Accelerating Church Growth*. Atlanta: Impact, 2010.

Brown, William H. *Bin Der Dun Dat*. Fort Collins, CO: Book's Mind, 2013. Kindle.

Buford, Bob. *Drucker & Me: What a Texas Entrepreneur Learned from the Father of Modern Management*. Brentwood, TN: Worthy, 2014.

Caldwell, Kirbyjon, and Walt Kallestad. *Entrepreneurial Faith: Launching Bold Initiatives to Expand God's Kingdom*. Colorado Springs: WaterBrook, 2004.

Callahan, Kennon L. *Twelve Keys to an Effective Church: Strategic Planning for Mission*. San Francisco: Harper & Row, 1983.

Carmichael, Ralph. *He's Everything to Me*. Waco: Word, 1986.

———. *He's Everything to Me Plus 53*. Waco: Lexicon Music, 1969.

———. *He's Everything to Me Plus 153*. Waco: Lexicon Music, 1974.

———. *The New Church Hymnal*. Waco: Lexicon Music, 1976.

Carothers, Merlin R. *Answers to Praise*. Plainfield, NJ: Logos International, 1972.

———. *Power in Praise*. Plainfield, NJ: Logos International, 1972.

———. *Praise Works!* Plainfield, NJ: Logos International, 1973.

———. *Prison to Praise*. Plainfield, NJ: Logos International, 1970.

Carson, Tim, and Kathy Carson. *So You're Thinking about Contemporary Worship*. St. Louis: Chalice, 1997.

Castle, Robert R. *So You've Been Asked to Develop a Worship Team*. Grand Rapids: CRC Publications, 1996.

Christensen, James L. *Contemporary Worship Services: A Sourcebook*. Old Tappan, NJ: Revell, 1971.

———. *New Ways to Worship: More Contemporary Worship Services*. Old Tappan, NJ: Revell, 1973.

Clark, Elmer T., ed. *The Journal and Letters of Francis Asbury*. 3 vols. Nashville: Abingdon, 1958.

Collins, Dori Erwin, and Scott C. Weidler. *Sound Decisions: Evaluating Contemporary Music for Lutheran Worship*. Minneapolis: Augsburg Fortress, 1997.

Conner, Kevin J. *The Tabernacle of David: The Presence of God as Experienced in the Tabernacle*. Vol. 2 of *Divine Habitation Trilogy*. Portland, OR: City Bible, 1976.

———. *The Tabernacle of Moses: The Riches of Redemption's Story as Revealed in the Tabernacle*. Vol. 1 of *Divine Habitation Trilogy*. Portland, OR: City Bible, 1976.

———. *The Temple of Solomon: The Glory of God as Displayed through the Temple*. Vol. 3 of *Divine Habitation Trilogy*. Portland, OR: City Bible, 1988.

———. *This Is My Story*. Vermont, VIC: Conner Ministries, 2007.

Cornwall, Judson. *Elements of Worship*. South Plainfield, NJ: Bridge, 1985.

———. "Into the Holy of Holies." In *The Spirit Is a-Movin': 16 Charismatic Descriptions of How, Where, and Why*, edited by R. Russell Bixler, 170–75. Carol Stream, IL: Creation House, 1974.

———. *Let God Arise*. Old Tappan, NJ: Revell, 1982.

———. *Let Us Abide*. Old Tappan, NJ: Revell, 1977.

———. *Let Us Draw Near*. Plainfield, NJ: Logos International, 1977.

———. *Let Us Praise*. Plainfield, NJ: Logos International, 1973.

———. *Let Us Worship: The Believer's Response to God*. South Plainfield, NJ: Bridge, 1983.

Couch, Helen F., and Sam S. Barefield. *Worship Sourcebook for Youth*. Nashville: Abingdon, 1962.

Cousins, Don. *Tomorrow's Church . . . Today!* Elk Grove Village, IL: Kukla, 1979.

[Crandall, Ron]. *Finding the Way Forward Session Worksheets*. Nashville: Discipleship Resources, 1980.

Crawford, Ruth D., and Percy B. Crawford, comps. *The Young People's Church of the Air Hymn Book*. Wheaton: Van Kampen, n.d.

Davis, Holland. *Let It Rise: A Manual for Worship*. Alachua, FL: Bridge-Logos, 2006.

Dudley, Carl S. *Where Have All Our People Gone? New Choices for Old Churches*. New York: Pilgrim, 1979.

Easum, William M. *The Church Growth Handbook*. Nashville: Abingdon, 1990.

Eiche, Jon F. *Guide to Sound Systems for Worship*. Milwaukee: Leonard, 1990.

Elliott, Ernest Eugene. *How to Fill the Pews*. Cincinnati: Standard, 1917.

Espinosa, Eddie. "Worship Leading." In *Worship Leaders Training Manual*, 55–83. Anaheim: Worship Resource Center/Vineyard Ministries International, 1987.

Farley, Todd. *The Silent Prophet: The Prophetic Ministry of the Human Body*. Shippensburg, PA: Destiny Image, 1989.

Farlow, Wenceslaus, Rich Fleming, and Mike Herron, eds. *Psalms, Hymns, and Spiritual Songs*. Portland, OR: Bible Temple, 1980.

Fettke, Tom, ed. *The Hymnal for Worship & Celebration*. Waco: Word Music, 1986.

Finn, Peter C., and James M. Schellman, eds. *Shaping English Liturgy*. Washington, DC: Pastoral Press, 1990.

Finney, Charles G. *Lectures on Revivals of Religion*. New York: Leavitt, Lord, 1835.

Fischer, Sharon Gardner. *I Remember . . . : The Birth of Calvary Chapel*. Privately published, 2014.

Forbes, Forrest. *God Hath Chosen: The Story of Jack Wyrtzen and the Word of Life Hour*. Reprinted in Joel A. Carpenter, ed. *The Youth for Christ Movement and Its Pioneers*, 54–60. New York: Garland, 1988.

Frankforter, A. Daniel. *Stones for Bread: A Critique of Contemporary Worship*. Louisville: Westminster John Knox, 2001.

Gaglardi, B. Maureen. *After This Manner*. Vancouver: Glad Tidings Temple, 1963.

———. *The Key of David*. Vancouver: Glad Tidings Temple, 1966.

———. *The Path of the Just: The Tabernacle of Moses*. Vancouver: New West, 1963.

Garlington, Joseph L. *Worship: The Pattern of Things in Heaven*. Shippensburg, PA: Destiny Image, 1997.

Garratt, David, and Dale Garratt, eds. *Scripture in Song*. Vol. 2, *Songs of the Kingdom*. Auckland, New Zealand: Scripture in Song, 1981.

Gentile, Ernest B. *Charismatic Catechism*. Harrison, AR: New Leaf, 1977.

———. *Your Sons & Daughters Shall Prophesy: Prophetic Gifts in Ministry Today*. Grand Rapids: Chosen Books, 1999.

Goodall, Norman, ed. *The Uppsala Report 1968: Official Report of the Fourth Assembly of the World Council of Churches Uppsala, July 4–20, 1968*. Geneva: World Council of Churches, 1968.

Gordon, Kayy, and Lois Neely. *God's Fire on Ice*. Plainfield: Logos International, 1977.

Green, Charles. "The Pathway of Praise." In *Spirit Filled Life Bible*, edited by Jack W. Hayford, xxix–xxx. Nashville: Nelson, 1991.

Griffing, Barry. "Releasing Charismatic Worship." In *An Anthology of Articles on Restoring Praise & Worship to the Church*, edited by David K. Blomgren, Dean Smith, and Douglas Christoffel, 91–98. Shippensburg, PA: Revival, 1989.

Gruits, Patricia Beall. *Understanding God*. Springdale, PA: Whitaker House, 1962.

Gustafson, Gerrit. "A Charismatic Theology of Worship." In *Twenty Centuries of Christian Worship*. Vol. 2 of *The Complete Library of Christian Worship*, edited by Robert E. Webber, 309–12. Nashville: Star Song, 1994.

Hall, G. Stanley. *Adolescence: Its Psychology and Its Relations to Physiology, Anthropology, Sociology, Sex, Crime, Religion and Education*. New York: Appleton, 1916.

Hamon, Bill. *The Eternal Church: A Prophetic Look at the Church—Her History, Restoration, and Destiny*. Rev. ed. Shippensburg, PA: Destiny Image, 2003.

Handbook of the Methodist Youth Fellowship. Nashville: Methodist Publishing House, 1953.

Harding, Joe A., and Ralph W. Mohney. *Vision 2000: Planning for Ministry into the Next Century*. Nashville: Discipleship Resources, 1991.

Haulk, Donnie. *God's Laws of Communication: Exploring the Physiology and Technology of Worship*. N.p.: AE Global Media, 2011.

Hawkins, Greg L., and Cally Parkinson. *Reveal: Where Are You?* Barrington, IL: Willow Creek Resources, 2007.

Hayford, Jack W. *The Charismatic Century: The Enduring Impact of the Azusa Street Revival*. New York: Warner Faith, 2006.

———. *The Church on the Way: Learning to Live in the Promise of Biblical Congregational Life*. Old Tappan, NJ: Chosen Books, 1983.

———, ed. *Hayford's Bible Handbook*. Nashville: Nelson, 1995.

———. *Manifest Presence: Expecting a Visitation of God's Grace through Music*. Grand Rapids: Chosen Books, 2005.

———, ed. *Spirit Filled Life Bible*. Nashville: Nelson, 1991.

Heinecke, Paul T., Kent R. Hunter, and David S. Luecke. *Courageous Churches: Refusing Decline, Inviting Growth*. St. Louis: Concordia, 1991.

Henderson, Patrick. "Praising God for What He Has Done, Worshipping Him for Who He Is." In *Messengers: Portraits of African American Ministers, Evangelists, Gospel Singers, and Other Messengers of the Word*, edited by David Ritz, 194–201. New York: Doubleday, 2005.

Hibbert, Vivien. *David's Tabernacle: God's Plan for Glory*. Texarkana, AR: Judah Books, 2015.

Hoey, Robert F., ed. *The Experimental Liturgy Book*. New York: Herder & Herder, 1969.

Hoge, Dean R., and David A. Roozen, eds. *Understanding Church Growth and Decline, 1950–1978*. New York: Pilgrim, 1979.

Horn, Henry E. *Worship in Crisis*. Philadelphia: Fortress, 1972.

Horner, R. Bruce. "The Function of Music in the Youth for Christ Program." MME thesis, Indiana University, 1970.

Horness, Joe. "Contemporary Music-Driven Worship." In *Exploring the Worship Spectrum: 6 Views*, edited by Paul A. Basden, 99–116. Grand Rapids: Zondervan, 2004.

Hughes, Chris, and Jennifer McSwain. *The Kadasha Workbook: Experiential Worship for the Next Generation*. Franklin, TN: Providence House, 2001.

Hunter, George G., III. *Church for the Unchurched*. Nashville: Abingdon, 1996.

———. *The Contagious Congregation: Frontiers in Evangelism and Church Growth*. Nashville: Abingdon, 1979.

———. *Finding the Way Forward*. Nashville: Discipleship Resources, 1980.

———. *To Spread the Power: Church Growth in the Wesleyan Spirit*. Nashville: Abingdon, 1987.

Hustad, Donald P. *Jubilate! Church Music in the Evangelical Tradition*. Carol Stream, IL: Hope, 1981.

Hybels, Bill. "Willow Creek Community Church and the Willow Creek Association." In *The New Apostolic Churches*, edited by C. Peter Wagner, 73–88. Ventura, CA: Regal, 1998.

Hybels, Lynne, and Bill Hybels. *Rediscovering Church: The Story and Vision of Willow Creek Community Church*. Grand Rapids: Zondervan, 1995.

Iverson, Dick. *The Journey: A Lifetime of Prophetic Moments*. Portland, OR: City Bible, 1995.

Iverson, Dick, and Bill Scheidler. *Present Day Truths*. Portland, OR: City Christian, 1976.

Johnson, Torrey, and Robert Cook. *Reaching Youth for Christ*. Chicago: Moody, 1944.

Jones, Stacey B. *(i)Pastor Hip-Hop: Bridging the Gap between Hip-Hop and the Christian Faith Community*. N.p.: One Communications, 2020.

Kallestad, Walt. *Entertainment Evangelism: Taking the Church Public*. Nashville: Abingdon, 1996.

———. "Entertainment Evangelism." DMin thesis, Fuller Theological Seminary, 1992.

Kelley, Dean M. *Why Conservative Churches Are Growing: A Study in Sociology of Religion*. New York: Harper & Row, 1972.

Kelligan, Reta. *Scripture Set to Music*. Lima, NY: Elim Bible Institute, 1952.

Kendrick, Graham. *Learning to Worship as a Way of Life*. Minneapolis: Bethany House, 1984.

Killinger, John. *Leave It to the Spirit: Commitment and Freedom in the New Liturgy*. New York: Harper & Row, 1971.

Kraeuter, Tom, ed. *More Things They Didn't Teach Me in Worship Leading School*. Lynnwood, WA: Emerald, 1998.

———, ed. *Things They Didn't Teach Me in Worship Leading School*. Lynnwood, WA: Emerald, 1995.

Kucera, Ralph, and Carl Tuttle. *Worship Seminar*. Privately published, n.d.

Larson, Mel. *Young Man on Fire: The Story of Torrey Johnson and Youth for Christ*. Chicago: Youth Publications, 1945.

———. *Youth for Christ*. Grand Rapids: Zondervan, 1947.

Law, Terry. *The Power of Praise and Worship*. Tulsa: Victory House, 1985.

Law, Terry, and Jim Gilbert. *The Power of Praise and Worship*. Exp. and rev. ed. Shippensburg, PA: Destiny Image, 2008.

Law, Terry, and Shirley Law. *Yet Will I Praise Him*. Old Tappan, NJ: Chosen Books, 1987.

Layzell, Hugh, and Audrey Layzell. *Sons of His Purpose: The Interweaving of the*

Ministry of Reg Layzell, and His Son, Hugh, during a Season of Revival. San Bernardino, CA: privately published, 2012.

Layzell, Reg. *The Pastor's Pen: Early Revival Writings of Pastor Reg. Layzell.* Compiled by B. Maureen Gaglardi. Vancouver: Glad Tidings Temple, 1965. Reprinted as *Pastor's Pen: Firsthand Accounts of the 1948 Prophetic Revival* [edited by Marion Peterson]. Privately published, 2019.

———. *Unto Perfection: The Truth about the Present Restoration Revival.* Mountlake Terrace, WA: King's Temple, 1979. Reprinted in *Pastor's Pen: Firsthand Accounts of the 1948 Prophetic Revival* [edited by Marion Peterson]. Privately published, 2019.

Liesch, Barry. *People in the Presence of God: Models and Directions for Worship.* Grand Rapids: Zondervan, 1988.

———. "A Structure Runs through It." In *Changing Lives through Preaching and Worship: 30 Strategies for Power Communication*, edited by Marshall Shelley, 244–54. Nashville: Moorings, 1995.

Litherland, Janet. *The Clown Ministry Handbook.* Colorado Springs: Meriwether, 1982.

Logan, Robert E. *Beyond Church Growth.* Grand Rapids: Revell, 1989.

Lorber, Richard, and Ernest Fladell. *The Gap.* New York: Signet, 1969.

Luecke, David S. *Apostolic Style and Lutheran Substance: Ten Years of Controversy over What Can Change.* Lima, OH: Fairway, 1999.

———. *Evangelical Style and Lutheran Substance: Facing America's Mission Challenge.* St. Louis: Concordia, 1988.

———. *The Other Story of Lutherans at Worship: Reclaiming Our Heritage of Diversity.* Tempe, AZ: Fellowship Ministries, 1995.

Martin, Ralph P. *The Worship of God: Some Theological, Pastoral, and Practical Reflections.* Grand Rapids: Eerdmans, 1982.

Mauro, Philip. *The Hope of Israel.* Boston: Hamilton Brothers, 1929.

McAllister, Judith. Conference teaching outlines. Privately published, 1991–97.

McGavran, Donald A., and Win Arn. *How to Grow a Church: Conversations about Church Growth.* Ventura, CA: Regal, 1973.

———. *Ten Steps for Church Growth.* New York: Harper & Row, 1977.

McGavran, Donald A., and George G. Hunter III. *Church Growth: Strategies That Work.* Nashville: Abingdon, 1980.

McPherson, Aimee Semple. *In the Service of the King: The Story of My Life.* New York: Boni and Liveright, 1927.

———. *This Is That: Personal Experiences, Sermons and Writings of Aimee Semple McPherson, Evangelist.* Los Angeles: Bridal Call, 1919.

McWilliams, Jeannie Hilton. *From the Past, to the Present, for Our Future.* Beaumont, TX: Sabine Tabernacle, 2005.

Meloon, Marion. *Ivan Spencer: Willow in the Wind.* Lima, NY: Elim Bible Institute, 1997.

Miller, Herb. *Fishing on the Asphalt: Effective Evangelism in Mainline Denominations.* St. Louis: Bethany, 1983.

———. *How to Build a Magnetic Church.* Nashville: Abingdon, 1987.

———. *The Vital Congregation.* Nashville: Abingdon, 1990.

Miller, Kim. *Handbook for Multi-sensory Worship.* Nashville: Abingdon, 1999.

Mira, Greg. *Victor or Victim: A Fresh Look at Spiritual Warfare.* Grandview, MO: Grace!, 1992.

Mohney, Ralph, and Nell Mohney. *Churches of Vision: Stories from the Five Jurisdictions of United Methodism.* Nashville: Discipleship Resources, 1990.

———. *Parable Churches: Stories of United Methodism's Ten Fastest Growing Churches.* Nashville: Discipleship Resources, 1989.

Morgenthaler, Sally. *Worship Evangelism: Inviting Unbelievers into the Presence of God.* Grand Rapids: Zondervan, 1995.

Munroe, Myles. *The Purpose and Power of Praise & Worship.* Shippensburg, PA: Destiny Image, 2000.

Murchison, Anne Ferrell. *Praise and Worship in Earth as It Is in Heaven.* Waco: Word, 1981.

Murren, Doug. *The Baby Boomerang: Catching Baby Boomers as They Return to Church*. Ventura, CA: Regal, 1990.

Nori, Don. *His Manifest Presence: Discovering Life within the Veil*. Shippensburg, PA: Destiny Image, 1988.

Owens, Buddy. *The Way of a Worshiper: Discover the Secret to Friendship with God*. Lake Forest, CA: Purpose Driven, 2002.

Owens, Jimmy, and Carol Owens. *Come Together: A Musical Experience in Love*. Waco: Lexicon Music, 1972.

Phifer, Stephen R. *Worship That Pleases God*. Victoria, BC: Trafford, 2005.

Powe, F. Douglas, Jr. *New Wine, New Wineskins: How African American Congregations Can Reach New Generations*. Nashville: Abingdon, 2012.

Powell, Marie Cole. *Guiding the Experience of Worship*. New York: Methodist Book Concern, 1935.

Rachinski, Howard. "From Praise to Worship." In *An Anthology of Articles on Restoring Praise & Worship to the Church*, edited by David K. Blomgren, Dean Smith, and Douglas Christoffel, 135–40. Shippensburg, PA: Revival, 1989.

Randolph, David James. *God's Party: A Guide to New Forms of Worship*. Nashville: Abingdon, 1975.

———. *Ventures in Worship*. 3 vols. Nashville: Abingdon, 1969–73.

Rising, Jon, comp. *The Latter Rain Movement of '48*. August 6, 2020. https://lrm1948.blogspot.com.

Roof, Wade Clark. *A Generation of Seekers: The Spiritual Journeys of the Baby Boom Generation*. San Francisco: HarperSanFrancisco, 1993.

Roozen, David A., and C. Kirk Hadaway, eds. *Church & Denominational Growth: What Does (and Does Not) Cause Growth or Decline*. Nashville: Abingdon, 1993.

Schaller, Lyle E. *44 Ways to Increase Church Attendance*. Nashville: Abingdon, 1988.

Schuller, Robert H. *My Journey: From an Iowa Farm to a Cathedral of Dreams*. San Francisco: HarperSanFrancisco, 2001.

———. *Your Church Has Real Possibilities!* Glendale, CA: Regal, 1974.

Shaffer, Floyd. *If I Were a Clown*. Minneapolis: Augsburg, 1984.

Shaffer, Floyd, and Penne Sewall. *Clown Ministry: A How-To Manual and Dozens of Skits for Service & Worship*. Loveland, CO: Group Books, 1984.

Sherrill, John L. *They Speak with Other Tongues*. Grand Rapids: Chosen Books, 1985.

Slaughter, Michael. *Out on the Edge: A Wake-Up Call for Church Leaders on the Edge of the Media Reformation*. Nashville: Abingdon, 1998.

———. *Spiritual Entrepreneurs: 6 Principles for Risking Renewal*. Nashville: Abingdon, 1994. Also published as *Beyond Playing Church: A Christ-Centered Environment for Church Renewal*. Anderson, IN: Bristol House, 1994.

Smith, Chuck, and Hugh Steven. *The Reproducers: New Life for Thousands*. Glendale, CA: Gospel Light, 1972. Republished, Philadelphia: Calvary Chapel of Philadelphia, 2011.

Smith, George. *The Harmony of the Divine Dispensations*. New York: Carlton and Porter, 1856.

Smith, H. Augustine, ed. *The New Hymnal for American Youth*. New York: Appleton-Century, 1930.

Sorge, Bob. *Exploring Worship: A Practical Guide to Praise and Worship*. Canandaigua, NY: Bob Sorge, 1987. Republished, Lee's Summit, MO: Oasis House, 2004.

Spiers, Phyllis C. *Spiritual Songs by the Spiers: Many New Latter Rain Choruses and Hymns*. Chicago: Philadelphia Book Concern, 1949.

Spurr, Thurlow. *Festival of Praise*. Waco: Lexicon Music, 1977.

Stevenson, John W. *The 2nd Flood: The Discipline of Worship*. Shippensburg, PA: Destiny Image, 1990.

Stevick, Daniel B. *Language in Worship: Reflections on a Crisis*. New York: Seabury, 1970.

Stewart, Barbara, ed. *Willow Creek Community Church: Church Leader's Handbook*. South Barrington, IL: Willow Creek Community Church, 1991.

Stewart, Carlyle Fielding. *African American Church Growth: 12 Principles for Prophetic Ministry*. Nashville: Abingdon, 1994.

Stone, Gladys. Songbook. Undated manuscript.

Stoneburner, Tony. "Emotional Resonance and Life Change in Worship." In *Multimedia Worship: A Model and Nine Viewpoints*, edited by Myron B. Bloy Jr., 133–44. New York: Seabury, 1969.

Strobel, Lee. *Inside the Mind of Unchurched Harry & Mary: How to Reach Friends and Family Who Avoid God and the Church*. Grand Rapids: Zondervan, 1993.

Taylor, Jack R. *The Hallelujah Factor*. Nashville: Broadman, 1983.

Teal, Rodney A. *Reflections on Praise & Worship from a Biblical Perspective*. Privately published, 1999. Reprinted in *Readings in African American Church Music and Worship*, edited by James Abbington, 2:547–59. Chicago: GIA, 2014.

Tomlin, Chris, and Darren Whitehead. *Holy Roar: 7 Words That Will Change the Way You Worship*. Brentwood, TN: Bowyer & Bow, 2017.

Townley, Cathy, and Mike Graham. *Come Celebrate! A Guide for Planning Contemporary Worship*. Nashville: Abingdon, 1995.

Towns, Elmer L. *An Inside Look at 10 of Today's Most Innovative Churches: What They're Doing, How They're Doing It & How You Can Apply Their Ideas in Your Church*. Ventura, CA: Regal, 1990.

Trombley, Charles. *How to Praise the Lord*. Harrison, AR: Fountain, 1976.

———. *Kicked Out of the Kingdom*. Springdale, PA: Whitaker House, 1974.

———. *Praise: Faith in Action*. Indianola, IA: Fountain, 1978.

Truscott, Graham. *Every Christian's Ministry*. Calgary: Gordon Donaldson Missionary Foundation, 1977.

———. *The Power of His Presence: The Restoration of the Tabernacle of David*. San Diego: Restoration Temple, 1969.

———. *You Shall Receive Power: A Fresh Study of the Holy Spirit in Light of the New Awakening in the Historic Churches*. Poona, India: New Life Centre, 1967.

Truscott, Graham, and Pamela Truscott. *Kiwis Can Fly! Celebrating over 50 Years of Marriage, Ministry and Miracles*. Privately published, 2013.

Tuttle, Carl. "Foundations of Praise and Worship." In *In Spirit and in Truth: Exploring Directions in Music in Worship Today*, edited by R. Sheldon, 133–50. London: Hodder & Stoughton, 1989.

———. "Introduction to Worship." In *Worship Leaders Training Manual*, 5–27. Anaheim: Worship Resource Center/Vineyard Ministries International, 1987.

———. *Reckless Mercy: A Trophy of God's Grace*. N.p.: Coaching Saints, 2017.

Ulmer, Kenneth C. *A New Thing: A Theological and Personal Look at the Full Gospel Baptist Church Fellowship*. Los Angeles: FaithWay, 1994.

———. "Transformational Worship in the Life of a Church." In *Worship That Changes Lives: Multidisciplinary and Congregational Perspectives on Spiritual Transformation*, edited by Alexis D. Abernethy, 181–96. Grand Rapids: Baker Academic, 2008.

United States Navy Chaplain Corps. *The Layman as a Leader of Worship*. Washington, DC: US Government Printing Office, 1969.

Vegh, Moses. *The Chronicles of Moses: The Acts of an Apostolic Journey*. Fort Wayne: Weaver, 2013.

Wagner, C. Peter. "Church Growth Research: The Paradigm and Its Applications." In *Understanding Church Growth and Decline, 1950–1978*, edited by Dean R. Hoge and David A. Roozen, 270–87. New York: Pilgrim, 1979.

———, ed. *The New Apostolic Churches: Rediscovering the New Testament Model of Leadership and Why It Is God's Desire for the Church Today*. Ventura, CA: Regal, 1998.

———. *Our Kind of People*. Atlanta: John Knox, 1979.

———. *Your Church Can Grow: Seven Vital Signs of a Healthy Congregation*. Ventura, CA: Regal, 1976.

Wagner, C. Peter, Win Arn, and Elmer Towns, eds. *Church Growth: State of the Art*. Wheaton: Tyndale, 1986.

Wardlaw, Don M. "Come to Our Liturgical Storehouse." In *Ventures in Worship 3*, edited by David James Randolph, 209–23. Nashville: Abingdon, 1973.

Warnock, George H. *The Feast of Tabernacles*. Springfield, MO: Bill Britton, 1951.

Warren, Rick (Richard Duane). "New Churches for a New Generation: Church Planting to Reach Baby Boomers; A Case Study; The Saddleback Valley Community Church." DMin thesis, Fuller Theological Seminary, 1993.

———. *The Purpose Driven Church: Growth without Compromising Your Message & Mission*. Grand Rapids: Zondervan, 1995.

Webber, Robert E., ed. *The Complete Library of Christian Worship*. 7 vols. Nashville: Star Song, 1993.

———. *Evangelicals on the Canterbury Trail: Why Evangelicals Are Attracted to the Liturgical Church*. Waco: Word, 1985.

White, James Emery. *Opening the Front Door: Worship and Church Growth*. Nashville: Convention, 1992.

———. *Rethinking the Church: A Challenge to Creative Redesign in an Age of Transition*. Rev. ed. Grand Rapids: Baker Books, 2003.

White, James F. *Christian Worship in Transition*. Nashville: Abingdon, 1976.

———. *New Forms of Worship*. Nashville: Abingdon, 1971.

———. *The Worldliness of Worship*. New York: Oxford University Press, 1967.

Wilke, Richard B. *And Are We Yet Alive? The Future of the United Methodist Church*. Nashville: Abingdon, 1986.

Williams, Don. *Call to the Streets*. Minneapolis: Augsburg, 1972.

Wilson, Len. *The Wired Church: Making Media Ministry*. Nashville: Abingdon, 1999.

Wilson-Bridges, Cheryl. *Deeper Praise: Music, Majesty, or Mayhem*. Lake Mary, FL: Creation House, 2016.

Wimber, John, ed. *Thoughts on Worship*. Anaheim: Vineyard Music, 1996.

———. *The Way In Is the Way On: John Wimber's Teachings and Writings on Life in Christ*. Atlanta: Ampelon, 2006.

———. "The Worship Experience." In *Worship Leaders Training Manual*, 171–83. Anaheim: Worship Resource Center/Vineyard Ministries International, 1987.

———. "Worship: Intimacy with God." In *Worship Conference*, 5–9. Anaheim: Vineyard Ministries International, 1989.

Witt, Marcos. *Enciende Una Luz*. Lake Mary, FL: Casa Creación, 2000.

———. *¿Que hacemos con estos músicos? Respuestas a los problemas que enfrenta la iglesia en cuanto al ministerio musical*. Nashville: Grupo Nelson, 1995.

——— (as J. Mark Witt). "Wanted: Christ-Like Musicians." In *An Anthology of Articles on Restoring Praise & Worship to the Church*, edited by David K. Blomgren, Dean Smith, and Douglas Christoffel, 151–54. Shippensburg, PA: Revival, 1989.

———. *A Worship-Filled Life: Making Worship a Way of Life Rather Than Just a Manner of Expression*. Orlando: Creation House, 1998. Originally published as *Adoremos*. Miami: Editorial Caribe, 1993.

Wohlgemuth, Paul W. *Rethinking Church Music*. Rev. ed. Carol Stream, IL: Hope, 1981.

Wright, Timothy. *A Community of Joy: How to Create Contemporary Worship*. Nashville: Abingdon, 1994.

Wright, Tim, and Jan Wright, eds. *Contemporary Worship: A Sourcebook for Spirited-Traditional, Praise and Seeker Services*. Nashville: Abingdon, 1997.

Wyrtzen, Jack, Carlton Booth, and Norman J. Clayton, comps. *Word of Life Chorus Melodies: For Your Young People's Meeting, Conference, Youth Rally and Sunday School*. Malverne, NY: Gospel Songs, 1947.

Secondary Material

Albrecht, Daniel E. "Worshiping and the Spirit: Transmuting Liturgy Pentecostally." In *The Spirit in Worship—Worship in the Spirit*, edited by Teresa Berger and Bryan D. Spinks, 223–44. Collegeville, MN: Liturgical Press, 2009.

Allen, L. Dean. *Rise Up, O Men of God: The Men and Religion Forward Movement and Promise Keepers*. Macon, GA: Mercer University Press, 2002.

Ambrose, Linda M. "Aimee Semple McPherson: Gender Theory, Worship, and the Arts." *Pneuma* 39, nos. 1–2 (2017): 105–22.

Anderson, Jonathan D. *Fifty Thousand Evangelists: Lutheran Youth in the Jesus Revolution*. Privately published, 2019.

Bacher, Robert, and Kenneth Inskeep. *Chasing Down a Rumor: The Death of Mainline Denominations*. Minneapolis: Augsburg Fortress, 2005.

Bains, David Ralph. "Contemporary Worship: Trends and Patterns in Christian America." In *Faith in America: Changes, Challenges, New Directions*, edited by Charles H. Lippy, 3:1–22. Westport, CT: Praeger, 2006.

———. "The Liturgical Impulse in Mid-Twentieth-Century American Mainline Protestantism." PhD diss., Harvard University, 1999.

Barnes, Zachary. "How Flow Became the Thing." In *Flow: The Ancient Way to Do Contemporary Worship*, edited by Lester Ruth, 13–23. Nashville: Abingdon, 2020.

Bartkowski, John P. *The Promise Keepers: Servants, Soldiers, and Godly Men*. New Brunswick, NJ: Rutgers University Press, 2004.

Bergler, Thomas E. "'I Found My Thrill': The Youth for Christ Movement and American Congregational Singing, 1940–1970." In *Wonderful Words of Life: Hymns in American Protestant History & Theology*, edited by Richard J. Mouw and Mark A. Noll, 123–49. Grand Rapids: Eerdmans, 2004.

———. *The Juvenilization of American Christianity*. Grand Rapids: Eerdmans, 2012.

Bishop, William Robert. "Christian Youth Musicals: 1967–1975." DMA diss., New Orleans Baptist Theological Seminary, 2015.

Bowler, Kate. *Blessed: A History of the American Prosperity Gospel*. Oxford: Oxford University Press, 2013.

Bowler, Kate, and Wen Reagan. "Bigger, Better, Louder: The Prosperity Gospel's Impact on Contemporary Christian Worship." *Religion and American Culture: A Journal of Interpretation* 24, no. 2 (Summer 2014): 186–230.

Brailsford, Ian. "Ripe for Harvest: American Youth Marketing, 1945–70." PhD diss., University of Auckland, 1999.

Bugnini, Annibale. *The Reform of the Liturgy 1948–1975*. Translated by Matthew J. O'Connell. Collegeville, MN: Liturgical Press, 1990.

Burgess, Stanley M., ed. *The New International Dictionary of Pentecostal and Charismatic Movements*. Rev. ed. Grand Rapids: Zondervan, 2002.

Busman, Joshua Kalin. "(Re)Sounding Passion: Listening to American Evangelical Worship Music, 1997–2015." PhD diss., University of North Carolina, 2015.

Bustraan, Richard. "The Jesus People Movement and the Charismatic Movement: A Case for Inclusion." *PentecoStudies* 10, no. 1 (2011): 29–49.

———. *The Jesus People Movement: A Story of Spiritual Revolution among the Hippies*. Eugene, OR: Pickwick, 2014.

Campbell, Ted A. *The Sky Is Falling, the Church Is Dying, and Other False Alarms*. Nashville: Abingdon, 2015.

Carpenter, Joel. "Geared to the Times, but Anchored to the Rock." *Christianity Today* 29, no. 16 (November 8, 1985): 44–47.

Cowan, Nelson. "Lay-Prophet-Priest: The Not-So-Fledgling 'Office' of the Worship Leader." *Liturgy* 32, no. 1 (2017): 24–31.

Crawford, Dan D. *A Thirst for Souls: The Life of Evangelist Percy B. Crawford (1902–1960)*. Selinsgrove, PA: Susquehanna University Press, 2010.

Dallam, Marie W. *Cowboy Christians*. Oxford: Oxford University Press, 2018.

Darrand, Tom Craig, and Anson Shupe. *Metaphors of Social Control in a Pentecostal Sect*. New York: Edwin Mellen, 1983.

Dawson, Connie. *John Wimber: His Life and Ministry*. Privately published, 2020.

Di Sabatino, David. *The Jesus People Movement: An Annotated Bibliography and General Resource*. Westport, CT: Greenwood, 1999.

Eatherton, Samuel. "The Introduction of Contemporary Worship Music into the Lutheran Church–Missouri Synod." *Concordia Historical Institute Quarterly* 92, no. 2 (Summer 2019): 27–48.

Ellingson, Stephen. *The Megachurch and the Mainline: Remaking Religious Tradition in the Twenty-First Century*. Chicago: University of Chicago Press, 2007.

Ellis, Christopher J. *Gathering: A Theology and Spirituality of Worship in Free Church Tradition*. London: SCM, 2004.

Eskridge, Larry. *God's Forever Family: The Jesus People Movement in America*. Oxford: Oxford University Press, 2013.

———. "Only Believe: Paul Rader and the Chicago Gospel Tabernacle, 1922–1933." Master's thesis, University of Maryland, 1985.

Farley, Michael A. "What Is 'Biblical' Worship? Biblical Hermeneutics and Evangelical Theologies of Worship." *Journal of the Evangelical Theological Society* 51, no. 3 (September 2008): 591–613.

Faupel, D. William. "The New Order of the Latter Rain: Restoration or Renewal?" In *Winds from the North: Canadian Contributions to the Pentecostal Movement*, edited by Michael Wilkinson and Peter Althouse, 239–63. Leiden: Brill, 2010.

Fromm, Charles E. (Chuck). "New Song to Contemporary Christian Music Entertainment." Master's thesis, Fuller Theological Seminary, 1996.

———. "Textual Communities and New Song in the Multimedia Age: The Routinization of Charisma in the Jesus Movement." PhD diss., Fuller Theological Seminary, 2006.

Groh, John E. *Air Force Chaplains, 1971–1980*. Vol. 4 of *Air Force Chaplains*. Washington, DC: Office, Chief of Air Force Chaplains, 1986.

Hamilton, Michael S. "A Generation Changes North American Hymnody." *Hymn* 52, no. 3 (July 2001): 11–21.

———. "The Triumph of the Praise Songs: How Guitars Beat Out the Organ in the Worship Wars." *Christianity Today* 43, no. 8 (July 12, 1999): 29–35.

Han, Chae-Dong. "Tradition and Reform in the Frontier Worship Tradition: A New Understanding of Charles G. Finney as Liturgical Reformer." PhD diss., Drew University, 2004.

Hardin, John Curran. "Retailing Religion: Business Promotionalism in American Christian Churches in the Twentieth Century." PhD diss., University of Maryland, 2011.

Hatch, Nathan O. *The Democratization of American Christianity*. New Haven: Yale University Press, 1989.

Heffley, Jeff. *God Goes to High School*. Waco: Word, 1970.

Higgins, Thomas W. "Kenn Gulliksen and the Beginning of the Vineyard Christian Fellowship." Master's thesis, Gordon-Conwell Theological Seminary, 2005.

———. "Kenn Gulliksen, John Wimber, and the Founding of the Vineyard Movement." *Pneuma* 34, no. 2 (2012): 208–28.

Hilborn, David, ed. *"Toronto" in Perspective: Papers on the New Charismatic Wave of the Mid 1990s*. Carlisle, UK: Acute, 2001.

Hinck, Joel. "Heavenly Harmony: An Audio Analysis of Corporate Singing in Tongues." *Pneuma* 40, nos. 1–2 (2018): 167–91.

Hine, Thomas. *The Rise and Fall of the American Teenager*. New York: Perennial, 2000.

Holdcroft, L. Thomas. "The New Order of the Latter Rain." *Pneuma* 2, no. 2 (Fall 1980): 46–60.

Hollander, Stanley C., and Richard Germain. *Was There a Pepsi Generation before Pepsi Discovered It? Youth-Based Segmentation in Marketing*. Lincolnwood, IL: NTC Business, 1992.

Horner, R. Bruce. "The Function of Music in the Youth for Christ Program." MME thesis, Indiana University, 1970.

Hunt, Stephen. *A History of the Charismatic Movement in Britain and the United States of America*. Lewiston, NY: Edwin Mellen, 2009.

Hutchinson, Mark. "The Latter Rain Movement and the Phenomenon of Global Return." In *Winds from the North: Canadian Contributions to the Pentecostal*

Movement, edited by Michael Wilkinson and Peter Althouse, 265–83. Leiden: Brill, 2010.

Ingalls, Monique M. "Awesome in This Place: Sound, Space, and Identity in Contemporary North American Evangelical Worship." PhD diss., University of Pennsylvania, 2008.

———. *Singing the Congregation: How Contemporary Worship Music Forms Evangelical Community*. Oxford: Oxford University Press, 2018.

———. "Transnational Connections, Musical Meaning, and the 1990s 'British Invasion' of North American Evangelical Worship Music." In *The Oxford Handbook of Music and World Christianities*, edited by Suzel Ana Reily and Jonathan M. Dueck, 425–48. Oxford: Oxford University Press, 2012.

Johnson, Birgitta J. "Back to the Heart of Worship: Praise and Worship Music in a Los Angeles African-American Megachurch." *Black Music Research Journal* 31, no. 1 (Spring 2011): 105–29.

———. "'Oh, for a Thousand Tongues to Sing': Music and Worship in African American Megachurches of Los Angeles, California." PhD diss., University of California Los Angeles, 2008.

———. "Singing Down Walls of Race, Ethnicity, and Tradition in an African American Megachurch." *Liturgy* 33, no. 3 (2018): 37–45.

———. "'This Is Not the Warm-Up Act!': How Praise and Worship Reflects Expanding Musical Traditions and Theology in a Bapticostal Charismatic African American Megachurch." In *The Spirit of Praise: Music and Worship in Global Pentecostal-Charismatic Christianity*, edited by Monique M. Ingalls and Amos Yong, 117–32. University Park: Pennsylvania State University Press, 2015.

Johnson, Todd E. "Disconnected Rituals: The Origins of the Seeker Service Movement." In *The Conviction of Things Not Seen: Worship and Ministry in the 21st Century*, edited by Todd E. Johnson, 53–66. Grand Rapids: Brazos, 2002.

Justice, Deborah R. "The Curious Longevity of the Traditional–Contemporary Divide: Mainline Musical Choices in Post–Worship War America." *Liturgy* 32, no. 1 (2017): 16–23.

———. "Mainline Protestantism and Contemporary versus Traditional Worship Music." In *The Oxford Handbook of Music and World Christianities*, edited by Suzel Ana Reily and Jonathan M. Dueck, 487–512. Oxford: Oxford University Press, 2016.

———. "Sonic Change, Social Change, Sacred Change: Music and the Reconfiguration of American Christianity." PhD diss., Indiana University, 2012.

Knowles, Brett. *The History of a New Zealand Pentecostal Movement*. Lewiston, NY: Edwin Mellen, 2000.

Lathrop, Gordon W. "New Pentecost or Joseph's Britches? Reflections on the History and Meaning of the Worship Order in the Megachurches." *Worship* 72, no. 6 (November 1998): 521–38.

Lim, Swee Hong. "Nashville and Sydney Are Not the World: The Transnational Migration of Sources for Chinese Contemporary Praise & Worship Songs." In *Essays on the History of Contemporary Praise and Worship*, edited by Lester Ruth, 149–59. Eugene, OR: Pickwick, 2020.

Lim, Swee Hong, and Lester Ruth. *Lovin' on Jesus: A Concise History of Contemporary Worship*. Nashville: Abingdon, 2017.

Mall, Andrew Theodore. "'The Stars Are Underground': Undergrounds, Mainstreams, and Christian Popular Music." PhD diss., University of Chicago, 2012.

Massa, Mark. *The American Catholic Revolution: How the Sixties Changed the Church Forever*. Oxford: Oxford University Press, 2010.

McClymond, Michael. "After Toronto: Randy Clark's Global Awakening, Heidi and Rolland Baker's Iris Ministries, and the Post-1990s Global Charismatic Networks." *Pneuma* 38, no. 1–2 (2016): 50–76.

McIntosh, Gary L. "Introduction: Why Church Growth Can't Be Ignored." In *Evaluating the Church Growth*

Movement, edited by Elmer Towns and Gary L. McIntosh, 7–28. Grand Rapids: Zondervan, 2004.

McWhorter, John. *Doing Our Own Thing: The Degradation of Language and Music and Why We Should, Like, Care.* New York: Gotham, 2003.

Meredith, Char. *It's a Sin to Bore a Kid: The Story of Young Life.* Waco: Word, 1978.

Miller, Donald E. *Reinventing American Protestantism: Christianity in the New Millennium.* Los Angeles: University of California Press, 1997.

Moir, Les. *Missing Jewel: The Worship Movement That Impacted the Nations.* Colorado Springs: David C. Cook, 2017.

Moore, S. David. *Pastor Jack: The Authorized Biography of Jack Hayford.* Colorado Springs: David C. Cook, 2020.

———. *The Shepherding Movement: Controversy and Charismatic Ecclesiology.* London: T&T Clark, 2003.

Mulder, Mark T., and Gerardo Martí. *The Glass Church: Robert H. Schuller, the Crystal Cathedral, and the Strain of Megachurch Ministry.* New Brunswick, NJ: Rutgers University Press, 2020.

Nation, Garry Dale. "The Hermeneutics of Pentecostal-Charismatic Restoration Theology: A Critical Analysis." PhD diss., Southwestern Baptist Theological Seminary, 1990.

Nekola, Anna E. "Between This World and the Next: The Musical 'Worship Wars' and Evangelical Ideology in the United States, 1960–2005." PhD diss., University of Wisconsin–Madison, 2009.

Nel, Marius. "Attempting to Develop a Pentecostal Theology of Worship." *Verbum et Ecclesia* 37, no. 1 (2016): 1–8.

O'Malley, John W. *What Happened at Vatican II.* Cambridge, MA: Belknap, 2008.

Ottaway, Jonathan. "Raising Up David's Tabernacle: Theological Hermeneutics as Authority for Theologies of Praise." In *Worship and Power: Liturgical Authority in Free Church Traditions*, edited by Sarah Johnson and Andrew Wymer. Eugene, OR: Cascade Books, forthcoming.

———. "The Rise of the Worship Degree: Pedagogical Changes in the Preparation of Church Musicians." In *Essays on the History of Contemporary Praise and Worship*, edited by Lester Ruth, 160–75. Eugene, OR: Pickwick, 2020.

———. "The Seven Hebrew Words for Praise: Pentecostal Interpretations of Scripture in Liturgical Theology." *Worship* (forthcoming.).

Palladino, Grace. *Teenagers: An American History.* New York: Basic Books, 1996.

Park, Andy, Lester Ruth, and Cindy Rethmeier. *Worshiping with the Anaheim Vineyard: The Emergence of Contemporary Worship.* Grand Rapids: Eerdmans, 2017.

Percy, Martyn. "Adventure and Atrophy in a Charismatic Movement: Returning to the 'Toronto Blessing.'" In *Practicing the Faith: The Ritual Life of Pentecostal-Charismatic Christians*, edited by Martin Lindhardt, 152–78. New York: Berghahn, 2011.

———. "The Morphology of Pilgrimage in the 'Toronto Blessing.'" *Religion* 28 (1998): 281–88.

———. "Sweet Rapture: Subliminal Eroticism in Contemporary Charismatic Worship." *Theology and Sexuality* 6 (March 1997): 71–106.

Perez, Adam. "'All Hail King Jesus': The *International Worship Symposium* and the Making of Praise and Worship History, 1977–1989." ThD diss., Duke Divinity School, 2021.

———. "Beyond the Guitar: The Keyboard as Lens into the History of Contemporary Praise and Worship." *Hymn* 70, no. 2 (Spring 2019): 18–26.

———. "Sounding God's Enthronement in Worship: The Early History and Theology of Integrity's Hosanna! Music." In *Essays on the History of Contemporary Praise & Worship*, edited by Lester Ruth, 74–94. Eugene, OR: Pickwick, 2020.

Phillips, L. Edward. *The Purpose, Pattern, and Character of Worship.* Nashville: Abingdon, 2020.

Pierce, Matthew Lawrence. "Redeeming Performance? The Question of Liturgical Audience." *Liturgy* 28, no. 1 (2013): 54–62.

Pilcher, Jane. "Mannheim's Sociology of Generations: An Undervalued Legacy."

British Journal of Sociology 45, no. 3 (September 1994): 481–95.

Pollard, Deborah Smith. *When the Church Becomes Your Party*. Detroit: Wayne State University Press, 2008.

Powers, Jonathan A. "Robert Webber: Preserving Traditional Worship through Contemporary Styles." In *Essays on the History of Contemporary Praise and Worship*, edited by Lester Ruth, 95–115. Eugene, OR: Pickwick, 2020.

Pritchard, Gregory A. "The Strategy of Willow Creek Community Church: A Study in the Sociology of Religion." PhD diss., Northwestern University, 1994.

———. *Willow Creek Seeker Services: Evaluating a New Way of Doing Church*. Grand Rapids: Baker, 1996.

Rabey, Steve. *Revival in Brownsville: Pensacola, Pentecostalism, and the Power of American Revivalism*. Nashville: Nelson, 1998.

Rady-Shaw, Julia. "Religion during the Second World War." Accessed February 5, 2021. https://wartimecanada.ca/essay /worshipping/religion-during-second -world-war.

Randlett, Paul Harrison. "Training Worship Leaders through the Worship Wars: A Study of the Development of Liberty University's Undergraduate Music and Worship Leadership Degree Programs from 1971 to 2018." PhD diss., Southern Baptist Theological Seminary, 2019.

Reagan, Wen. "A Beautiful Noise: A History of Contemporary Worship Music in Modern America." PhD diss., Duke University, 2015.

———. "Christian Copyright Licensing, Inc." In *The Encyclopedia of Christianity in the United States*, edited by George Thomas Kurian and Mark A. Lamport, 529–31. Lanham, MD: Rowman & Littlefield, 2016.

Redman, Robb. *The Great Worship Awakening: Singing a New Song in the Postmodern Church*. San Francisco: Jossey-Bass, 2002.

Riss, Richard M. "The Latter Rain Movement of 1948." *Pneuma* 4, no. 1 (1982): 32–45.

———. *Latter Rain: The Latter Rain Movement of 1948 and the Mid-Twentieth Century Evangelical Awakening*. Mississauga, ON: Honeycomb Visual Productions, 1987.

———. "The New Order of the Latter Rain: A Look at the Revival Movement on Its 40th Anniversary." *Assemblies of God Heritage* 7, no. 3 (Fall 1987): 15–19.

———. *A Survey of 20th-Century Revival Movements in North America*. Peabody, MA: Hendrickson, 1988.

Riss, Richard M., and Kathryn Riss. *Images of Revival: Another Wave Rolls In*. Shippensburg, PA: Revival, 1997.

Rogers, Mark. "End Times Innovator: Paul Rader and Evangelical Missions." *International Bulletin of Missionary Research* 37, no. 1 (January 2013): 17–24.

Roso, Joseph, Anna Holleman, and Mark Chaves. "Changing Worship Practices in American Congregations." *Journal for the Scientific Study of Religion* 59, no. 4 (December 2020). https://doi.org/10.1111 /jssr.12682.

Ruth, Lester. "Divine, Human, or Devilish? The State of the Question on the Writing of the History of Contemporary Worship." *Worship* 88, no. 4 (July 2014): 290–310.

———, ed. *Essays on the History of Contemporary Praise & Worship*. Eugene, OR: Pickwick, 2020.

———. "Introduction: The Importance and History of Contemporary Praise & Worship." In *Essays on the History of Contemporary Praise & Worship*, edited by Lester Ruth, 1–12. Eugene, OR: Pickwick, 2020.

———. "*Lex Agendi, Lex Orandi*: Toward an Understanding of Seeker Services as a New Kind of Liturgy." *Worship* 70, no. 5 (September 1996): 386–405.

———. *A Little Heaven Below: Worship at Early Methodist Quarterly Meetings*. Nashville: Kingswood Books, 2000.

———. "Methodological Insights for the Historiography of Contemporary Praise & Worship." In *Essays on the History of Contemporary Praise & Worship*, edited by Lester Ruth, 176–92. Eugene, OR: Pickwick, 2020.

Sargeant, Kimon Howland. *Seeker Churches: Promoting Traditional Religion in a Nontraditional Way.* New Brunswick, NJ: Rutgers University Press, 2000.

Schmidt, Leigh E. *Holy Fairs: Scottish Communions and American Revivals in the Early Modern Period.* Princeton: Princeton University Press, 1989.

Sigler, R. Matthew. "James F. White, Grady Hardin, and Methodist 'Contemporary' Worship in the 1970s." In *Essays on the History of Contemporary Praise and Worship,* edited by Lester Ruth, 13–33. Eugene, OR: Pickwick, 2020.

———. *Methodist Worship: Mediating the Wesleyan Liturgical Heritage.* New York: Routledge, 2019.

Smith, Ted A. *The New Measures: A Theological History of Democratic Practice.* Cambridge: Cambridge University Press, 2007.

Snyder, Graydon F., and Doreen M. McFarlane. *The People Are Holy: The History and Theology of Free Church Worship.* Macon, GA: Mercer University Press, 2005.

Snyder, James L. *Paul Rader: Portrait of an Evangelist (1879–1938).* Ocala, FL: Fellowship Ministries, 2003.

Stallsmith, Glenn. "The Path to a Second Service: Mainline Decline, Church Growth, and Apostolic Leadership." In *Essays on the History of Contemporary Praise and Worship,* edited by Lester Ruth, 55–73. Eugene, OR: Pickwick, 2020.

Stowe, David W. *No Sympathy for the Devil: Christian Pop Music and the Transformation of American Evangelicalism.* Chapel Hill: University of North Carolina Press, 2011.

Sutton, Matthew Avery. *Aimee Semple McPherson and the Resurrection of Christian America.* Cambridge, MA: Harvard University Press, 2007.

Tanis, Gretchen Schoon. *Making Jesus Attractive: The Ministry and Message of Young Life.* Eugene, OR: Pickwick, 2016.

Taves, Ann. *Fits, Trances and Visions: Experiencing Religion and Explaining Experience from Wesley to James.* Princeton: Princeton University Press, 1999.

Tedlow, Richard S. *New and Improved: The Story of Mass Marketing in America.* New York: Basic Books, 1990.

Vachon, Brian. *A Time to Be Born.* Englewood Cliffs, NJ: Prentice-Hall, 1972.

Wacker, Grant. *America's Pastor: Billy Graham and the Shaping of a Nation.* Cambridge, MA: Belknap, 2014.

Weaver, C. Douglas. *Baptists and the Holy Spirit: The Contested History with Holiness-Pentecostal-Charismatic Movements.* Waco: Baylor University Press, 2019.

White, James F. *Christian Worship in North America: A Retrospective, 1955–1995.* Collegeville, MN: Liturgical Press, 1997.

———. *Protestant Worship: Traditions in Transition.* Louisville: Westminster John Knox, 1989.

Wigger, John H. *Taking Heaven by Storm: Methodism and the Rise of Popular Christianity in America.* Oxford: Oxford University Press, 1998.

Wilford, Justin G. *Sacred Subdivisions: The Postsuburban Transformation of American Evangelicalism.* New York: New York University Press, 2012.

Winston, Diane. *Red-Hot and Righteous: The Urban Religion of the Salvation Army.* Cambridge, MA: Harvard University Press, 1999.

Wohl, Robert. *The Generation of 1914.* Cambridge, MA: Harvard University Press, 1979.

Wong, Connie Oi-Yan. "Singing the Gospel Chinese Style: 'Praise and Worship' Music in the Asian Pacific." PhD diss., University of California, 2006.

name index

subject index

Made in the USA
Middletown, DE
27 December 2024